BOYS BE™

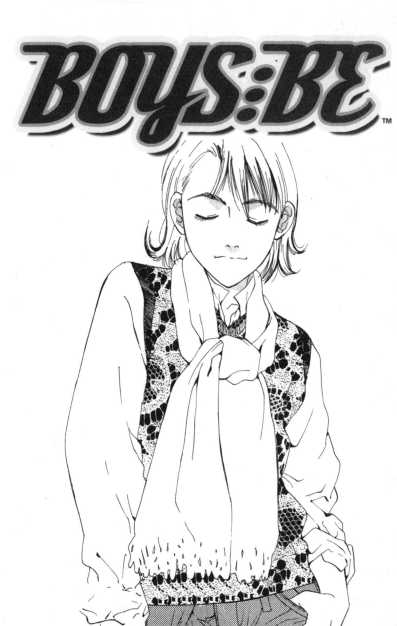

BOYS BE Second Season Vol. 5
Written by Masahiro Itabashi
Illustrated by Hiroyuki Tamakoshi

Translation - Katherine Schilling
Copy Editor - Suzanne Waldman
Retouch and Lettering - Benchcomix
Production Artist - James Lee
Cover Design - Kyle Plummer

Editor - Carol Fox
Digital Imaging Manager - Chris Buford
Pre-Press Manager - Antonio DePietro
Production Managers - Jennifer Miller and Mutsumi Miyazaki
Art Director - Matt Alford
Managing Editor - Jill Freshney
VP of Production - Ron Klamert
Editor-in-Chief - Mike Kiley
President and C.O.O. - John Parker
Publisher and C.E.O. - Stuart Levy

A  Manga

TOKYOPOP Inc.
5900 Wilshire Blvd. Suite 2000
Los Angeles, CA 90036

E-mail: info@TOKYOPOP.com
Come visit us online at www.TOKYOPOP.com

© 1997 Masahiro Itabashi and Hiroyuki Tamakoshi. All Rights Reserved. First published in Japan in 1997 by Kodansha Ltd., Tokyo English publication rights arranged through Kodansha Ltd.

English text copyright ©2005 TOKYOPOP Inc.

All rights reserved. No portion of this book may be reproduced or transmitted in any form or by any means without written permission from the copyright holders. This manga is a work of fiction. Any resemblance to actual events or locales or persons, living or dead, is entirely coincidental.

ISBN: 1-59532-103-9

First TOKYOPOP printing: July 2005
10 9 8 7 6 5 4 3 2 1
Printed in the USA

BOYS BE Second Season
Vol. 5

Writer
Masahiro Itabashi

Artist
Hiroyuki Tamakoshi

HAMBURG // LONDON // LOS ANGELES // TOKYO

CONTENTS

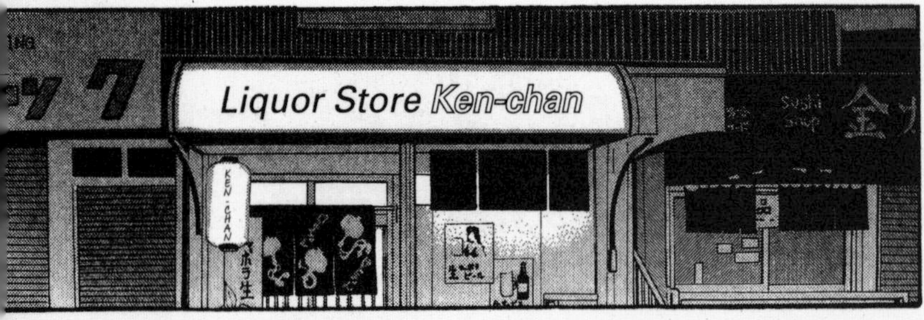

Liquor Store Ken-chan
KEN-CHAN

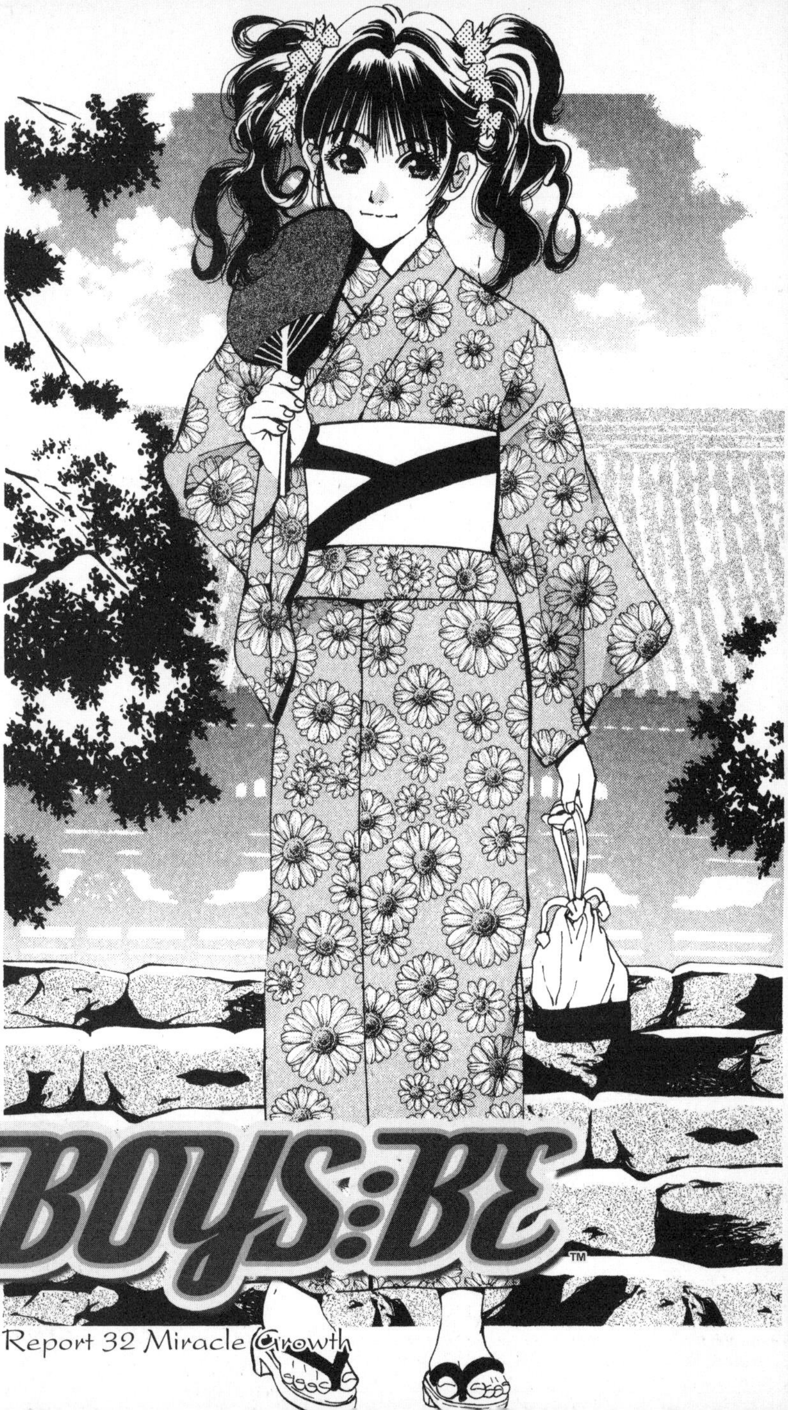
BOYS:BE™
Report 32 Miracle Growth

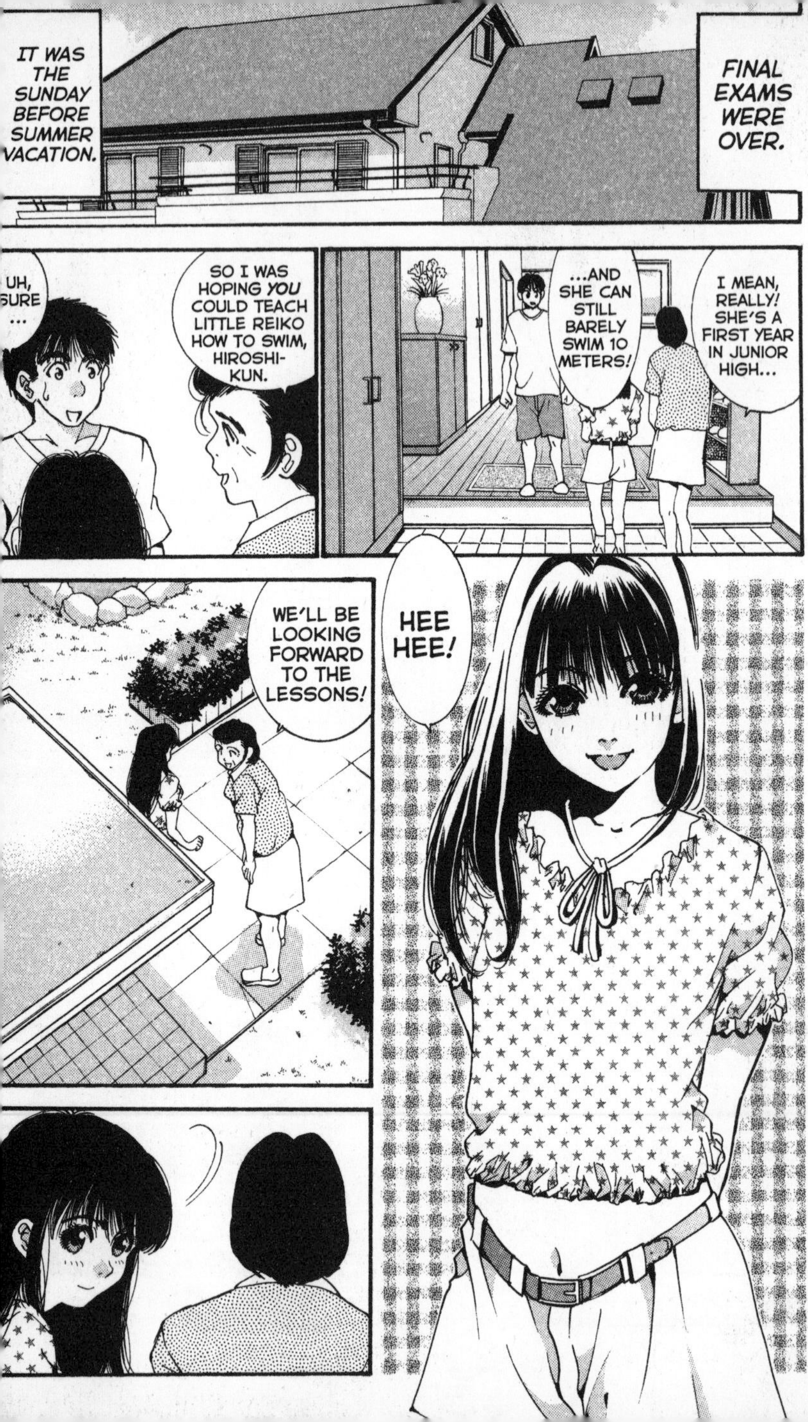
FINAL EXAMS WERE OVER.
IT WAS THE SUNDAY BEFORE SUMMER VACATION.
I MEAN, REALLY! SHE'S A FIRST YEAR IN JUNIOR HIGH...
...AND SHE CAN STILL BARELY SWIM 10 METERS!
SO I WAS HOPING YOU COULD TEACH LITTLE REIKO HOW TO SWIM, HIROSHI-KUN.
UH, SURE...
HEE HEE!
WE'LL BE LOOKING FORWARD TO THE LESSONS!

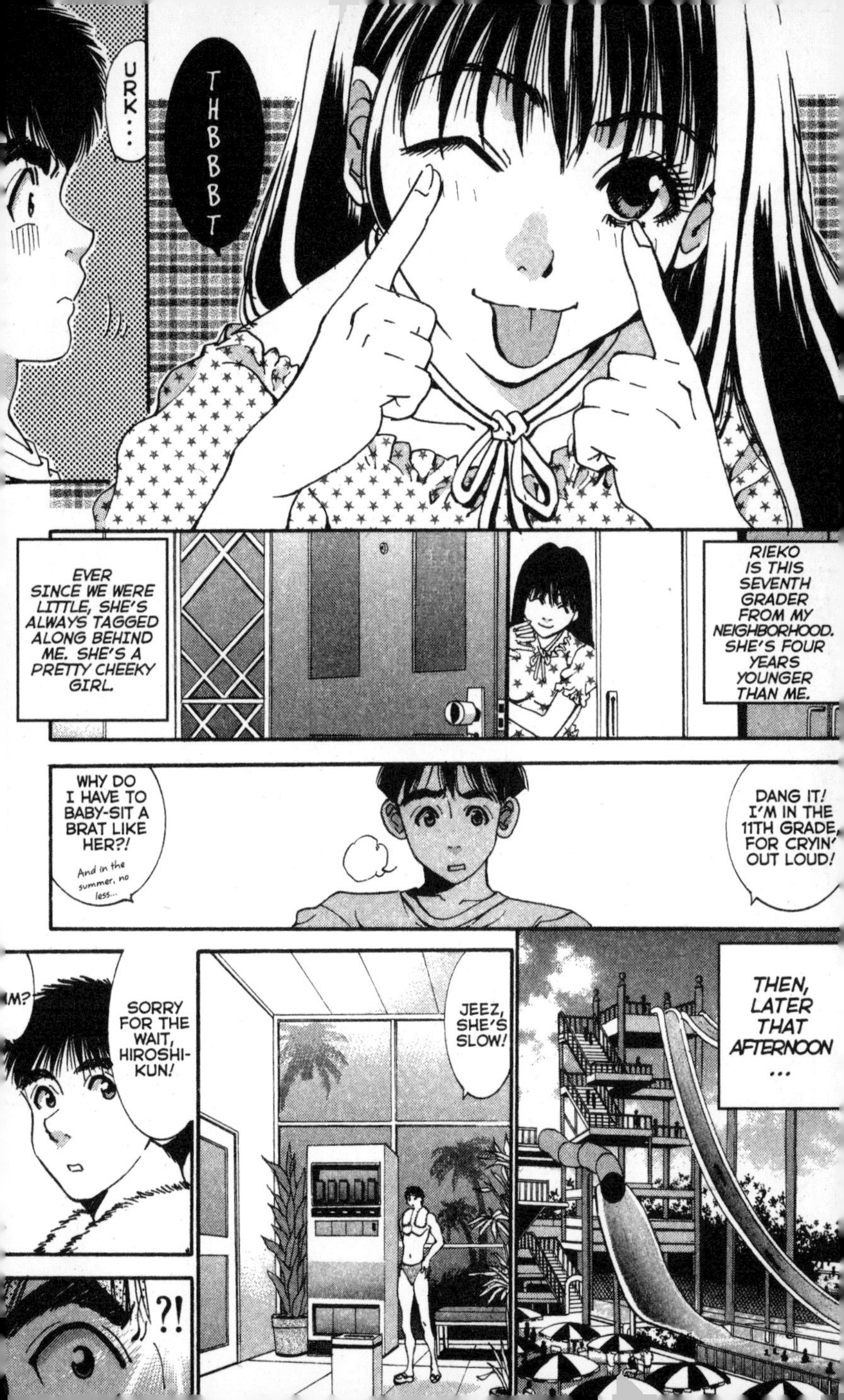
THBBBT
URK...
RIEKO IS THIS SEVENTH GRADER FROM MY NEIGHBORHOOD. SHE'S FOUR YEARS YOUNGER THAN ME.
EVER SINCE WE WERE LITTLE, SHE'S ALWAYS TAGGED ALONG BEHIND ME. SHE'S A PRETTY CHEEKY GIRL.
DANG IT! I'M IN THE 11TH GRADE, FOR CRYIN' OUT LOUD!
WHY DO I HAVE TO BABY-SIT A BRAT LIKE HER?!
And in the summer, no less...
THEN, LATER THAT AFTERNOON...
JEEZ, SHE'S SLOW!
M?
SORRY FOR THE WAIT, HIROSHI-KUN!
?!

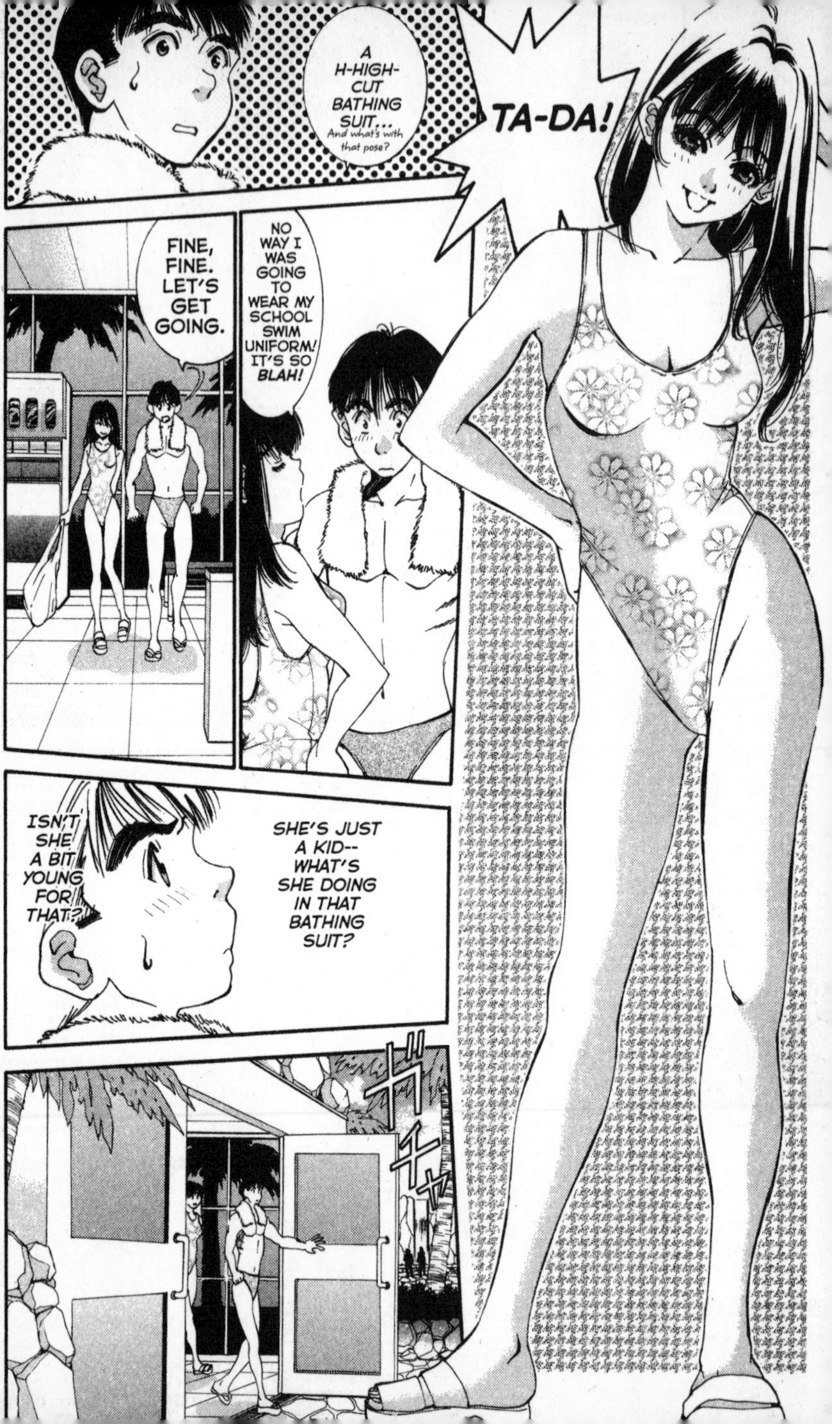
TA-DA!
A H-HIGH-CUT BATHING SUIT...
And what's with that pose?
NO WAY I WAS GOING TO WEAR MY SCHOOL SWIM UNIFORM! IT'S SO *BLAH!*
FINE, FINE. LET'S GET GOING.
SHE'S JUST A KID-- WHAT'S SHE DOING IN THAT BATHING SUIT?
ISN'T SHE A BIT YOUNG FOR THAT?

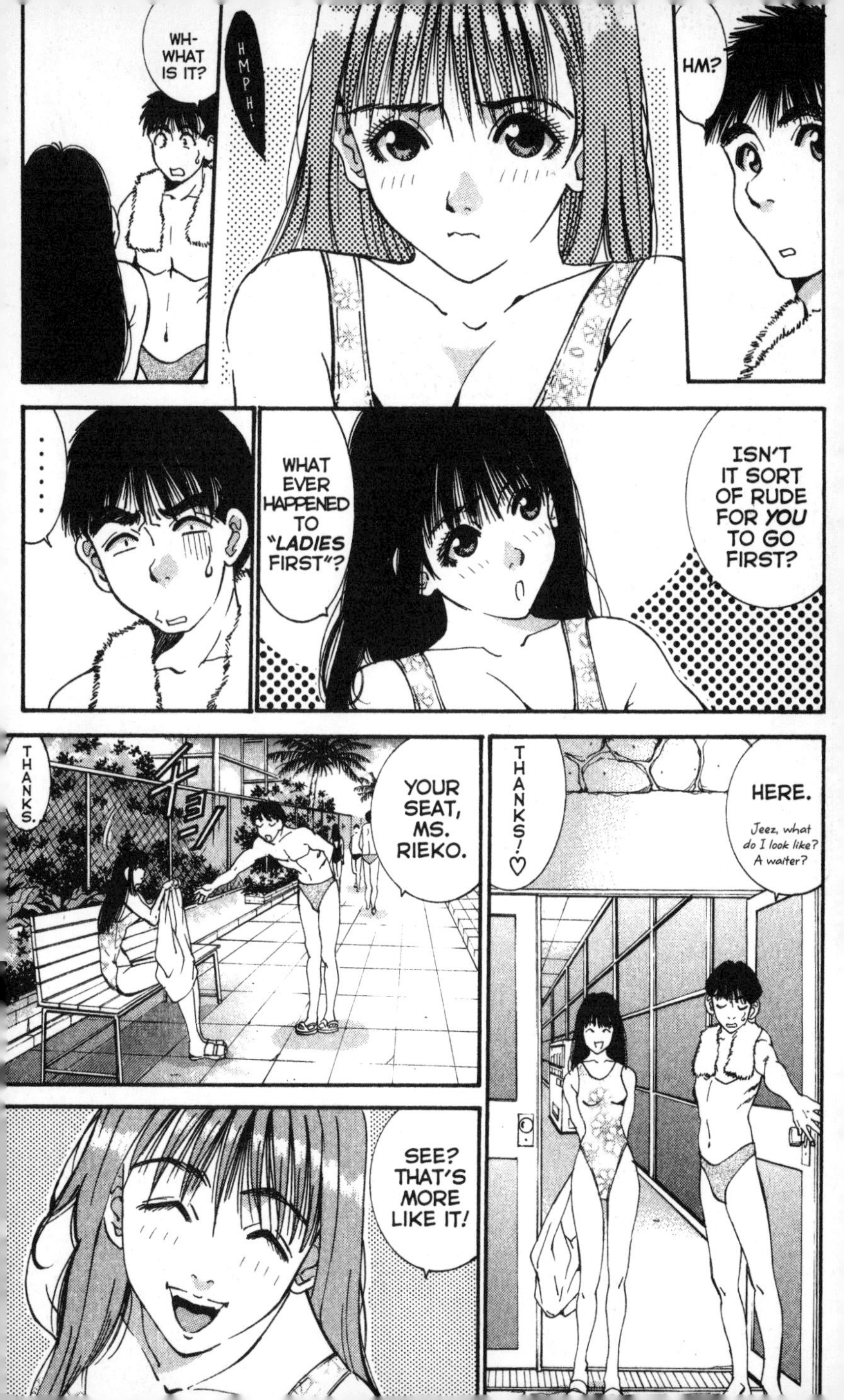
HM?
HMPH!
WH- WHAT IS IT?
ISN'T IT SORT OF RUDE FOR *YOU* TO GO FIRST?
WHAT EVER HAPPENED TO "*LADIES* FIRST"?
......
HERE.
Jeez, what do I look like? A waiter?
THANKS!♡
YOUR SEAT, MS. RIEKO.
THANKS.
SEE? THAT'S MORE LIKE IT!

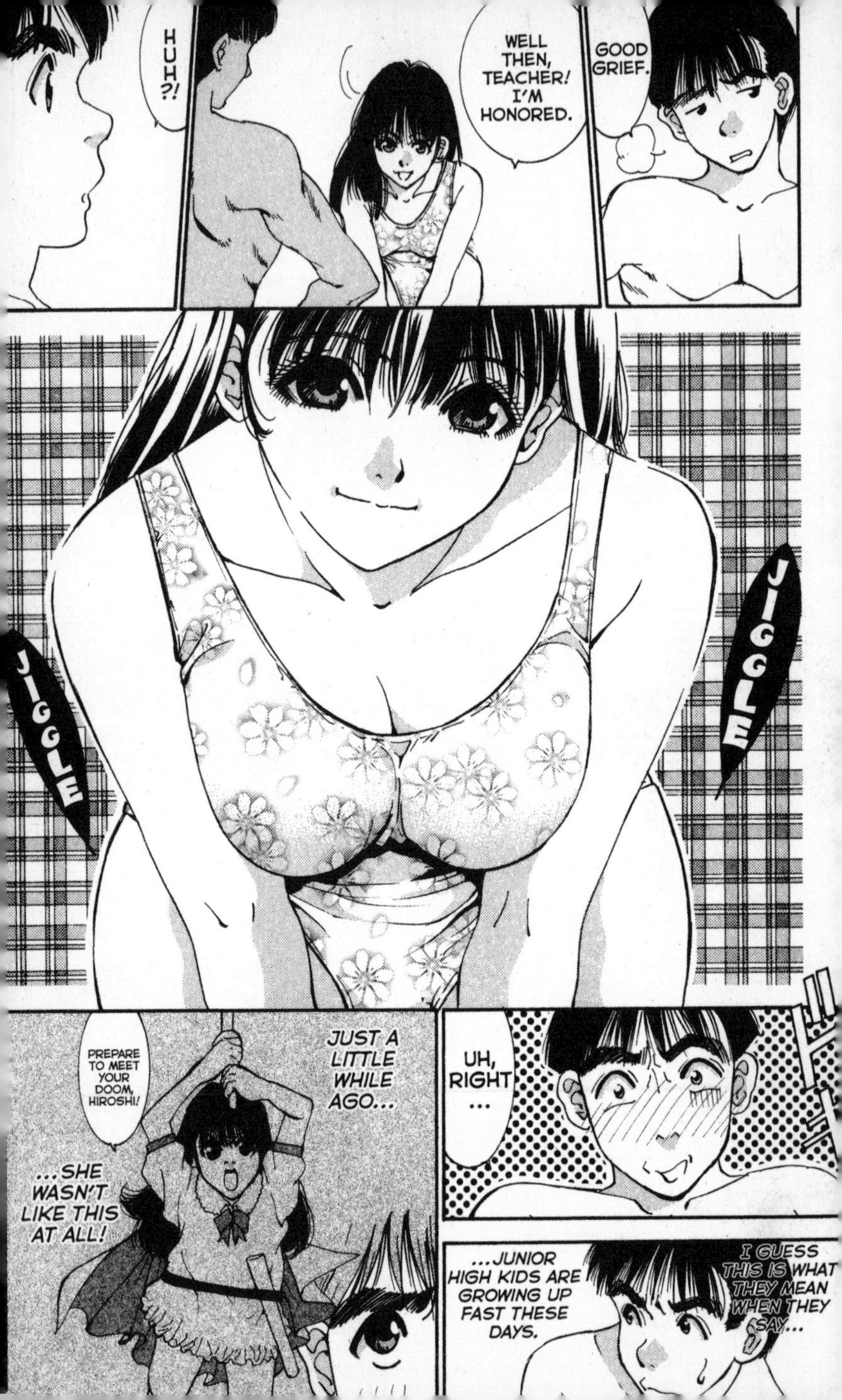
GOOD GRIEF.
WELL THEN, TEACHER! I'M HONORED.
HUH?!
JIGGLE
JIGGLE
UH, RIGHT ...
I GUESS THIS IS WHAT THEY MEAN WHEN THEY SAY...
...JUNIOR HIGH KIDS ARE GROWING UP FAST THESE DAYS.
JUST A LITTLE WHILE AGO...
PREPARE TO MEET YOUR DOOM, HIROSHI!
...SHE WASN'T LIKE THIS AT ALL!

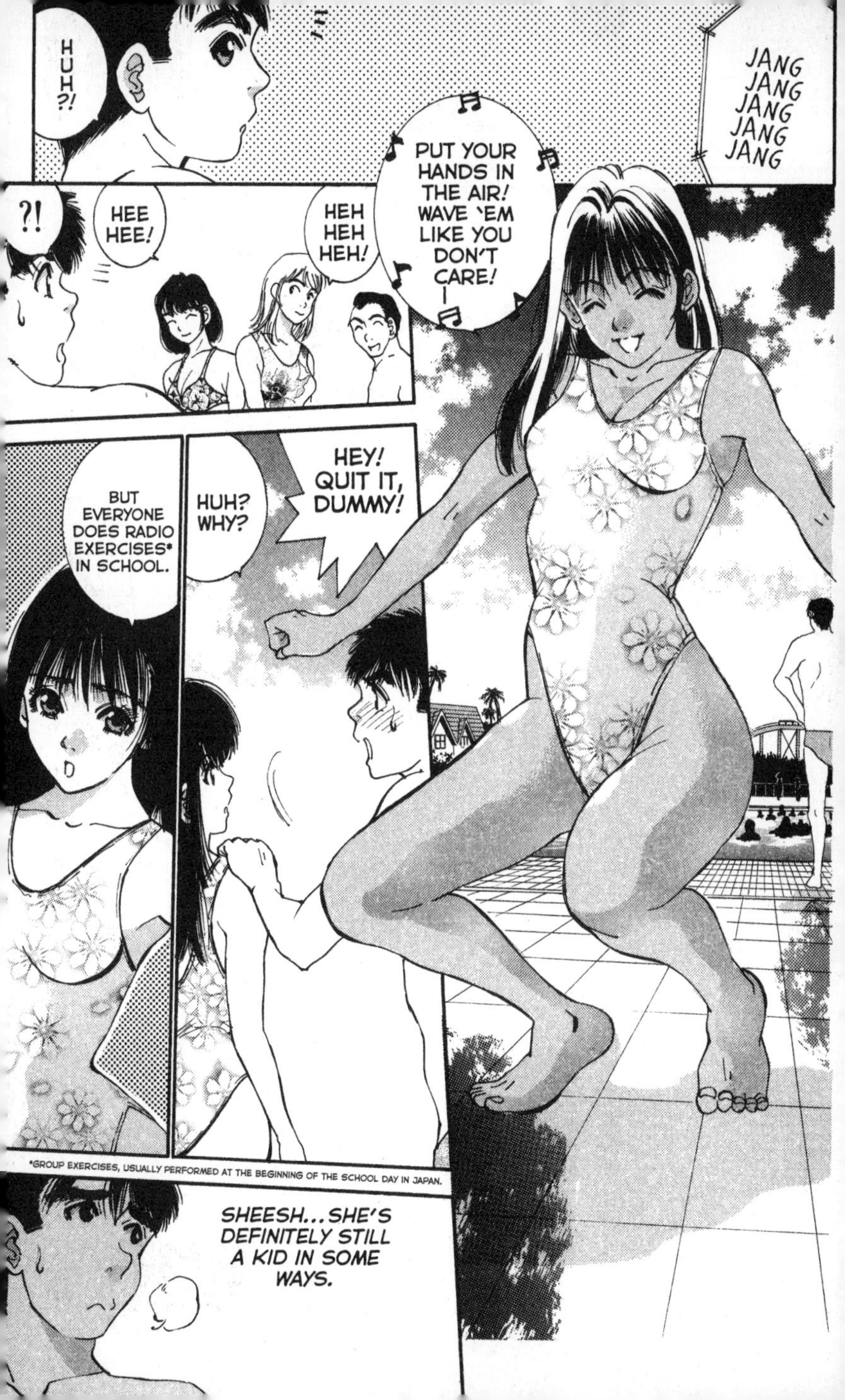
JANG JANG JANG JANG JANG
HUH?!
PUT YOUR HANDS IN THE AIR! WAVE 'EM LIKE YOU DON'T CARE!
HEH HEH HEH!
HEE HEE!
?!
HEY! QUIT IT, DUMMY!
HUH? WHY?
BUT EVERYONE DOES RADIO EXERCISES* IN SCHOOL.
SHEESH...SHE'S DEFINITELY STILL A KID IN SOME WAYS.

*GROUP EXERCISES, USUALLY PERFORMED AT THE BEGINNING OF THE SCHOOL DAY IN JAPAN.

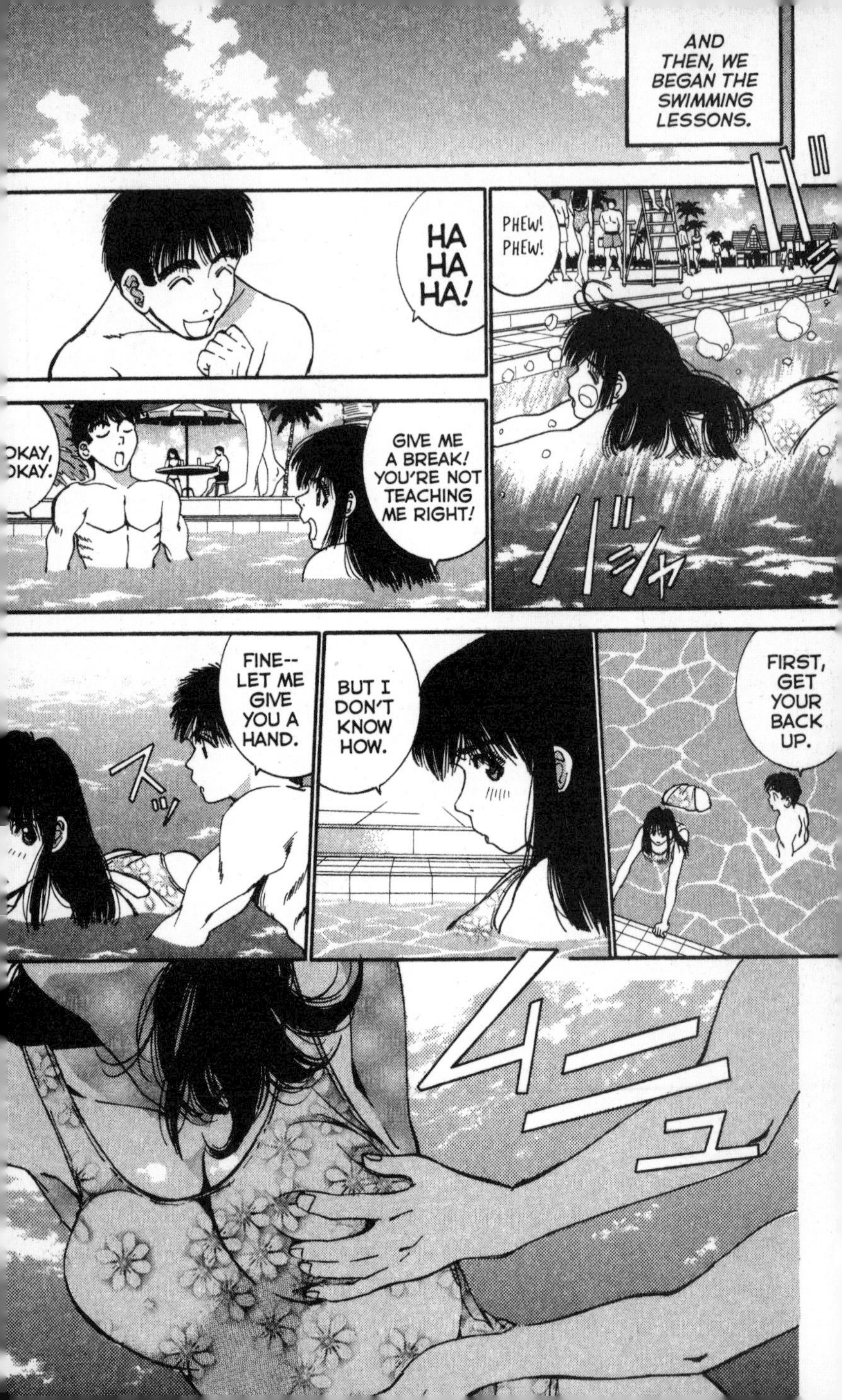
AND THEN, WE BEGAN THE SWIMMING LESSONS.
PHEW! PHEW!
バシャ
HA HA HA!
GIVE ME A BREAK! YOU'RE NOT TEACHING ME RIGHT!
OKAY, OKAY.
FIRST, GET YOUR BACK UP.
BUT I DON'T KNOW HOW.
FINE-- LET ME GIVE YOU A HAND.
スッ
ムニュ

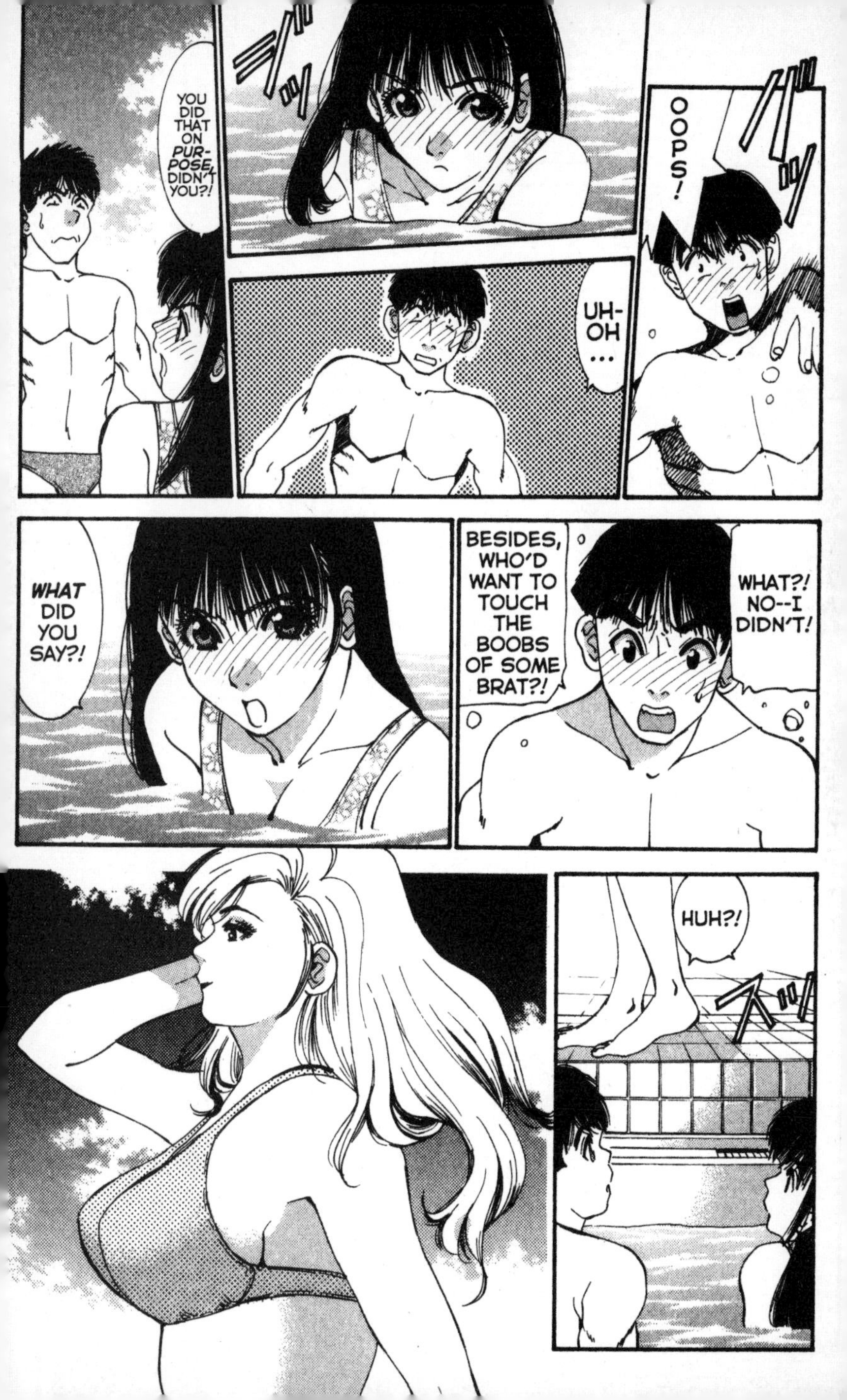
OOPS!
UH-OH ...
YOU DID THAT ON PURPOSE, DIDN'T YOU?!
WHAT?! NO--I DIDN'T!
BESIDES, WHO'D WANT TO TOUCH THE BOOBS OF SOME BRAT?!
WHAT DID YOU SAY?!
HUH?!

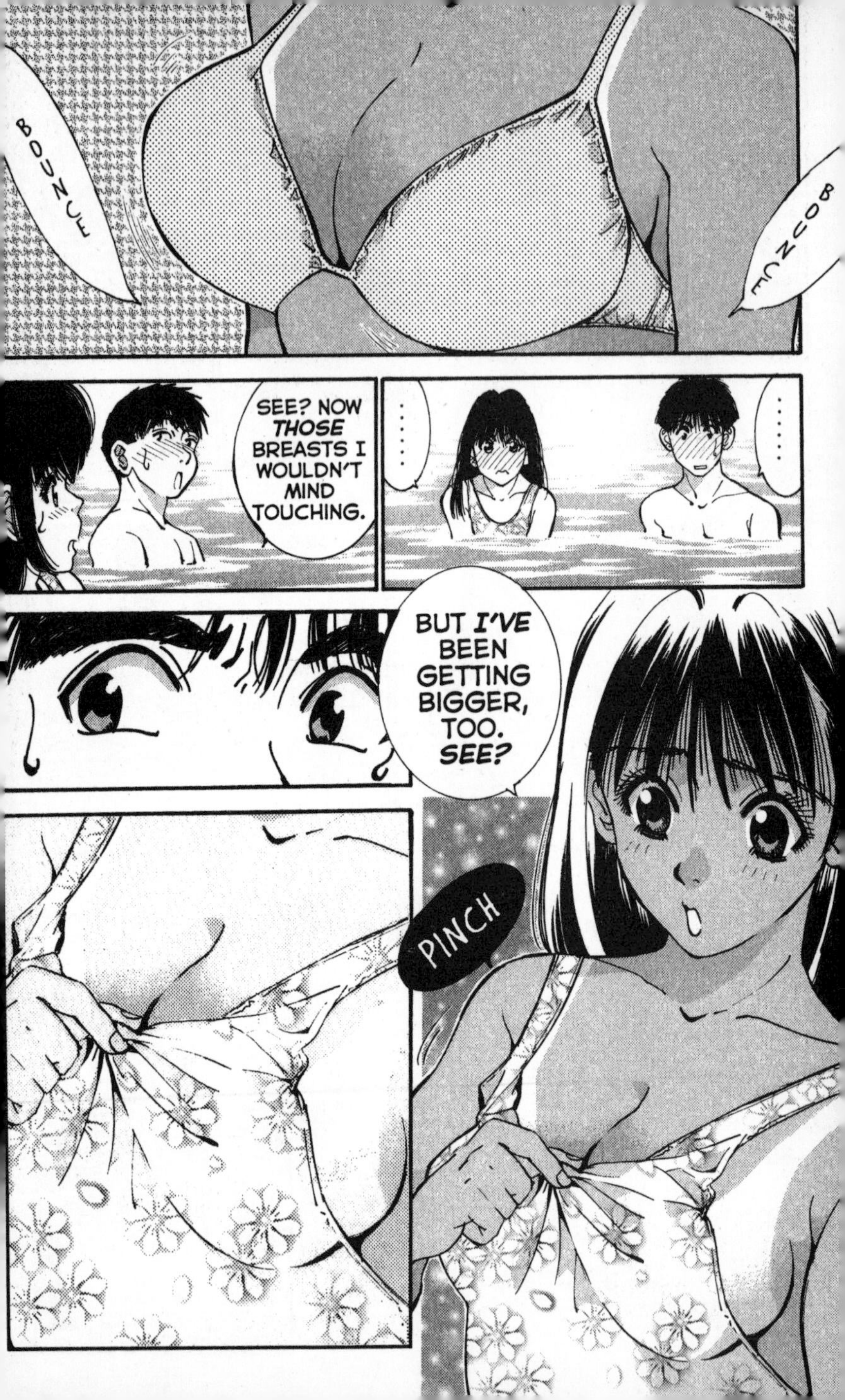
BOUNCE
BOUNCE
......
......
SEE? NOW *THOSE* BREASTS I WOULDN'T MIND TOUCHING.
BUT *I'VE* BEEN GETTING BIGGER, TOO. *SEE?*
PINCH

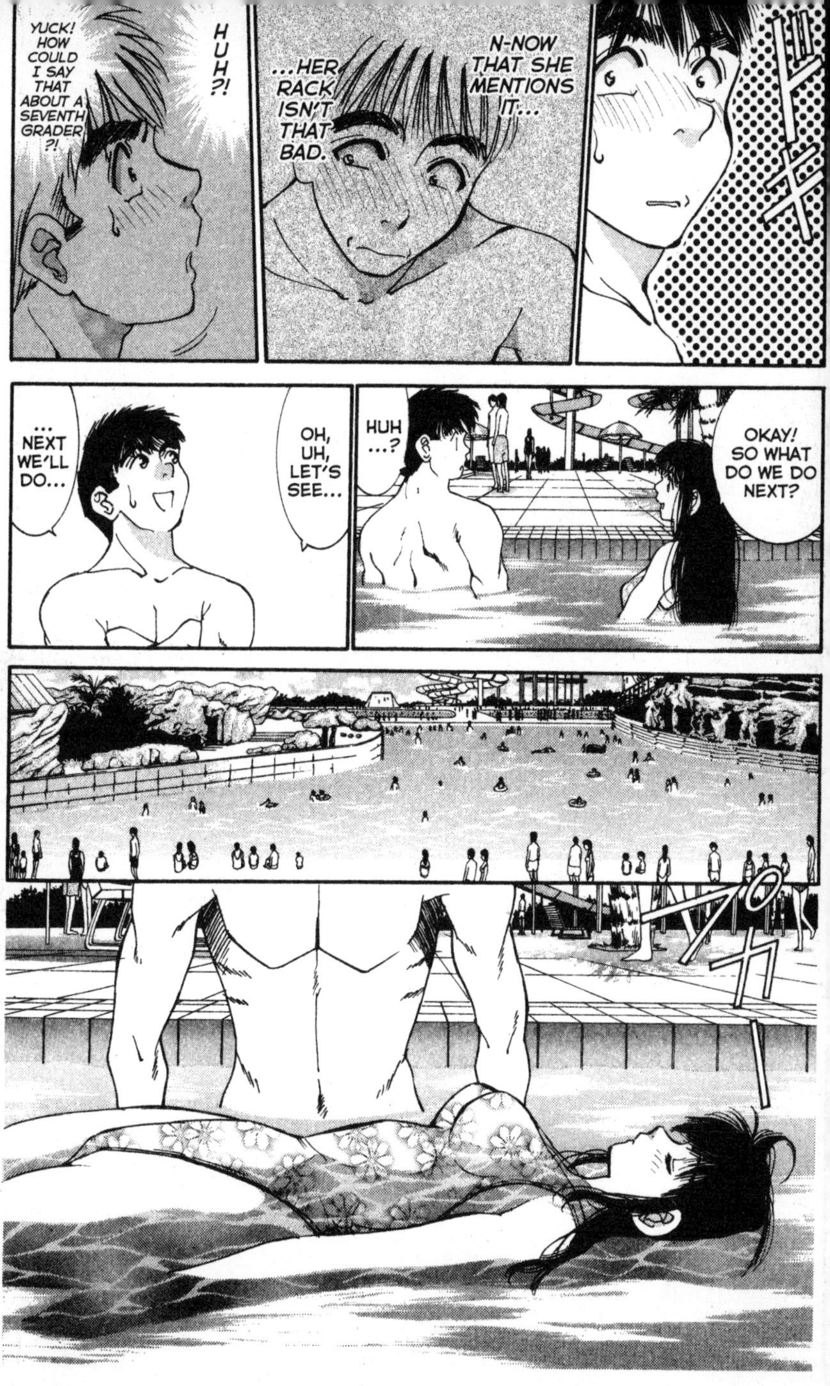
N-NOW THAT SHE MENTIONS IT...
...HER RACK ISN'T THAT BAD.
HUH?!
YUCK! HOW COULD I SAY THAT ABOUT A SEVENTH GRADER?!
OKAY! SO WHAT DO WE DO NEXT?
HUH ...?
OH, UH, LET'S SEE...
... NEXT WE'LL DO...

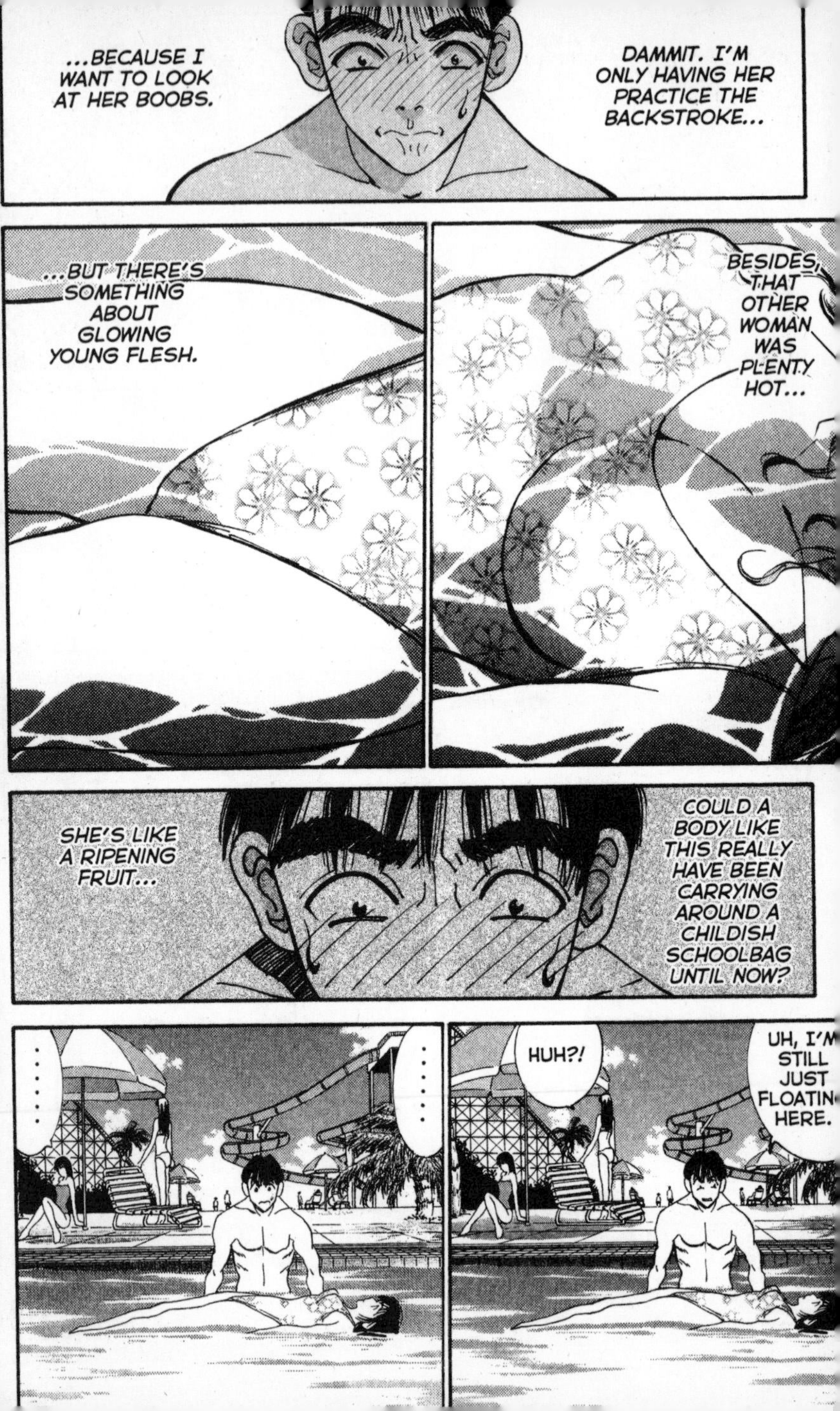
DAMMIT. I'M ONLY HAVING HER PRACTICE THE BACKSTROKE...
...BECAUSE I WANT TO LOOK AT HER BOOBS.
BESIDES, THAT OTHER WOMAN WAS PLENTY HOT...
...BUT THERE'S SOMETHING ABOUT GLOWING YOUNG FLESH.
COULD A BODY LIKE THIS REALLY HAVE BEEN CARRYING AROUND A CHILDISH SCHOOLBAG UNTIL NOW?
SHE'S LIKE A RIPENING FRUIT...
UH, I'M STILL JUST FLOATIN HERE.
HUH?!
......
......

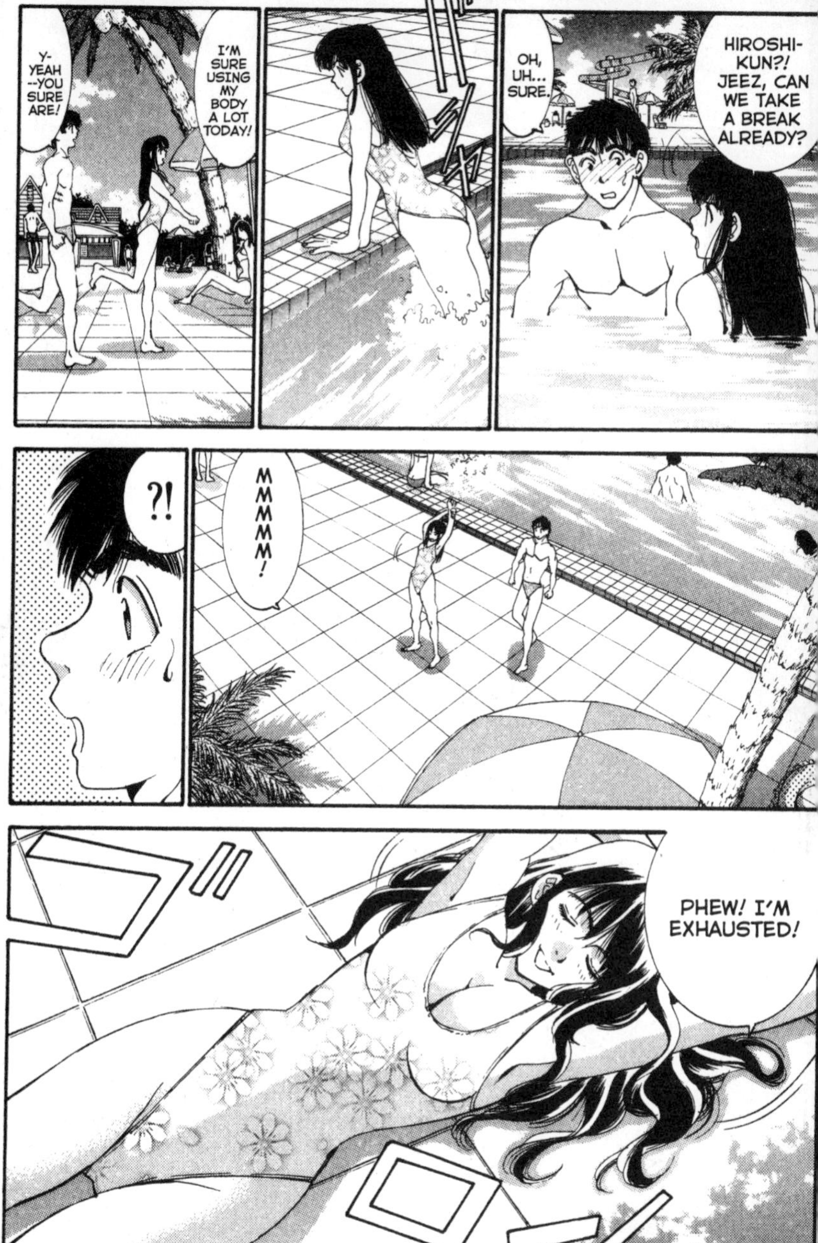

HIROSHI-KUN?! JEEZ, CAN WE TAKE A BREAK ALREADY?
OH, UH... SURE.
I'M SURE USING MY BODY A LOT TODAY!
Y-YEAH--YOU SURE ARE!
MMMMM!
?!
PHEW! I'M EXHAUSTED!

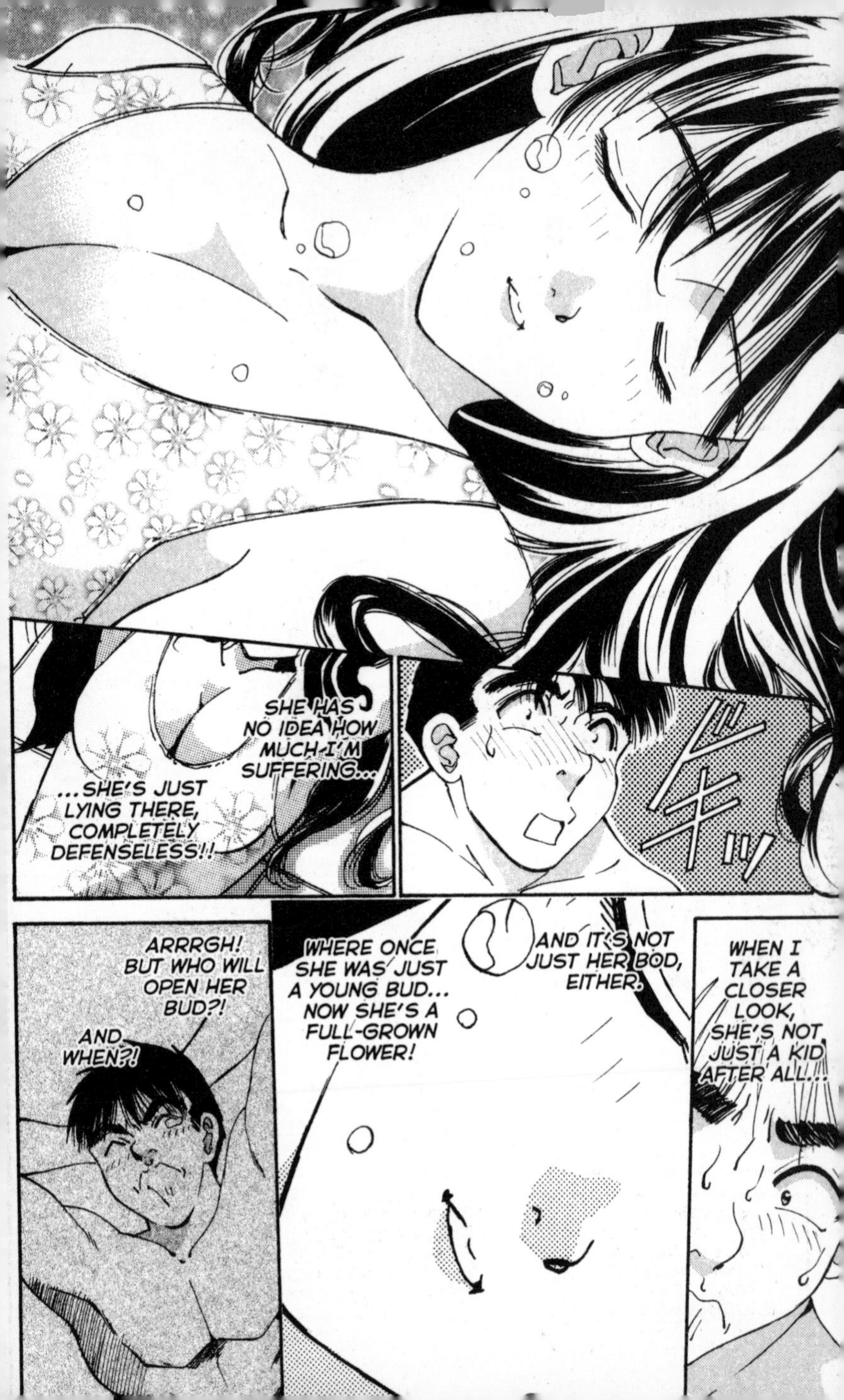
ドキッ
SHE HAS NO IDEA HOW MUCH I'M SUFFERING...
...SHE'S JUST LYING THERE, COMPLETELY DEFENSELESS!!
WHEN I TAKE A CLOSER LOOK, SHE'S NOT JUST A KID AFTER ALL...
AND IT'S NOT JUST HER BOD, EITHER.
WHERE ONCE SHE WAS JUST A YOUNG BUD... NOW SHE'S A FULL-GROWN FLOWER!
ARRRGH! BUT WHO WILL OPEN HER BUD?!
AND WHEN?!

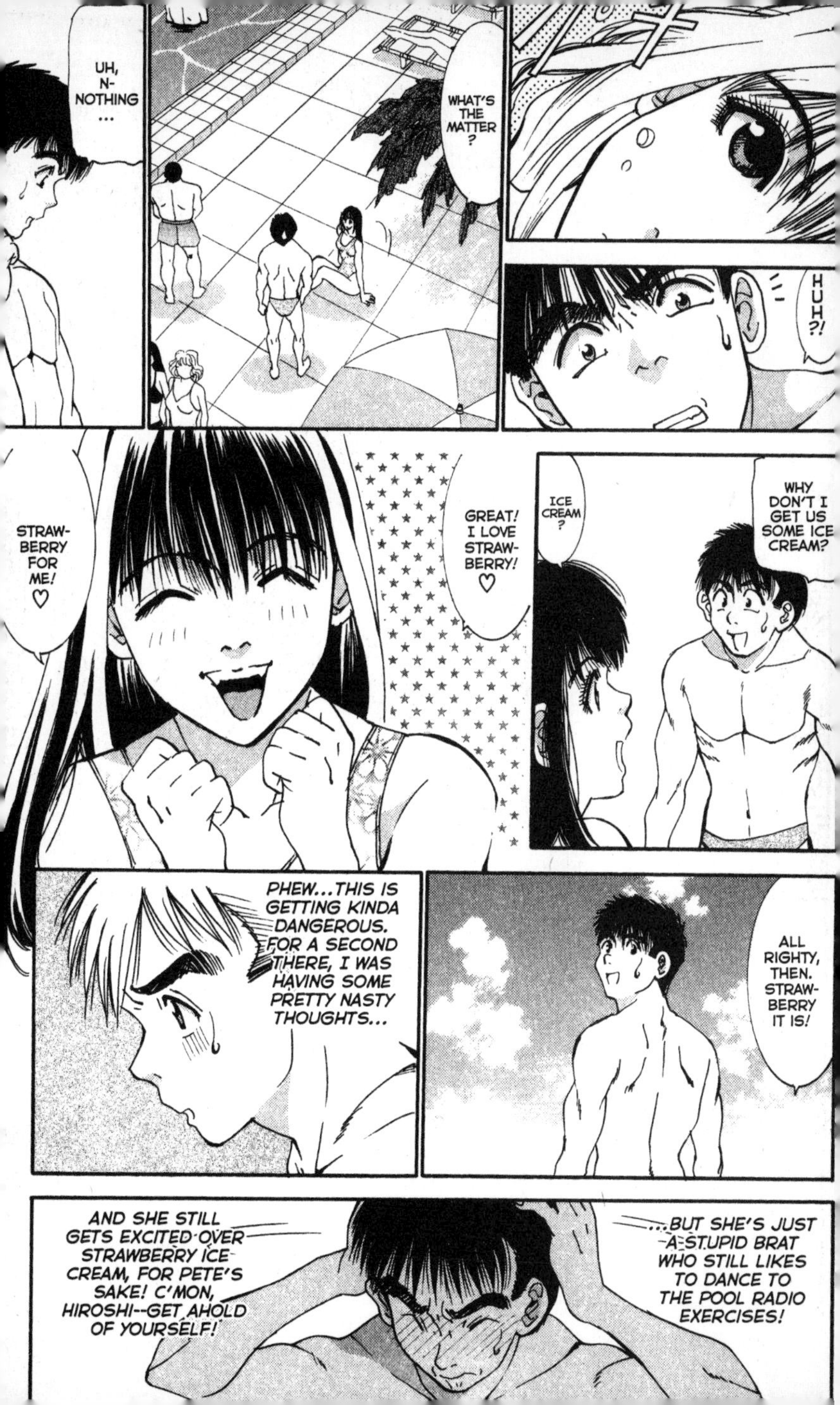
HUH?!
WHAT'S THE MATTER?
UH, N-NOTHING...
WHY DON'T I GET US SOME ICE CREAM?
ICE CREAM?
GREAT! I LOVE STRAWBERRY! ♡
STRAWBERRY FOR ME! ♡
ALL RIGHTY, THEN. STRAWBERRY IT IS!
PHEW...THIS IS GETTING KINDA DANGEROUS. FOR A SECOND THERE, I WAS HAVING SOME PRETTY NASTY THOUGHTS...
...BUT SHE'S JUST A STUPID BRAT WHO STILL LIKES TO DANCE TO THE POOL RADIO EXERCISES!
AND SHE STILL GETS EXCITED OVER STRAWBERRY ICE CREAM, FOR PETE'S SAKE! C'MON, HIROSHI--GET AHOLD OF YOURSELF!

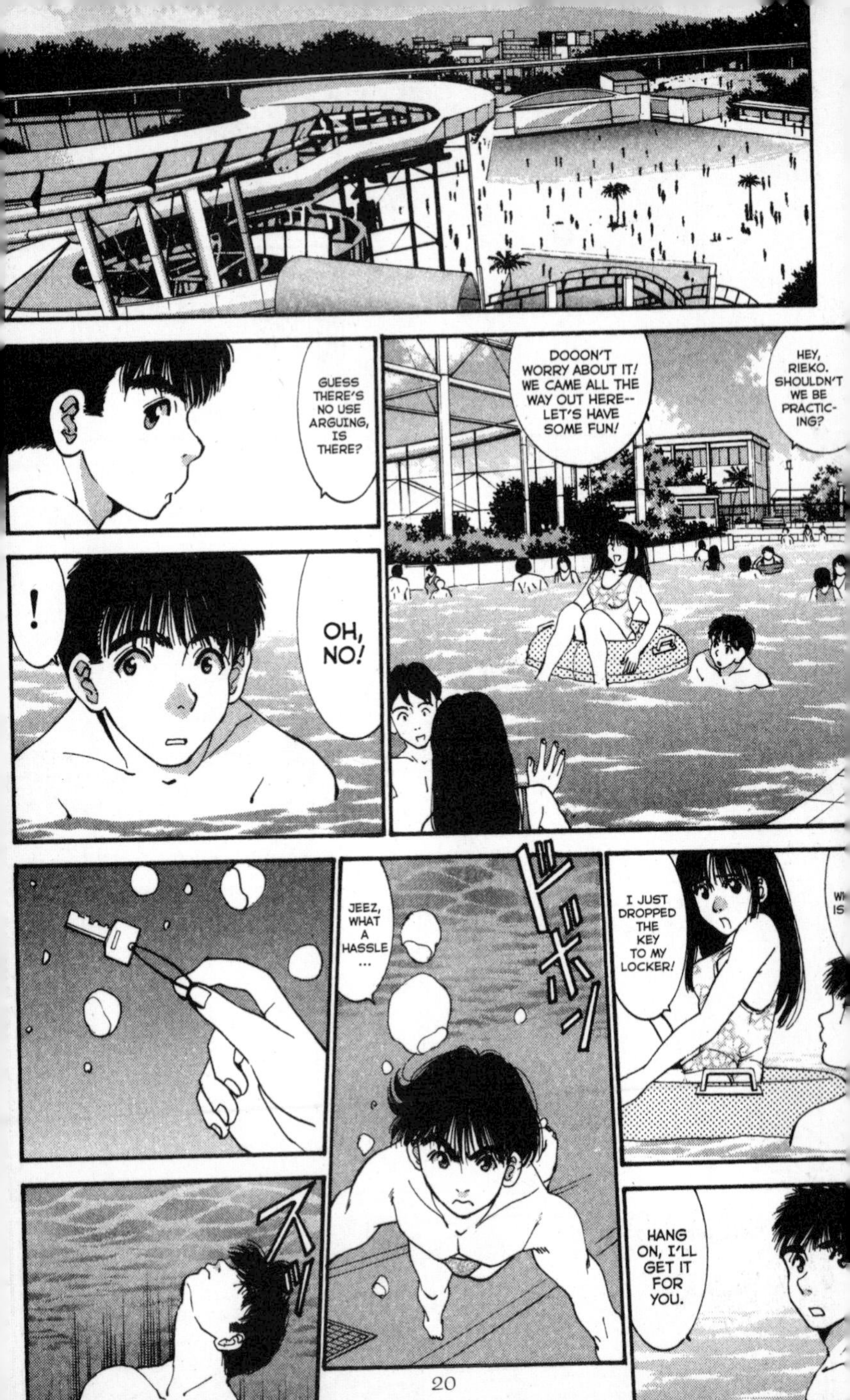
HEY, RIEKO. SHOULDN'T WE BE PRACTIC-ING?
DOOON'T WORRY ABOUT IT! WE CAME ALL THE WAY OUT HERE-- LET'S HAVE SOME FUN!
GUESS THERE'S NO USE ARGUING, IS THERE?
OH, NO!
!
I JUST DROPPED THE KEY TO MY LOCKER!
HANG ON, I'LL GET IT FOR YOU.
JEEZ, WHAT A HASSLE ...

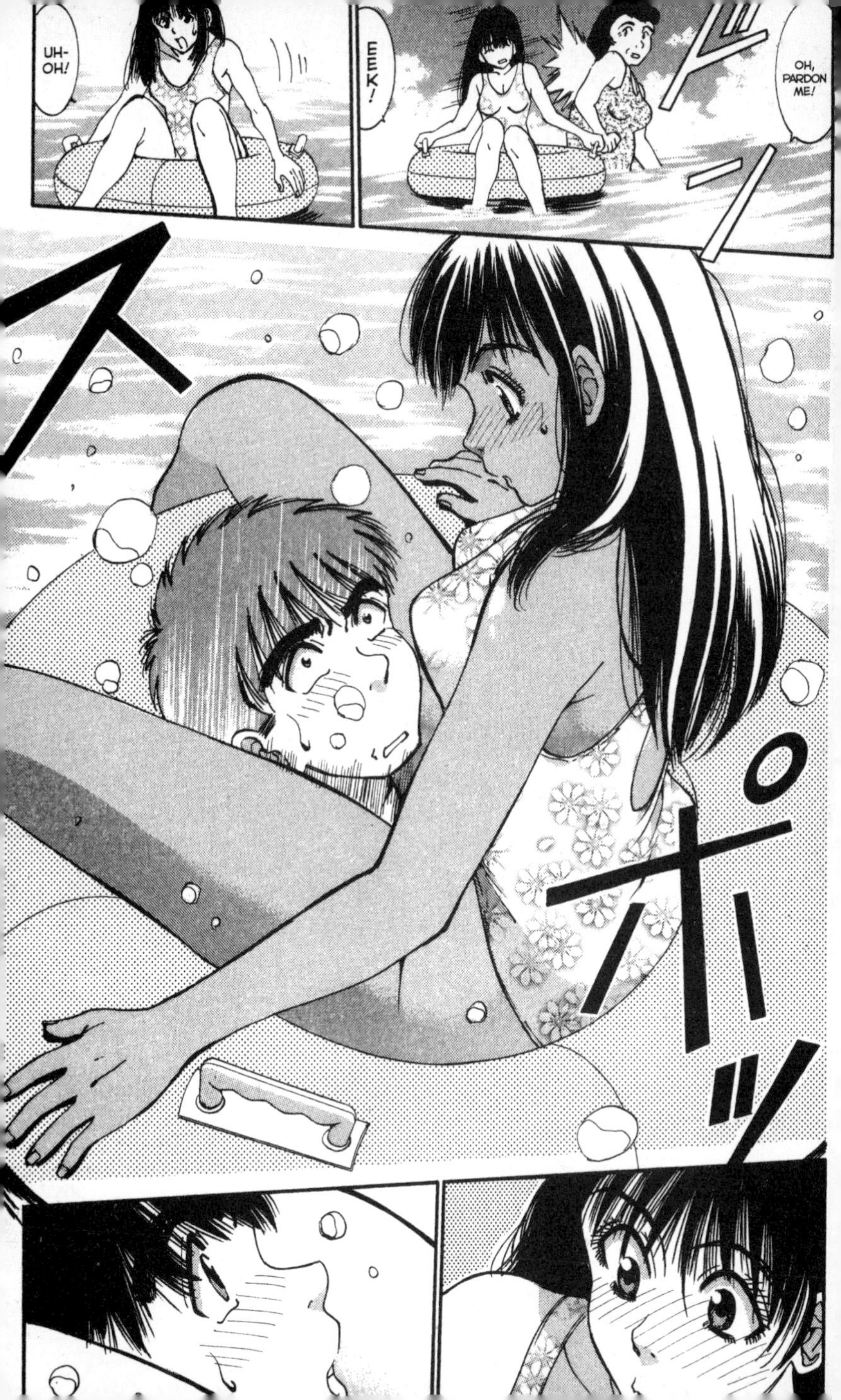
OH, PARDON ME!
EEK!
UH-OH!

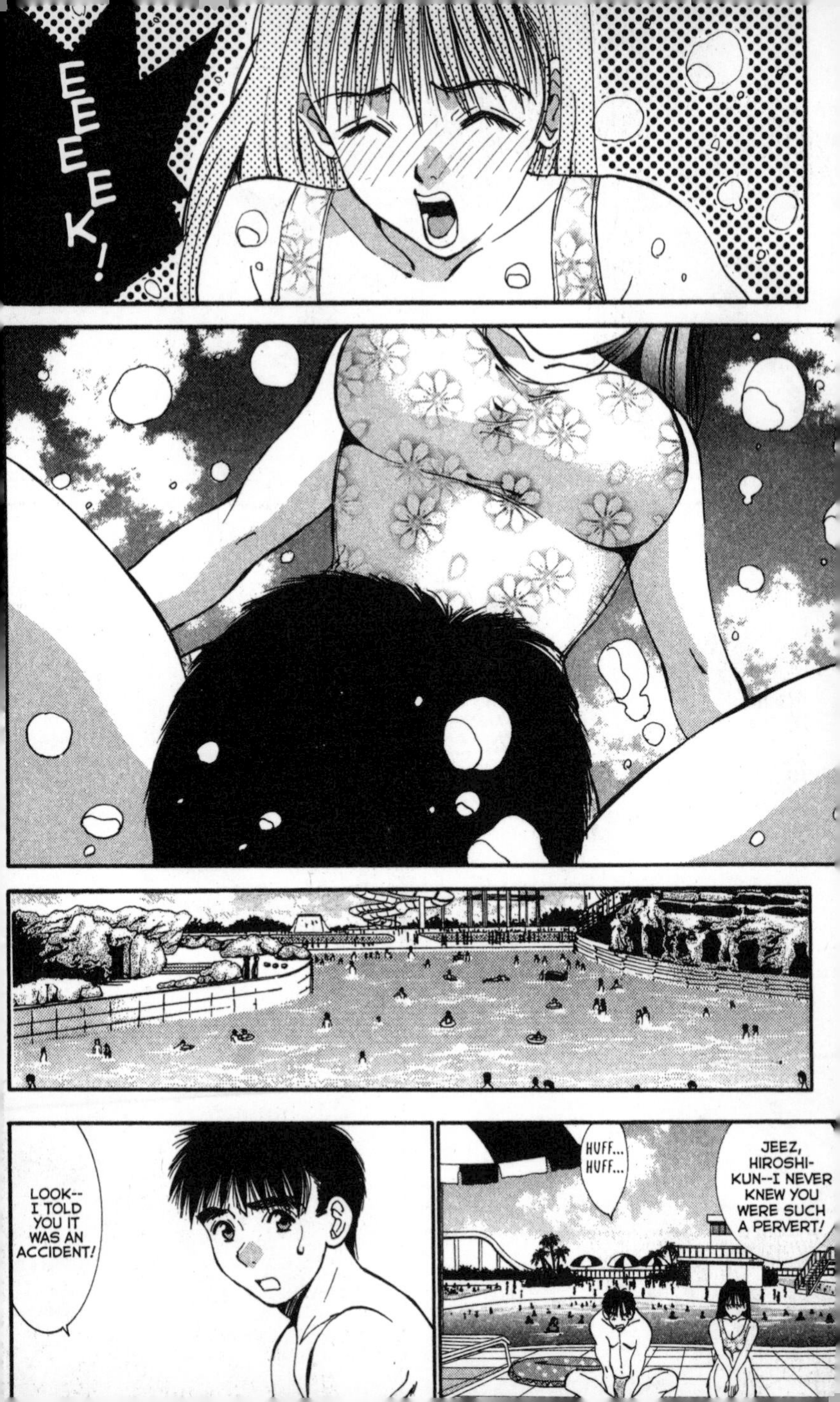
EEEEK!
JEEZ, HIROSHI-KUN--I NEVER KNEW YOU WERE SUCH A PERVERT!
HUFF... HUFF...
LOOK-- I TOLD YOU IT WAS AN ACCIDENT!

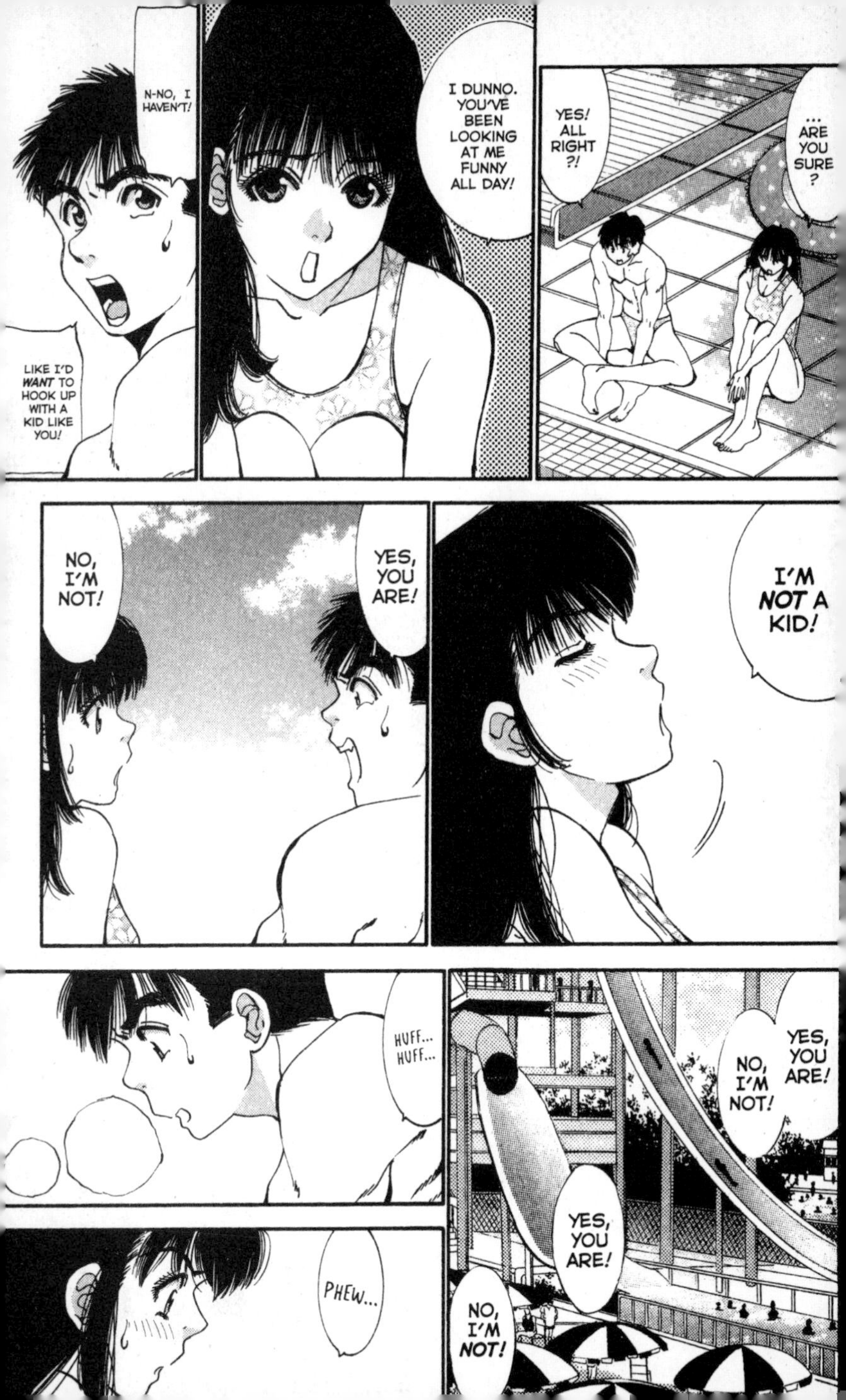
... ARE YOU SURE?
YES! ALL RIGHT?!
I DUNNO. YOU'VE BEEN LOOKING AT ME FUNNY ALL DAY!
N-NO, I HAVEN'T!
LIKE I'D *WANT* TO HOOK UP WITH A KID LIKE YOU!
I'M *NOT* A KID!
YES, YOU ARE!
NO, I'M NOT!
YES, YOU ARE!
NO, I'M NOT!
YES, YOU ARE!
NO, I'M *NOT*!
HUFF... HUFF...
PHEW...

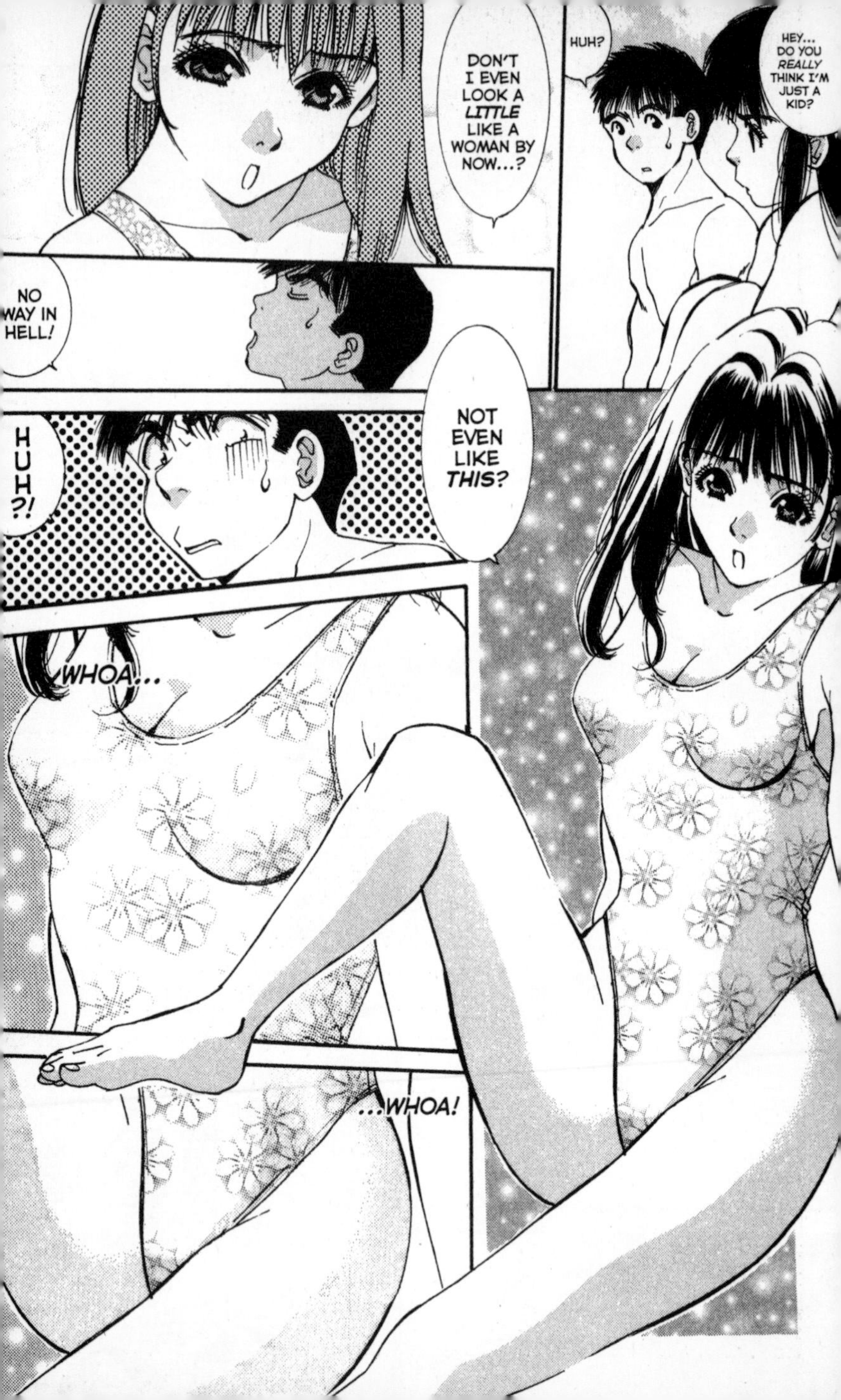
HEY... DO YOU *REALLY* THINK I'M JUST A KID?
HUH?
DON'T I EVEN LOOK A *LITTLE* LIKE A WOMAN BY NOW...?
NO WAY IN HELL!
NOT EVEN LIKE *THIS?*
HUH?!
WHOA...
...WHOA!

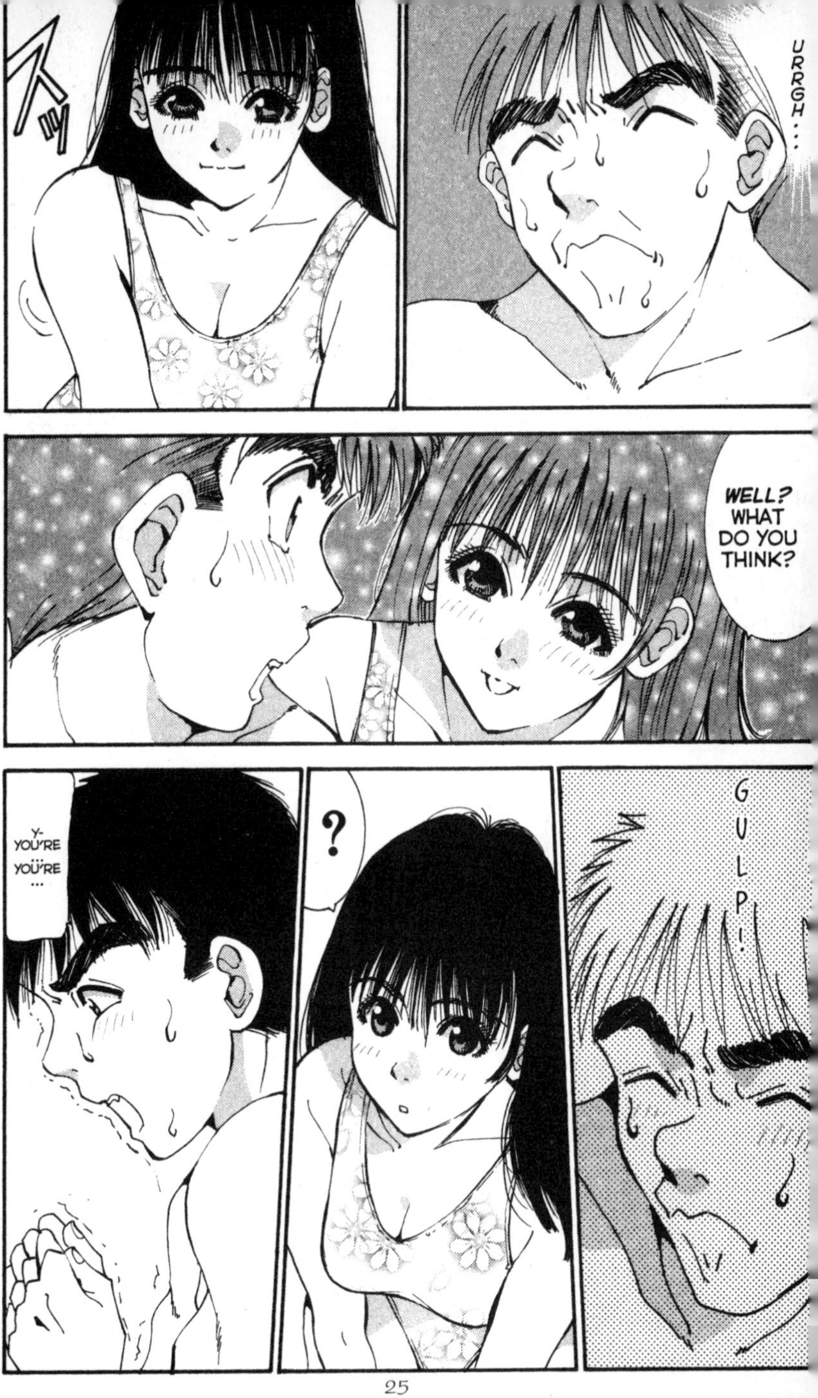

URRGH...
スッ
WELL? WHAT DO YOU THINK?
GULP!
?
Y- YOU'RE... YOU'RE...

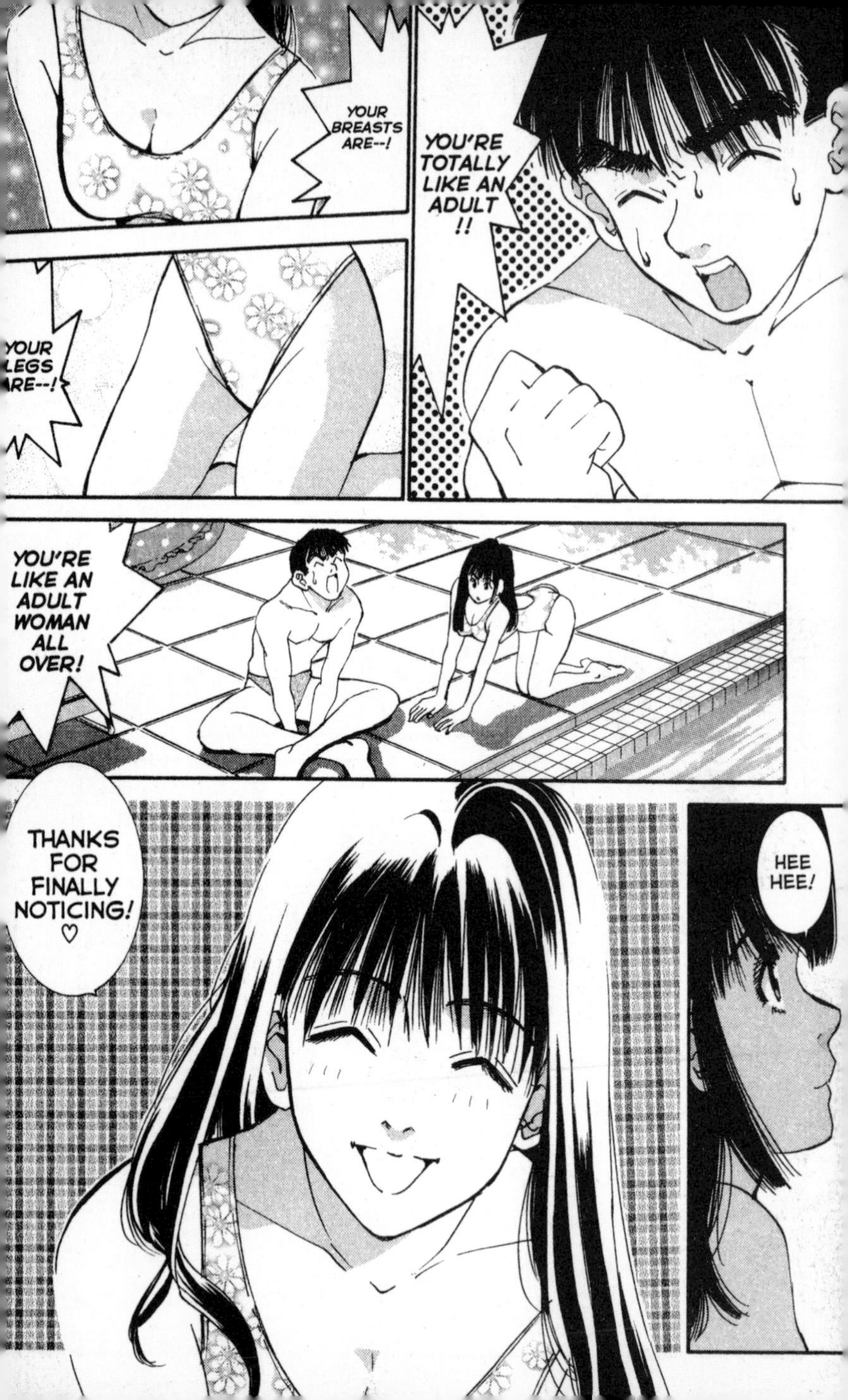
YOU'RE TOTALLY LIKE AN ADULT !!
YOUR BREASTS ARE--!
YOUR LEGS ARE--!
YOU'RE LIKE AN ADULT WOMAN ALL OVER!
HEE HEE!
THANKS FOR FINALLY NOTICING! ♡

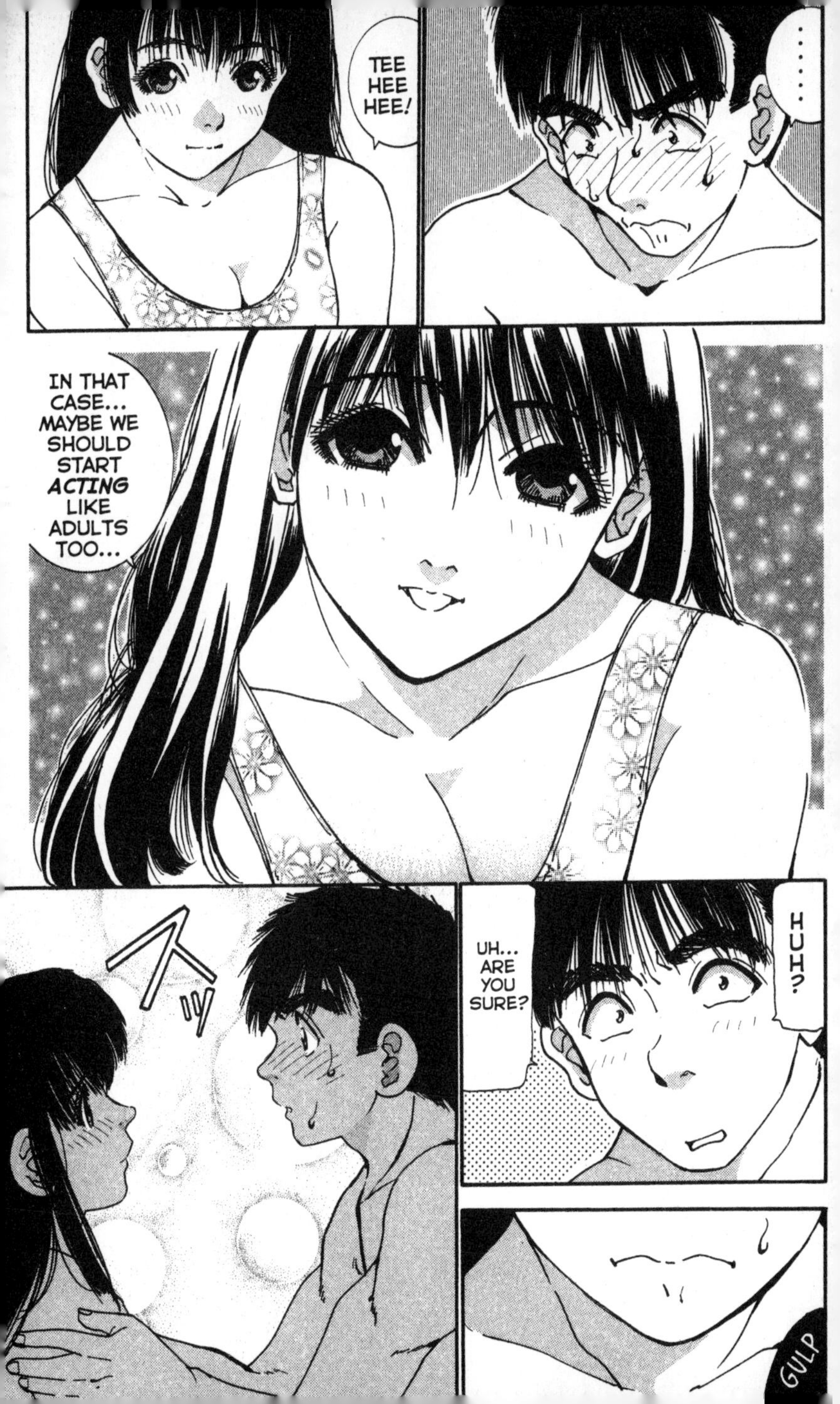
......
TEE HEE HEE!
IN THAT CASE... MAYBE WE SHOULD START *ACTING* LIKE ADULTS TOO...
HUH?
UH... ARE YOU SURE?
GULP

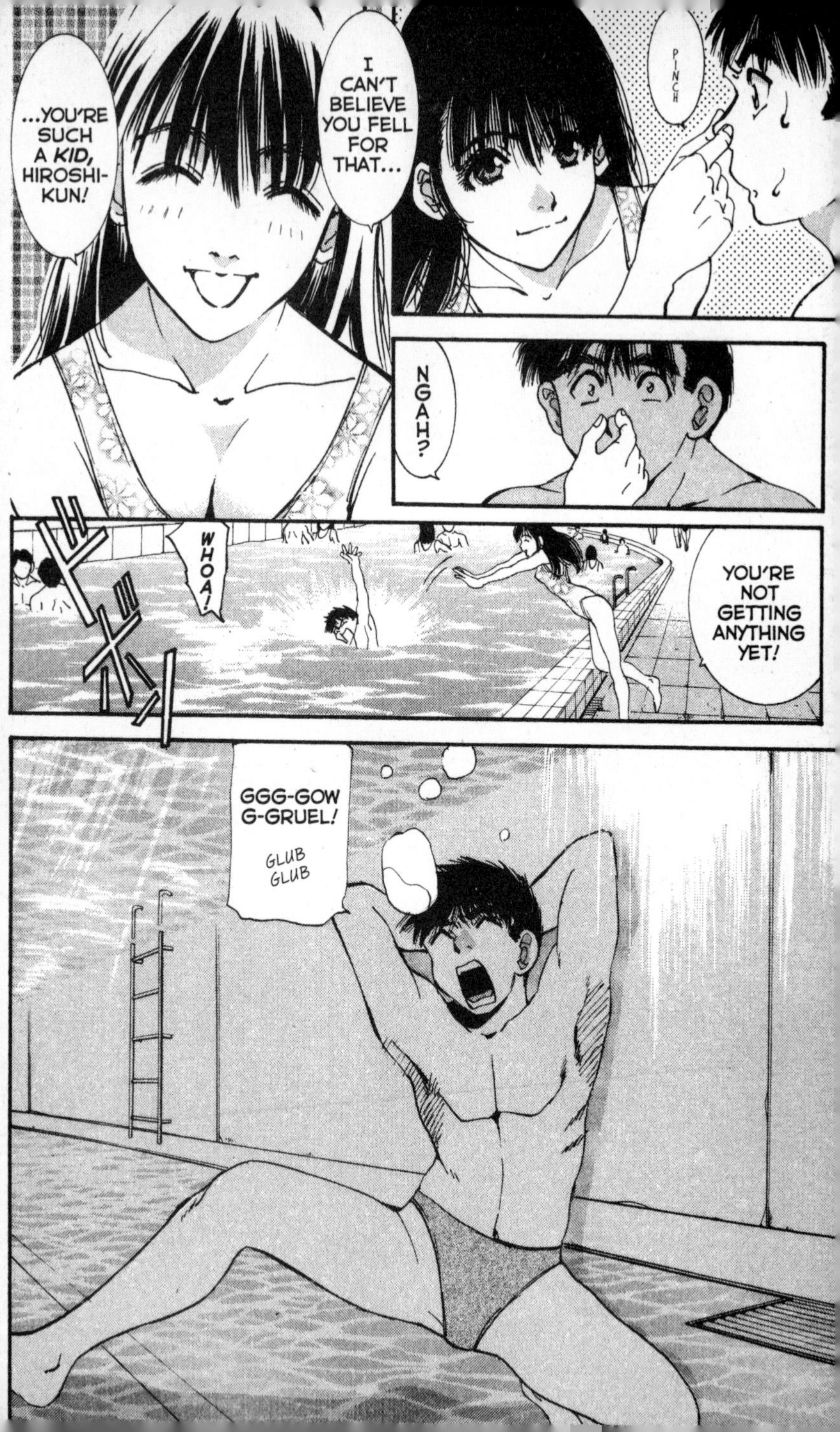

PINCH
I CAN'T BELIEVE YOU FELL FOR THAT...
NGAH?
...YOU'RE SUCH A *KID*, HIROSHI-KUN!
YOU'RE NOT GETTING ANYTHING YET!
WHOA!
GGG-GOW G-GRUEL!
GLUB GLUB

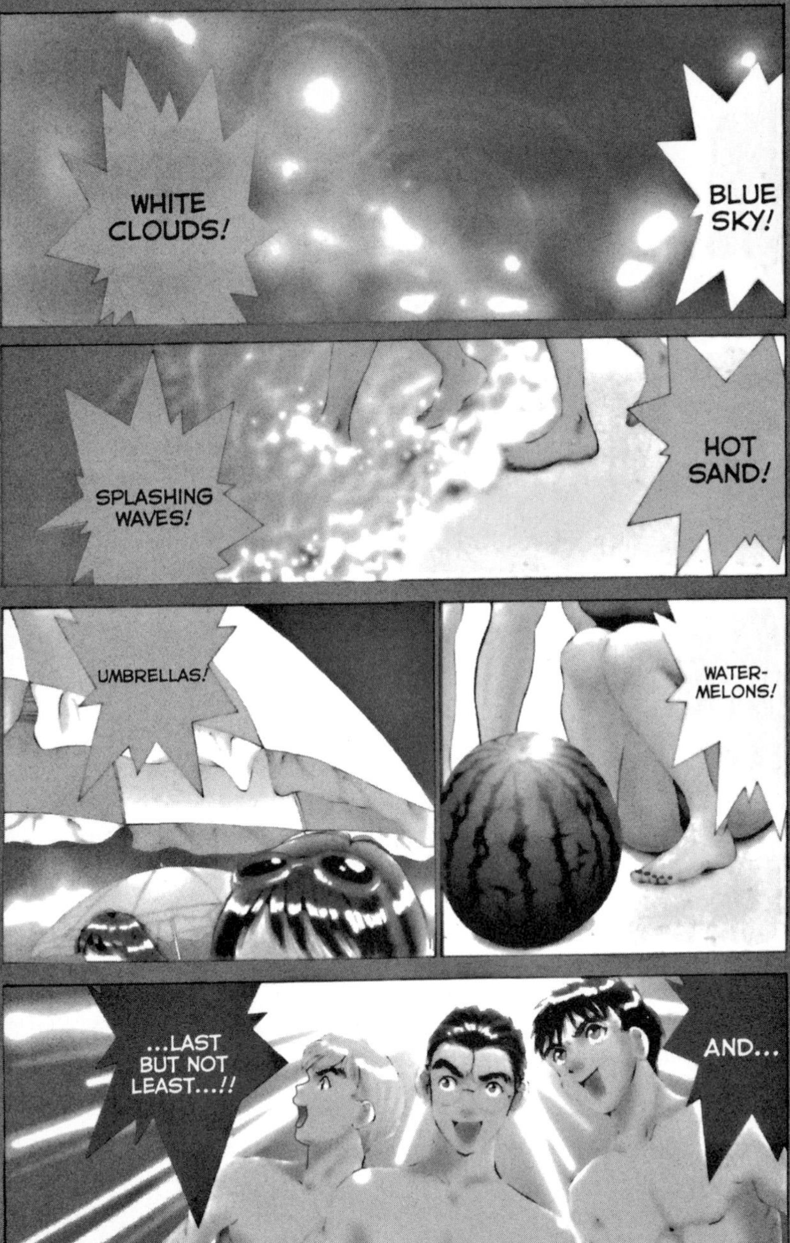
BLUE SKY!
WHITE CLOUDS!
HOT SAND!
SPLASHING WAVES!
WATER-MELONS!
UMBRELLAS!
AND...
...LAST BUT NOT LEAST...!!

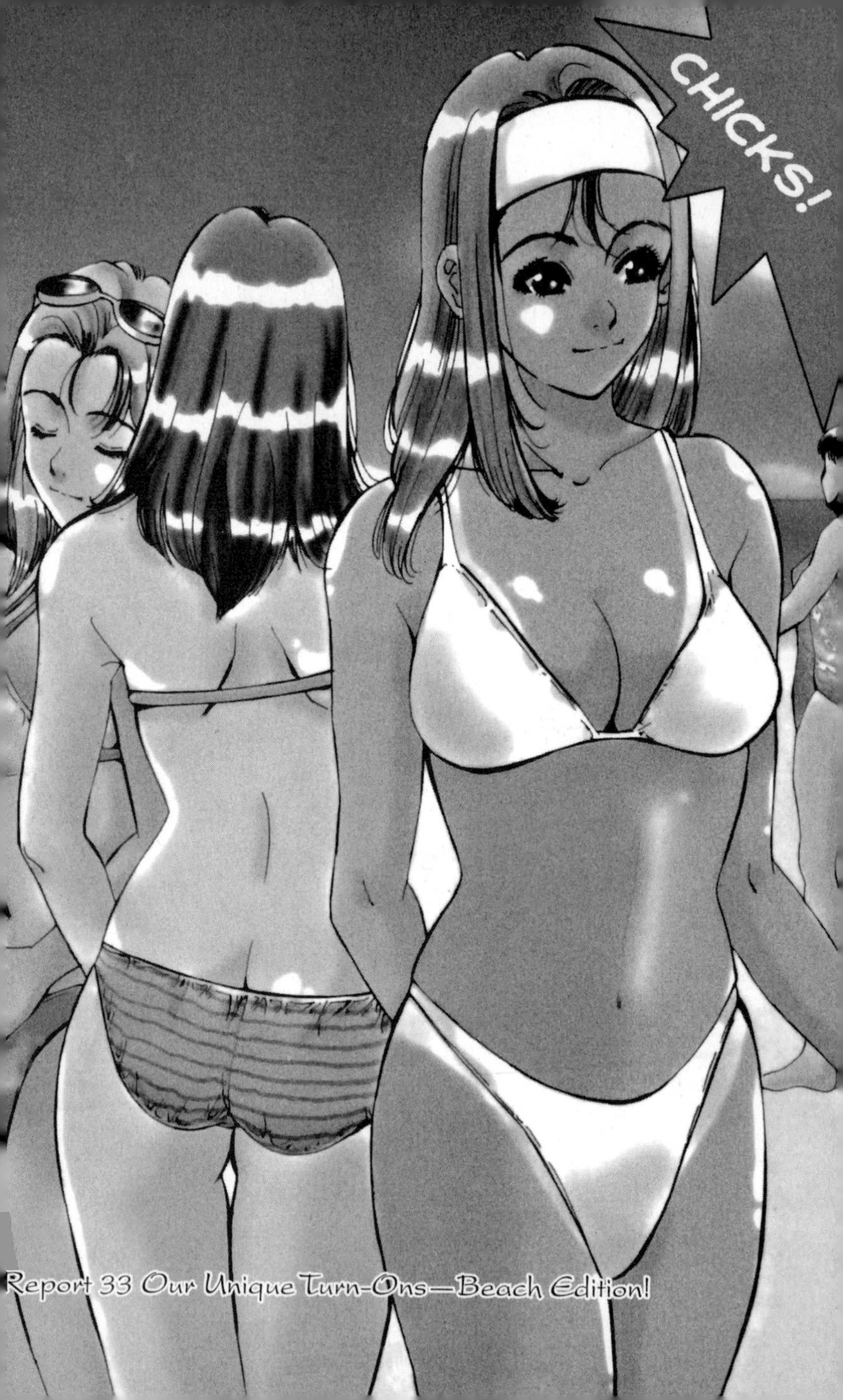
CHICKS!

Report 33 Our Unique Turn-Ons—Beach Edition!

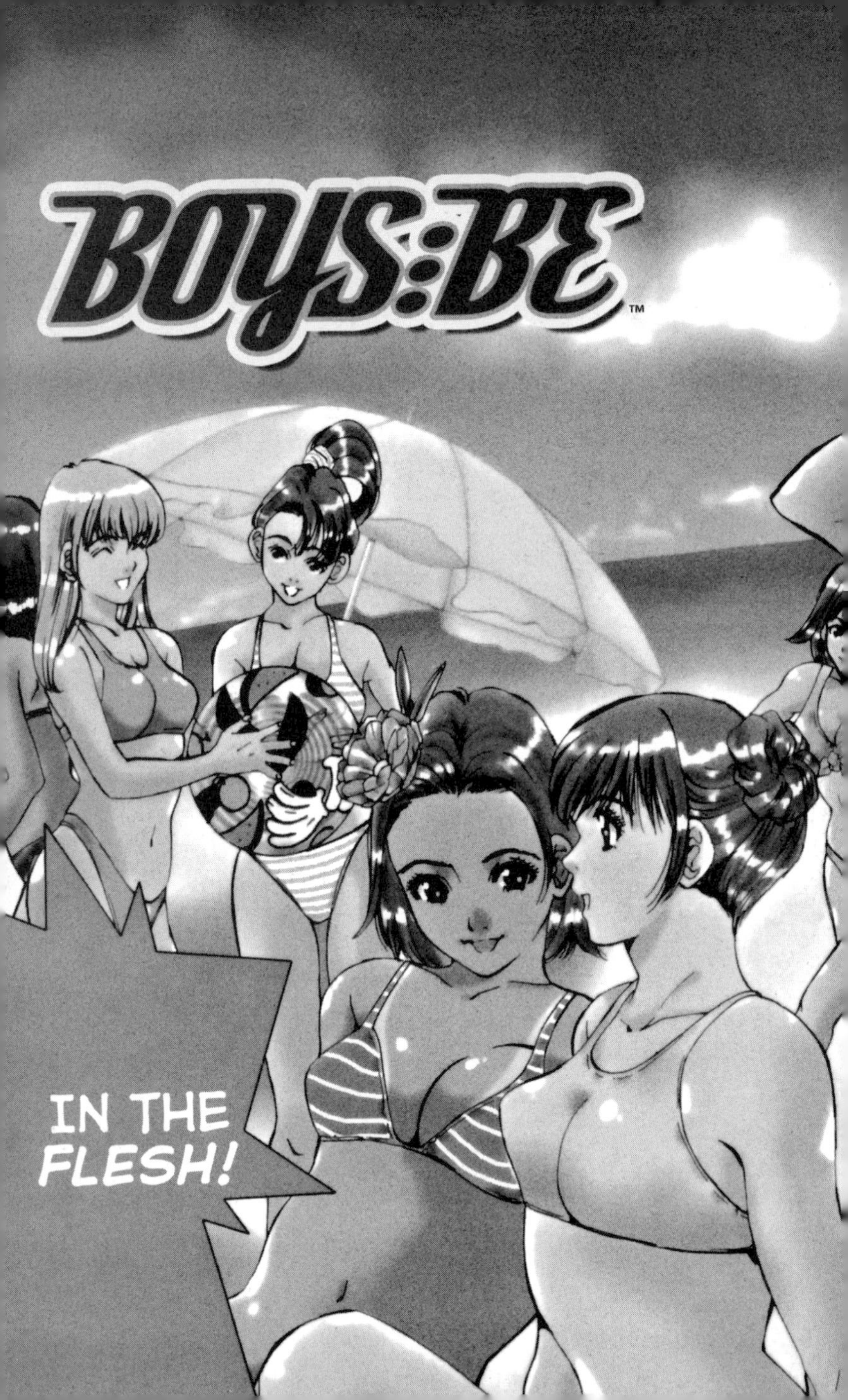
BOYS BE™
IN THE FLESH!

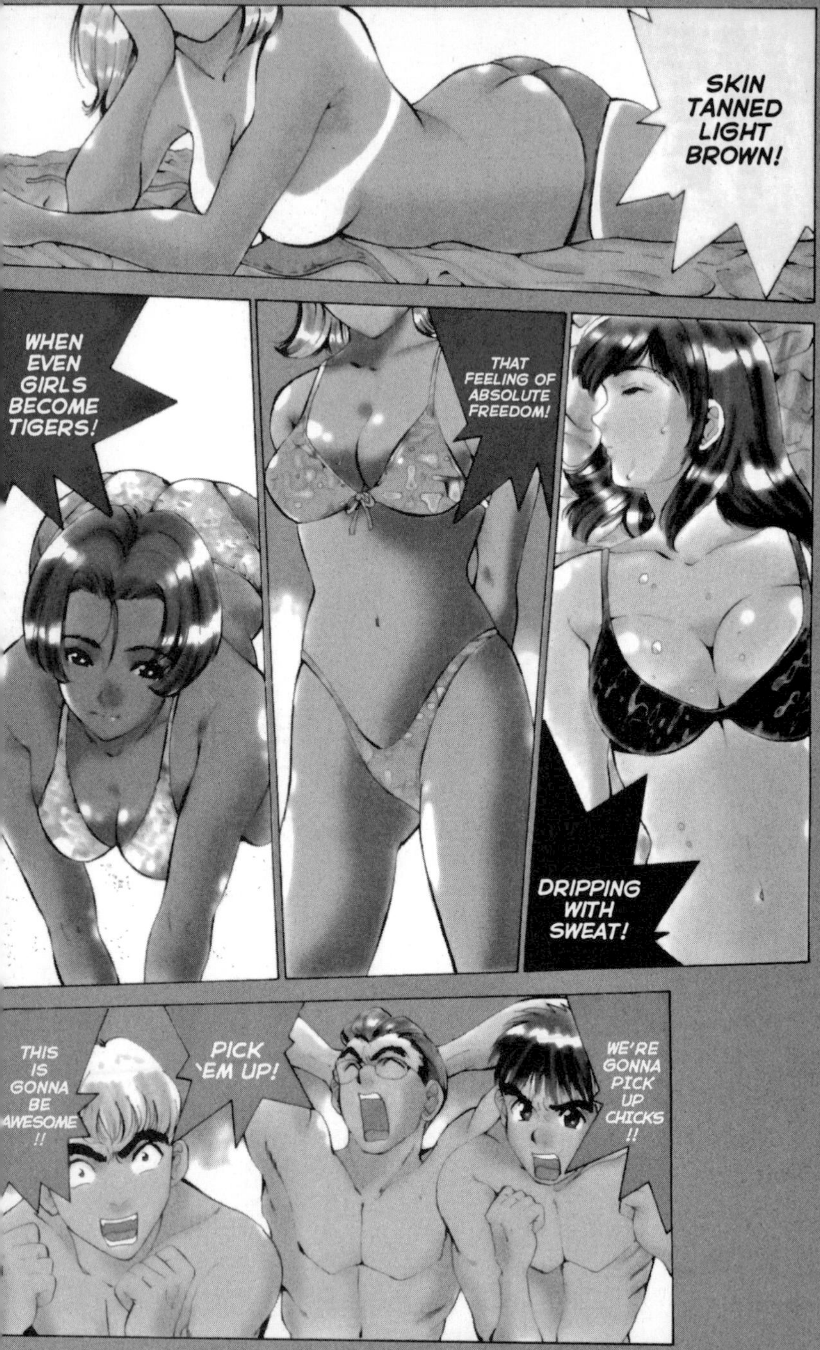
SKIN TANNED LIGHT BROWN!
DRIPPING WITH SWEAT!
THAT FEELING OF ABSOLUTE FREEDOM!
WHEN EVEN GIRLS BECOME TIGERS!
WE'RE GONNA PICK UP CHICKS!!
PICK 'EM UP!
THIS IS GONNA BE AWESOME!!

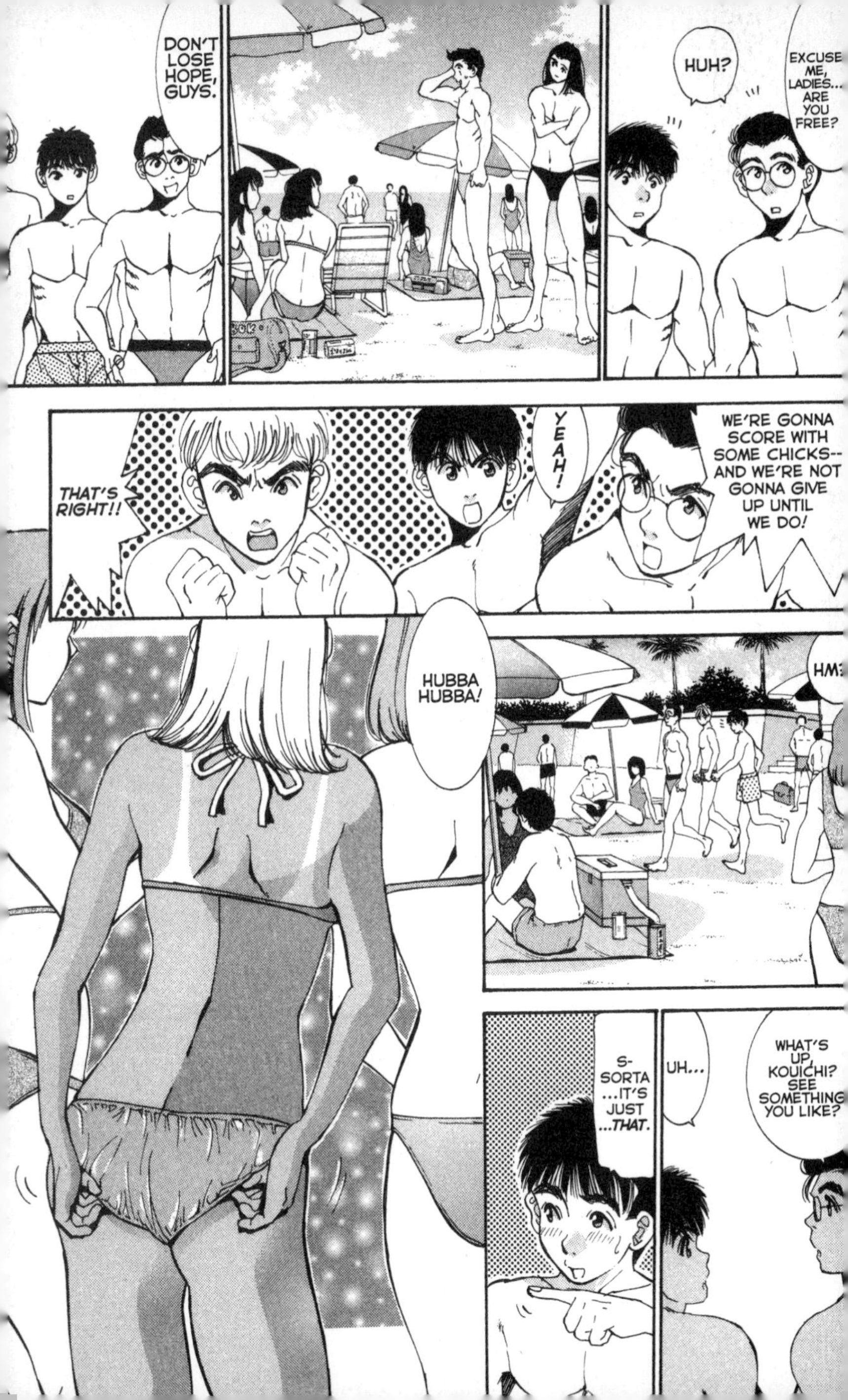
EXCUSE ME, LADIES... ARE YOU FREE?
HUH?
DON'T LOSE HOPE, GUYS.
WE'RE GONNA SCORE WITH SOME CHICKS--AND WE'RE NOT GONNA GIVE UP UNTIL WE DO!
YEAH!
THAT'S RIGHT!!
HM?
WHAT'S UP, KOUICHI? SEE SOMETHING YOU LIKE?
UH...
S-SORTA ...IT'S JUST ...*THAT*.
HUBBA HUBBA!

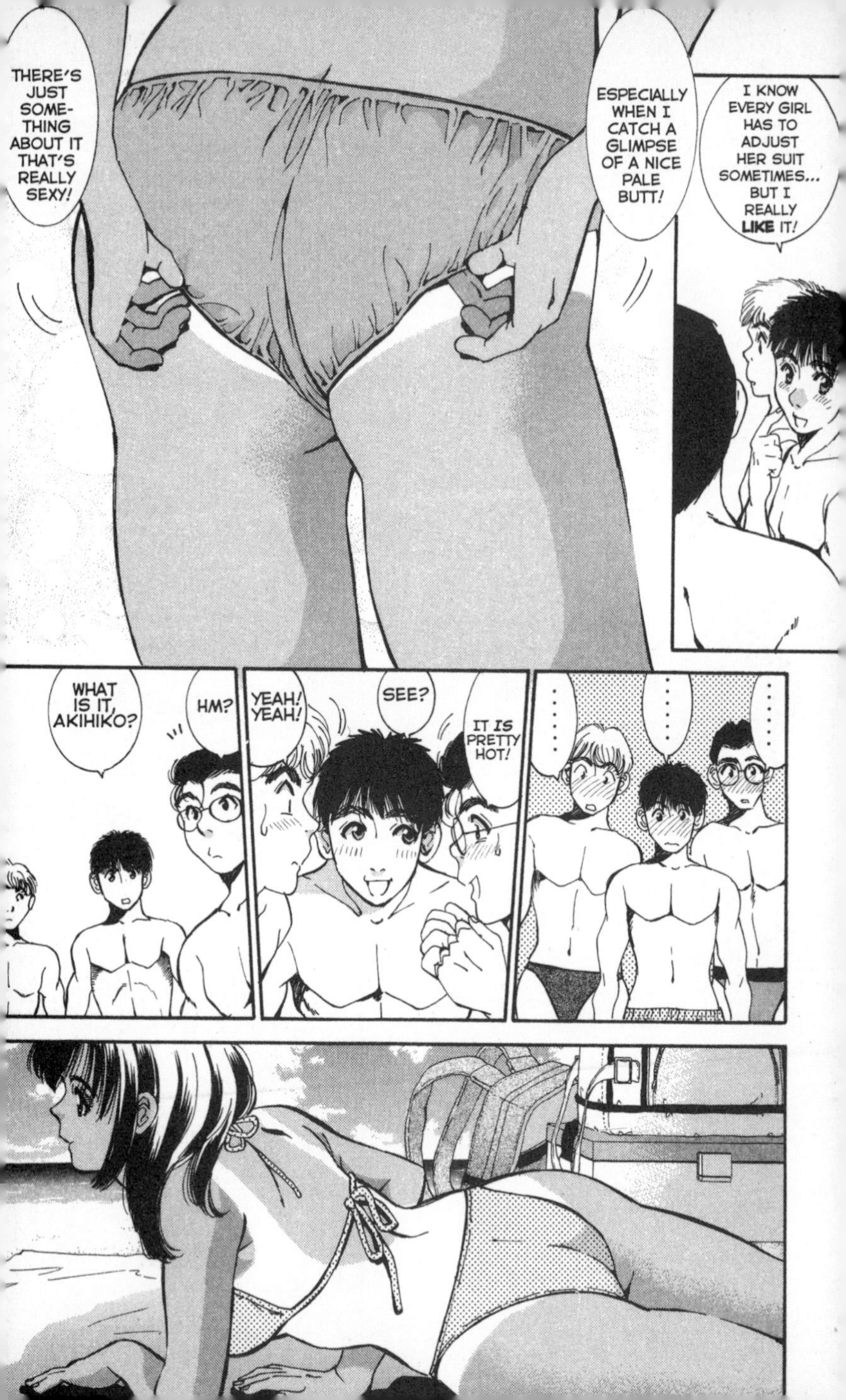
I KNOW EVERY GIRL HAS TO ADJUST HER SUIT SOMETIMES... BUT I REALLY **LIKE** IT!
ESPECIALLY WHEN I CATCH A GLIMPSE OF A NICE PALE BUTT!
THERE'S JUST SOMETHING ABOUT IT THAT'S REALLY SEXY!
......
......
......
IT *IS* PRETTY HOT!
SEE?
YEAH! YEAH!
HM?
WHAT IS IT, AKIHIKO?

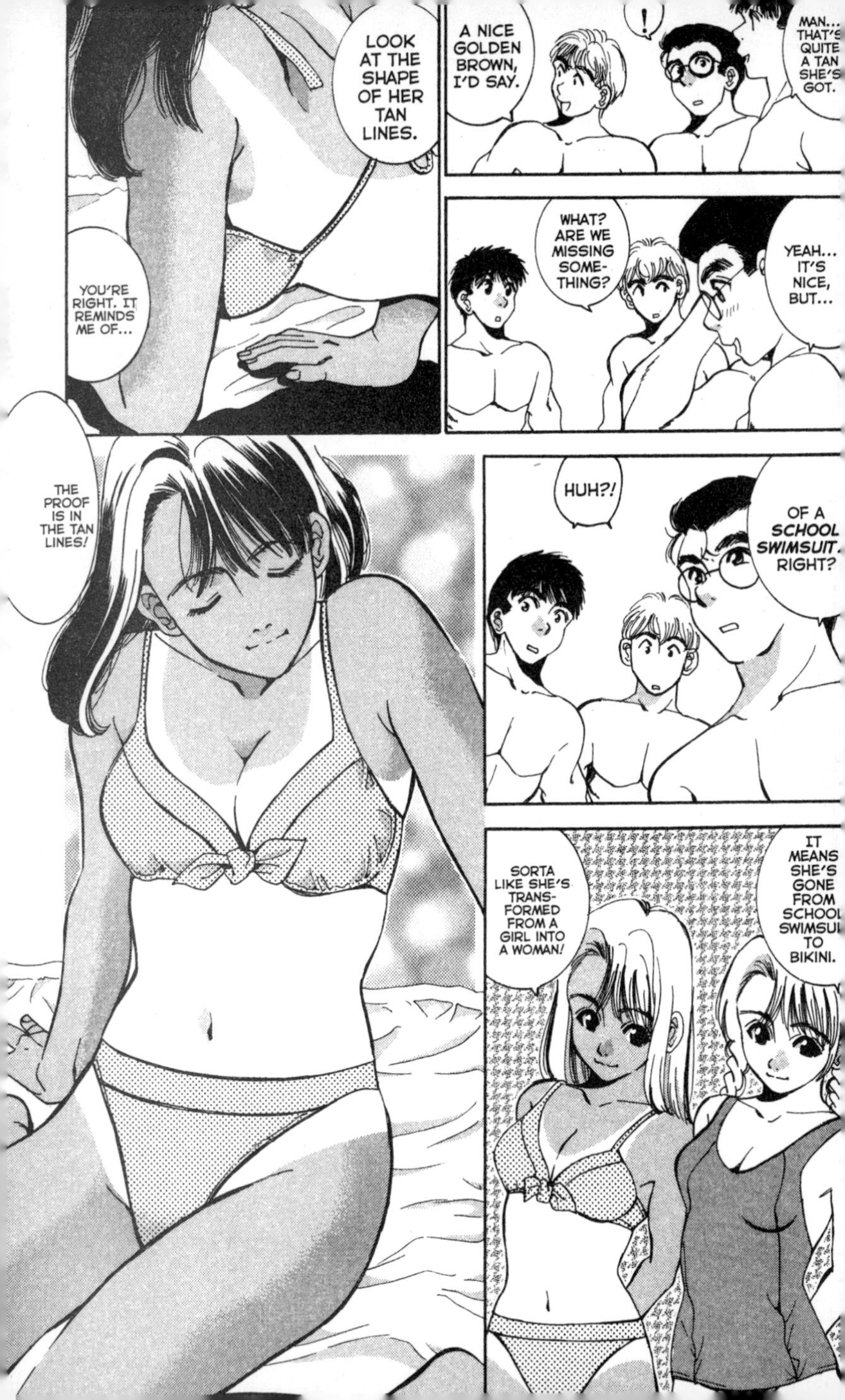
MAN... THAT'S QUITE A TAN SHE'S GOT.
!
A NICE GOLDEN BROWN, I'D SAY.
YEAH... IT'S NICE, BUT...
WHAT? ARE WE MISSING SOME-THING?
LOOK AT THE SHAPE OF HER TAN LINES.
YOU'RE RIGHT. IT REMINDS ME OF...
OF A *SCHOOL SWIMSUIT*, RIGHT?
HUH?!
IT MEANS SHE'S GONE FROM SCHOOL SWIMSUIT TO BIKINI.
SORTA LIKE SHE'S TRANS-FORMED FROM A GIRL INTO A WOMAN!
THE PROOF IS IN THE TAN LINES!

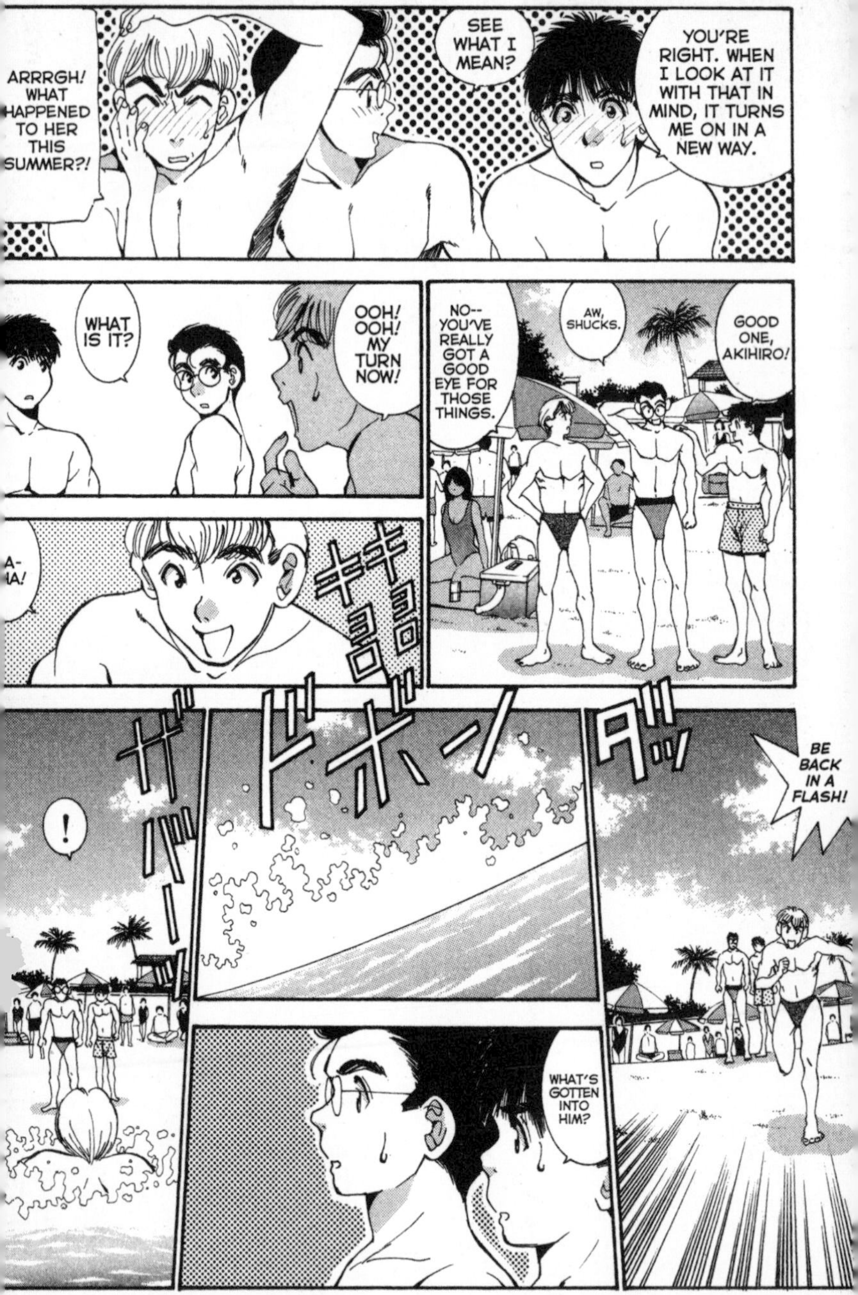
YOU'RE RIGHT. WHEN I LOOK AT IT WITH THAT IN MIND, IT TURNS ME ON IN A NEW WAY.
SEE WHAT I MEAN?
ARRRGH! WHAT HAPPENED TO HER THIS SUMMER?!
GOOD ONE, AKIHIRO!
AW, SHUCKS.
NO-- YOU'VE REALLY GOT A GOOD EYE FOR THOSE THINGS.
OOH! OOH! MY TURN NOW!
WHAT IS IT?
キョロキョロ
A- HA!
BE BACK IN A FLASH!
ダッ
ドボーン
WHAT'S GOTTEN INTO HIM?
ザバーッ
!

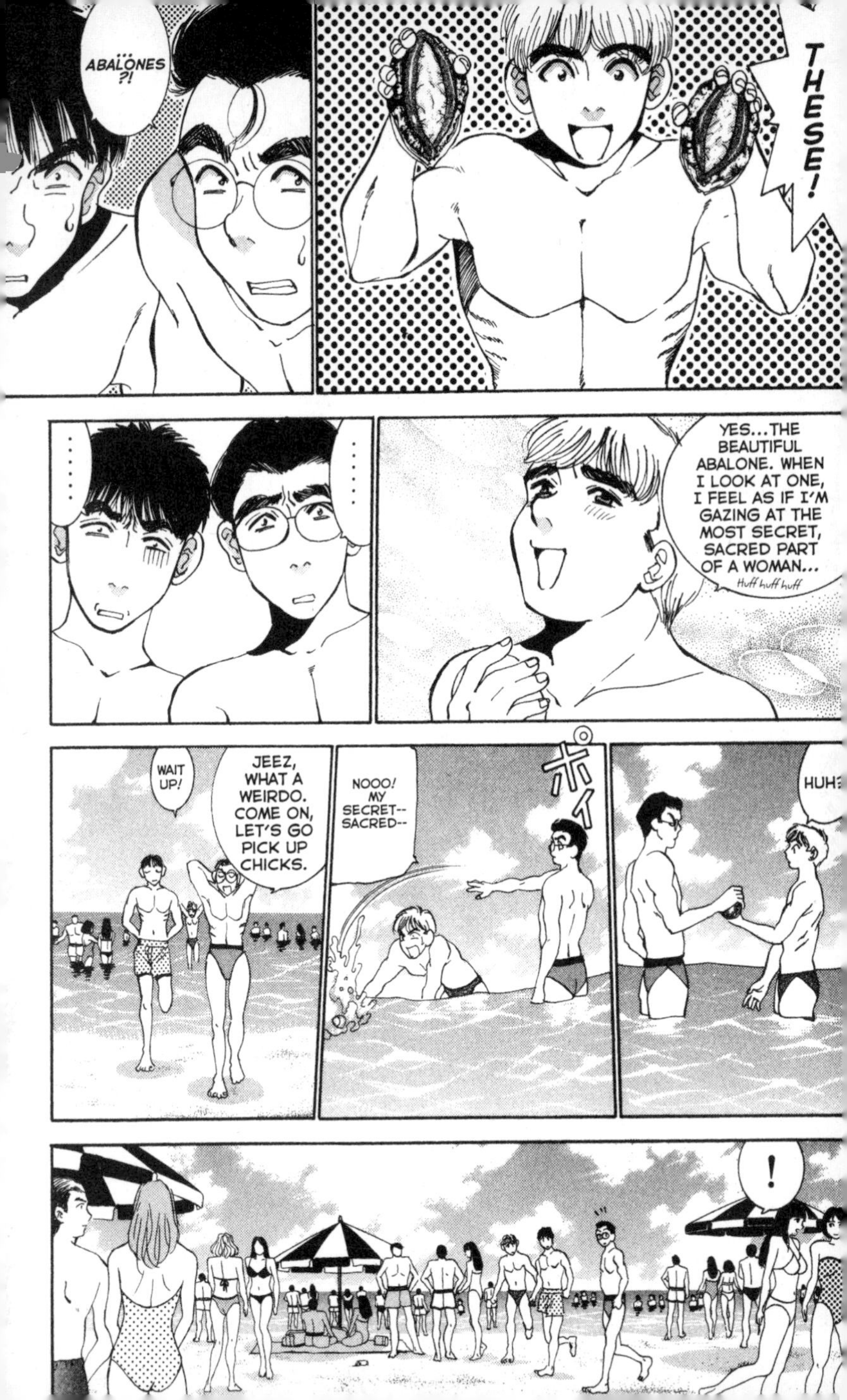
THESE!
...ABALONES ?!
YES...THE BEAUTIFUL ABALONE. WHEN I LOOK AT ONE, I FEEL AS IF I'M GAZING AT THE MOST SECRET, SACRED PART OF A WOMAN...
Huff huff huff
......
......
HUH?
ポイ
NOOO! MY SECRET-- SACRED--
JEEZ, WHAT A WEIRDO. COME ON, LET'S GO PICK UP CHICKS.
WAIT UP!
!

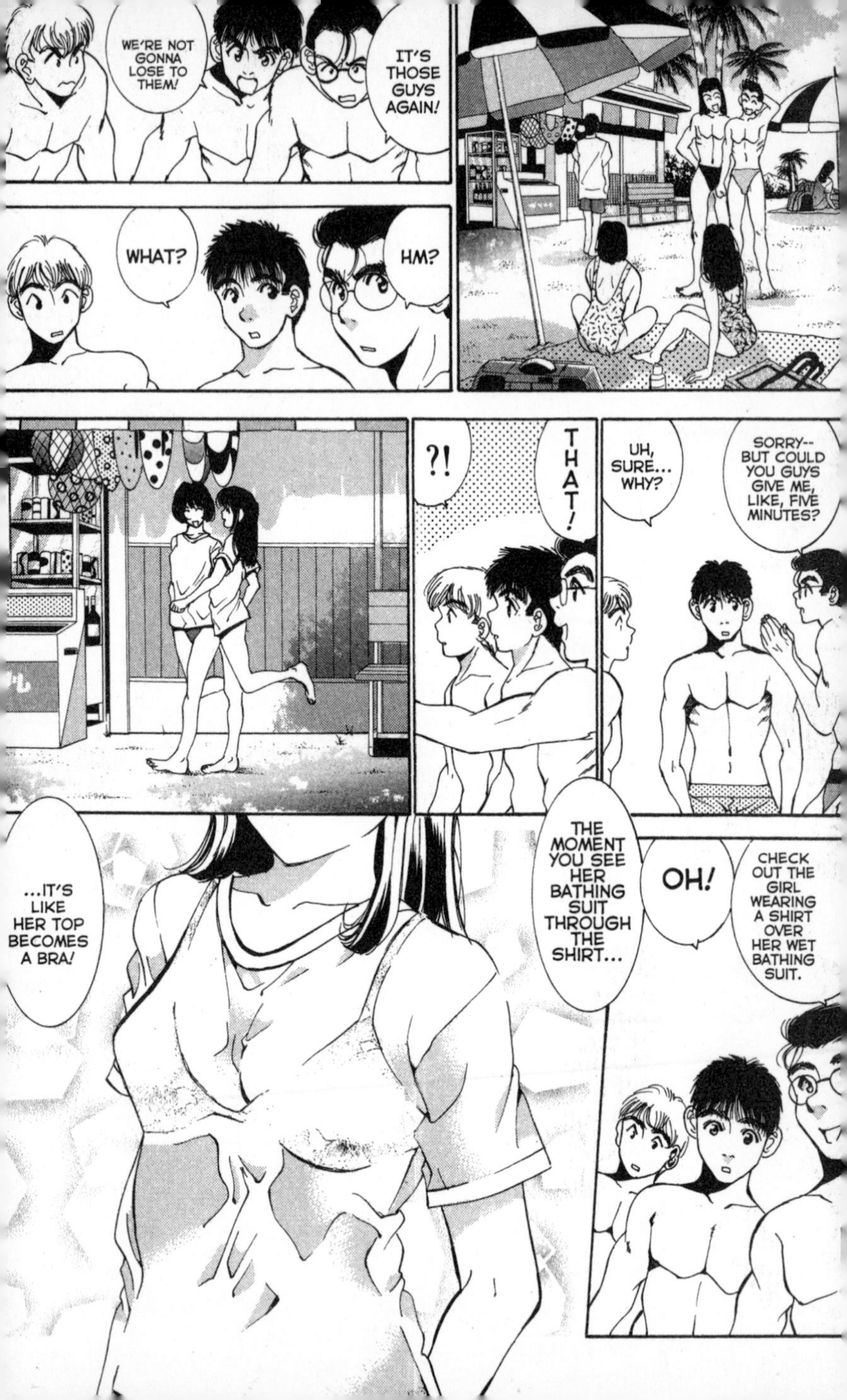

IT'S THOSE GUYS AGAIN!
WE'RE NOT GONNA LOSE TO THEM!
HM?
WHAT?
SORRY-- BUT COULD YOU GUYS GIVE ME, LIKE, FIVE MINUTES?
UH, SURE... WHY?
THAT!
?!
CHECK OUT THE GIRL WEARING A SHIRT OVER HER WET BATHING SUIT.
OH!
THE MOMENT YOU SEE HER BATHING SUIT THROUGH THE SHIRT...
...IT'S LIKE HER TOP BECOMES A BRA!

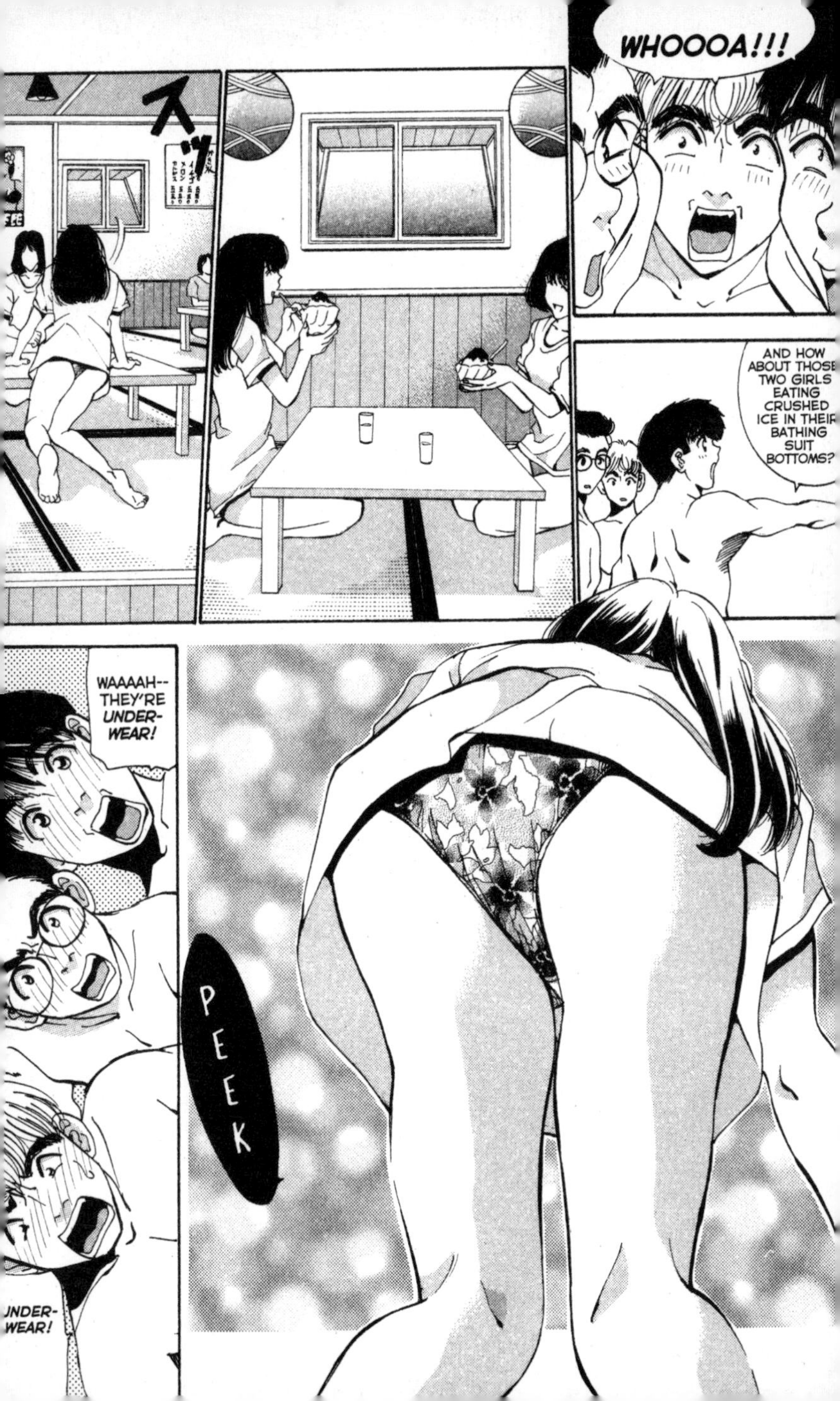

WHOOOA!!!
AND HOW ABOUT THOSE TWO GIRLS EATING CRUSHED ICE IN THEIR BATHING SUIT BOTTOMS?
スッ
PEEK
WAAAAH-- THEY'RE UNDER-WEAR!
UNDER-WEAR!

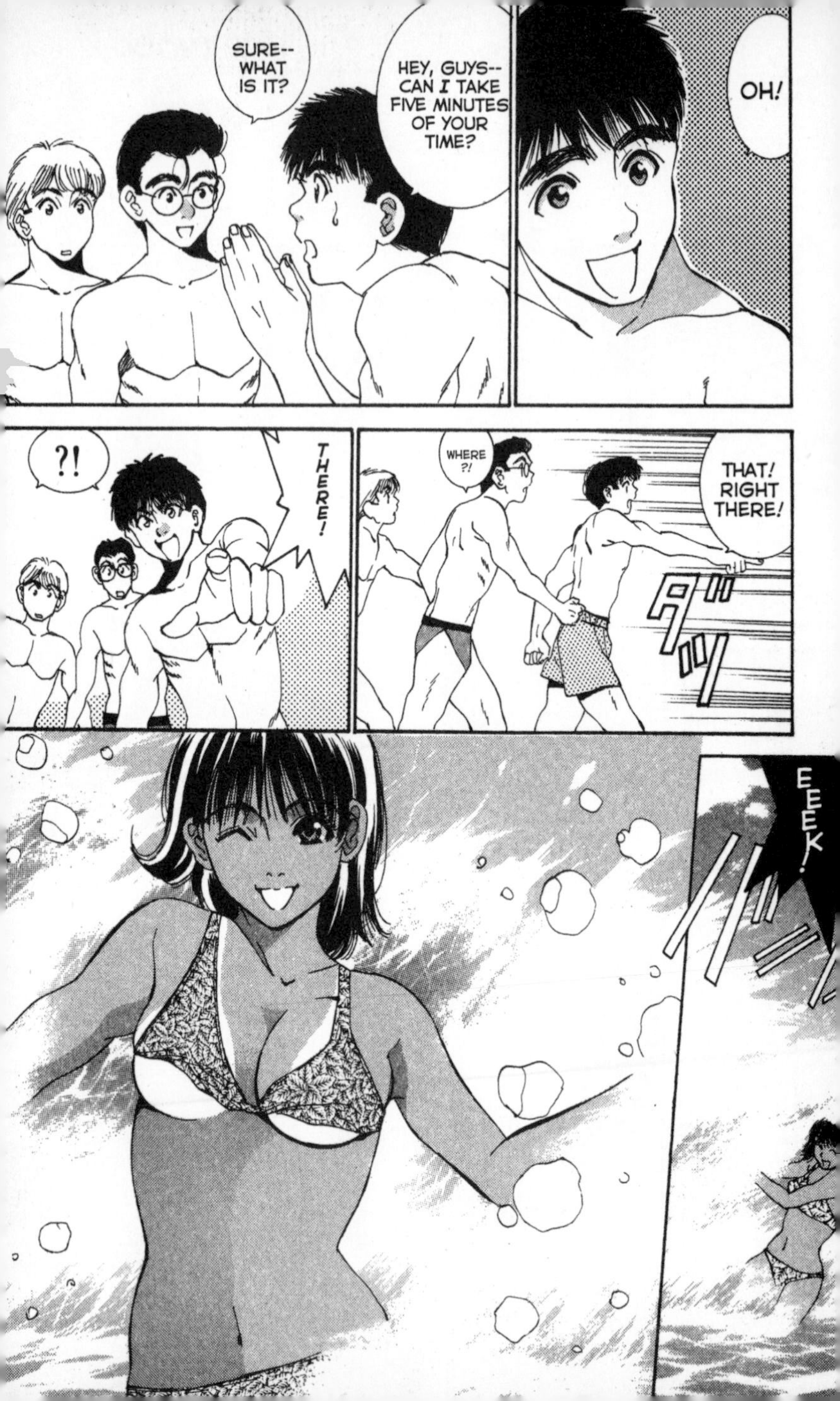

OH!
HEY, GUYS-- CAN I TAKE FIVE MINUTES OF YOUR TIME?
SURE-- WHAT IS IT?
THAT! RIGHT THERE!
WHERE ?!
ダッ
THERE!
?!
EEEK!

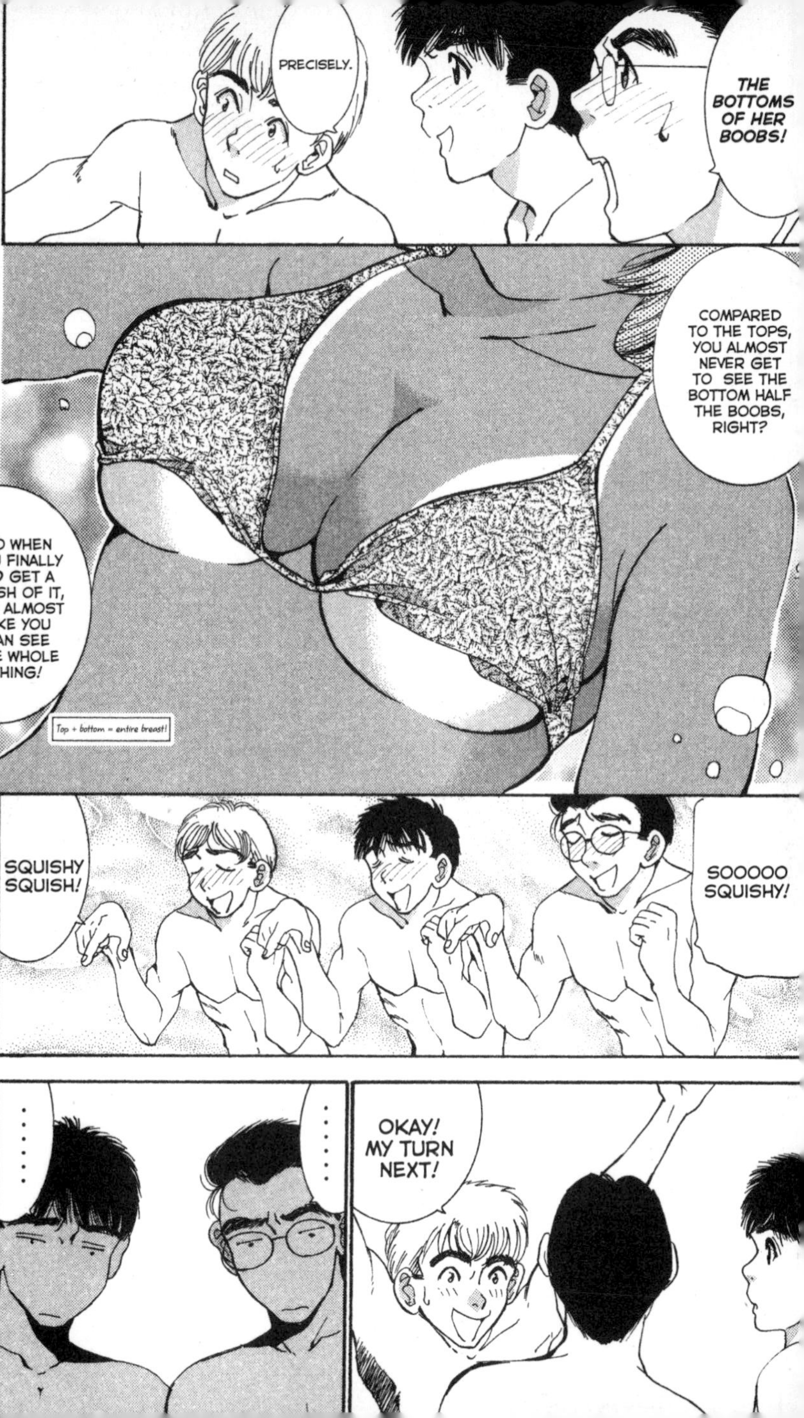
THE BOTTOMS OF HER BOOBS!
PRECISELY.
COMPARED TO THE TOPS, YOU ALMOST NEVER GET TO SEE THE BOTTOM HALF THE BOOBS, RIGHT?
SO WHEN YOU FINALLY *DO* GET A FLASH OF IT, IT'S ALMOST LIKE YOU CAN SEE THE WHOLE THING!
Top + bottom = entire breast!
SOOOOO SQUISHY!
SQUISHY SQUISH!
OKAY! MY TURN NEXT!
......
......

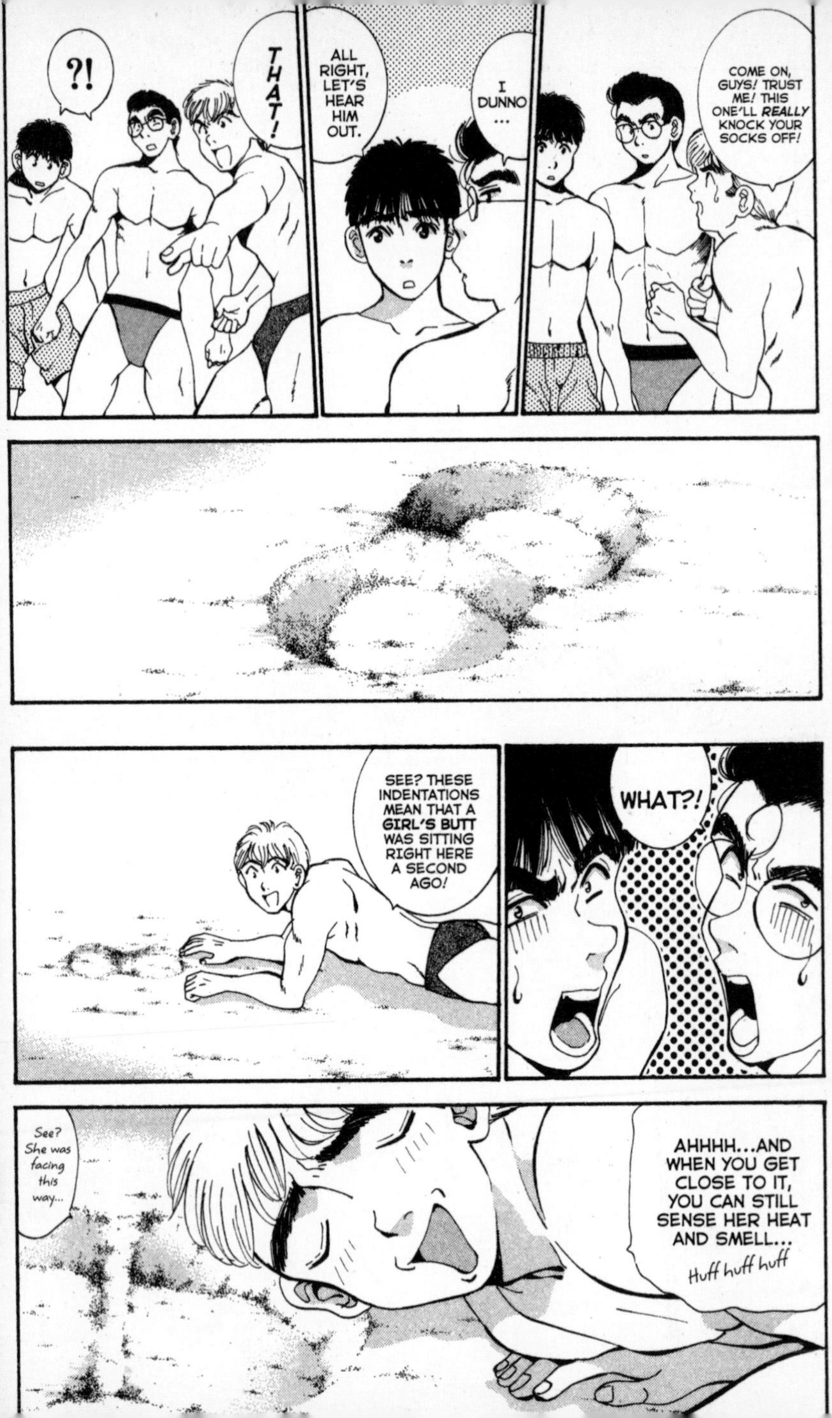
COME ON, GUYS! TRUST ME! THIS ONE'LL REALLY KNOCK YOUR SOCKS OFF!
I DUNNO ...
ALL RIGHT, LET'S HEAR HIM OUT.
THAT!
?!
WHAT?!
SEE? THESE INDENTATIONS MEAN THAT A GIRL'S BUTT WAS SITTING RIGHT HERE A SECOND AGO!
AHHHH...AND WHEN YOU GET CLOSE TO IT, YOU CAN STILL SENSE HER HEAT AND SMELL...
Huff huff huff
See? She was facing this way...

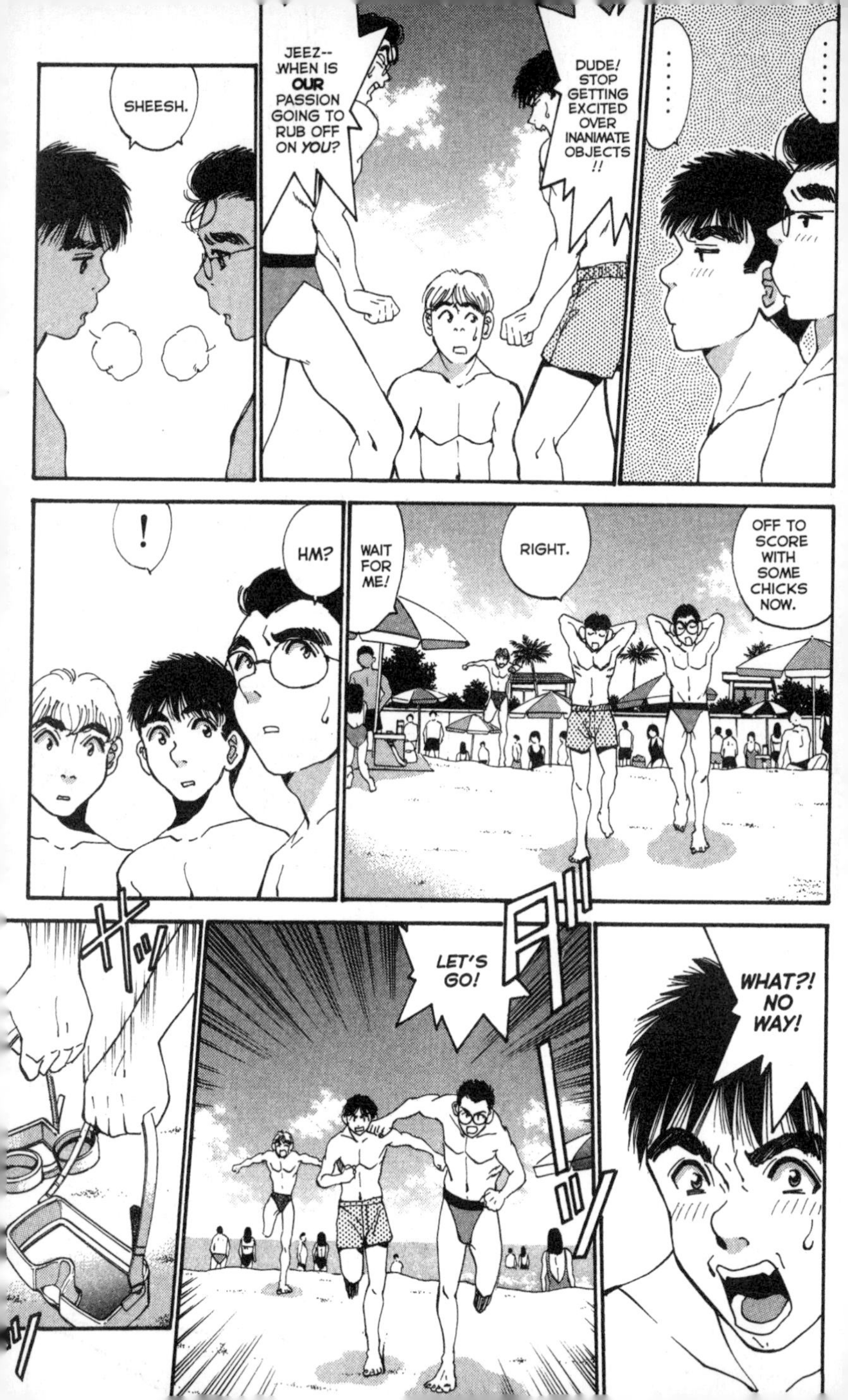
......
......
DUDE! STOP GETTING EXCITED OVER INANIMATE OBJECTS !!
JEEZ-- WHEN IS OUR PASSION GOING TO RUB OFF ON YOU?
SHEESH.
OFF TO SCORE WITH SOME CHICKS NOW.
RIGHT.
WAIT FOR ME!
HM?
!
WHAT?! NO WAY!
LET'S GO!

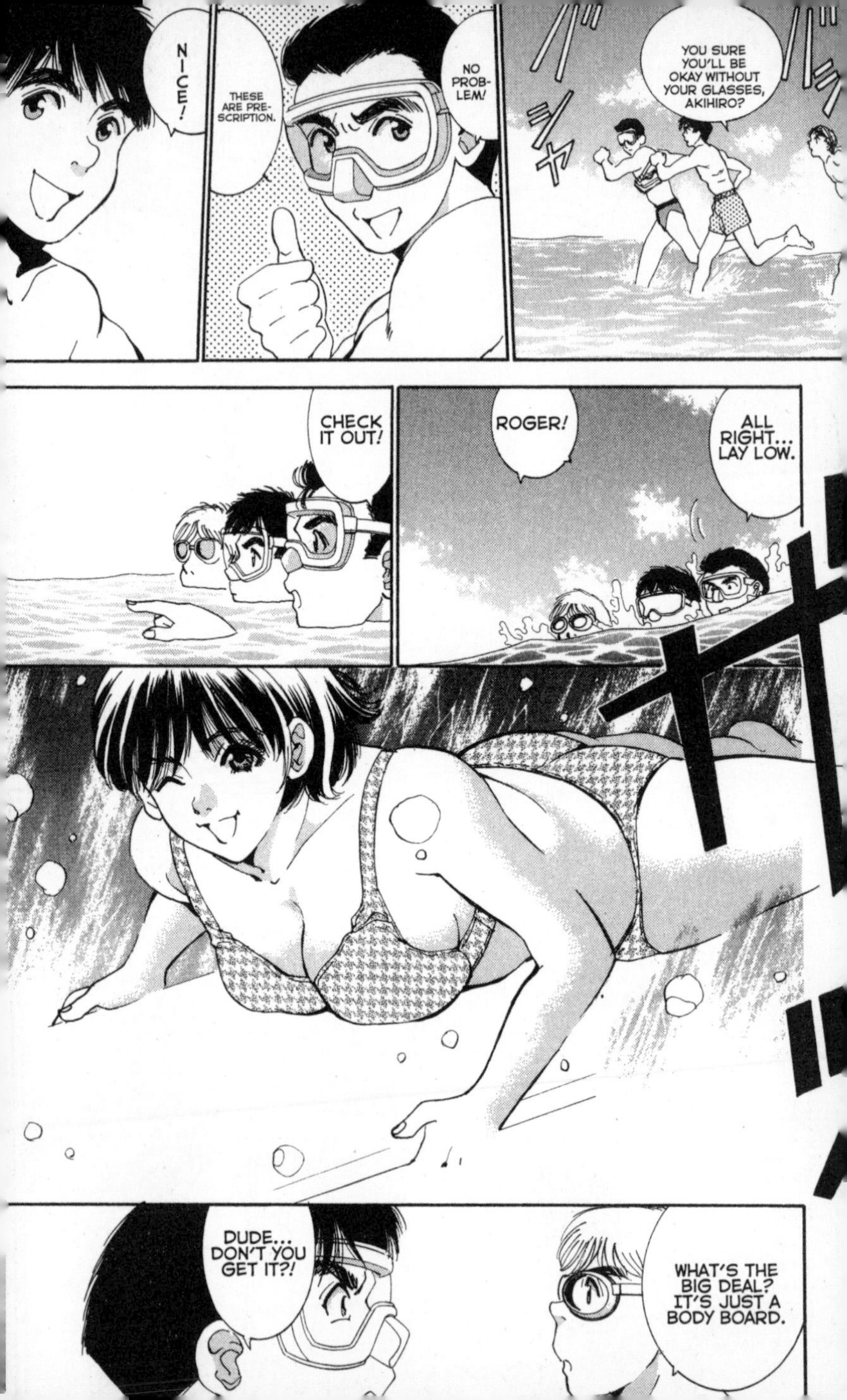
YOU SURE YOU'LL BE OKAY WITHOUT YOUR GLASSES, AKIHIRO?
NO PROB-LEM!
THESE ARE PRE-SCRIPTION.
NICE!
ALL RIGHT... LAY LOW.
ROGER!
CHECK IT OUT!
WHAT'S THE BIG DEAL? IT'S JUST A BODY BOARD.
DUDE... DON'T YOU GET IT?!

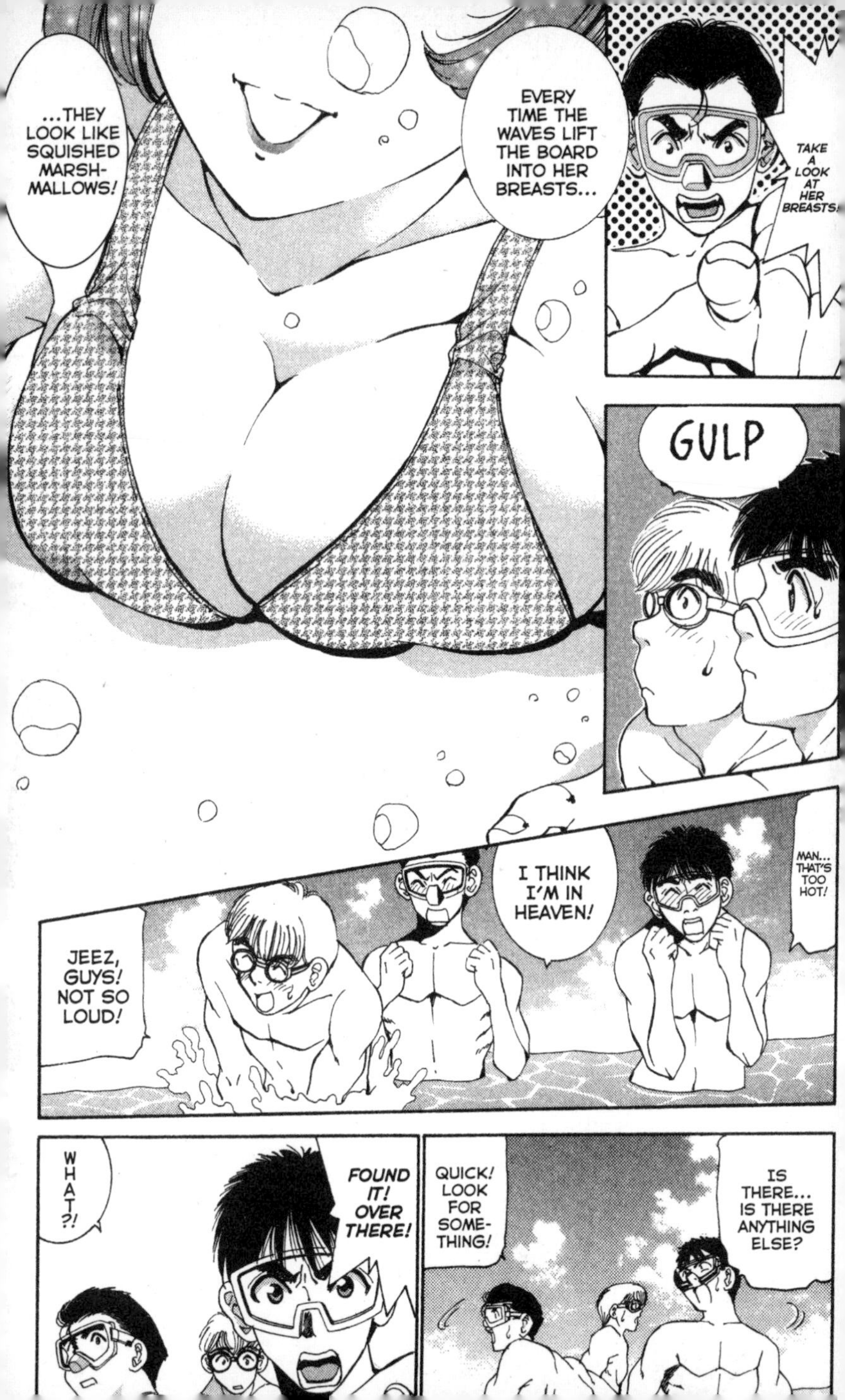
TAKE A LOOK AT HER BREASTS!
EVERY TIME THE WAVES LIFT THE BOARD INTO HER BREASTS...
...THEY LOOK LIKE SQUISHED MARSHMALLOWS!
GULP
MAN... THAT'S TOO HOT!
I THINK I'M IN HEAVEN!
JEEZ, GUYS! NOT SO LOUD!
IS THERE... IS THERE ANYTHING ELSE?
QUICK! LOOK FOR SOMETHING!
FOUND IT! OVER THERE!
WHAT?!

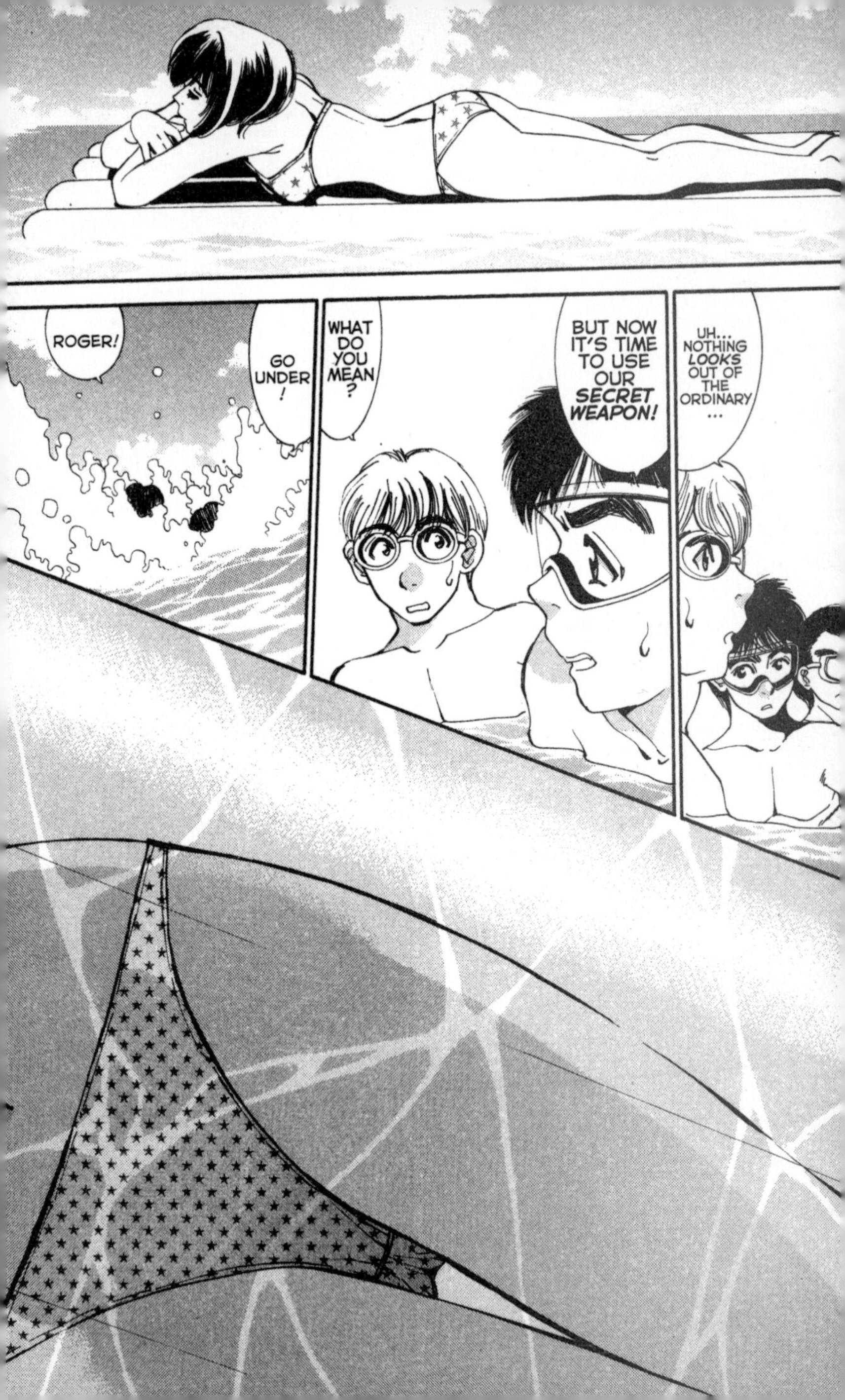
UH... NOTHING LOOKS OUT OF THE ORDINARY...
BUT NOW IT'S TIME TO USE OUR SECRET WEAPON!
WHAT DO YOU MEAN?
GO UNDER!
ROGER!

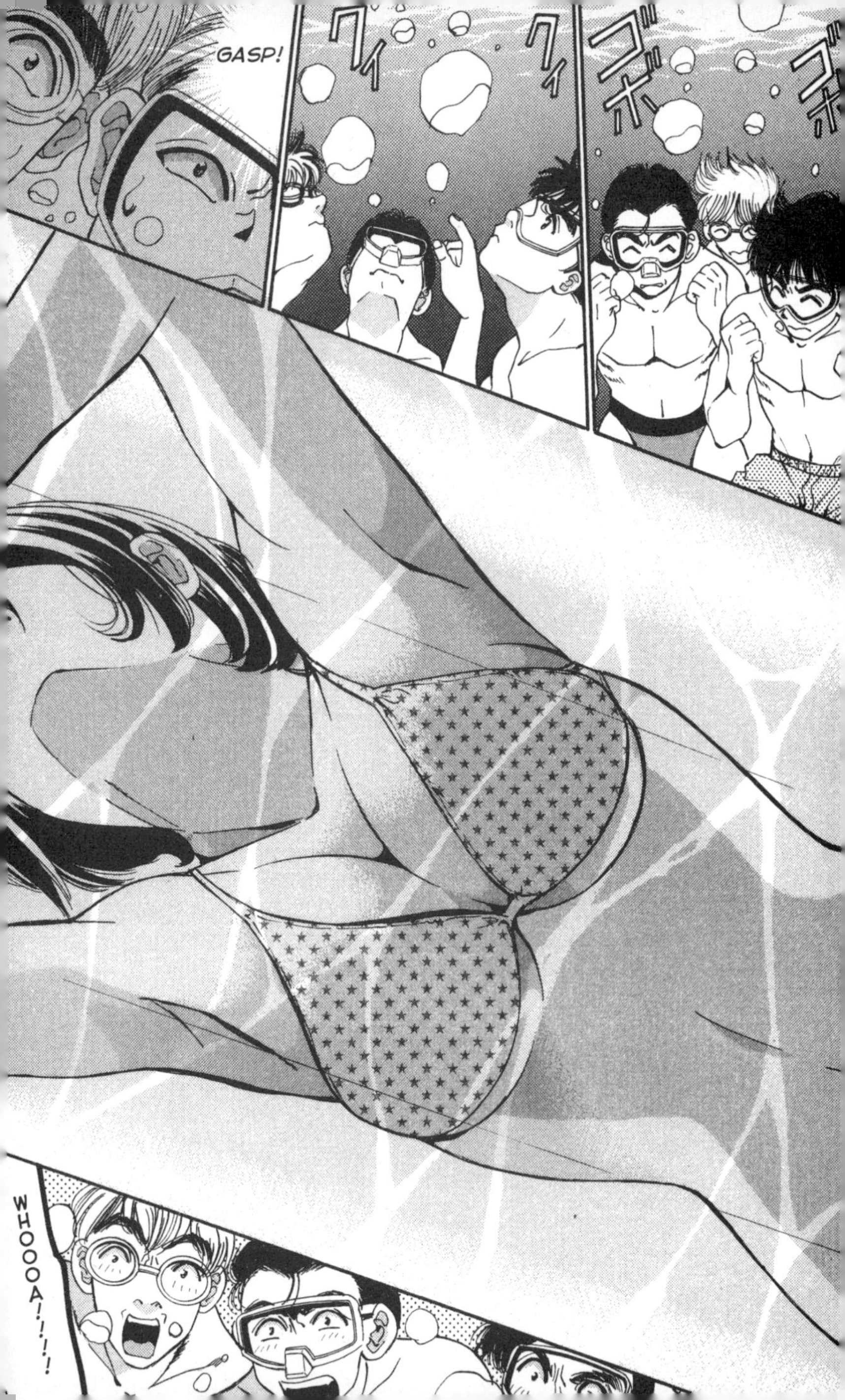
ゴボ
ゴボ
クィ
クィ
GASP!
WHOOOA!!!!!

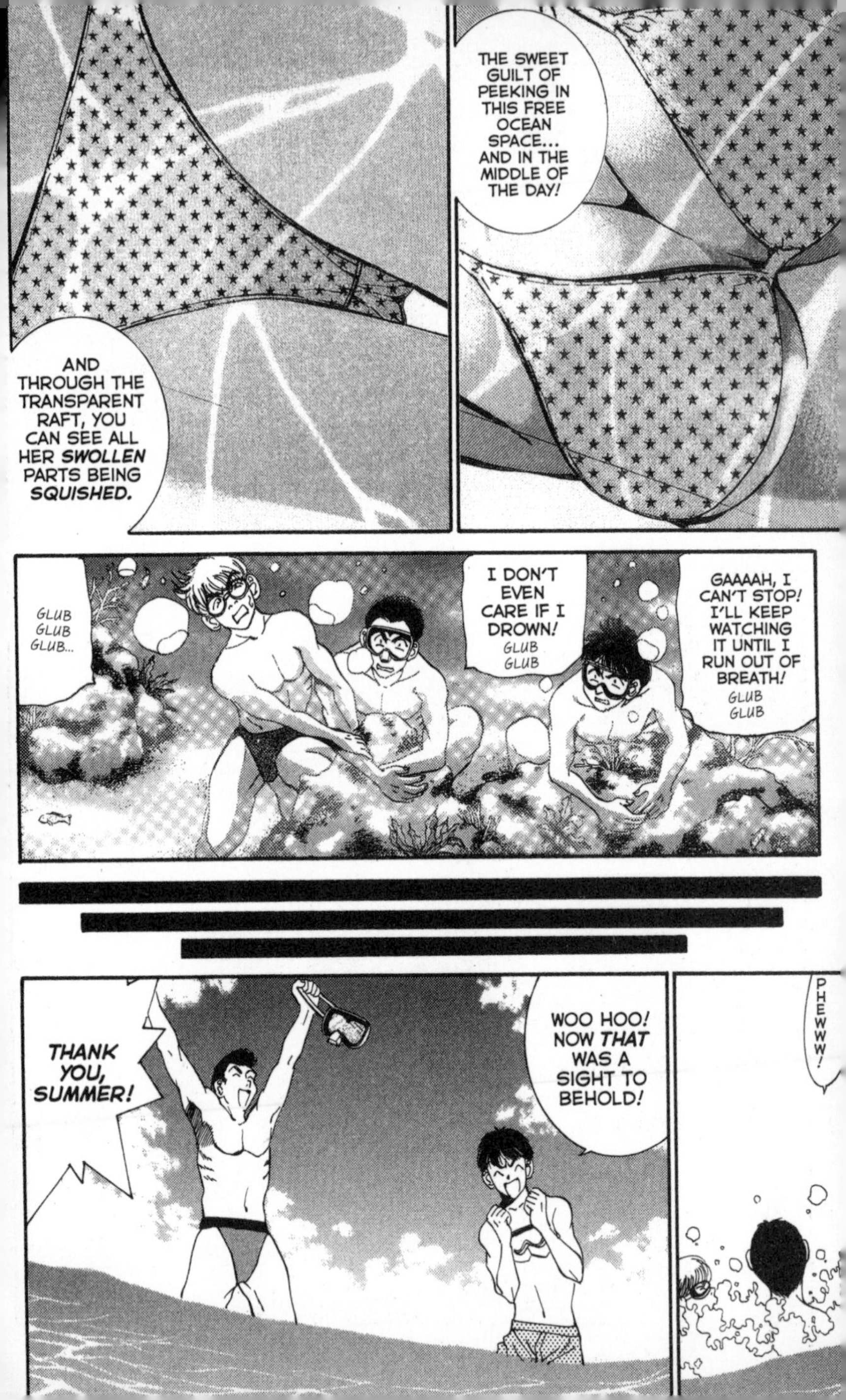
THE SWEET GUILT OF PEEKING IN THIS FREE OCEAN SPACE... AND IN THE MIDDLE OF THE DAY!
AND THROUGH THE TRANSPARENT RAFT, YOU CAN SEE ALL HER *SWOLLEN* PARTS BEING *SQUISHED.*
GAAAAH, I CAN'T STOP! I'LL KEEP WATCHING IT UNTIL I RUN OUT OF BREATH!
GLUB GLUB
I DON'T EVEN CARE IF I DROWN!
GLUB GLUB
GLUB GLUB GLUB...
PHEWWW!
WOO HOO! NOW *THAT* WAS A SIGHT TO BEHOLD!
THANK YOU, SUMMER!

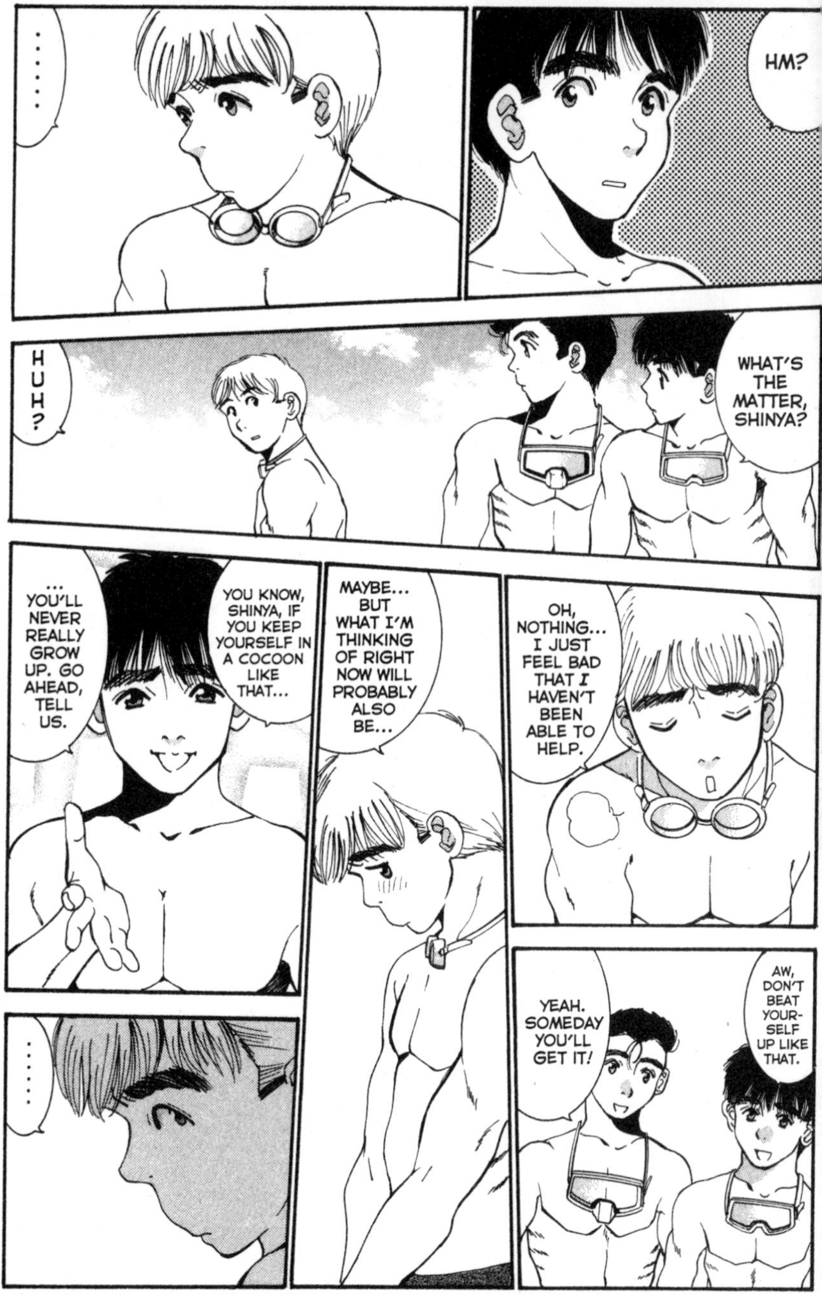
HM?
....
WHAT'S THE MATTER, SHINYA?
HUH?
OH, NOTHING... I JUST FEEL BAD THAT I HAVEN'T BEEN ABLE TO HELP.
AW, DON'T BEAT YOURSELF UP LIKE THAT.
YEAH. SOMEDAY YOU'LL GET IT!
MAYBE... BUT WHAT I'M THINKING OF RIGHT NOW WILL PROBABLY ALSO BE...
YOU KNOW, SHINYA, IF YOU KEEP YOURSELF IN A COCOON LIKE THAT...
... YOU'LL NEVER REALLY GROW UP. GO AHEAD, TELL US.
......

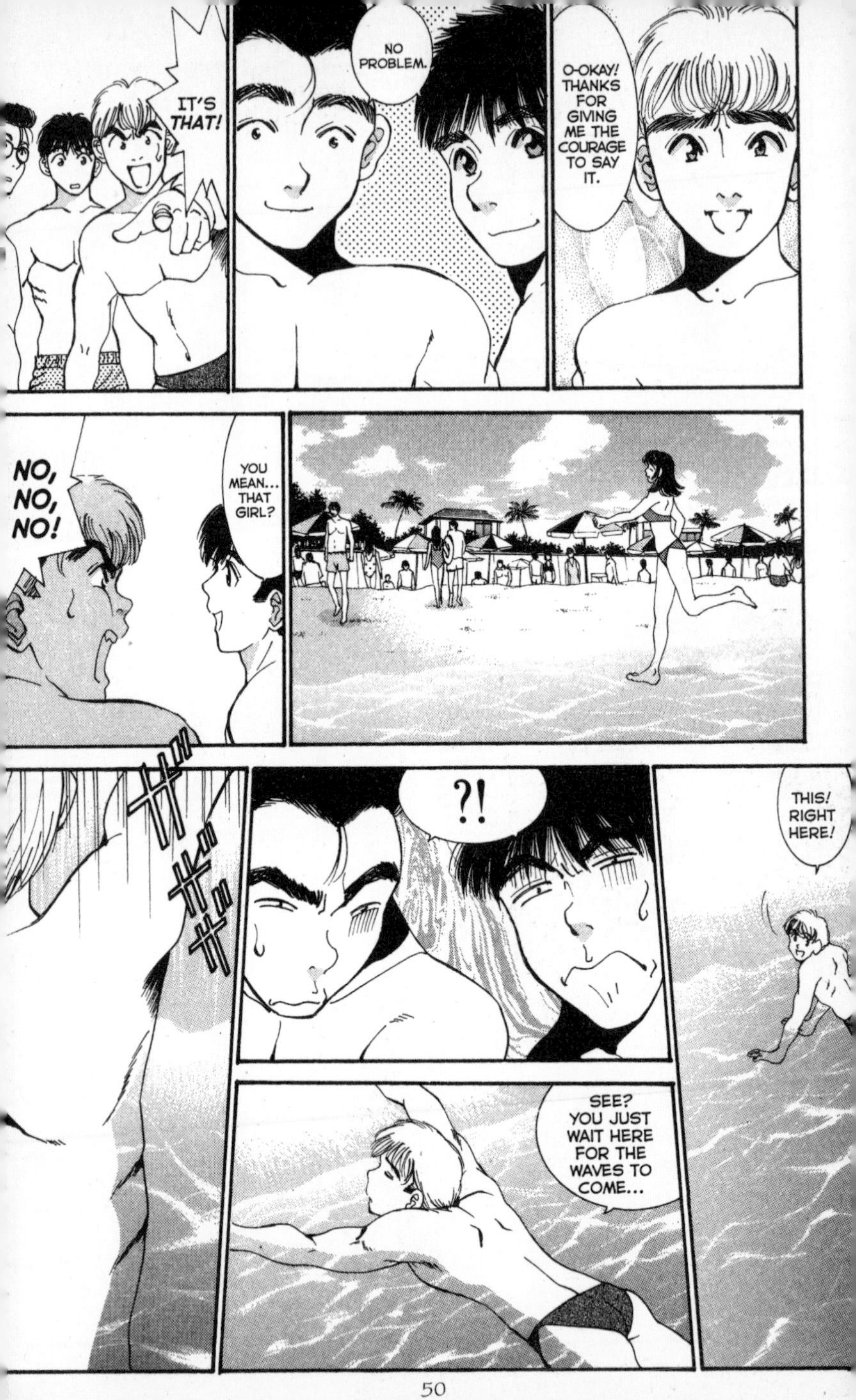
O-OKAY! THANKS FOR GIVING ME THE COURAGE TO SAY IT.
NO PROBLEM.
IT'S *THAT*!
YOU MEAN... THAT GIRL?
NO, NO, NO!
THIS! RIGHT HERE!
?!
SEE? YOU JUST WAIT HERE FOR THE WAVES TO COME...

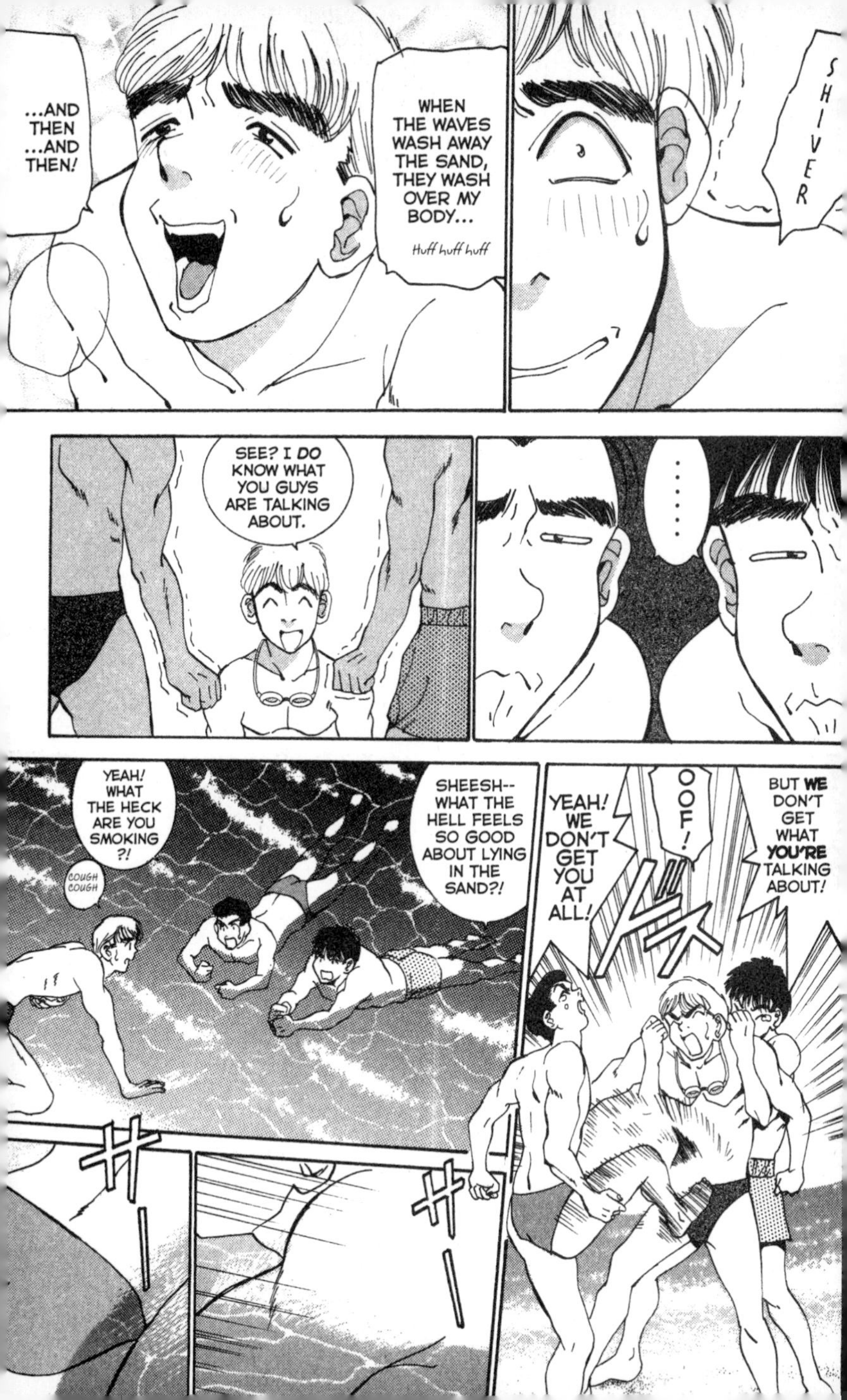
SHIVER
WHEN THE WAVES WASH AWAY THE SAND, THEY WASH OVER MY BODY...
Huff huff huff
...AND THEN ...AND THEN!
......
SEE? I DO KNOW WHAT YOU GUYS ARE TALKING ABOUT.
BUT WE DON'T GET WHAT YOU'RE TALKING ABOUT!
OOF!
YEAH! WE DON'T GET YOU AT ALL!
SHEESH-- WHAT THE HELL FEELS SO GOOD ABOUT LYING IN THE SAND?!
YEAH! WHAT THE HECK ARE YOU SMOKING?!
COUGH COUGH

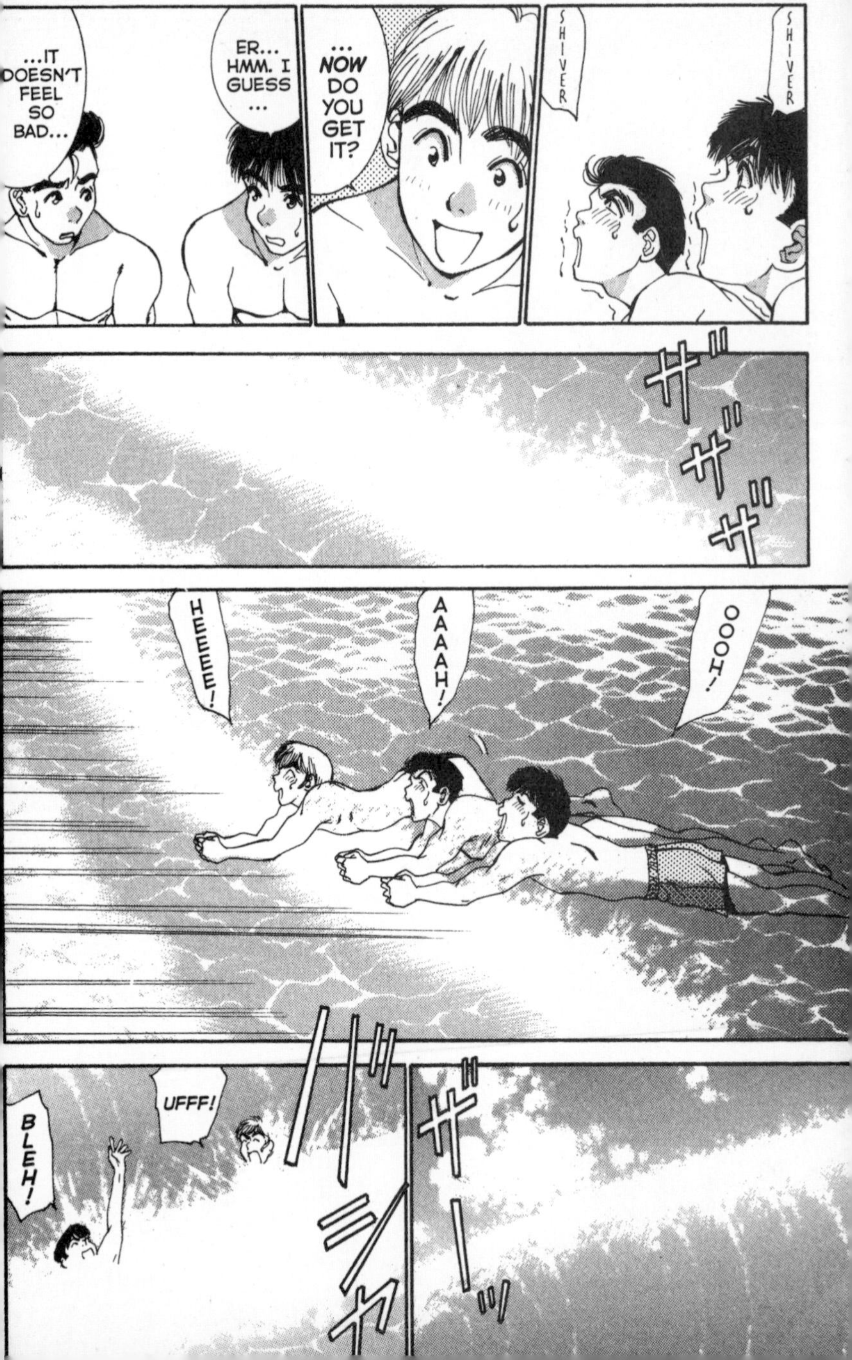
SHIVER
SHIVER
... NOW DO YOU GET IT?
ER... HMM. I GUESS ...
...IT DOESN'T FEEL SO BAD...
OOOH!
AAAAH!
HEEEEE!
UFFF!
BLEH!

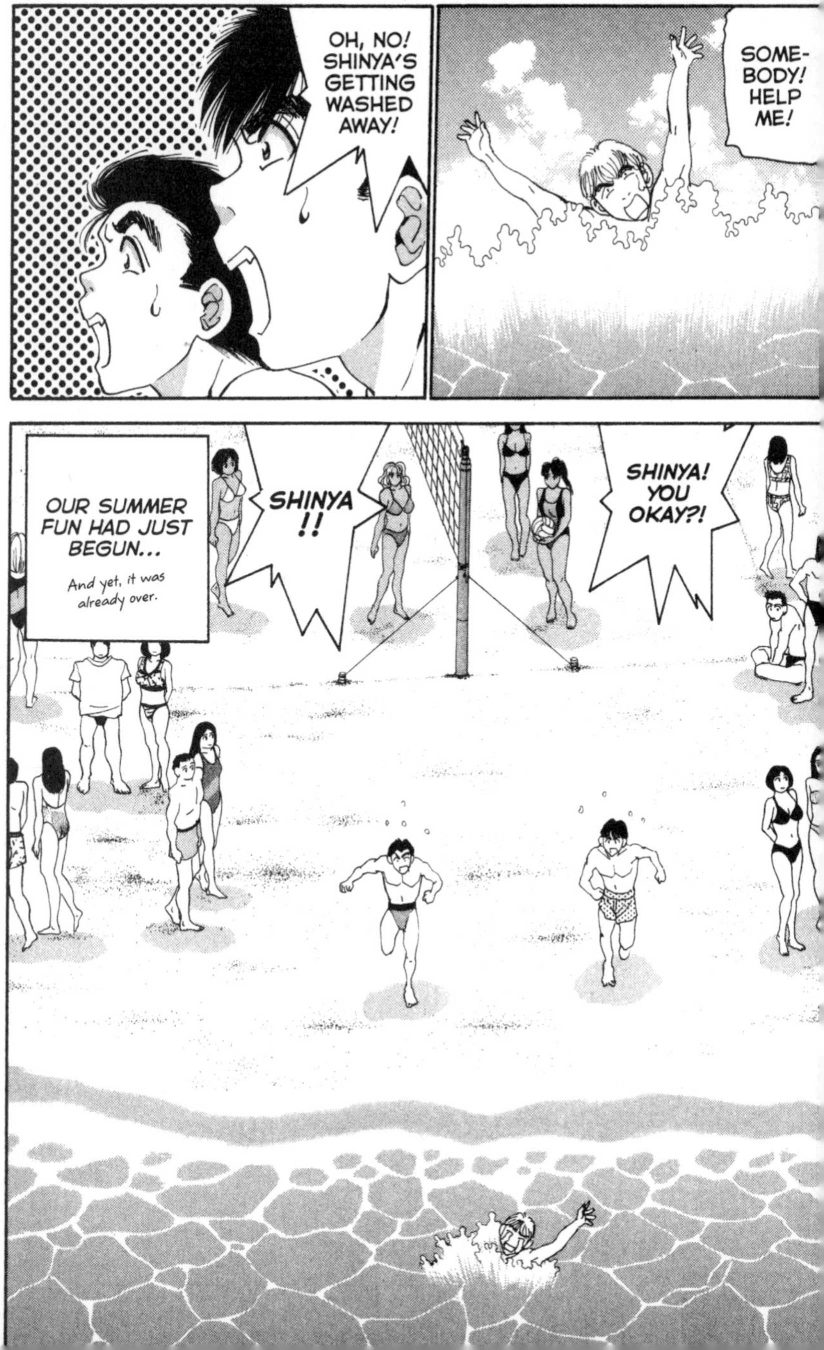
SOME-BODY! HELP ME!
OH, NO! SHINYA'S GETTING WASHED AWAY!
SHINYA! YOU OKAY?!
SHINYA!!
OUR SUMMER FUN HAD JUST BEGUN...
And yet, it was already over.

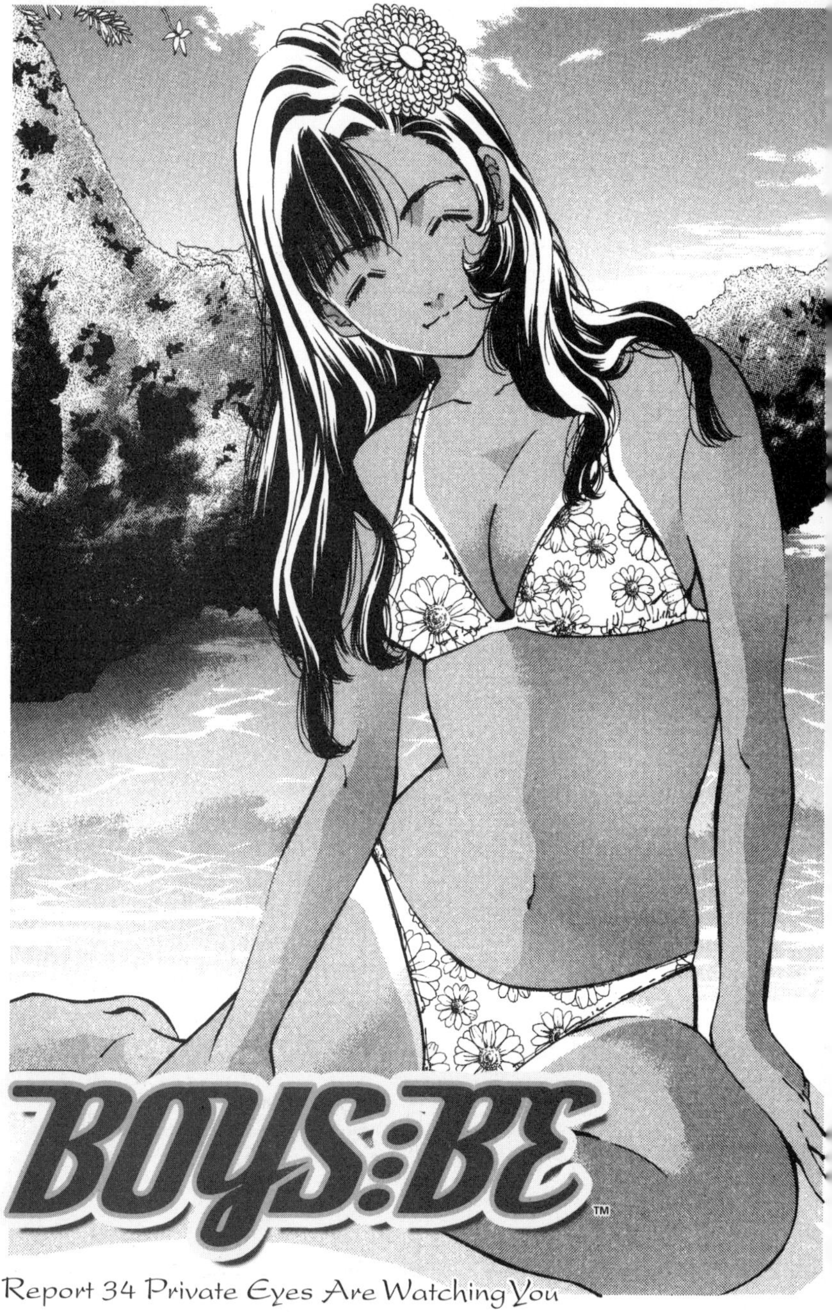
BOYS BE
Report 34 Private Eyes Are Watching You

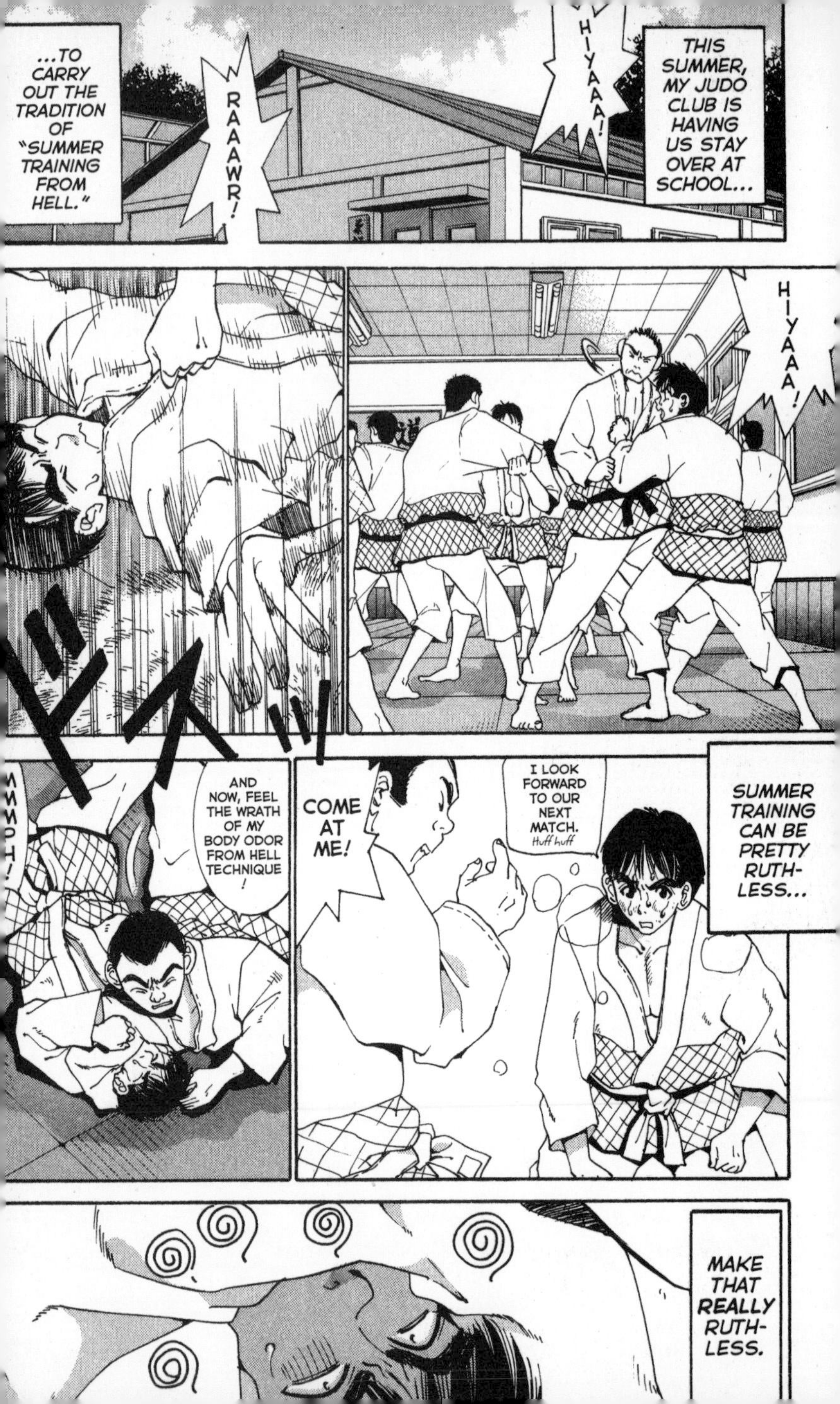
THIS SUMMER, MY JUDO CLUB IS HAVING US STAY OVER AT SCHOOL...
HIYAAAA!
RAAAAWR!
...TO CARRY OUT THE TRADITION OF "SUMMER TRAINING FROM HELL."
HIYAAA!
SUMMER TRAINING CAN BE PRETTY RUTH-LESS...
I LOOK FORWARD TO OUR NEXT MATCH. Huff huff
COME AT ME!
AND NOW, FEEL THE WRATH OF MY BODY ODOR FROM HELL TECHNIQUE!
MMMPH!
MAKE THAT REALLY RUTH-LESS.

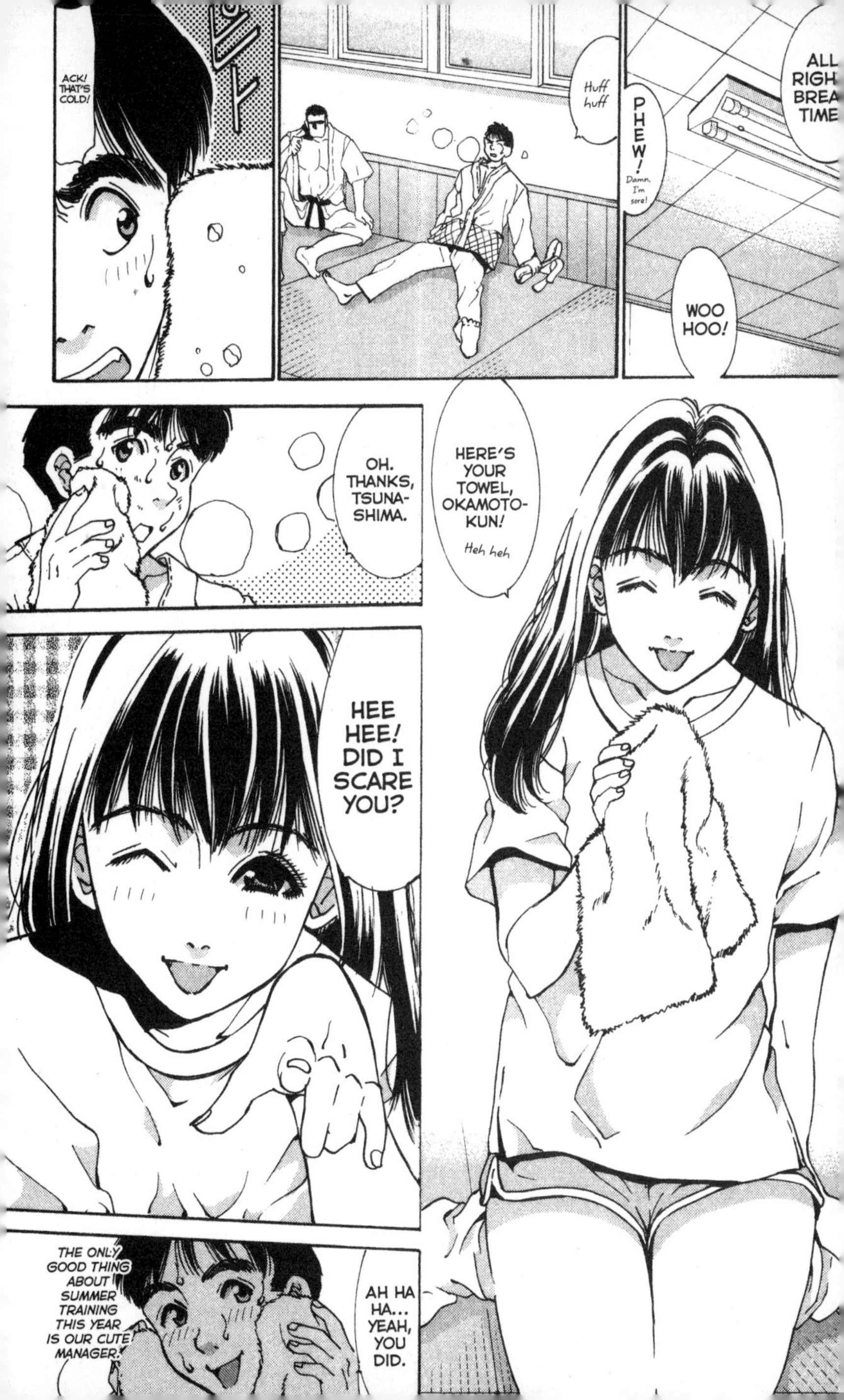
ALL RIGH BREA TIME
WOO HOO!
PHEW!
Damn, I'm sore!
Huff huff
ACK! THAT'S COLD!
HERE'S YOUR TOWEL, OKAMOTO-KUN!
Heh heh
OH. THANKS, TSUNA-SHIMA.
HEE HEE! DID I SCARE YOU?
AH HA HA... YEAH, YOU DID.
THE ONLY GOOD THING ABOUT SUMMER TRAINING THIS YEAR IS OUR CUTE MANAGER.

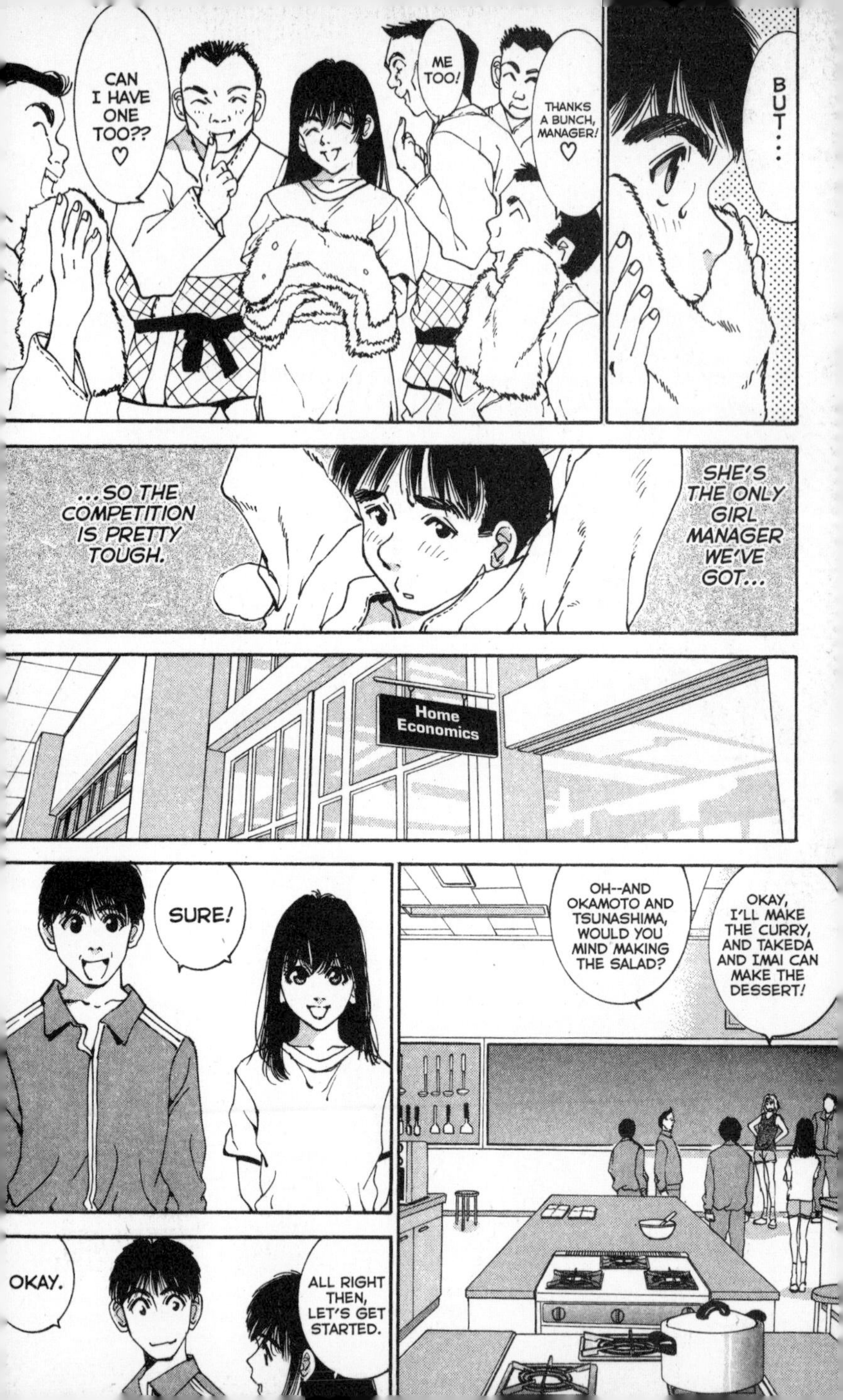
BUT...
THANKS A BUNCH, MANAGER! ♡
ME TOO!
CAN I HAVE ONE TOO?? ♡
SHE'S THE ONLY GIRL MANAGER WE'VE GOT...
...SO THE COMPETITION IS PRETTY TOUGH.
Home Economics
OKAY, I'LL MAKE THE CURRY, AND TAKEDA AND IMAI CAN MAKE THE DESSERT!
OH--AND OKAMOTO AND TSUNASHIMA, WOULD YOU MIND MAKING THE SALAD?
SURE!
ALL RIGHT THEN, LET'S GET STARTED.
OKAY.

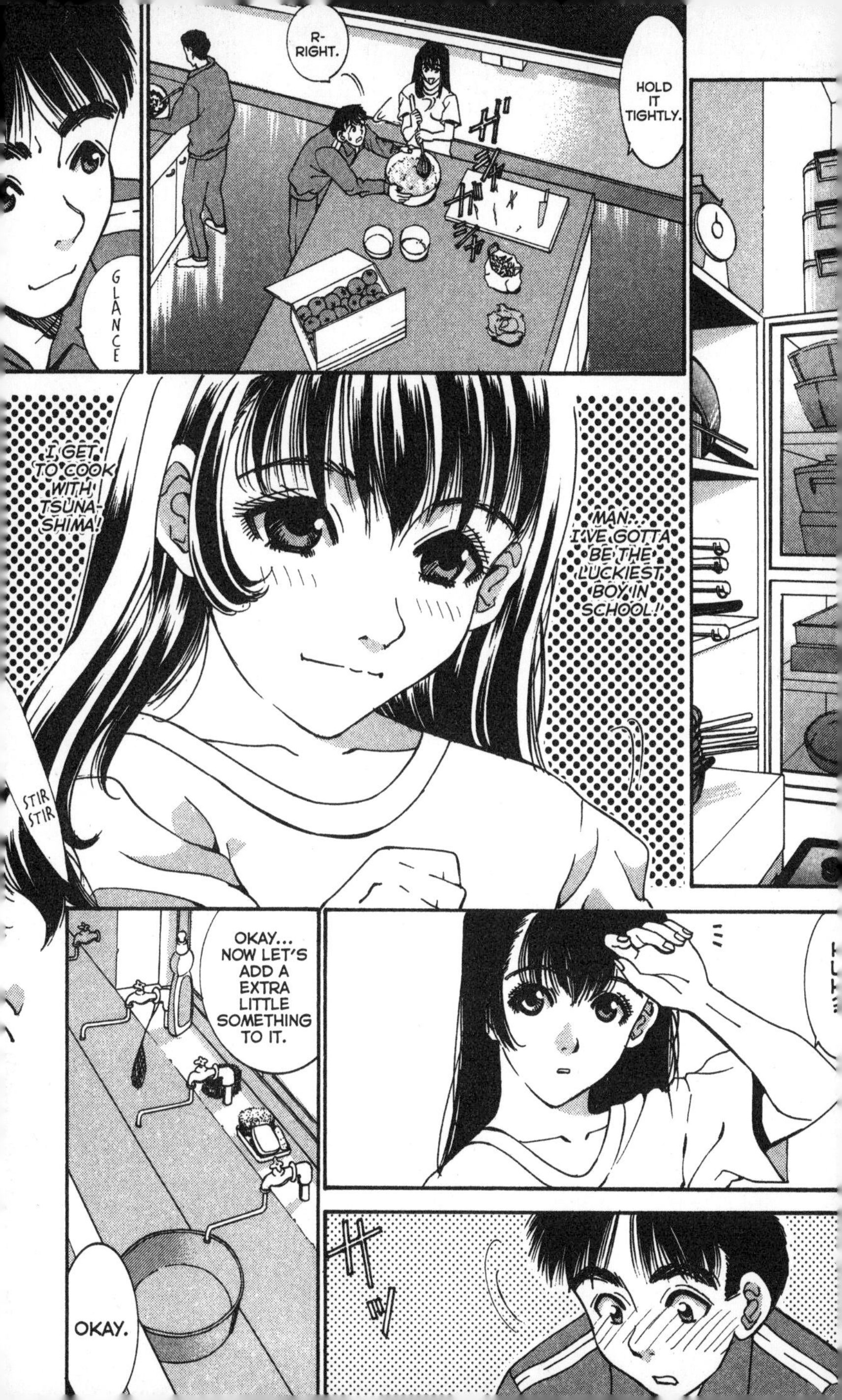

HOLD IT TIGHTLY.
R-RIGHT.
GLANCE
MAN... I'VE GOTTA BE THE LUCKIEST BOY IN SCHOOL!
I GET TO COOK WITH TSUNA-SHIMA!
STIR STIR
OKAY... NOW LET'S ADD A EXTRA LITTLE SOMETHING TO IT.
OKAY.

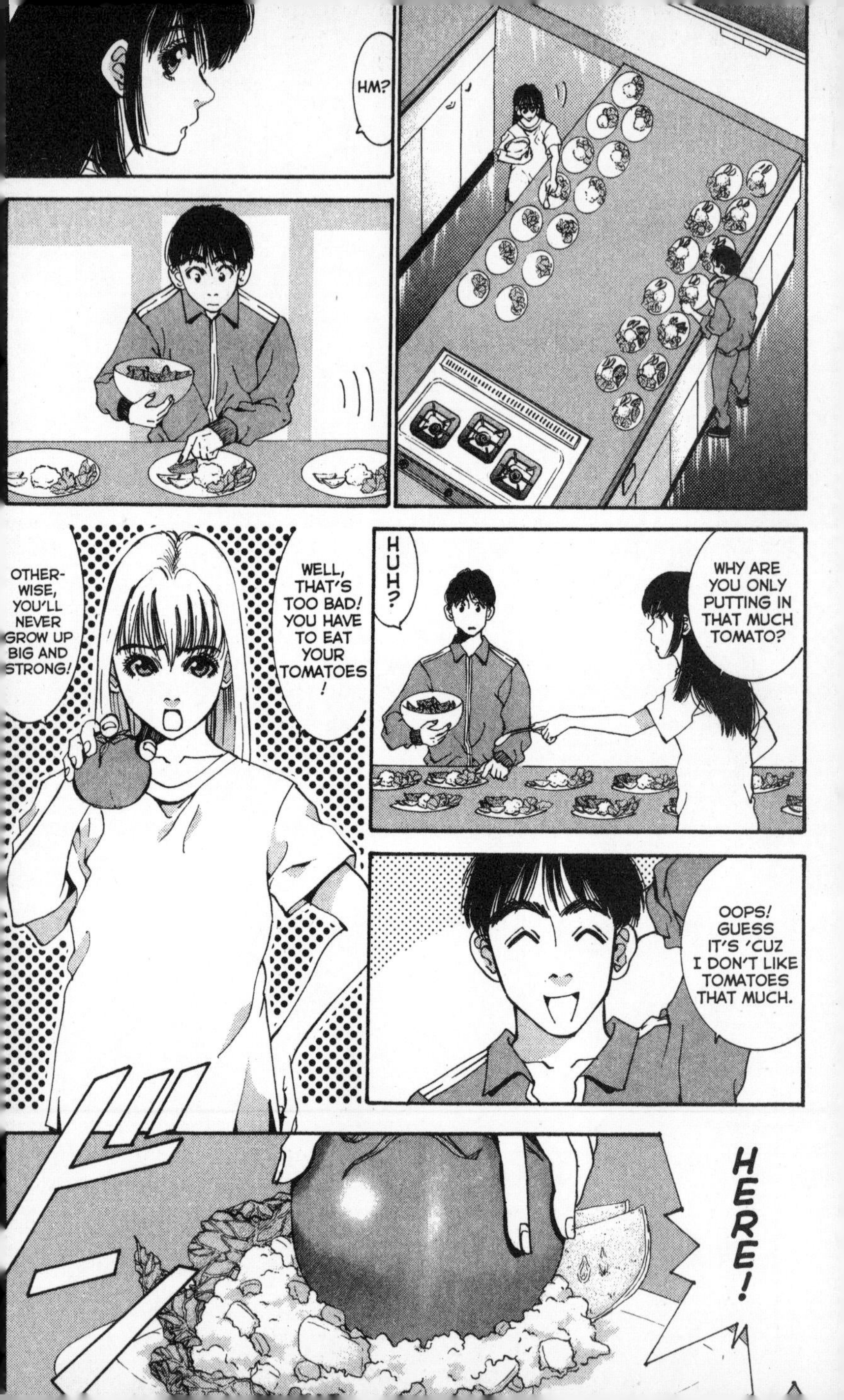
HM?
WHY ARE YOU ONLY PUTTING IN THAT MUCH TOMATO?
HUH?
OOPS! GUESS IT'S 'CUZ I DON'T LIKE TOMATOES THAT MUCH.
WELL, THAT'S TOO BAD! YOU HAVE TO EAT YOUR TOMATOES!
OTHER-WISE, YOU'LL NEVER GROW UP BIG AND STRONG!
HERE!

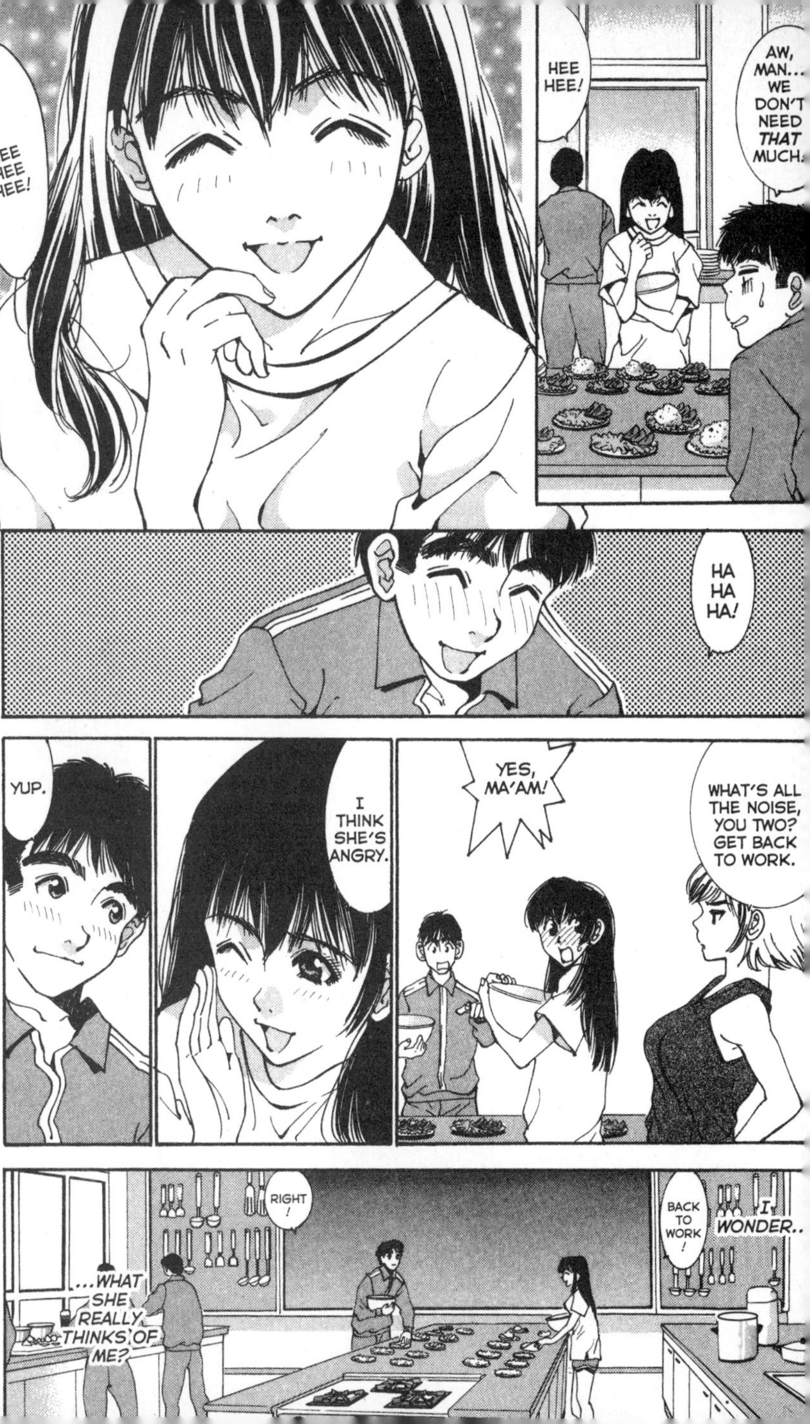
AW, MAN... WE DON'T NEED *THAT* MUCH.
HEE HEE!
HEE HEE HEE!
HA HA HA!
WHAT'S ALL THE NOISE, YOU TWO? GET BACK TO WORK.
YES, MA'AM!
I THINK SHE'S ANGRY.
YUP.
I WONDER..
BACK TO WORK!
RIGHT!
...WHAT SHE REALLY THINKS OF ME?

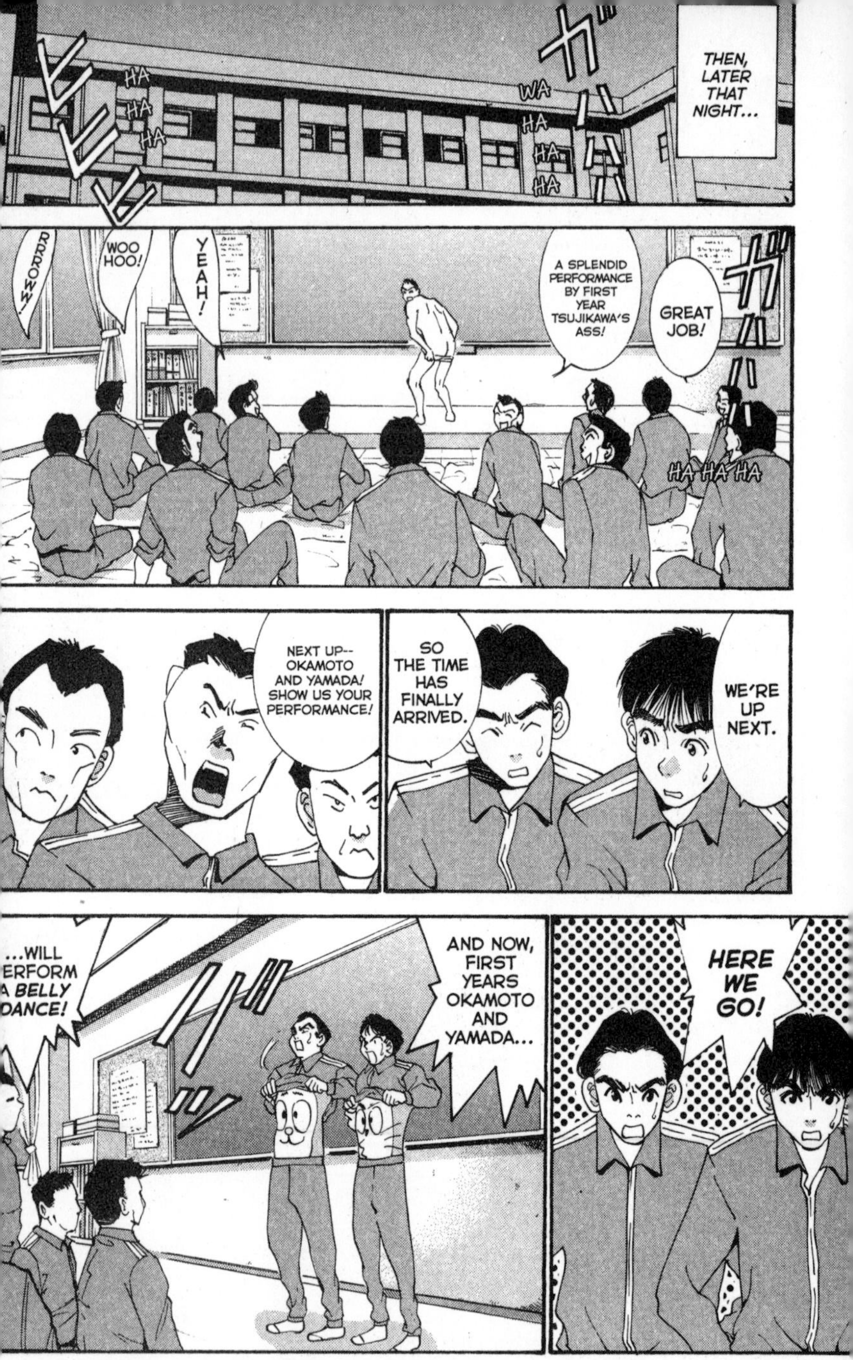
THEN, LATER THAT NIGHT...
WA HA HA HA
HA HA HA
GREAT JOB!
A SPLENDID PERFORMANCE BY FIRST YEAR TSUJIKAWA'S ASS!
HA HA HA
YEAH!
WOO HOO!
RRROWW!
WE'RE UP NEXT.
SO THE TIME HAS FINALLY ARRIVED.
NEXT UP-- OKAMOTO AND YAMADA! SHOW US YOUR PERFORMANCE!
HERE WE GO!
AND NOW, FIRST YEARS OKAMOTO AND YAMADA...
...WILL ERFORM A BELLY DANCE!

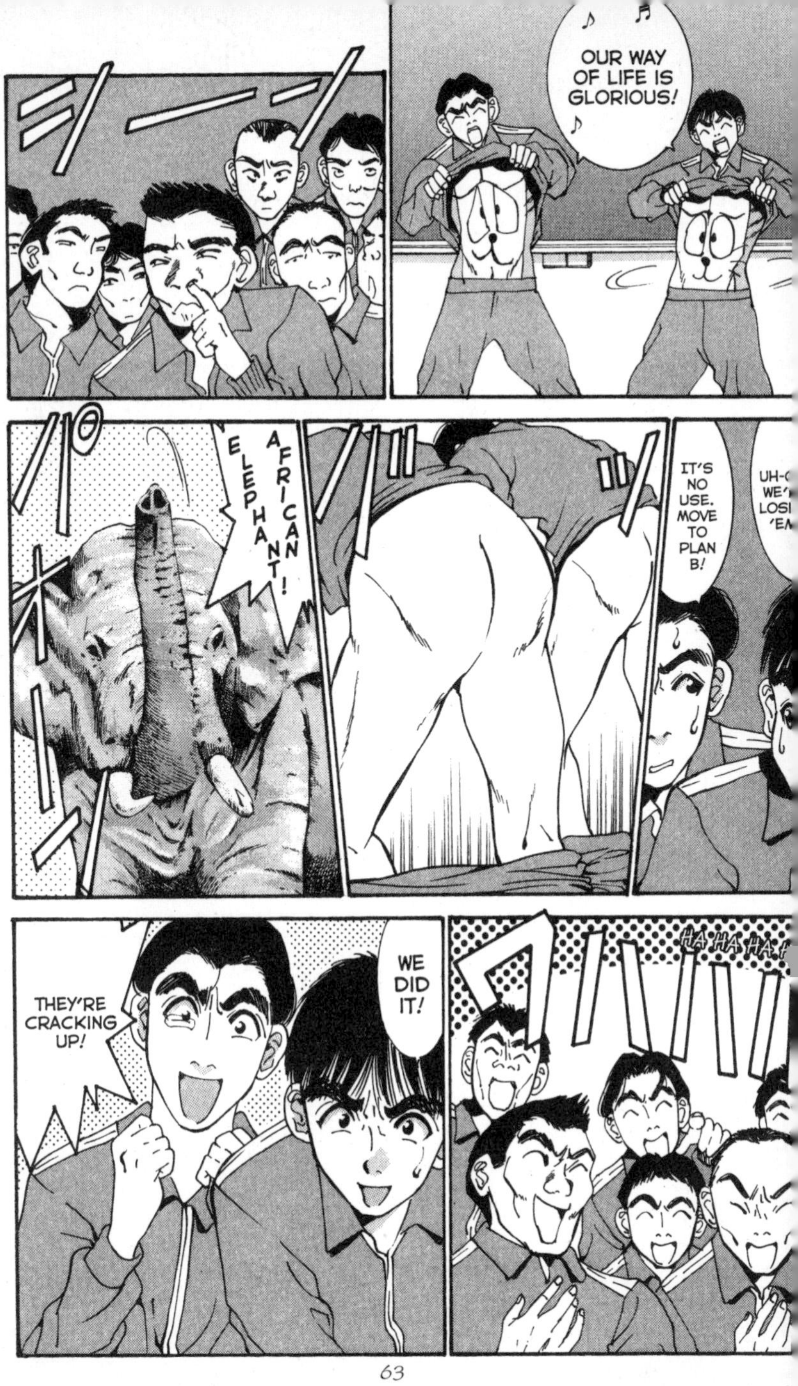
OUR WAY OF LIFE IS GLORIOUS!
IT'S NO USE. MOVE TO PLAN B!
AFRICAN ELEPHANT!
HA HA HA
WE DID IT!
THEY'RE CRACKING UP!

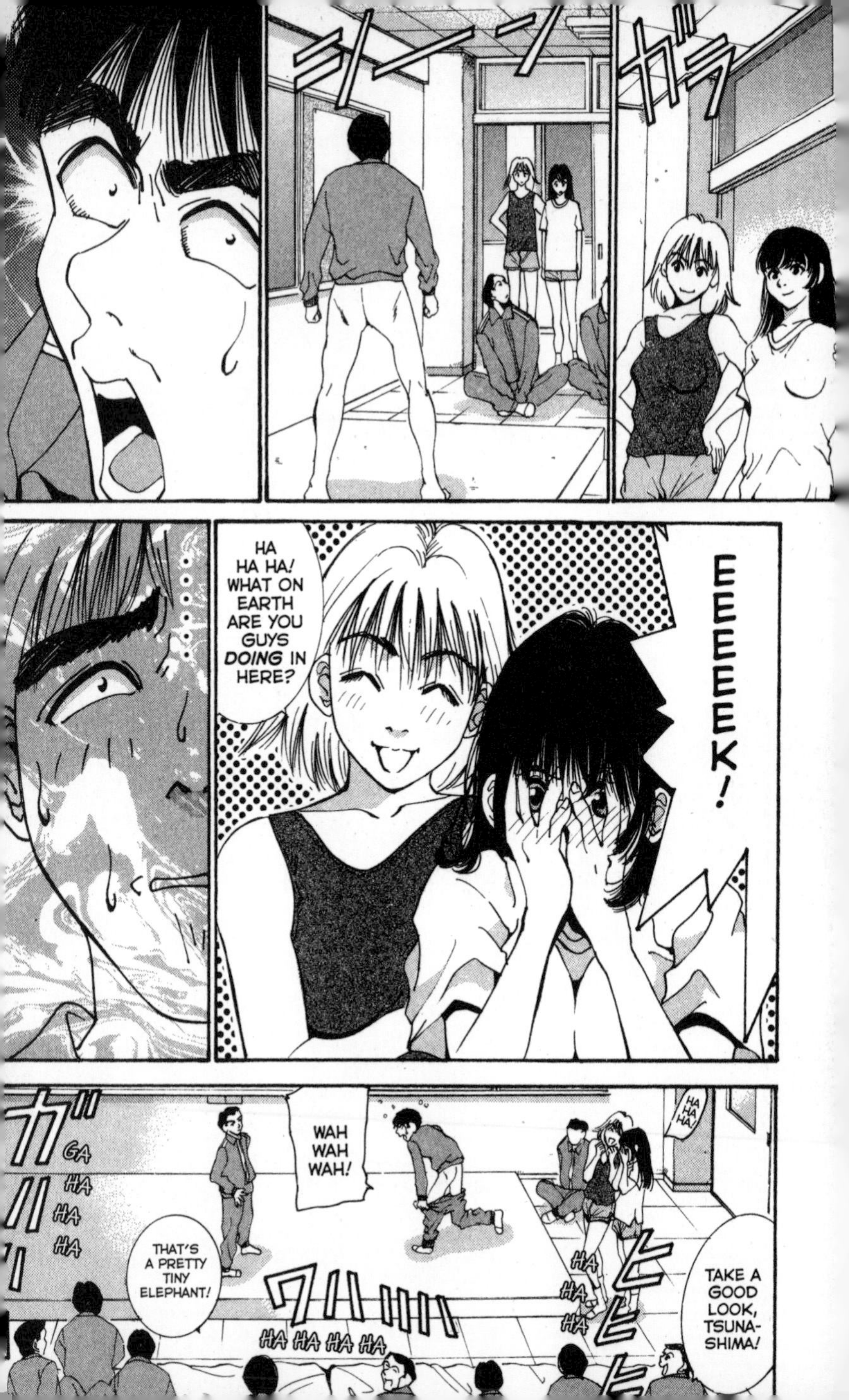
ガラ
シーン
EEEEEK!
HA HA HA! WHAT ON EARTH ARE YOU GUYS DOING IN HERE?
TAKE A GOOD LOOK, TSUNA-SHIMA!
ヒヒヒ
HA HA HA
HA HA HA!
WAH WAH WAH!
ワハハハ
HA HA HA HA
THAT'S A PRETTY TINY ELEPHANT!
ガハハハ
GA HA HA HA

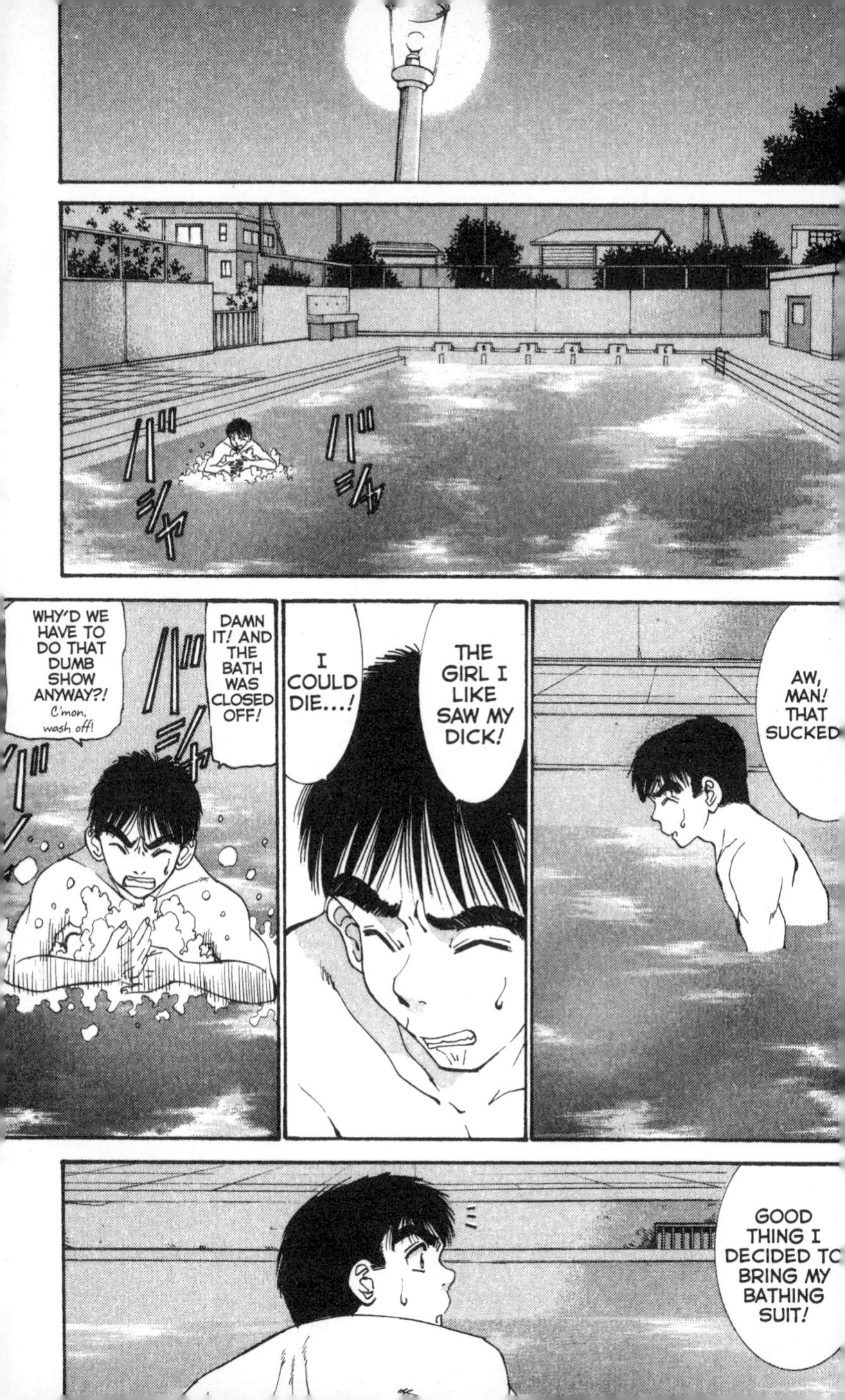
バシャ
バシャ
AW, MAN! THAT SUCKED
THE GIRL I LIKE SAW MY DICK!
I COULD DIE...!
DAMN IT! AND THE BATH WAS CLOSED OFF!
WHY'D WE HAVE TO DO THAT DUMB SHOW ANYWAY?!
C'mon, wash off!
GOOD THING I DECIDED TO BRING MY BATHING SUIT!

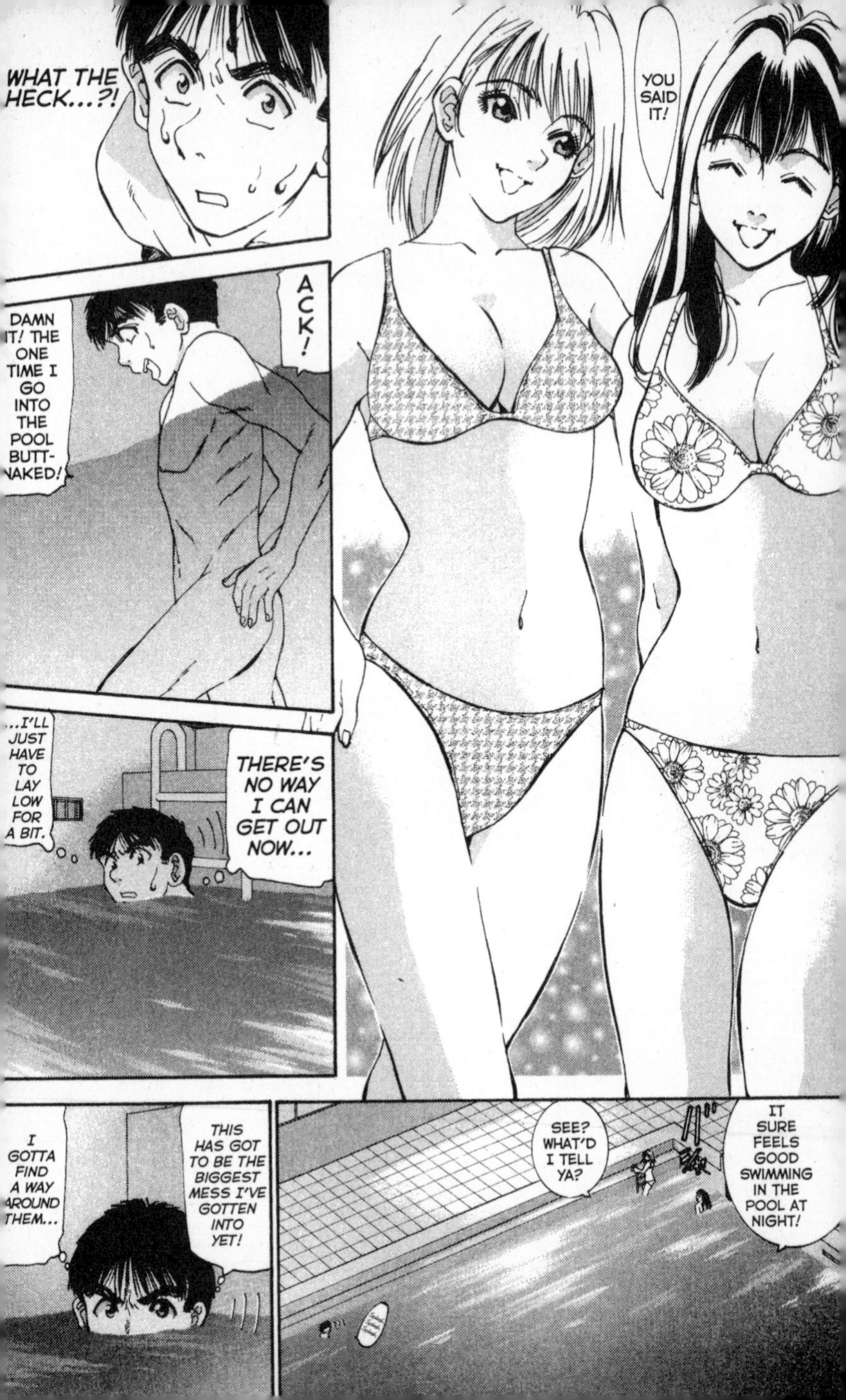
YOU SAID IT!
WHAT THE HECK...?!
ACK!
DAMN IT! THE ONE TIME I GO INTO THE POOL BUTT-NAKED!
THERE'S NO WAY I CAN GET OUT NOW...
...I'LL JUST HAVE TO LAY LOW FOR A BIT.
IT SURE FEELS GOOD SWIMMING IN THE POOL AT NIGHT!
SEE? WHAT'D I TELL YA?
THIS HAS GOT TO BE THE BIGGEST MESS I'VE GOTTEN INTO YET!
I GOTTA FIND A WAY AROUND THEM...

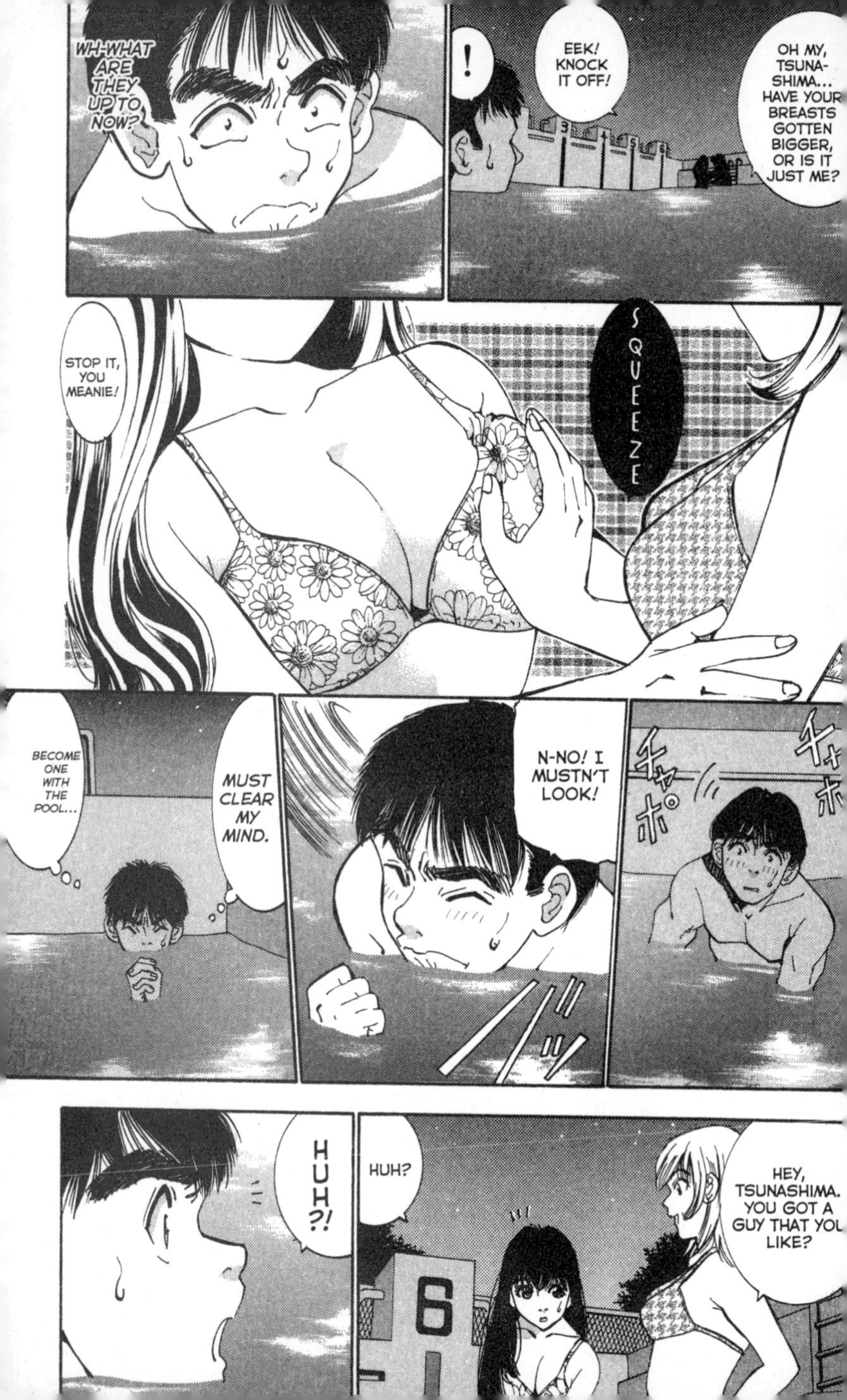
OH MY, TSUNASHIMA... HAVE YOUR BREASTS GOTTEN BIGGER, OR IS IT JUST ME?
EEK! KNOCK IT OFF!
!
WH-WHAT ARE THEY UP TO NOW?
SQUEEZE
STOP IT, YOU MEANIE!
N-NO! I MUSTN'T LOOK!
MUST CLEAR MY MIND.
BECOME ONE WITH THE POOL...
HEY, TSUNASHIMA. YOU GOT A GUY THAT YOU LIKE?
HUH?
HUH?!

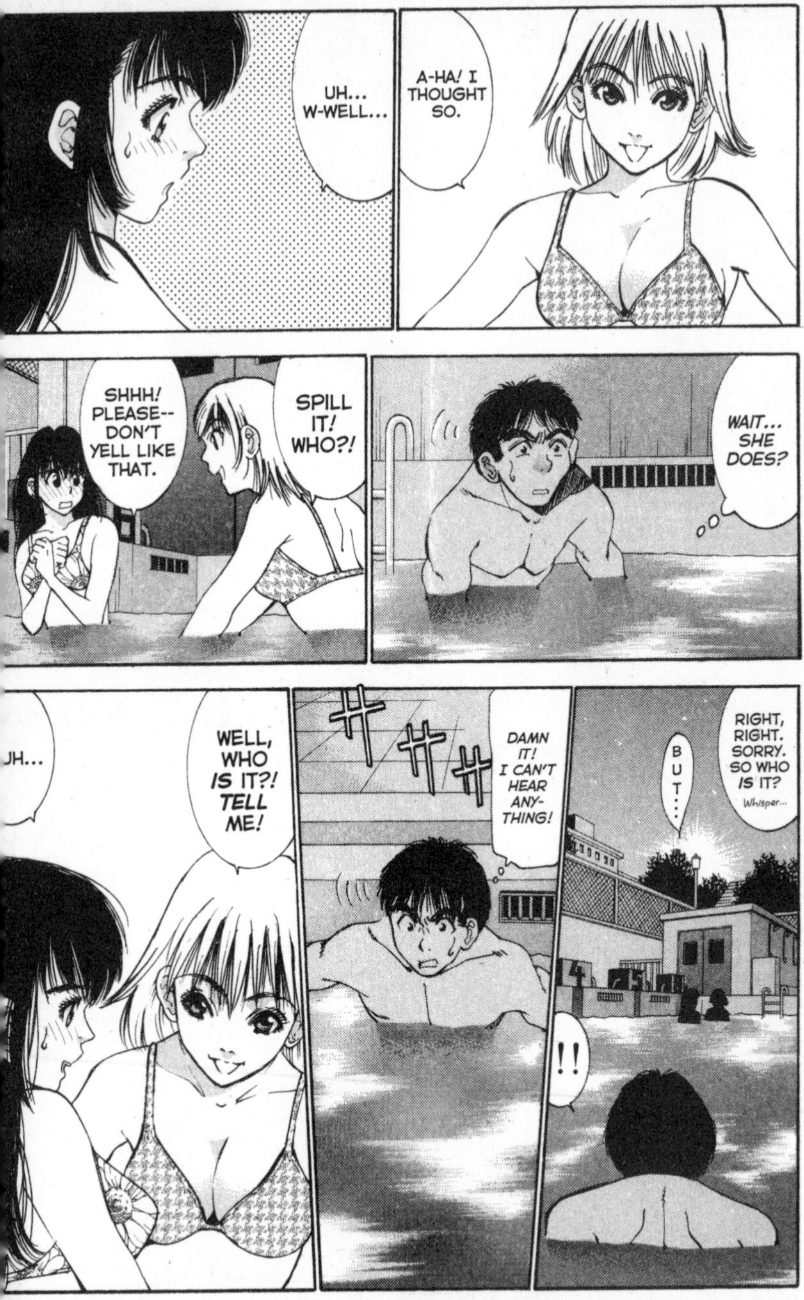

A-HA! I THOUGHT SO.
UH... W-WELL...
WAIT... SHE DOES?
SPILL IT! WHO?!
SHHH! PLEASE-- DON'T YELL LIKE THAT.
RIGHT, RIGHT. SORRY. SO WHO IS IT?
Whisper...
BUT...
!!
DAMN IT! I CAN'T HEAR ANY-THING!
WELL, WHO IS IT?! TELL ME!
UH...

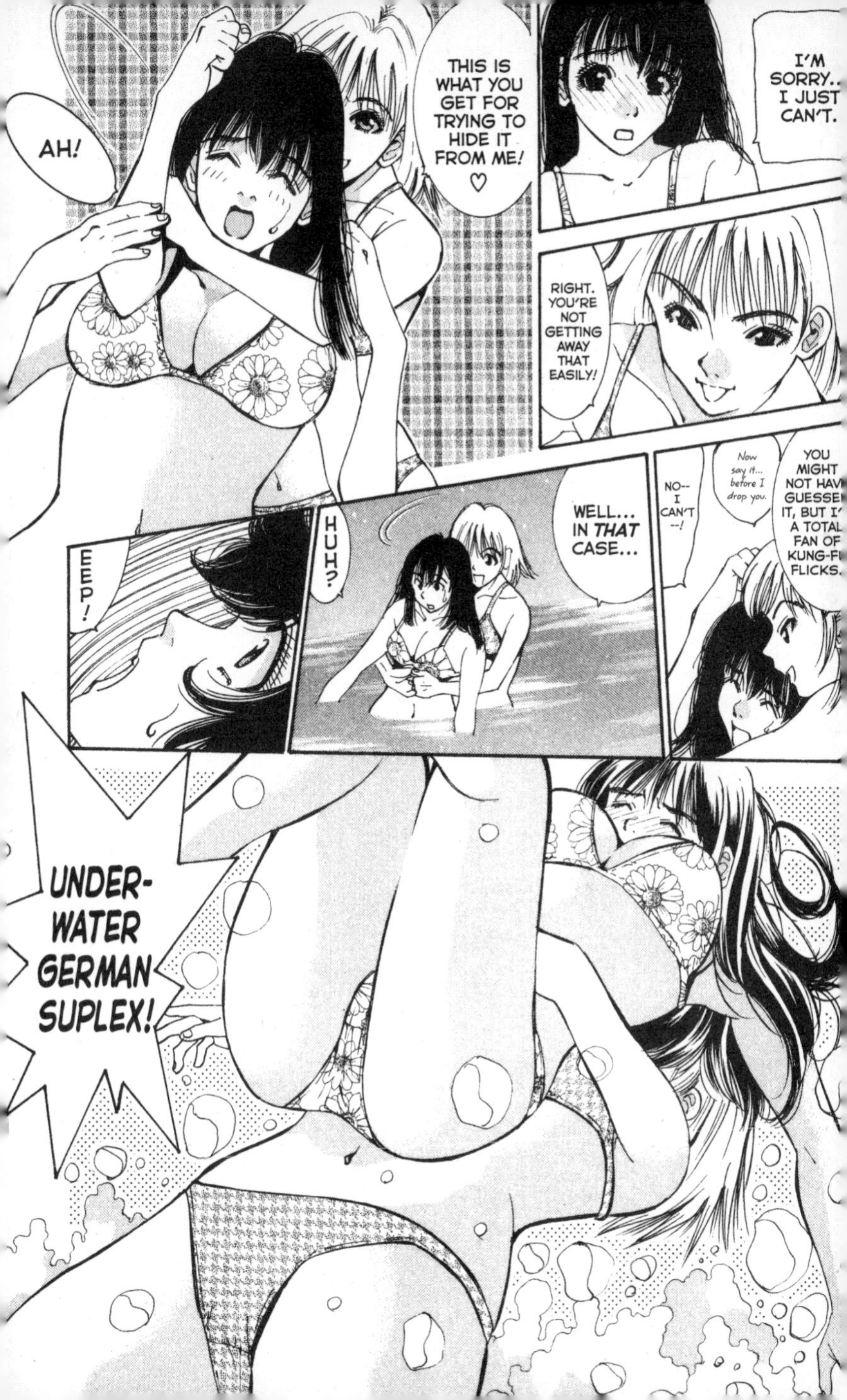
I'M SORRY.. I JUST CAN'T.
RIGHT. YOU'RE NOT GETTING AWAY THAT EASILY!
THIS IS WHAT YOU GET FOR TRYING TO HIDE IT FROM ME! ♡
AH!
YOU MIGHT NOT HAV GUESSE IT, BUT I' A TOTAL FAN OF KUNG-F FLICKS.
Now say it... before I drop you.
NO-- I CAN'T --!
WELL... IN *THAT* CASE...
HUH?
EEP!
UNDER-WATER GERMAN SUPLEX!

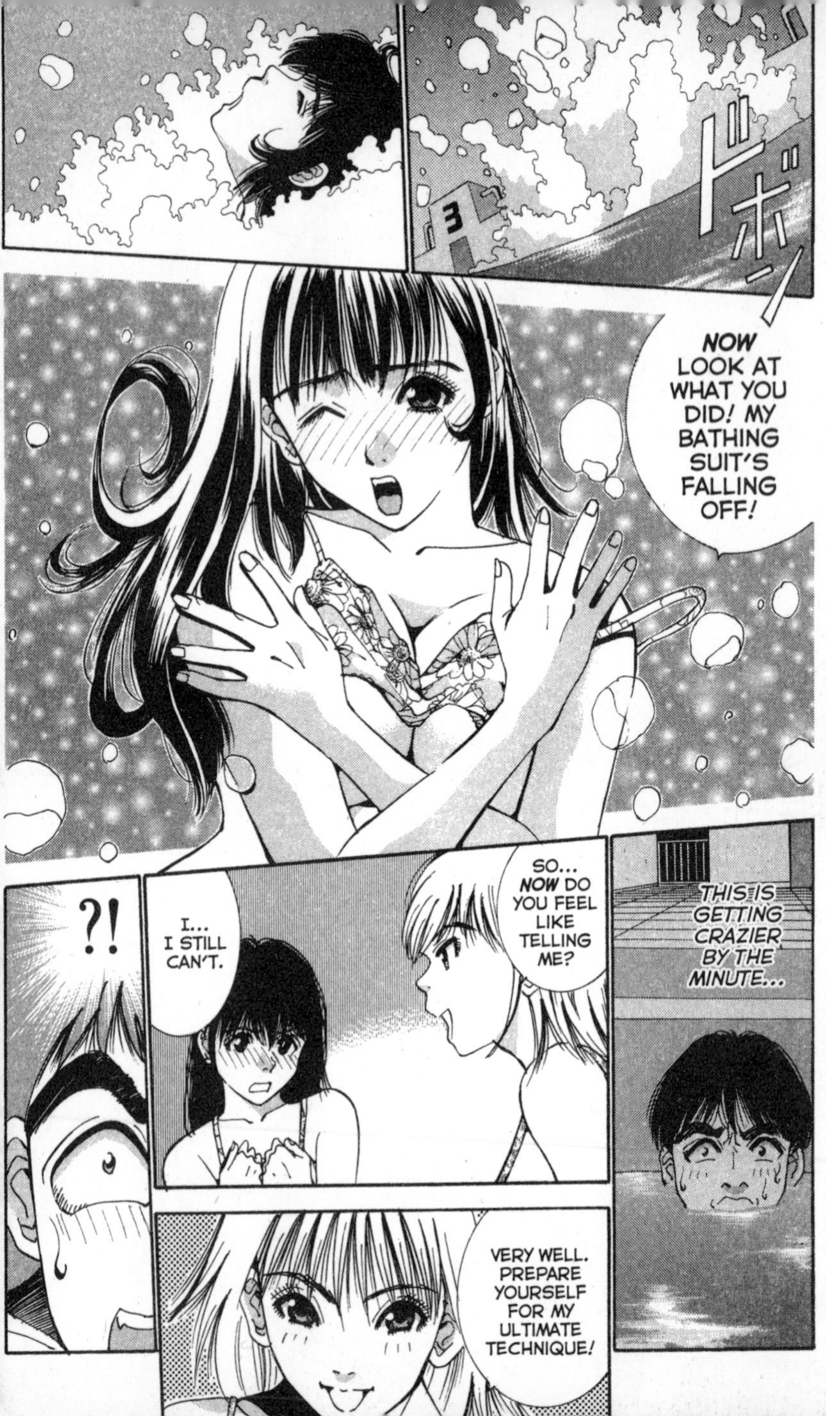
ドボン
NOW LOOK AT WHAT YOU DID! MY BATHING SUIT'S FALLING OFF!
THIS IS GETTING CRAZIER BY THE MINUTE...
SO... NOW DO YOU FEEL LIKE TELLING ME?
I... I STILL CAN'T.
VERY WELL. PREPARE YOURSELF FOR MY ULTIMATE TECHNIQUE!
?!

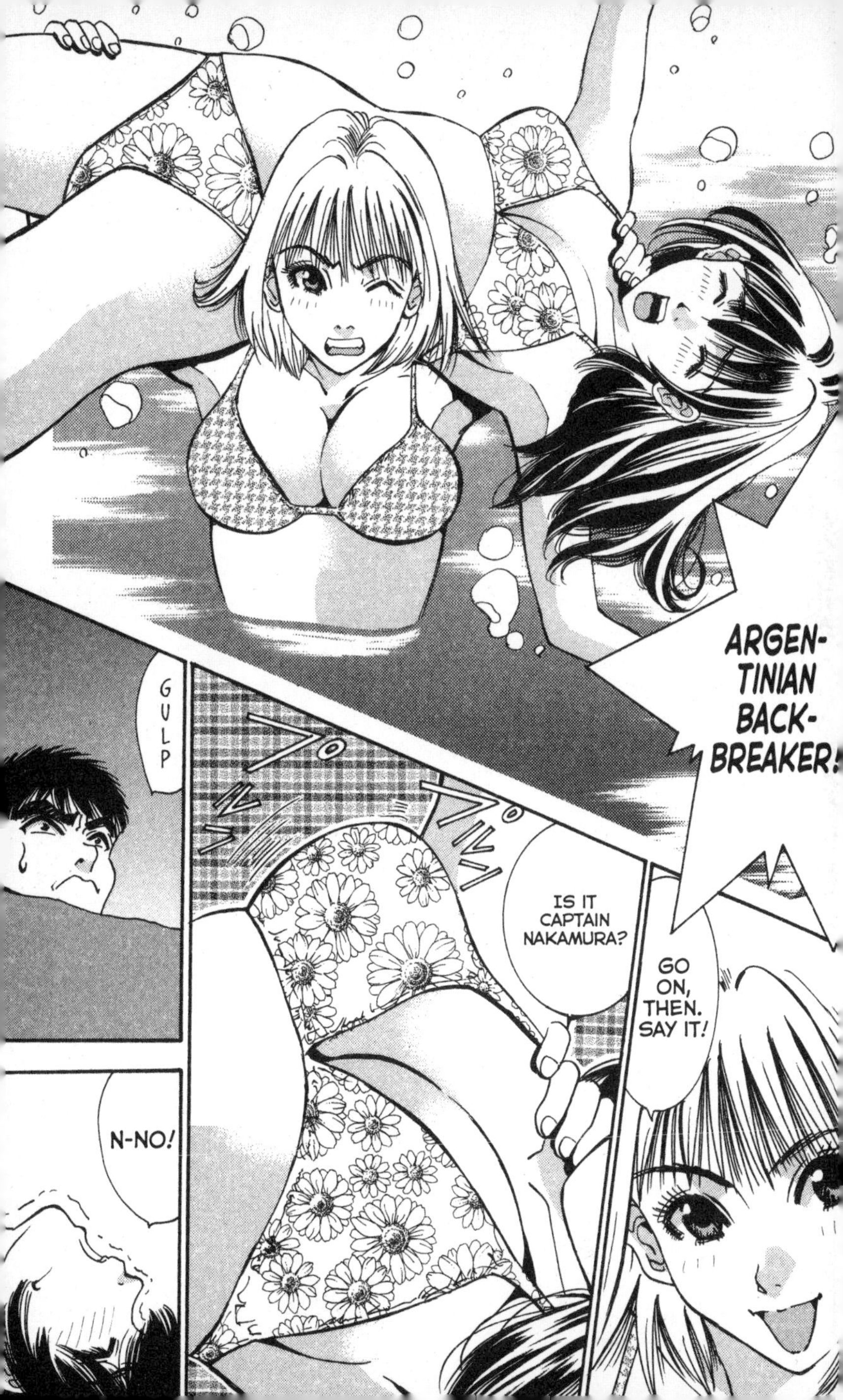
ARGEN-TINIAN BACK-BREAKER!
GO ON, THEN. SAY IT!
IS IT CAPTAIN NAKAMURA?
GULP
N-NO!

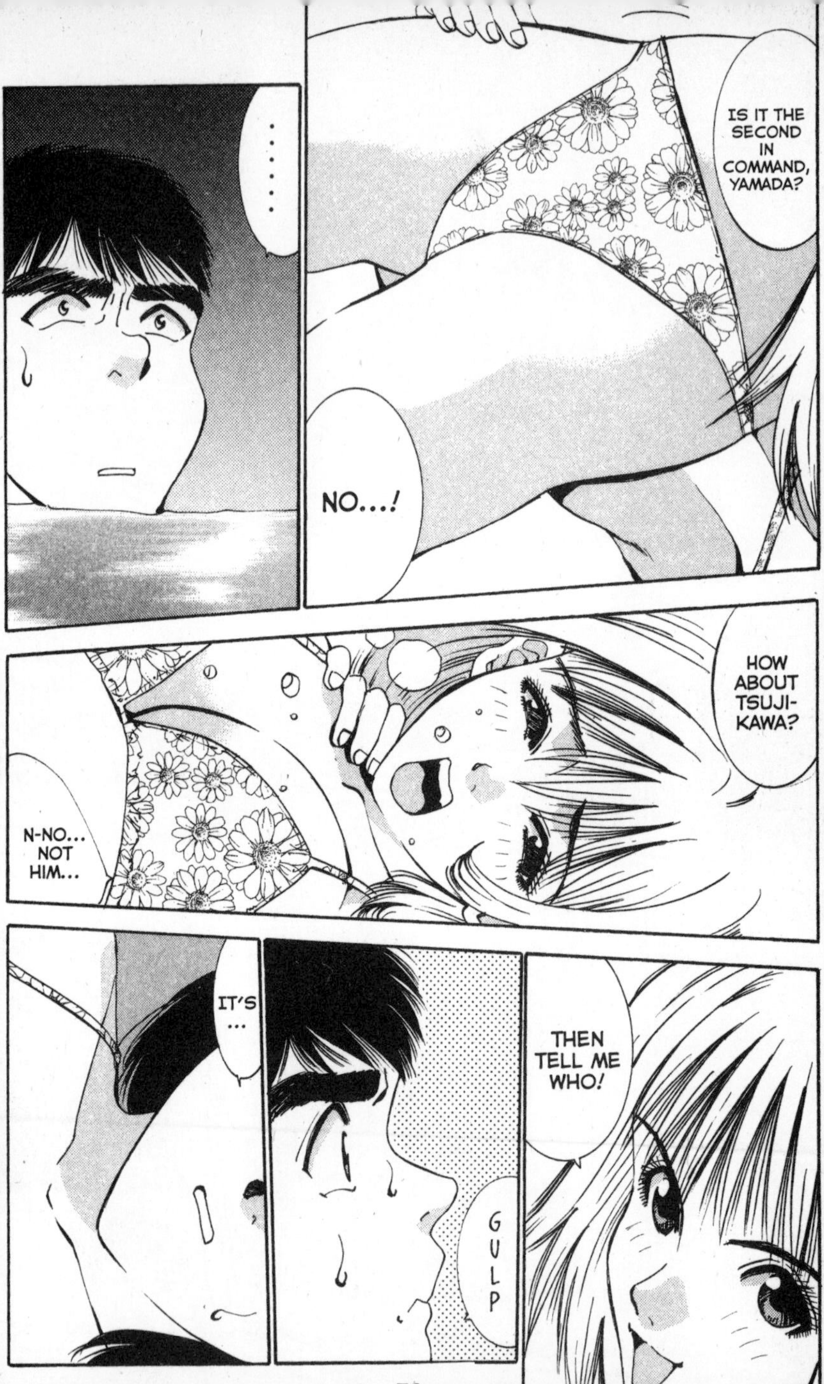
IS IT THE SECOND IN COMMAND, YAMADA?
NO...!
......
HOW ABOUT TSUJI-KAWA?
N-NO... NOT HIM...
THEN TELL ME WHO!
GULP
IT'S ...

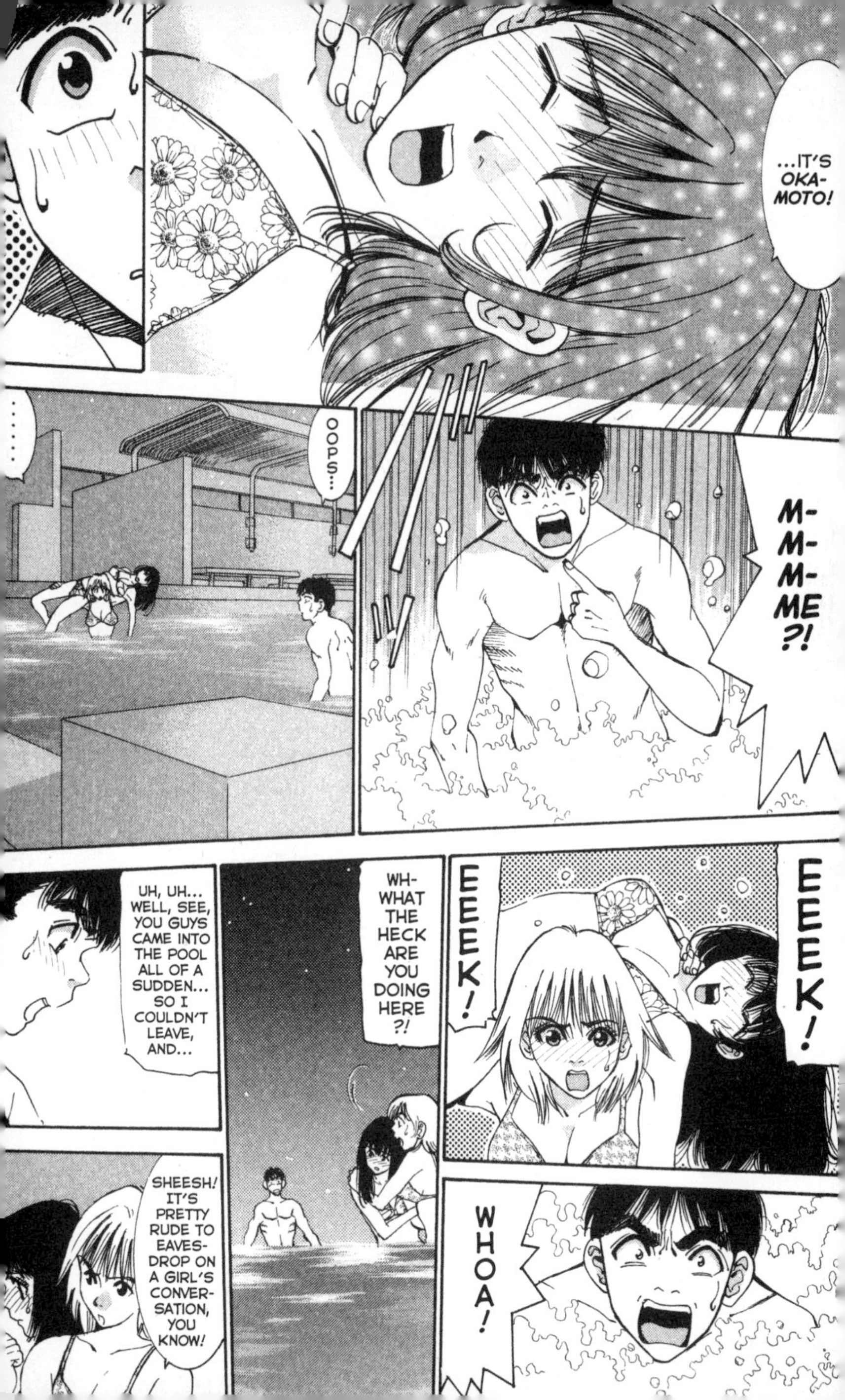
...IT'S OKA-MOTO!
M-M-M-ME?!
OOPS...
......
EEEEK!
EEEEK!
WHOA!
WH-WHAT THE HECK ARE YOU DOING HERE?!
UH, UH... WELL, SEE, YOU GUYS CAME INTO THE POOL ALL OF A SUDDEN... SO I COULDN'T LEAVE, AND...
SHEESH! IT'S PRETTY RUDE TO EAVES-DROP ON A GIRL'S CONVER-SATION, YOU KNOW!

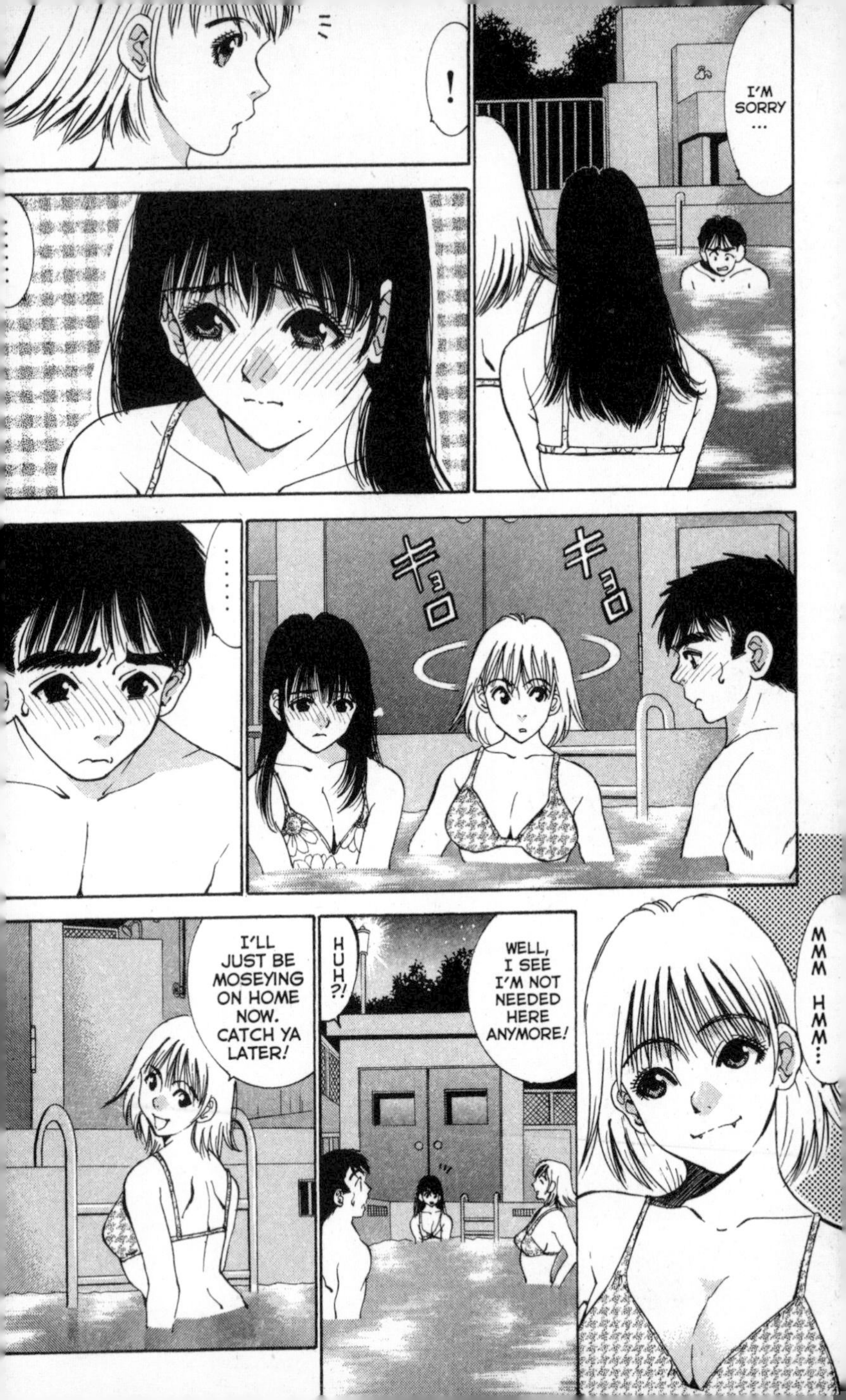
I'M SORRY ...
!
......
キョロ
キョロ
......
MMM HMM...
WELL, I SEE I'M NOT NEEDED HERE ANYMORE!
HUH?!
I'LL JUST BE MOSEYING ON HOME NOW. CATCH YA LATER!

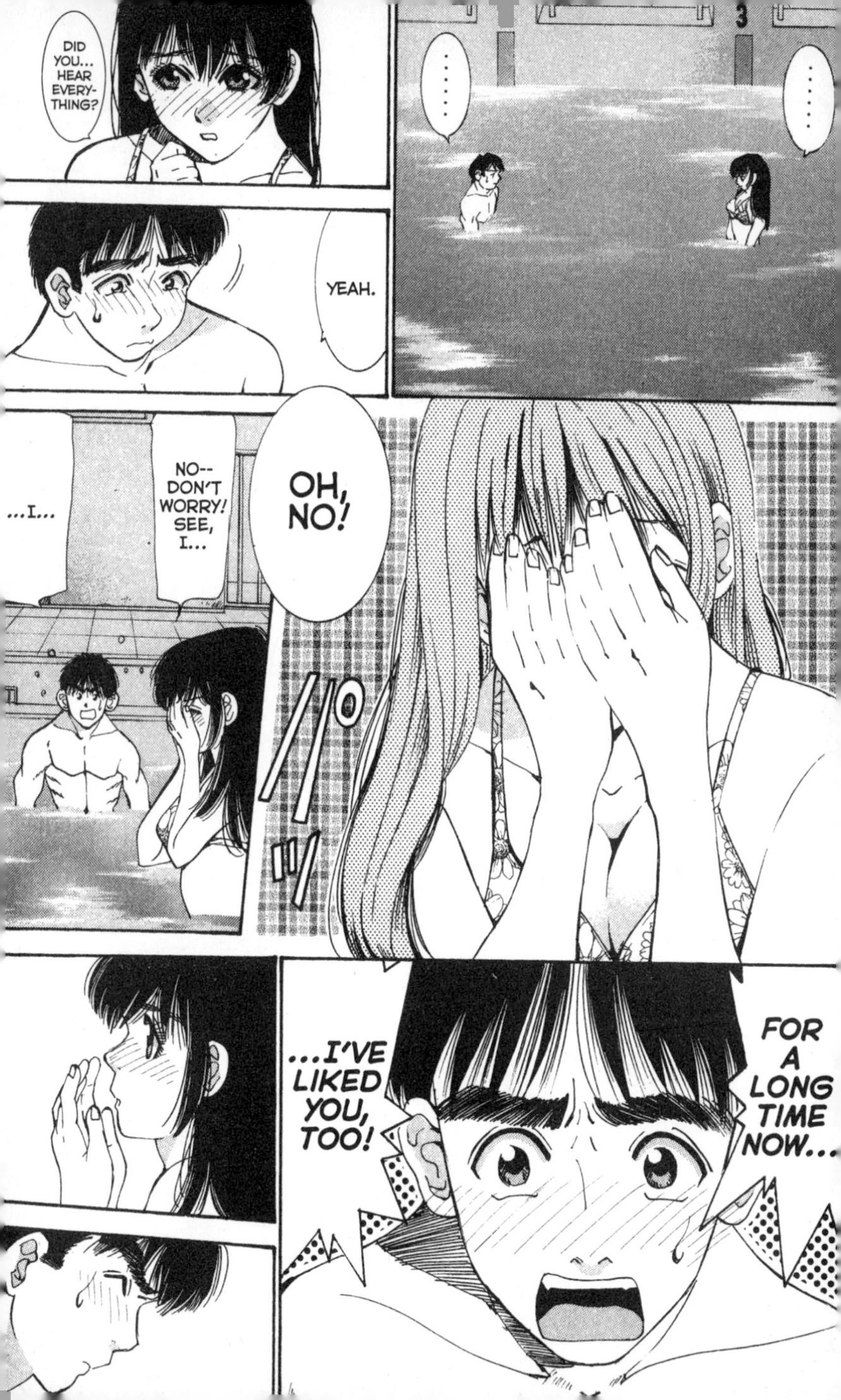

......
......
DID YOU... HEAR EVERY-THING?
YEAH.
OH, NO!
NO-- DON'T WORRY! SEE, I...
...I...
FOR A LONG TIME NOW...
...I'VE LIKED YOU, TOO!

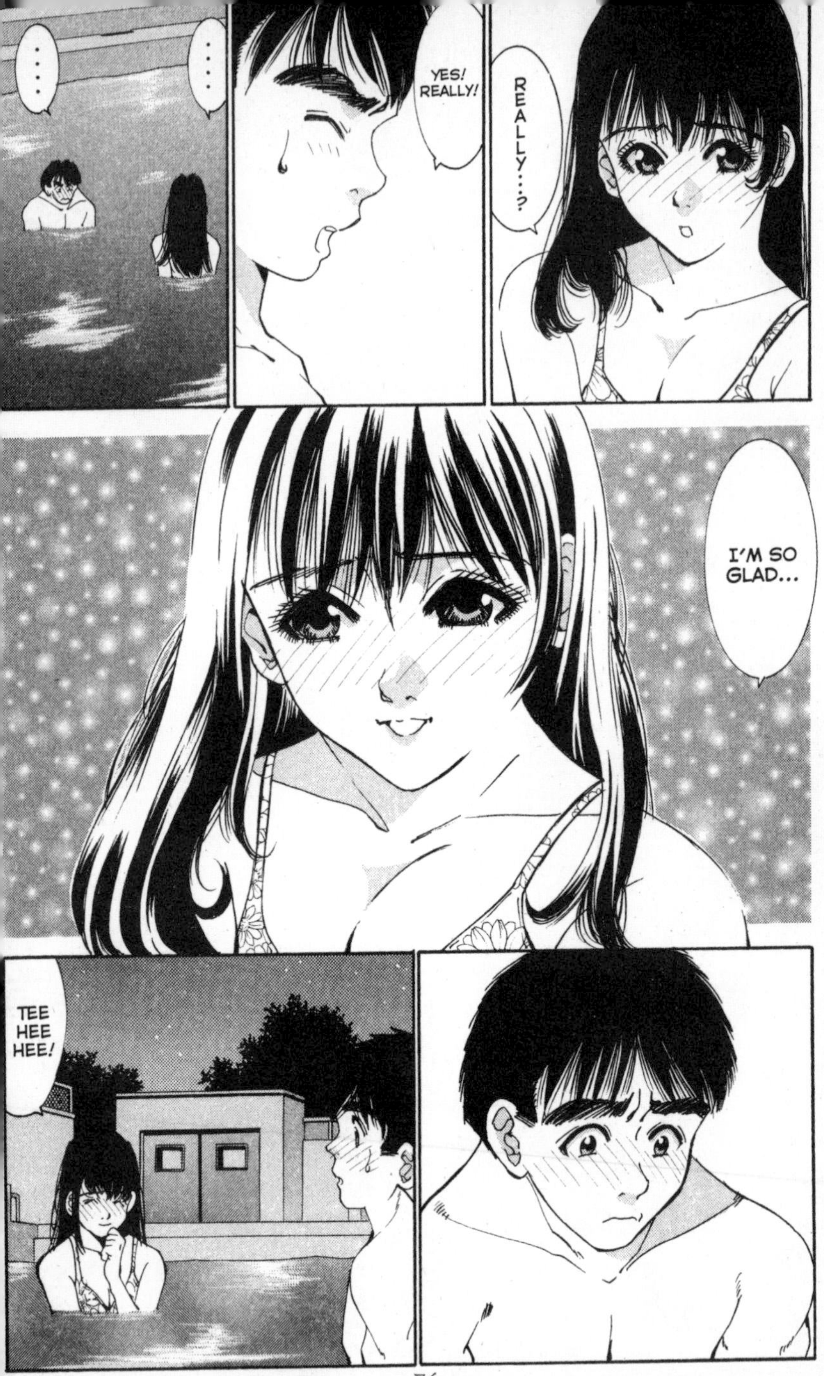
REALLY...?
YES! REALLY!
....
....
I'M SO GLAD...
TEE HEE HEE!

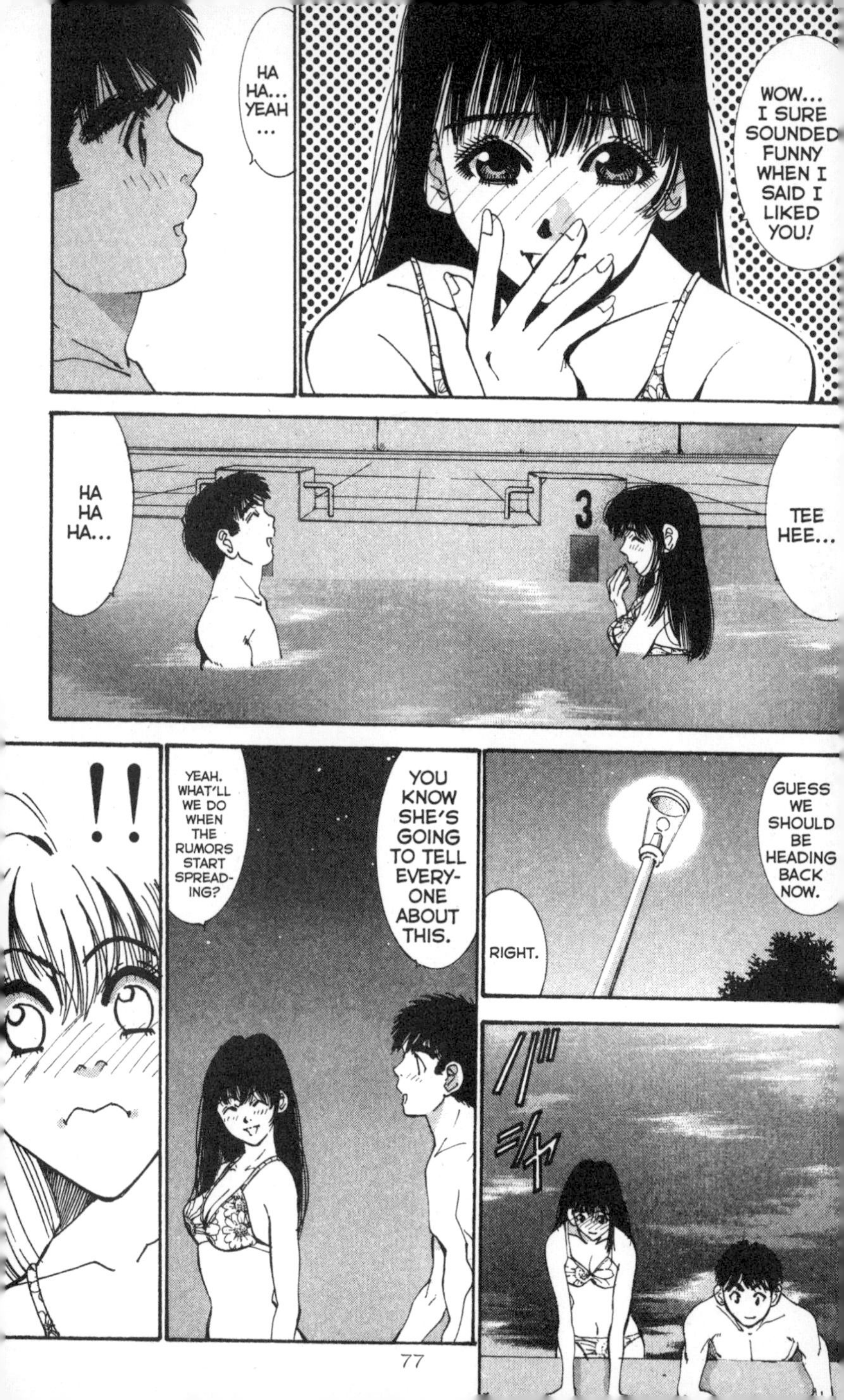
WOW... I SURE SOUNDED FUNNY WHEN I SAID I LIKED YOU!
HA HA... YEAH...
TEE HEE...
HA HA HA...
GUESS WE SHOULD BE HEADING BACK NOW.
RIGHT.
バシャ
YOU KNOW SHE'S GOING TO TELL EVERY-ONE ABOUT THIS.
YEAH. WHAT'LL WE DO WHEN THE RUMORS START SPREAD-ING?
!!

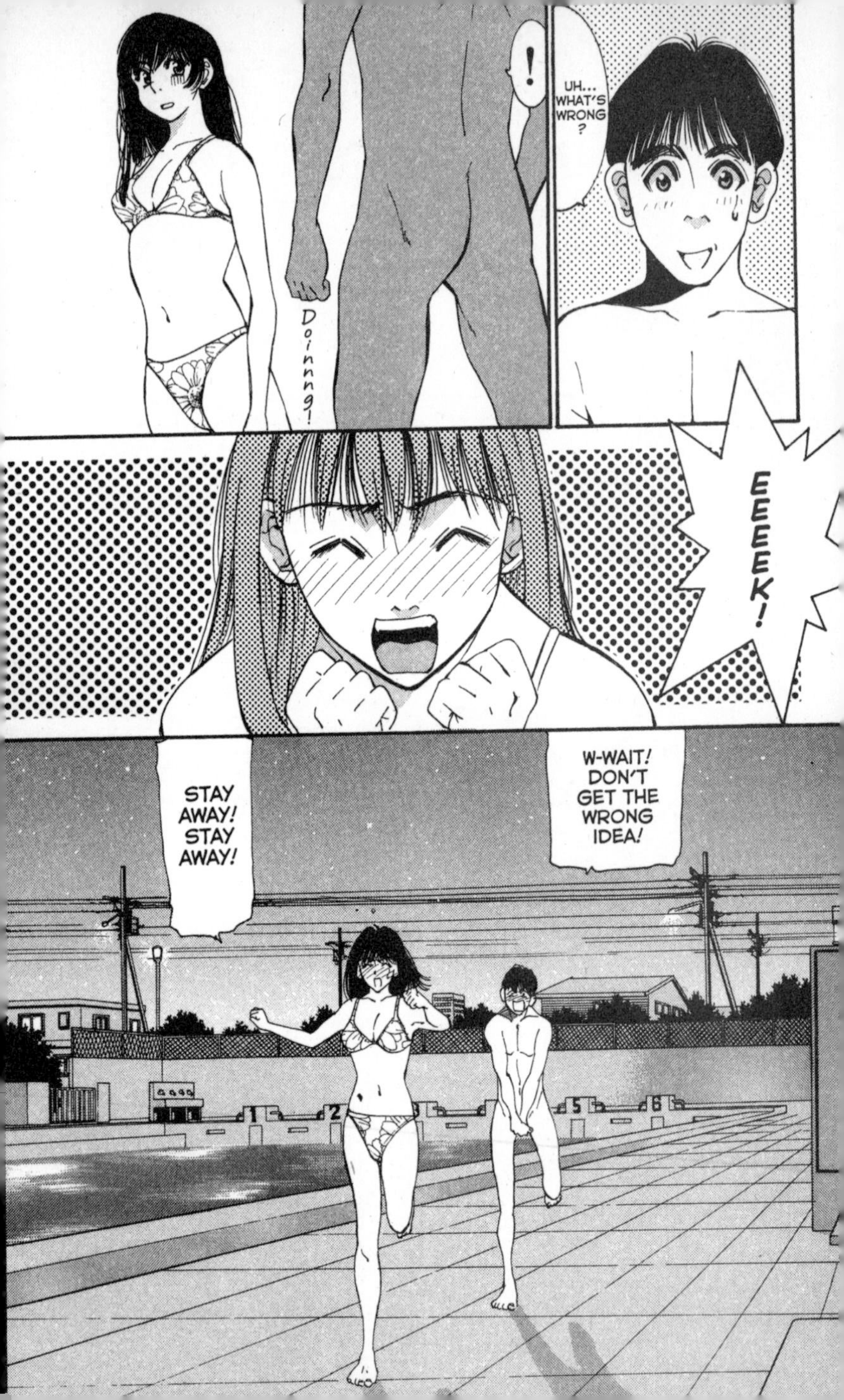
UH... WHAT'S WRONG?
!
Doinnng!
EEEEK!
W-WAIT! DON'T GET THE WRONG IDEA!
STAY AWAY! STAY AWAY!

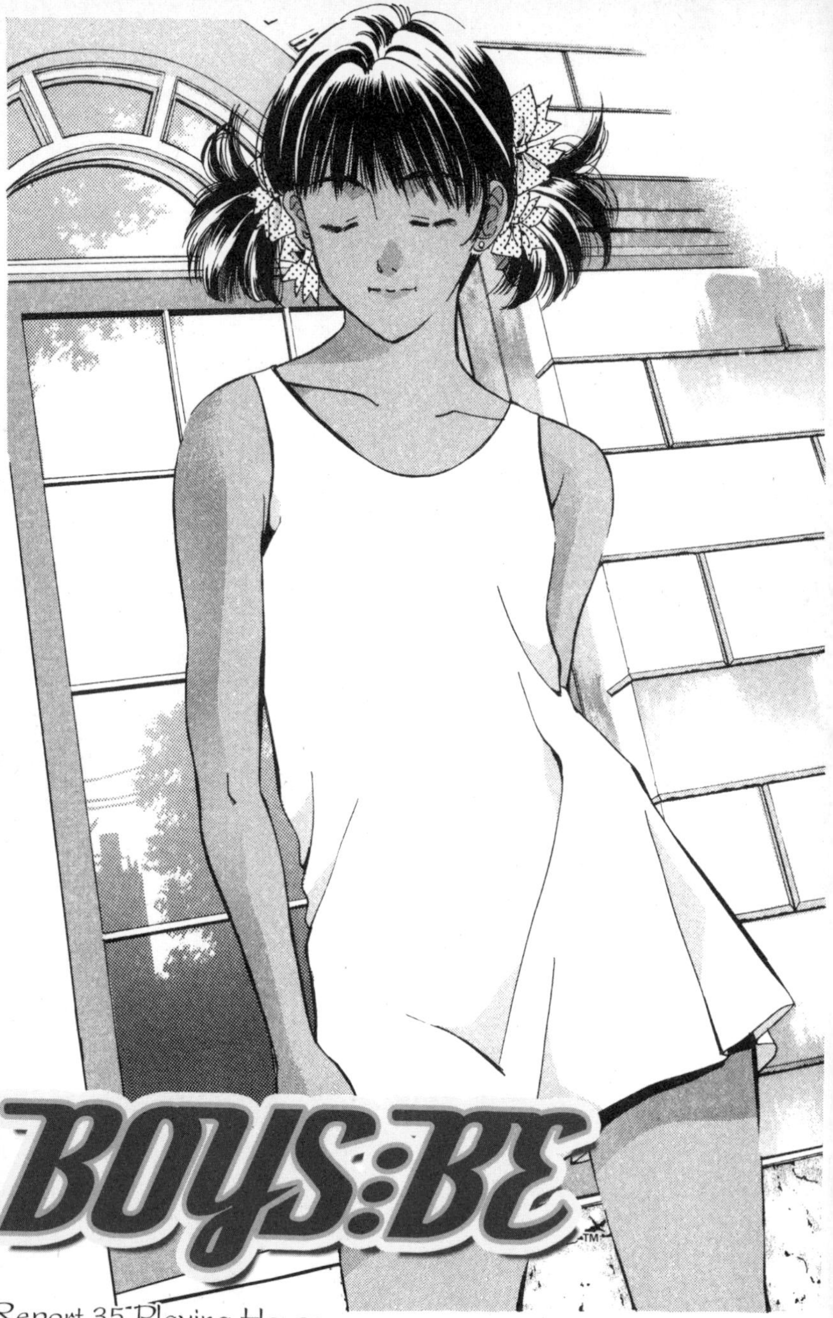
BOYS BE

Report 35 Playing House

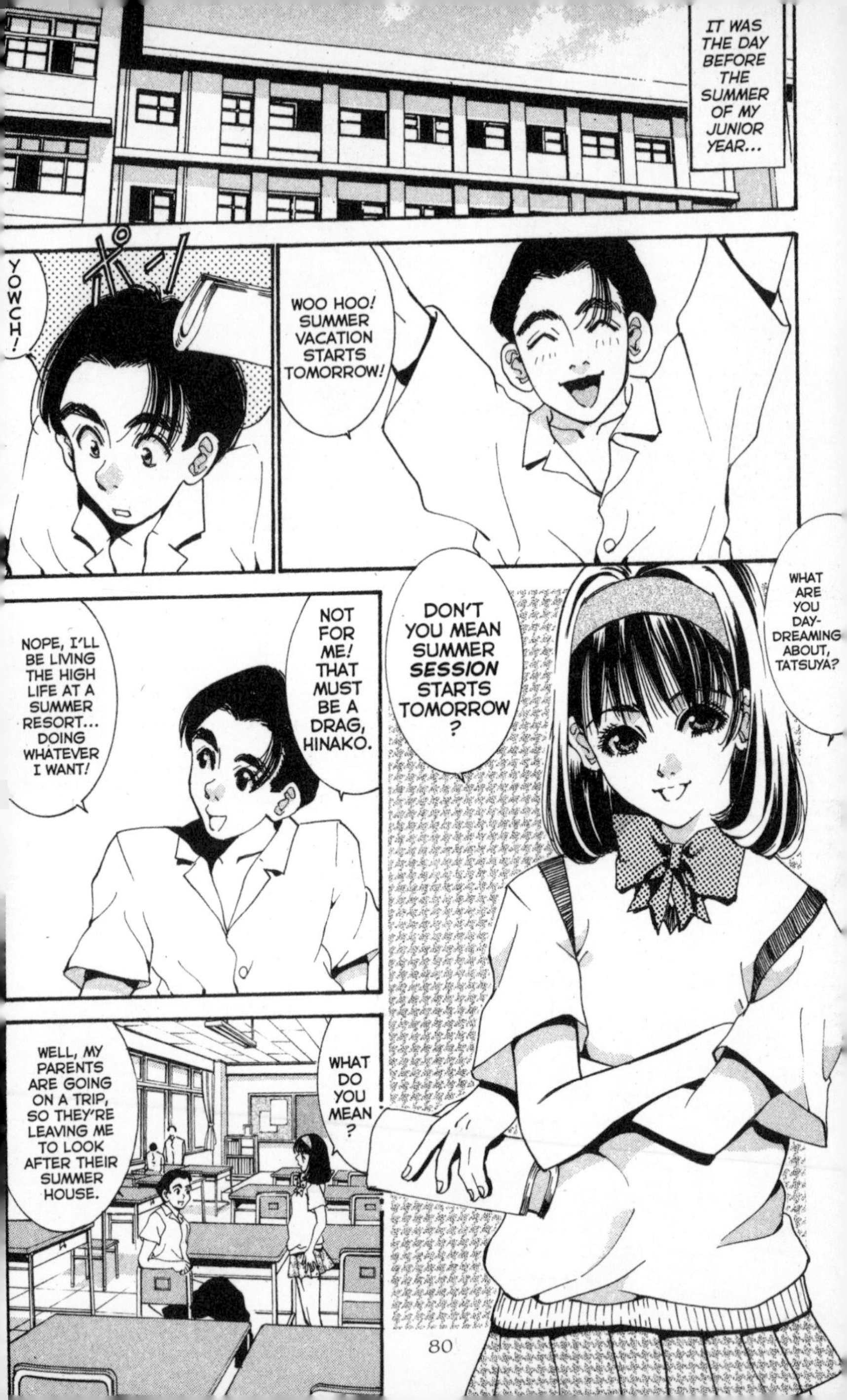
IT WAS THE DAY BEFORE THE SUMMER OF MY JUNIOR YEAR...
WOO HOO! SUMMER VACATION STARTS TOMORROW!
YOWCH!
WHAT ARE YOU DAY-DREAMING ABOUT, TATSUYA?
DON'T YOU MEAN SUMMER *SESSION* STARTS TOMORROW?
NOT FOR ME! THAT MUST BE A DRAG, HINAKO.
NOPE, I'LL BE LIVING THE HIGH LIFE AT A SUMMER RESORT... DOING WHATEVER I WANT!
WHAT DO YOU MEAN?
WELL, MY PARENTS ARE GOING ON A TRIP, SO THEY'RE LEAVING ME TO LOOK AFTER THEIR SUMMER HOUSE.

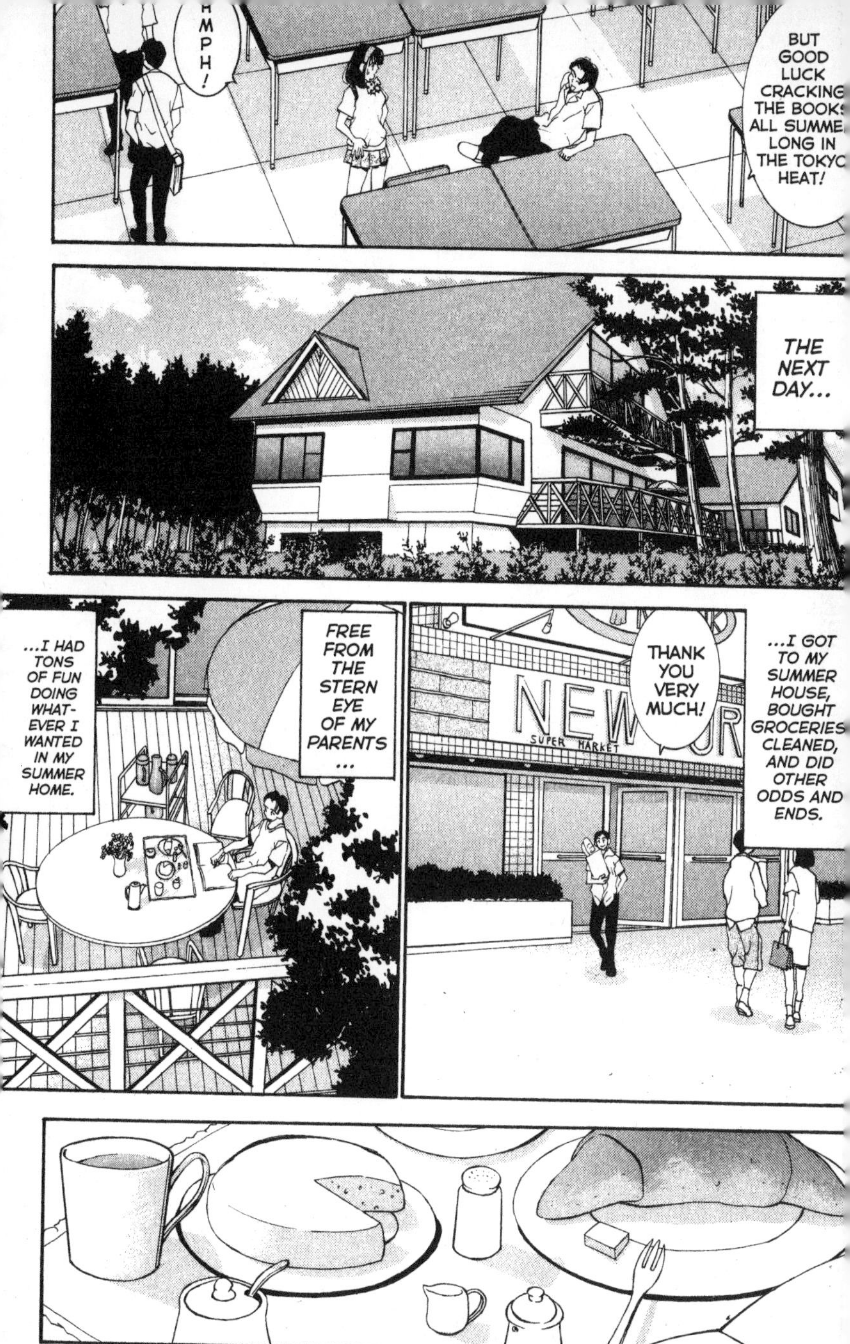
BUT GOOD LUCK CRACKING THE BOOKS ALL SUMME LONG IN THE TOKYO HEAT!
HMPH!
THE NEXT DAY...
...I GOT TO MY SUMMER HOUSE, BOUGHT GROCERIES CLEANED, AND DID OTHER ODDS AND ENDS.
THANK YOU VERY MUCH!
NEW
SUPER MARKET
FREE FROM THE STERN EYE OF MY PARENTS ...
...I HAD TONS OF FUN DOING WHAT-EVER I WANTED IN MY SUMMER HOME.

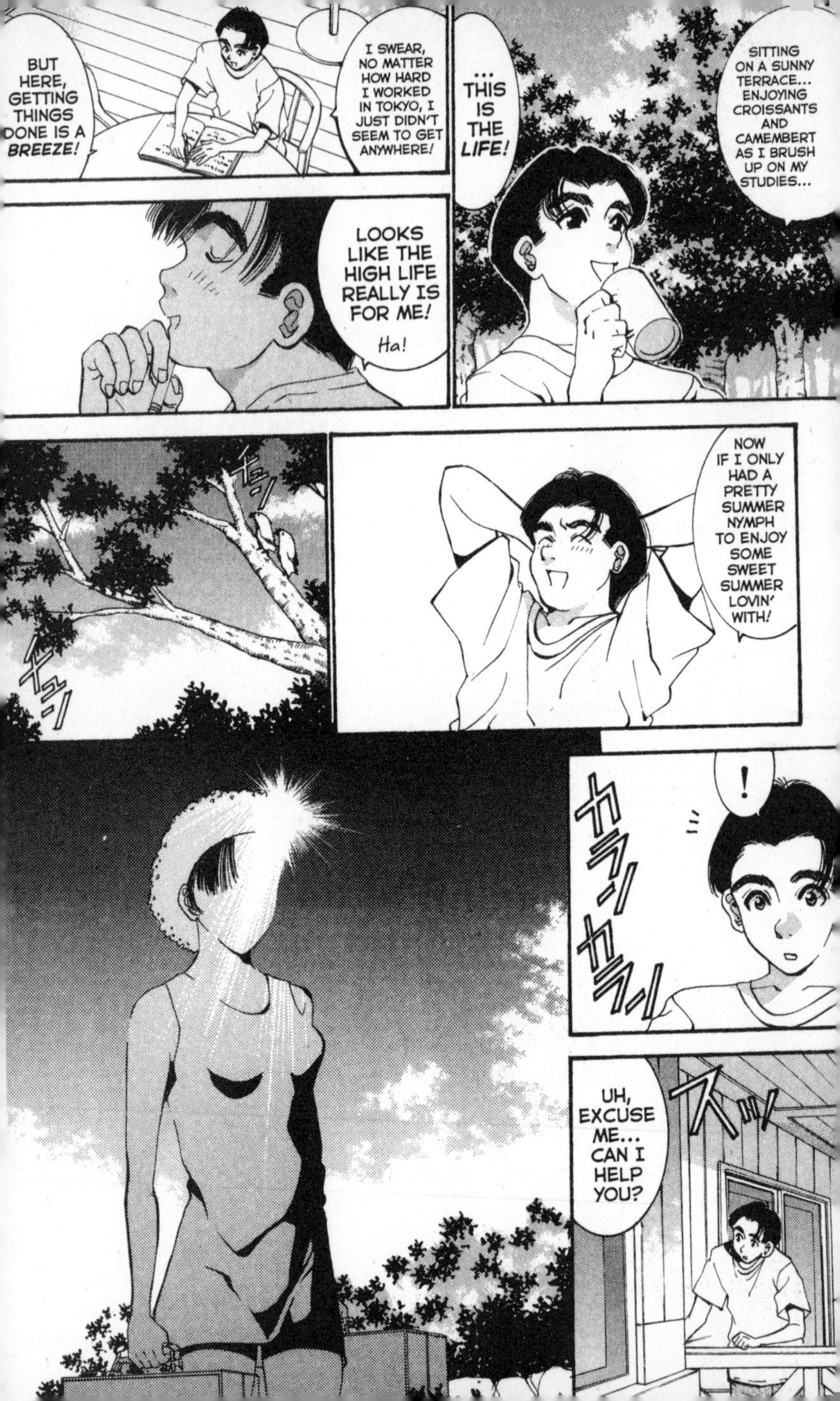
SITTING ON A SUNNY TERRACE... ENJOYING CROISSANTS AND CAMEMBERT AS I BRUSH UP ON MY STUDIES...
...THIS IS THE *LIFE!*
I SWEAR, NO MATTER HOW HARD I WORKED IN TOKYO, I JUST DIDN'T SEEM TO GET ANYWHERE!
BUT HERE, GETTING THINGS DONE IS A *BREEZE!*
LOOKS LIKE THE HIGH LIFE REALLY IS FOR ME!
Ha!
NOW IF I ONLY HAD A PRETTY SUMMER NYMPH TO ENJOY SOME SWEET SUMMER LOVIN' WITH!
!
UH, EXCUSE ME... CAN I HELP YOU?

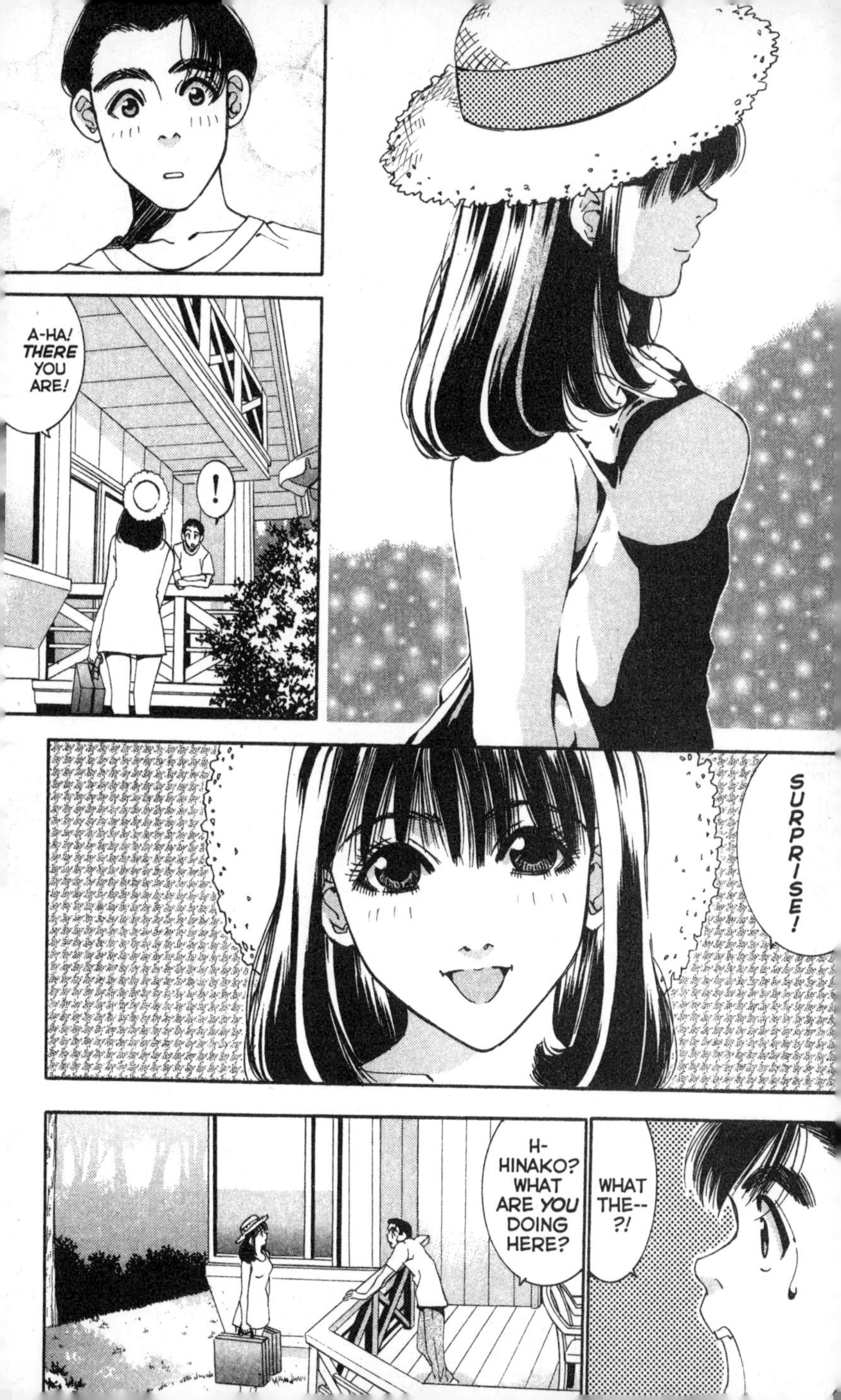
A-HA! *THERE* YOU ARE!
!
SURPRISE!
WHAT THE--?!
H-HINAKO? WHAT ARE *YOU* DOING HERE?

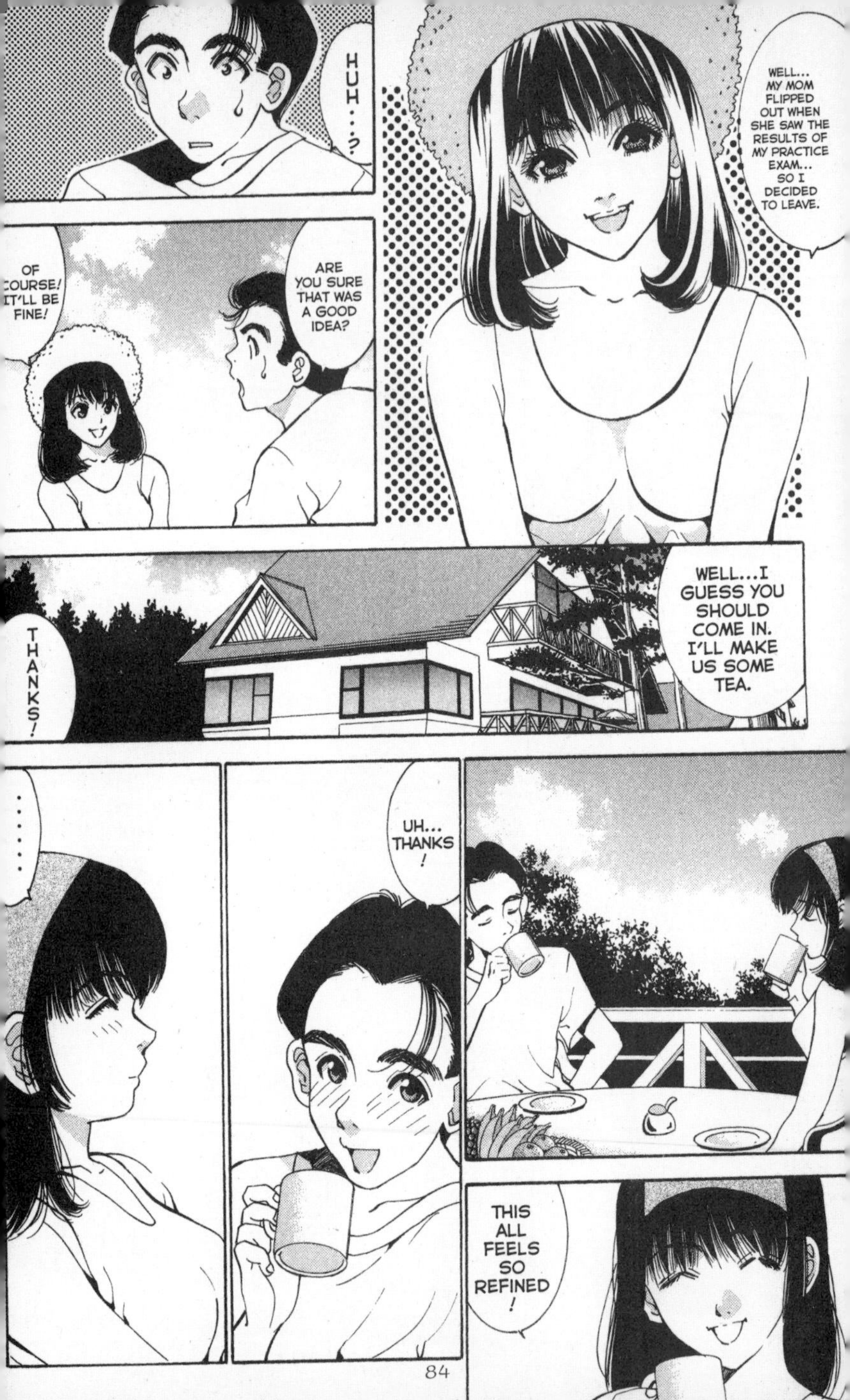
WELL... MY MOM FLIPPED OUT WHEN SHE SAW THE RESULTS OF MY PRACTICE EXAM... SO I DECIDED TO LEAVE.
HUH...?
ARE YOU SURE THAT WAS A GOOD IDEA?
OF COURSE! IT'LL BE FINE!
WELL...I GUESS YOU SHOULD COME IN. I'LL MAKE US SOME TEA.
THANKS!
THIS ALL FEELS SO REFINED!
UH... THANKS!
......

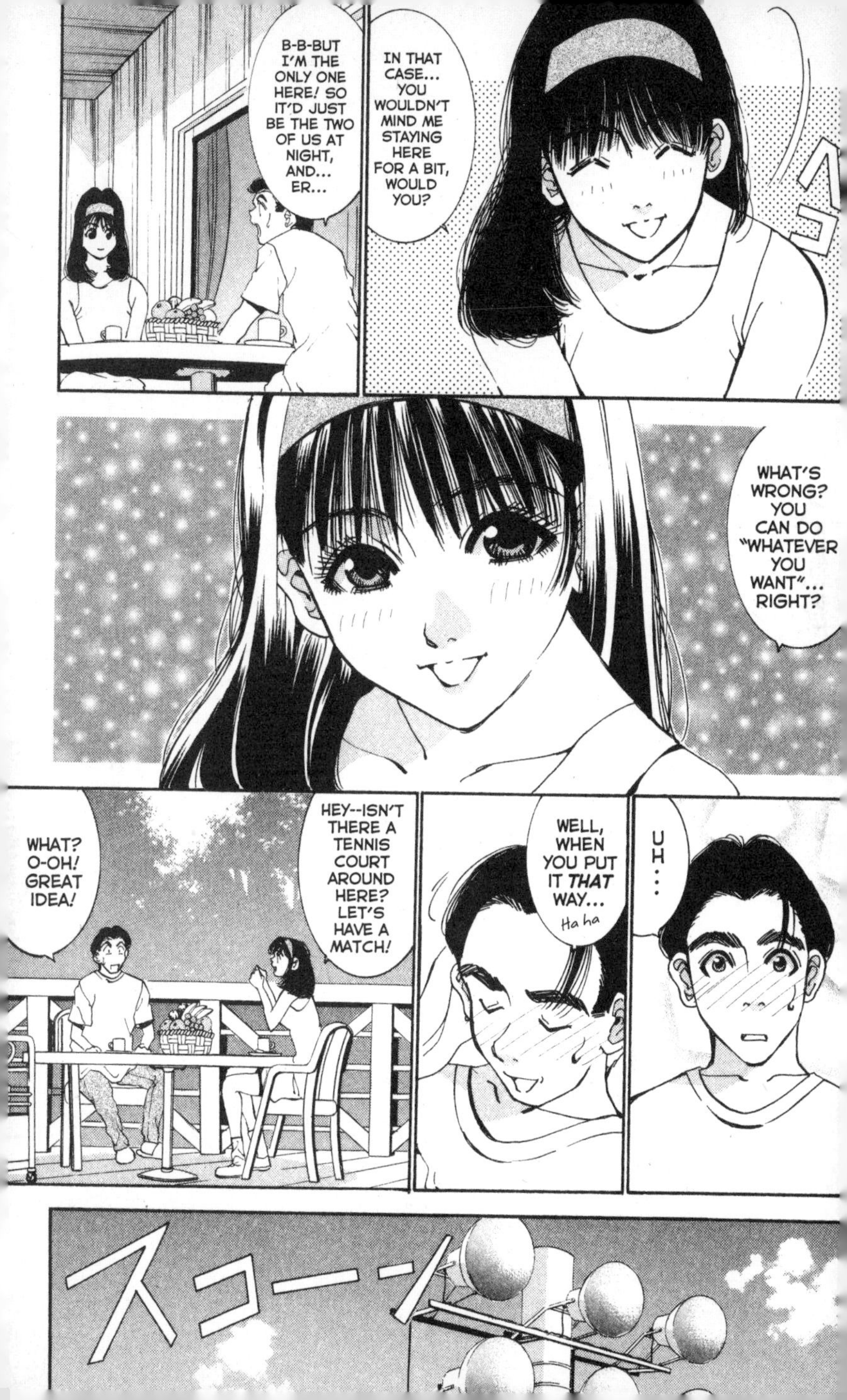
IN THAT CASE... YOU WOULDN'T MIND ME STAYING HERE FOR A BIT, WOULD YOU?
B-B-BUT I'M THE ONLY ONE HERE! SO IT'D JUST BE THE TWO OF US AT NIGHT, AND... ER...
WHAT'S WRONG? YOU CAN DO "WHATEVER YOU WANT"... RIGHT?
UH...
WELL, WHEN YOU PUT IT *THAT* WAY...
Ha ha
HEY--ISN'T THERE A TENNIS COURT AROUND HERE? LET'S HAVE A MATCH!
WHAT? O-OH! GREAT IDEA!
スコーー

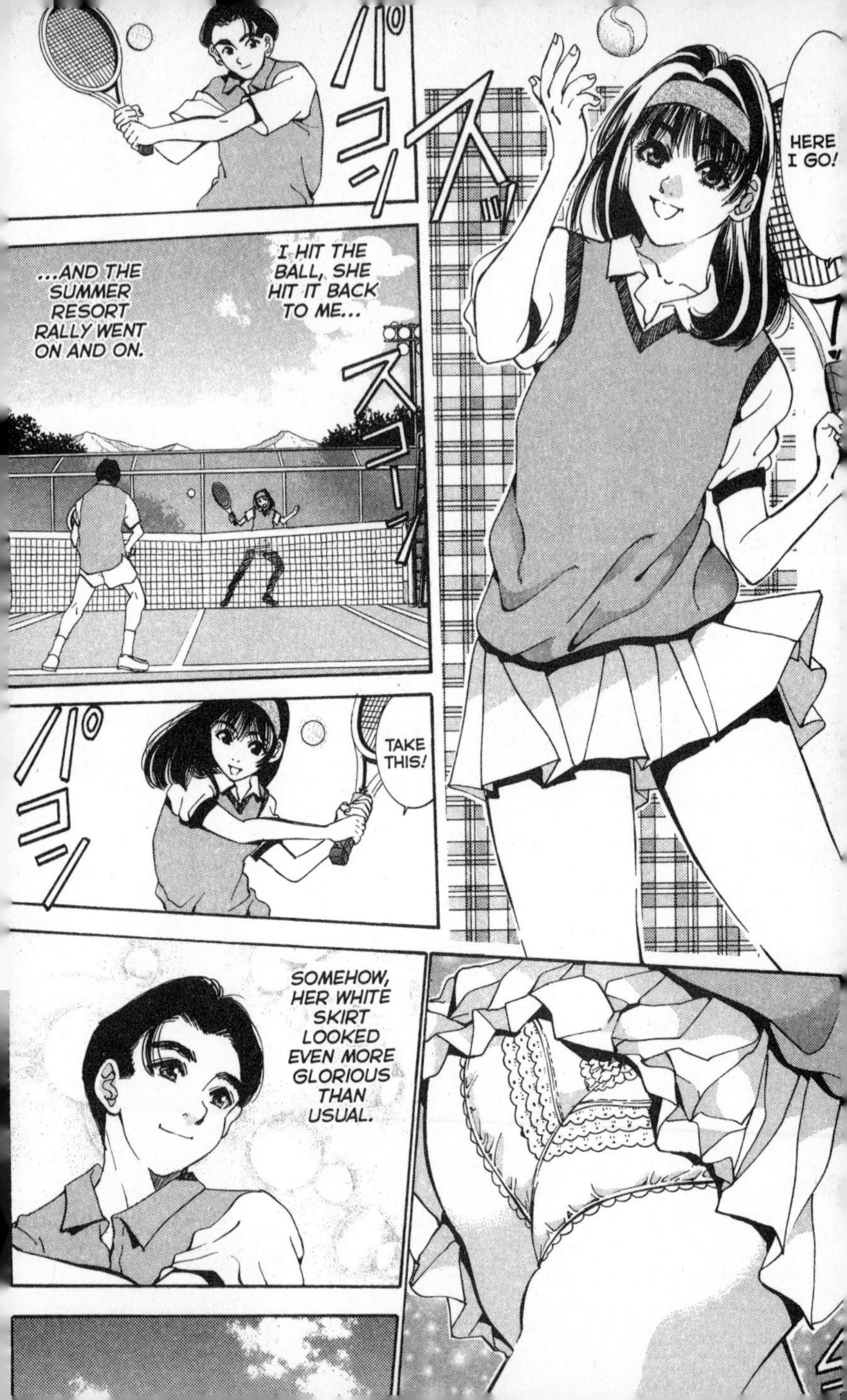
HERE I GO!
I HIT THE BALL, SHE HIT IT BACK TO ME...
...AND THE SUMMER RESORT RALLY WENT ON AND ON.
TAKE THIS!
SOMEHOW, HER WHITE SKIRT LOOKED EVEN MORE GLORIOUS THAN USUAL.

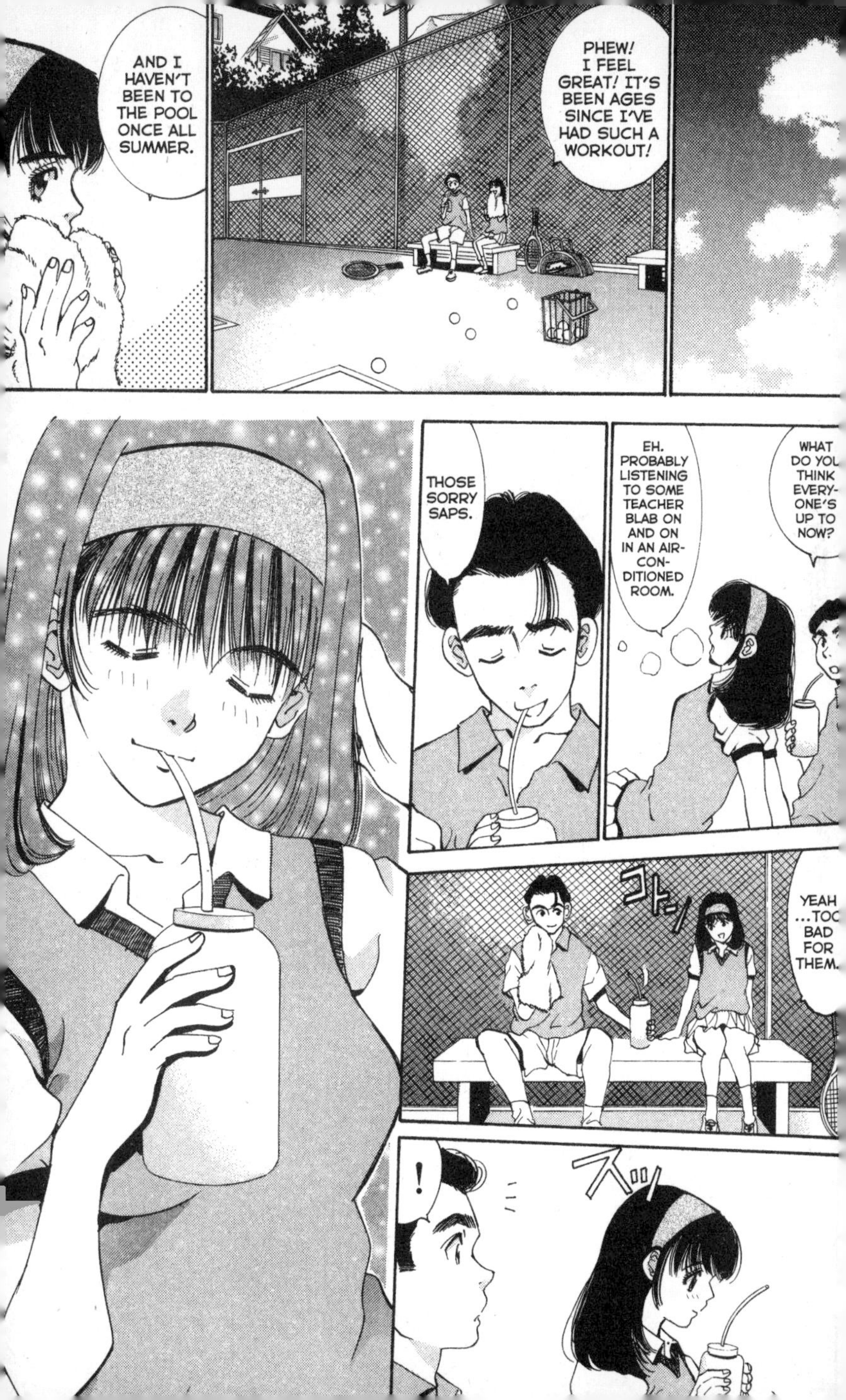
PHEW! I FEEL GREAT! IT'S BEEN AGES SINCE I'VE HAD SUCH A WORKOUT!
AND I HAVEN'T BEEN TO THE POOL ONCE ALL SUMMER.
WHAT DO YOU THINK EVERYONE'S UP TO NOW?
EH. PROBABLY LISTENING TO SOME TEACHER BLAB ON AND ON IN AN AIR-CONDITIONED ROOM.
THOSE SORRY SAPS.
YEAH ...TOO BAD FOR THEM.
!

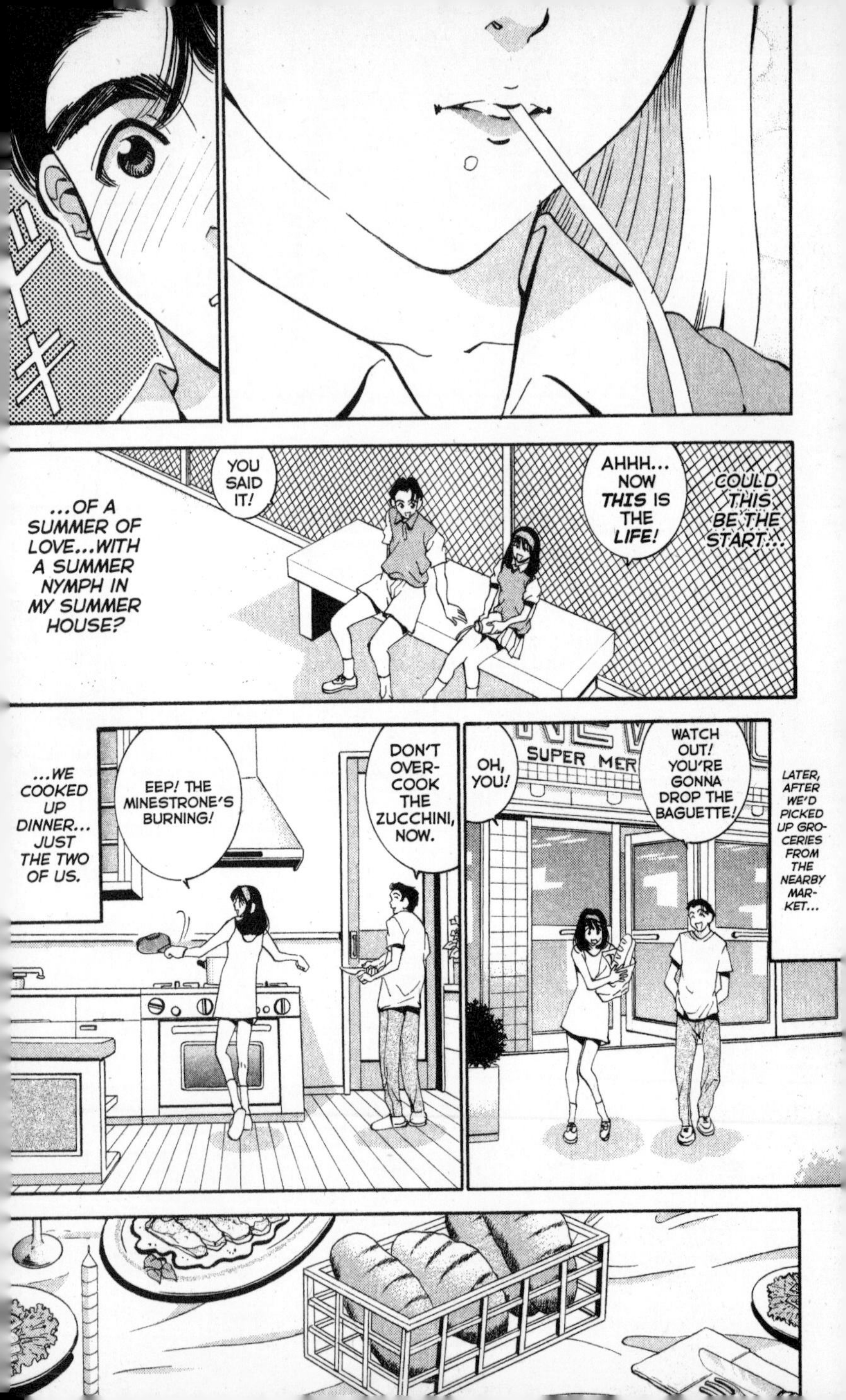
COULD THIS BE THE START...
AHHH... NOW *THIS* IS THE *LIFE!*
YOU SAID IT!
...OF A SUMMER OF LOVE...WITH A SUMMER NYMPH IN MY SUMMER HOUSE?
LATER, AFTER WE'D PICKED UP GROCERIES FROM THE NEARBY MARKET...
WATCH OUT! YOU'RE GONNA DROP THE BAGUETTE!
SUPER MER
OH, YOU!
DON'T OVERCOOK THE ZUCCHINI, NOW.
EEP! THE MINESTRONE'S BURNING!
...WE COOKED UP DINNER... JUST THE TWO OF US.

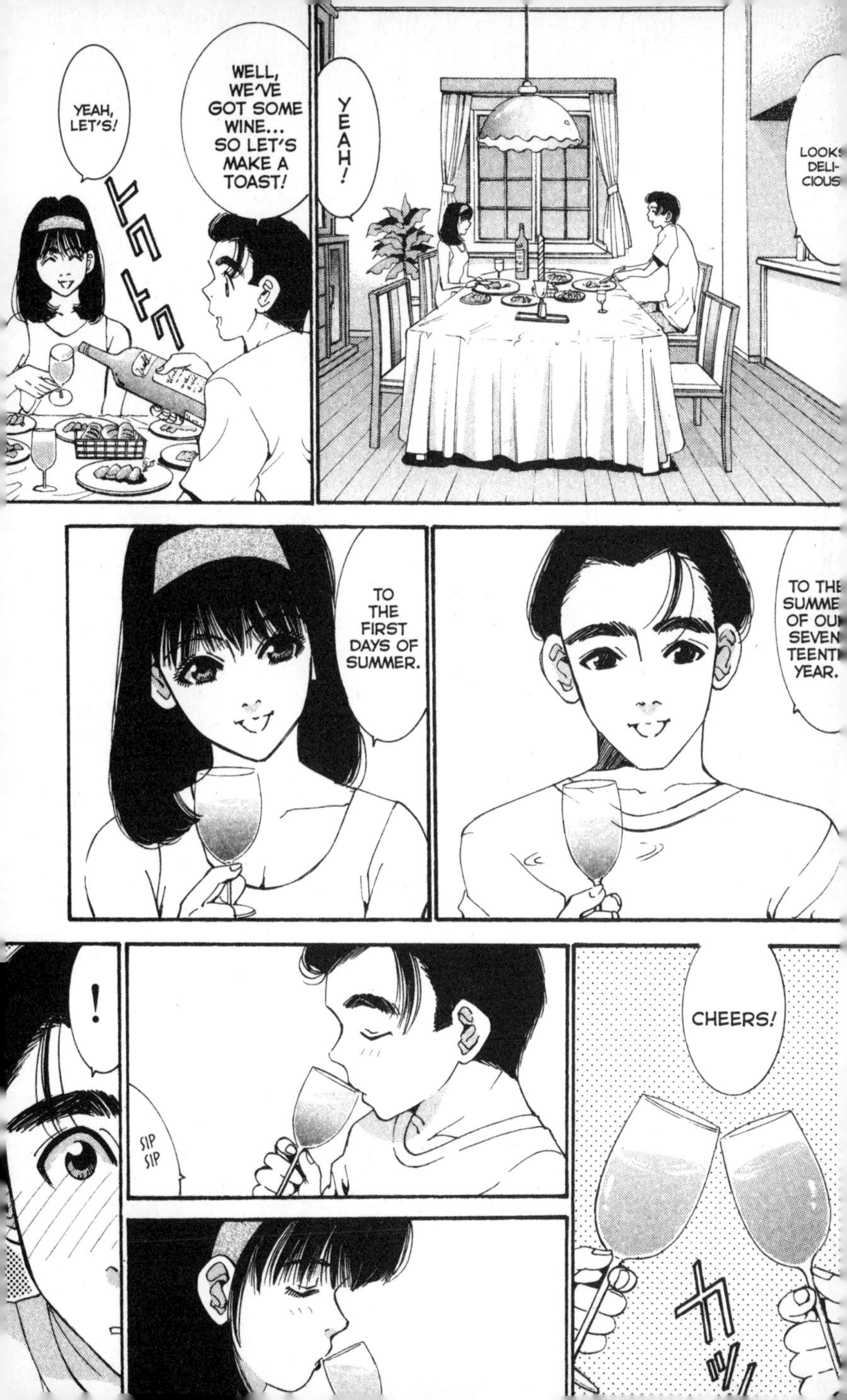

LOOKS DELI- CIOUS
YEAH!
WELL, WE'VE GOT SOME WINE... SO LET'S MAKE A TOAST!
YEAH, LET'S!
トクトク
TO THE SUMME OF OU SEVEN TEENT YEAR.
TO THE FIRST DAYS OF SUMMER.
CHEERS!
カツ
SIP SIP
!

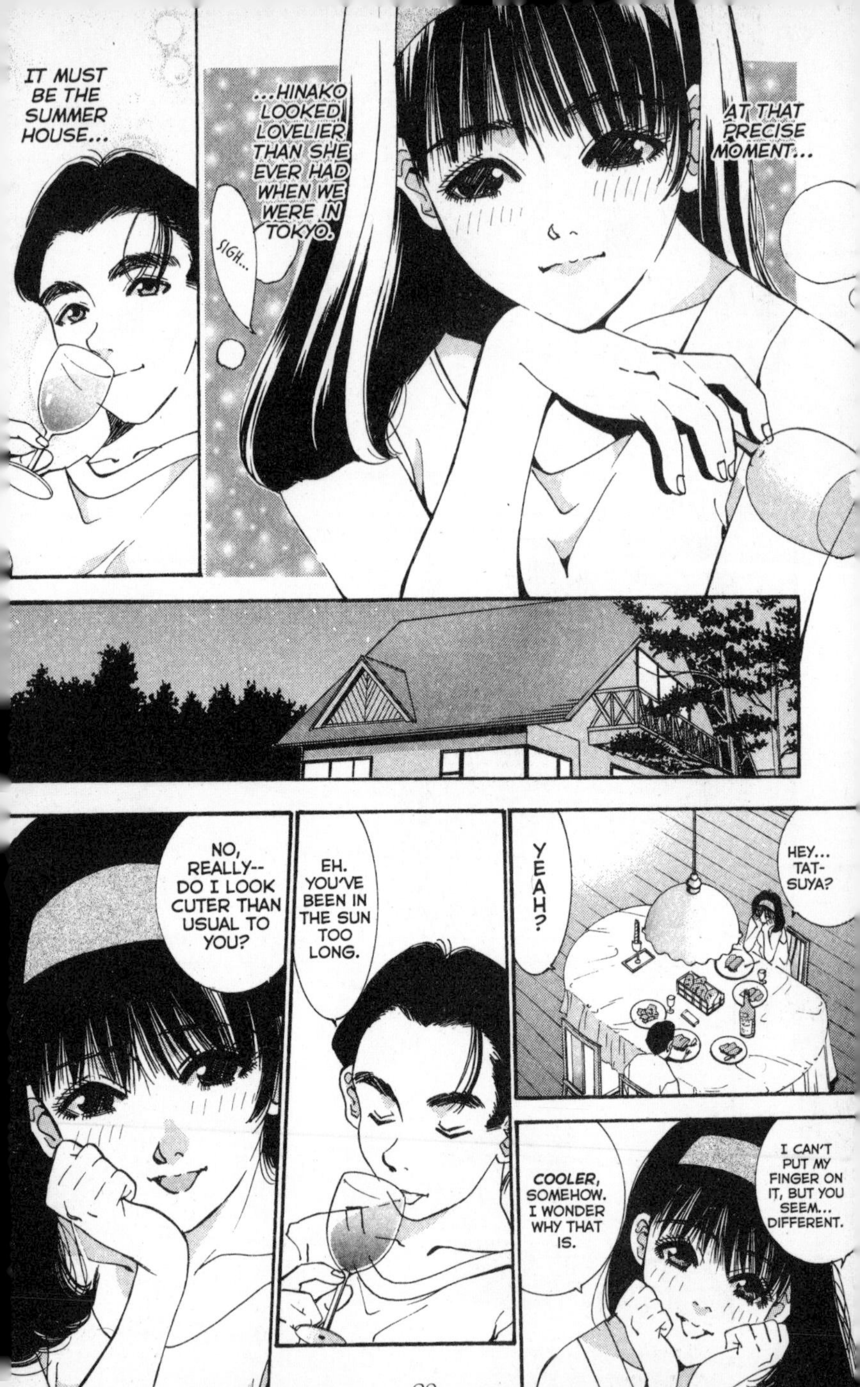
AT THAT PRECISE MOMENT...
...HINAKO LOOKED LOVELIER THAN SHE EVER HAD WHEN WE WERE IN TOKYO.
IT MUST BE THE SUMMER HOUSE...
SIGH...
HEY... TAT-SUYA?
YEAH?
I CAN'T PUT MY FINGER ON IT, BUT YOU SEEM... DIFFERENT.
COOLER, SOMEHOW. I WONDER WHY THAT IS.
EH. YOU'VE BEEN IN THE SUN TOO LONG.
NO, REALLY-- DO I LOOK CUTER THAN USUAL TO YOU?

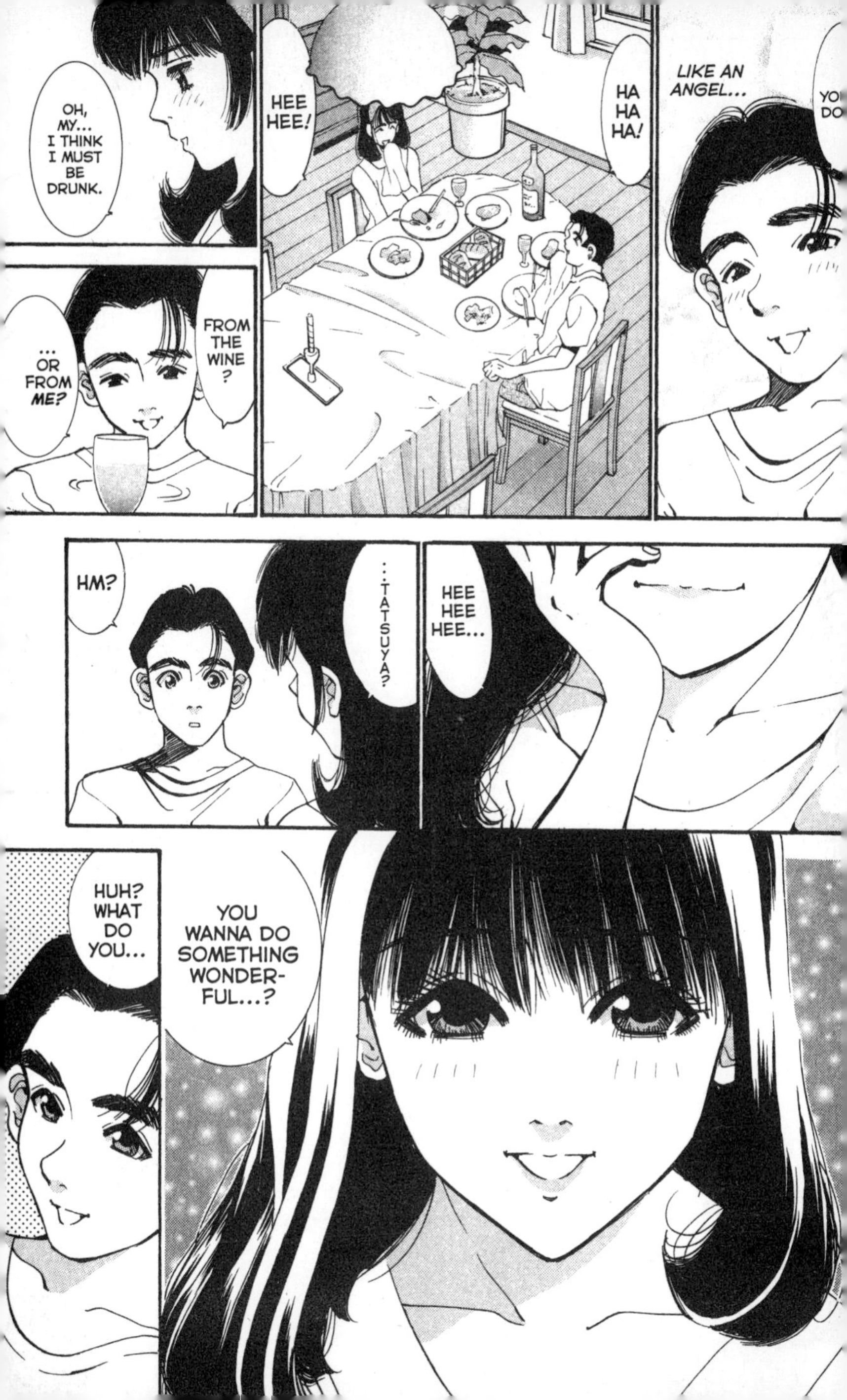
LIKE AN ANGEL...
HA HA HA!
HEE HEE!
OH, MY... I THINK I MUST BE DRUNK.
FROM THE WINE?
...OR FROM ME?
HEE HEE HEE...
...TATSUYA?
HM?
YOU WANNA DO SOMETHING WONDER-FUL...?
HUH? WHAT DO YOU...

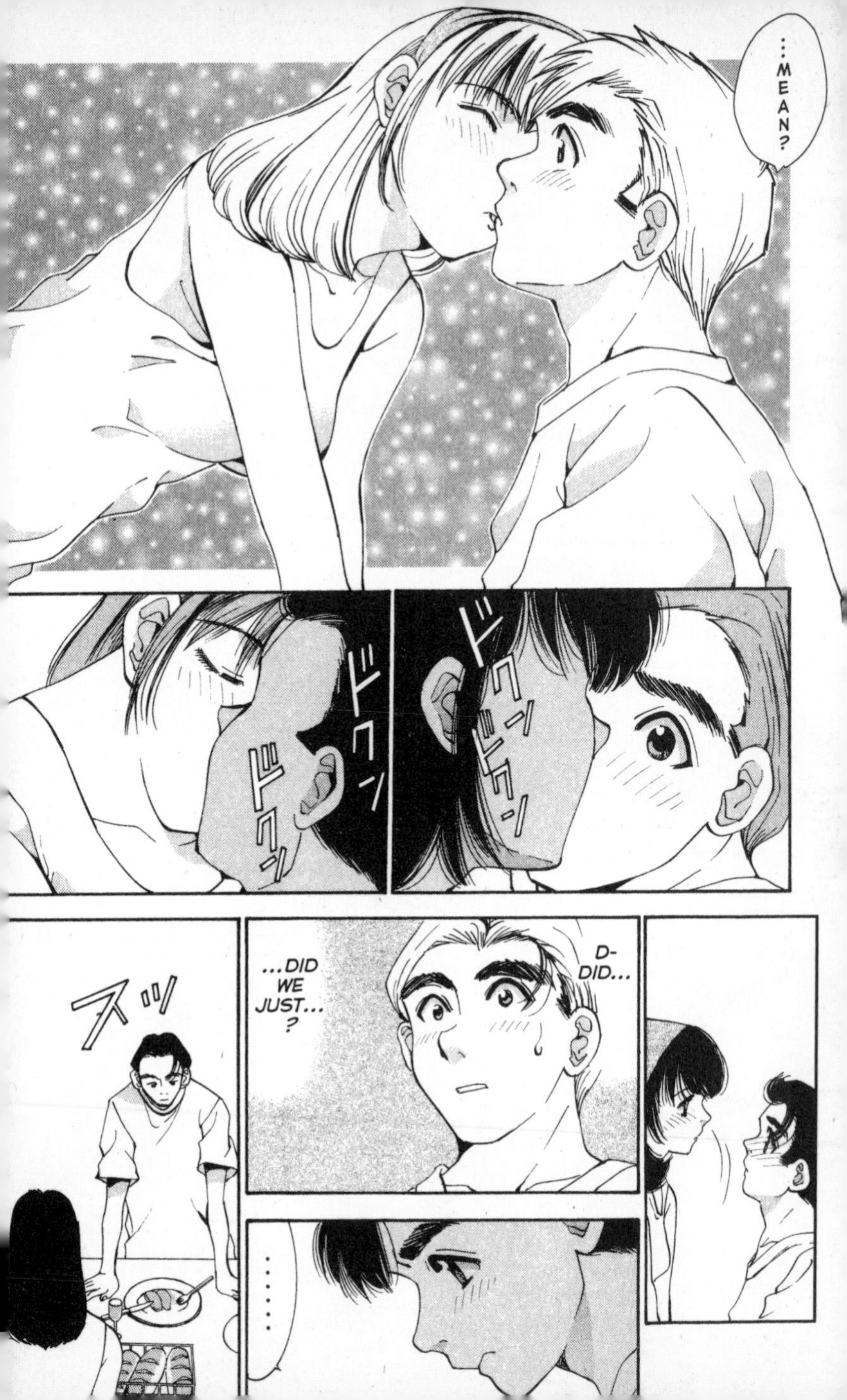
...MEAN?
D- DID...
...DID WE JUST...?
......
スッ

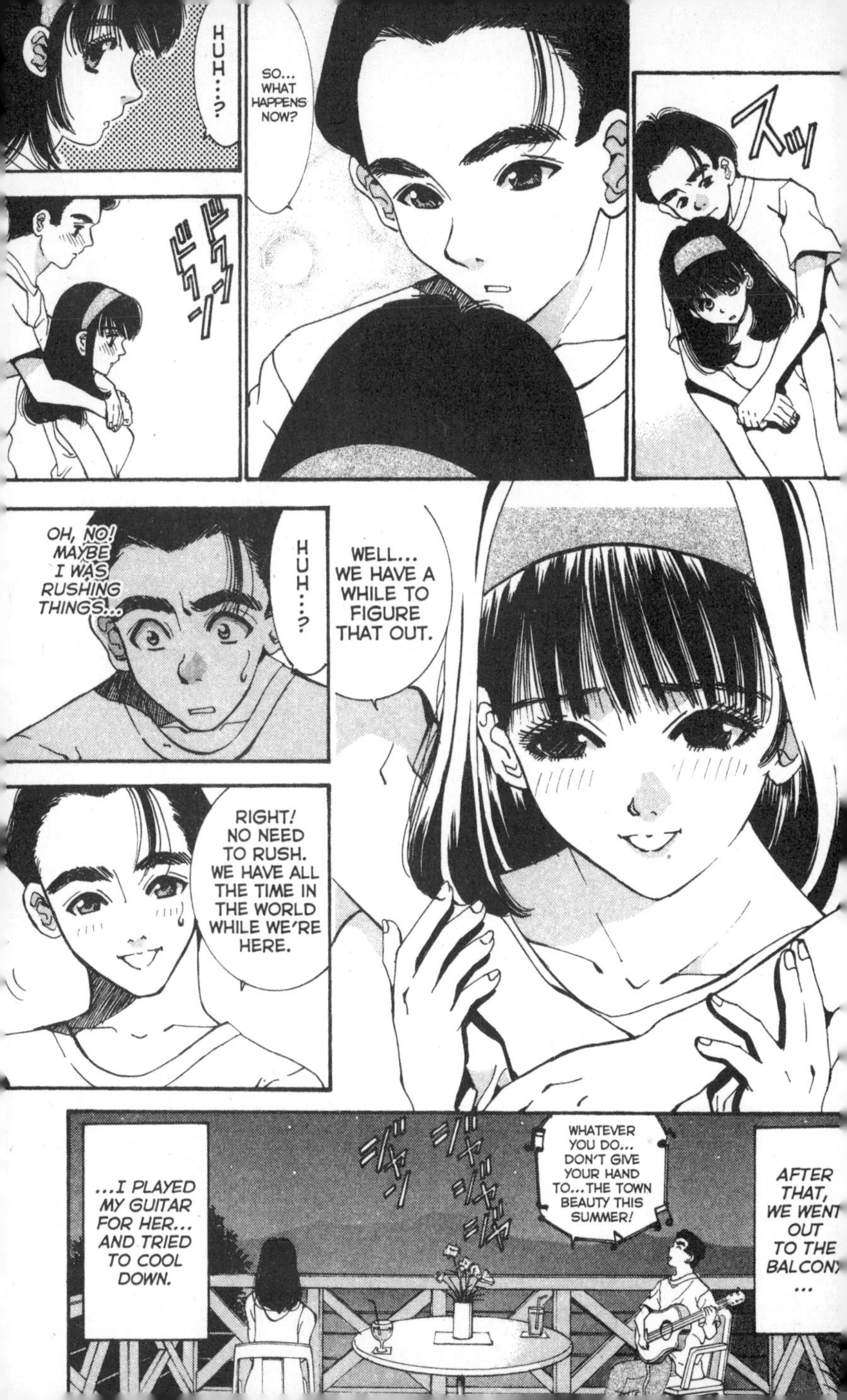
SO... WHAT HAPPENS NOW?
HUH...?
HUH...?
WELL... WE HAVE A WHILE TO FIGURE THAT OUT.
OH, NO! MAYBE I WAS RUSHING THINGS...
RIGHT! NO NEED TO RUSH. WE HAVE ALL THE TIME IN THE WORLD WHILE WE'RE HERE.
AFTER THAT, WE WENT OUT TO THE BALCONY...
WHATEVER YOU DO... DON'T GIVE YOUR HAND TO... THE TOWN BEAUTY THIS SUMMER!
...I PLAYED MY GUITAR FOR HER... AND TRIED TO COOL DOWN.

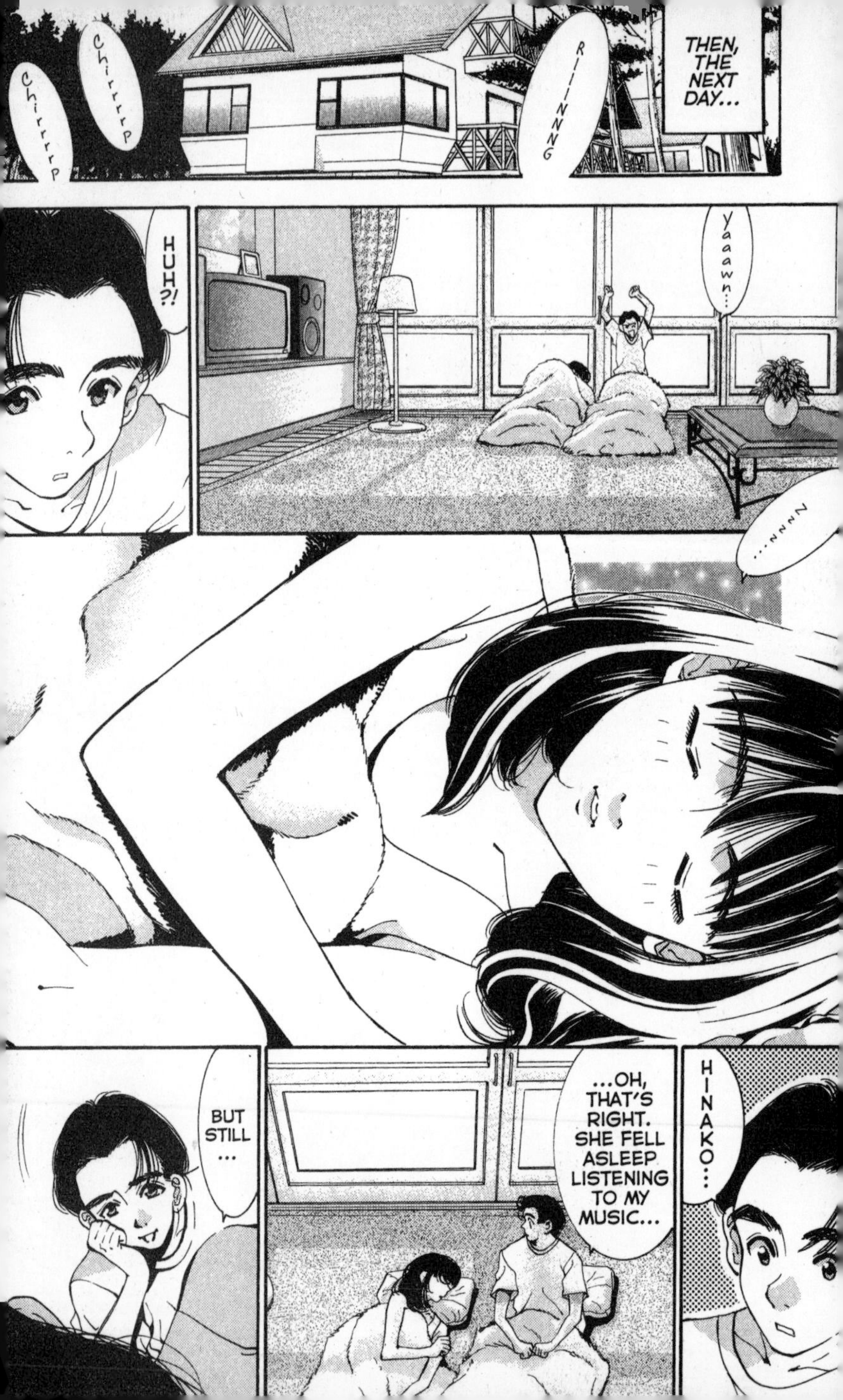

THEN, THE NEXT DAY...
RIIINNNG
Chirrrrp
Chirrrrp
Yaaawn...
HUH?!
Znnn...
HINAKO...
...OH, THAT'S RIGHT. SHE FELL ASLEEP LISTENING TO MY MUSIC...
BUT STILL ...

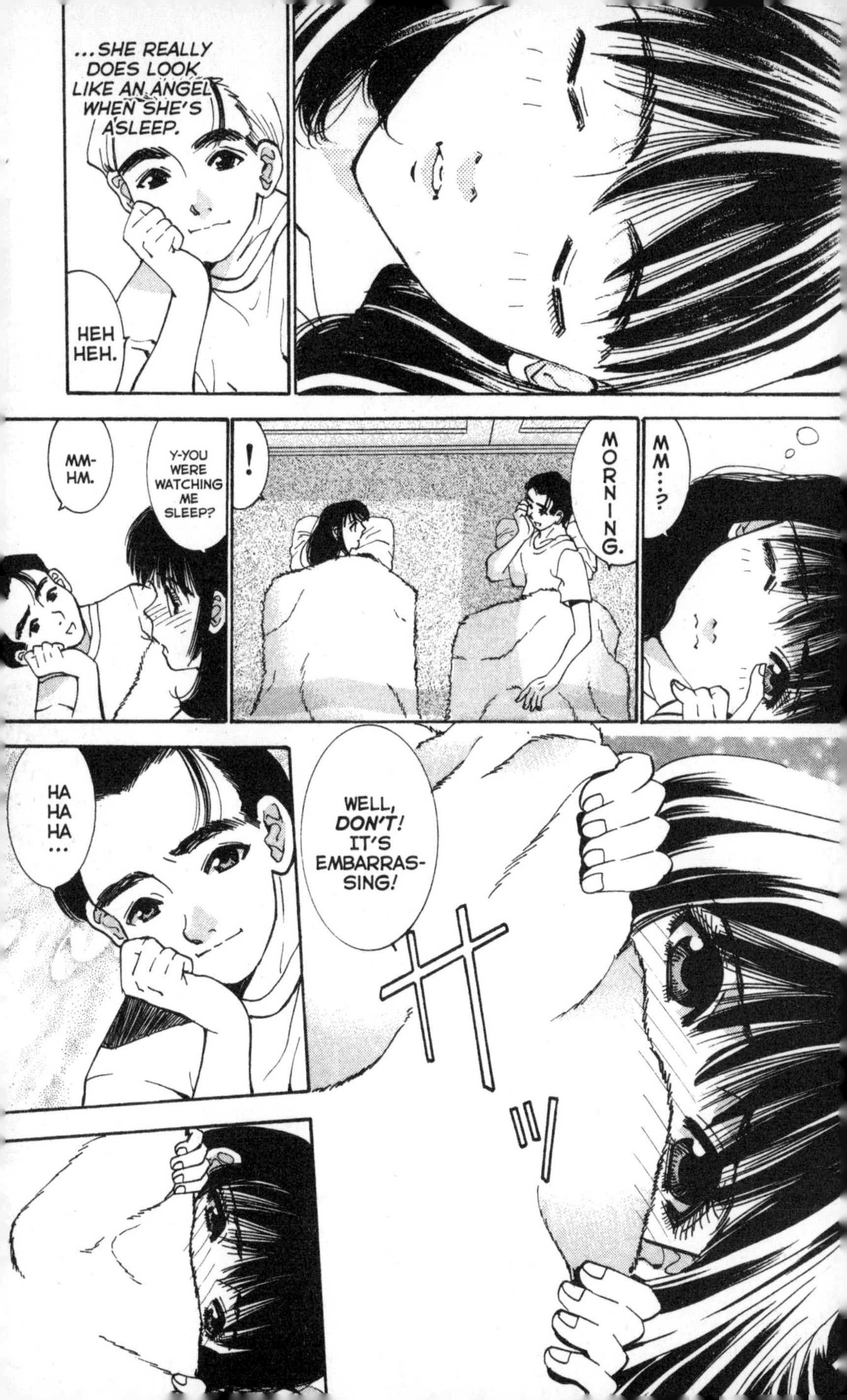
...SHE REALLY DOES LOOK LIKE AN ANGEL WHEN SHE'S ASLEEP.
HEH HEH.
MM...?
MORNING.
!
Y-YOU WERE WATCHING ME SLEEP?
MM-HM.
WELL, ***DON'T!*** IT'S EMBARRAS-SING!
HA HA HA ...

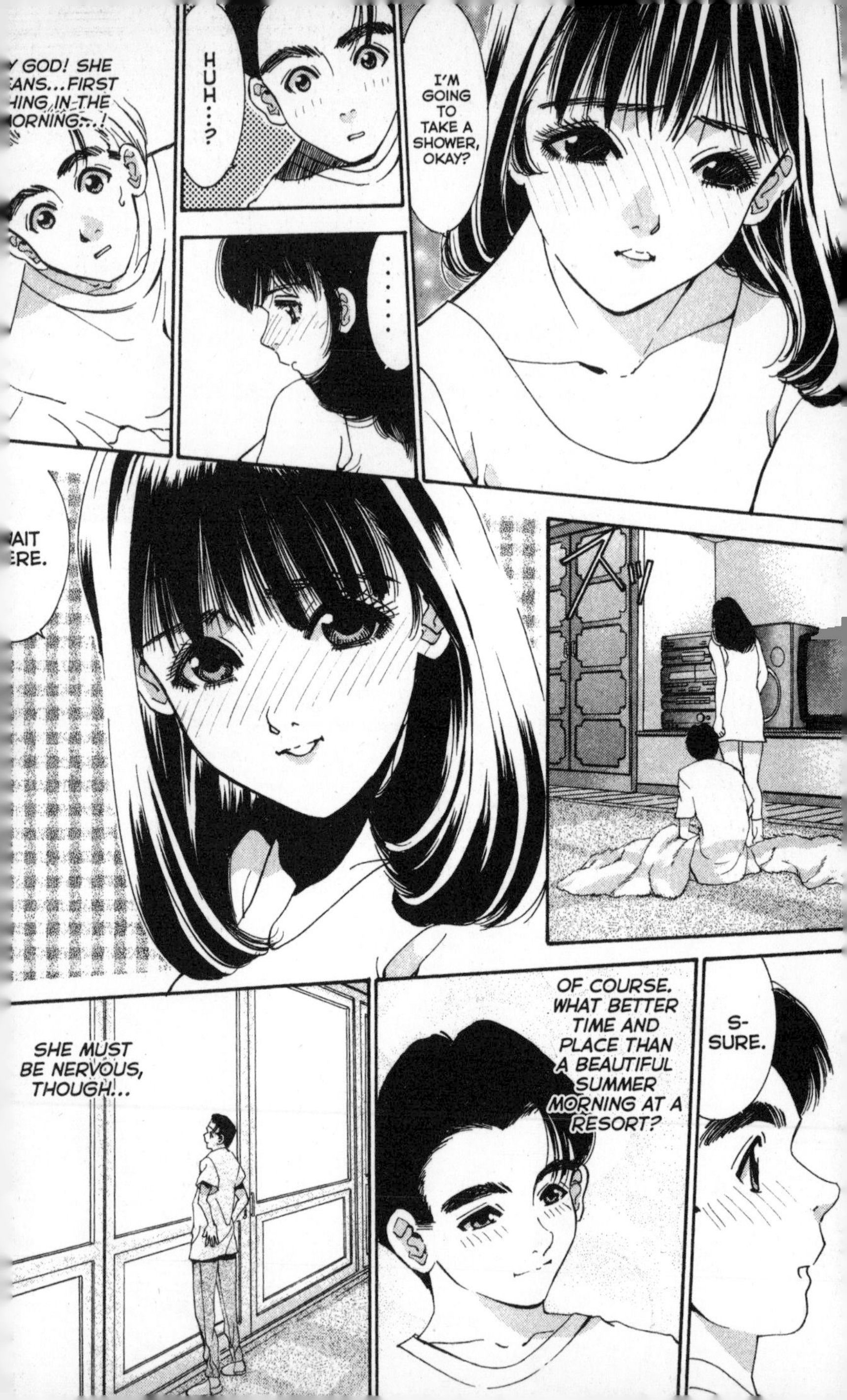
I'M GOING TO TAKE A SHOWER, OKAY?
HUH...?
......
Y GOD! SHE EANS...FIRST HING IN THE ORNING...!
AIT ERE.
S- SURE.
OF COURSE. WHAT BETTER TIME AND PLACE THAN A BEAUTIFUL SUMMER MORNING AT A RESORT?
SHE MUST BE NERVOUS, THOUGH...

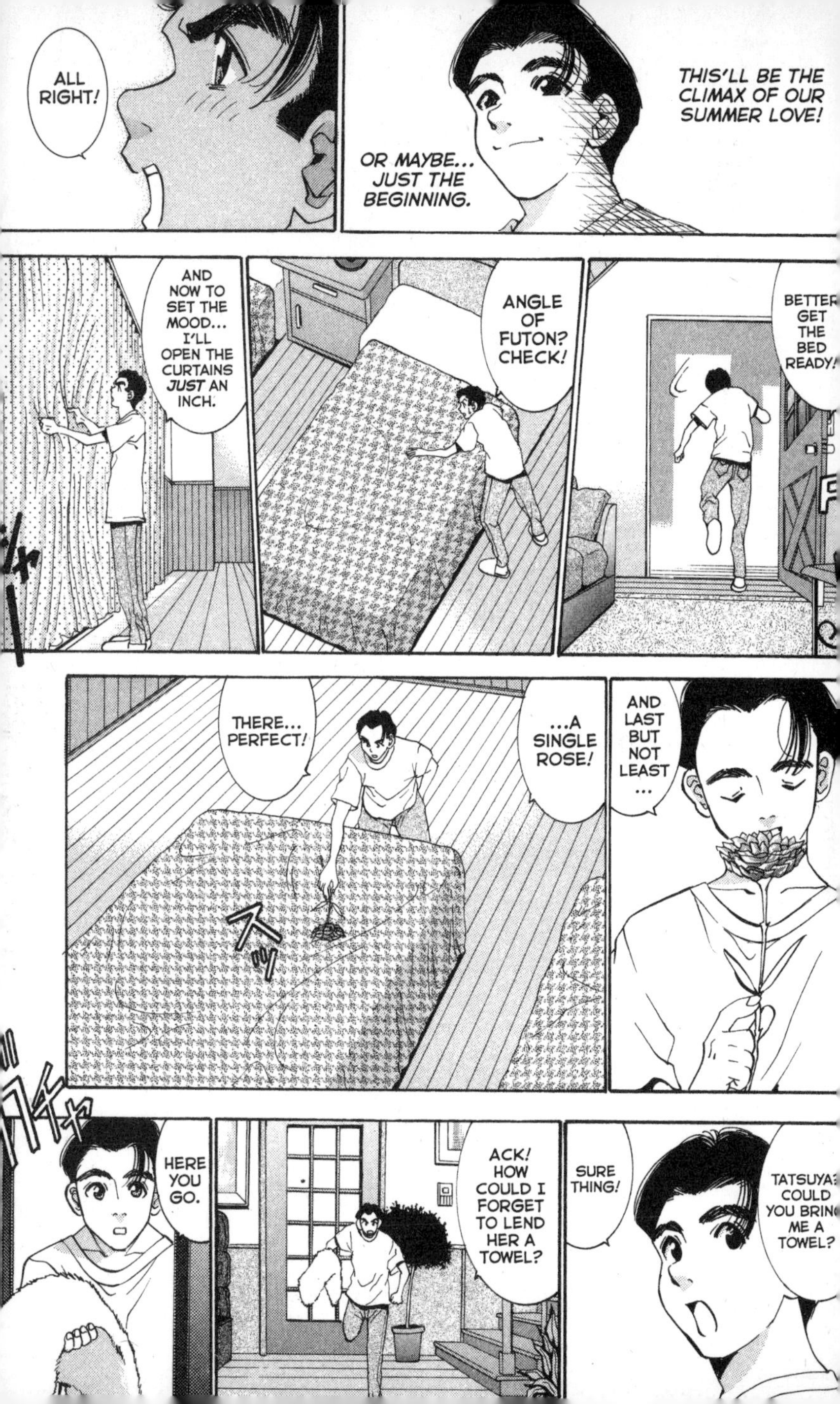

THIS'LL BE THE CLIMAX OF OUR SUMMER LOVE!
OR MAYBE... JUST THE BEGINNING.
ALL RIGHT!
BETTER GET THE BED READY!
ANGLE OF FUTON? CHECK!
AND NOW TO SET THE MOOD... I'LL OPEN THE CURTAINS *JUST* AN INCH.
AND LAST BUT NOT LEAST...
...A SINGLE ROSE!
THERE... PERFECT!
TATSUYA? COULD YOU BRING ME A TOWEL?
SURE THING!
ACK! HOW COULD I FORGET TO LEND HER A TOWEL?
HERE YOU GO.

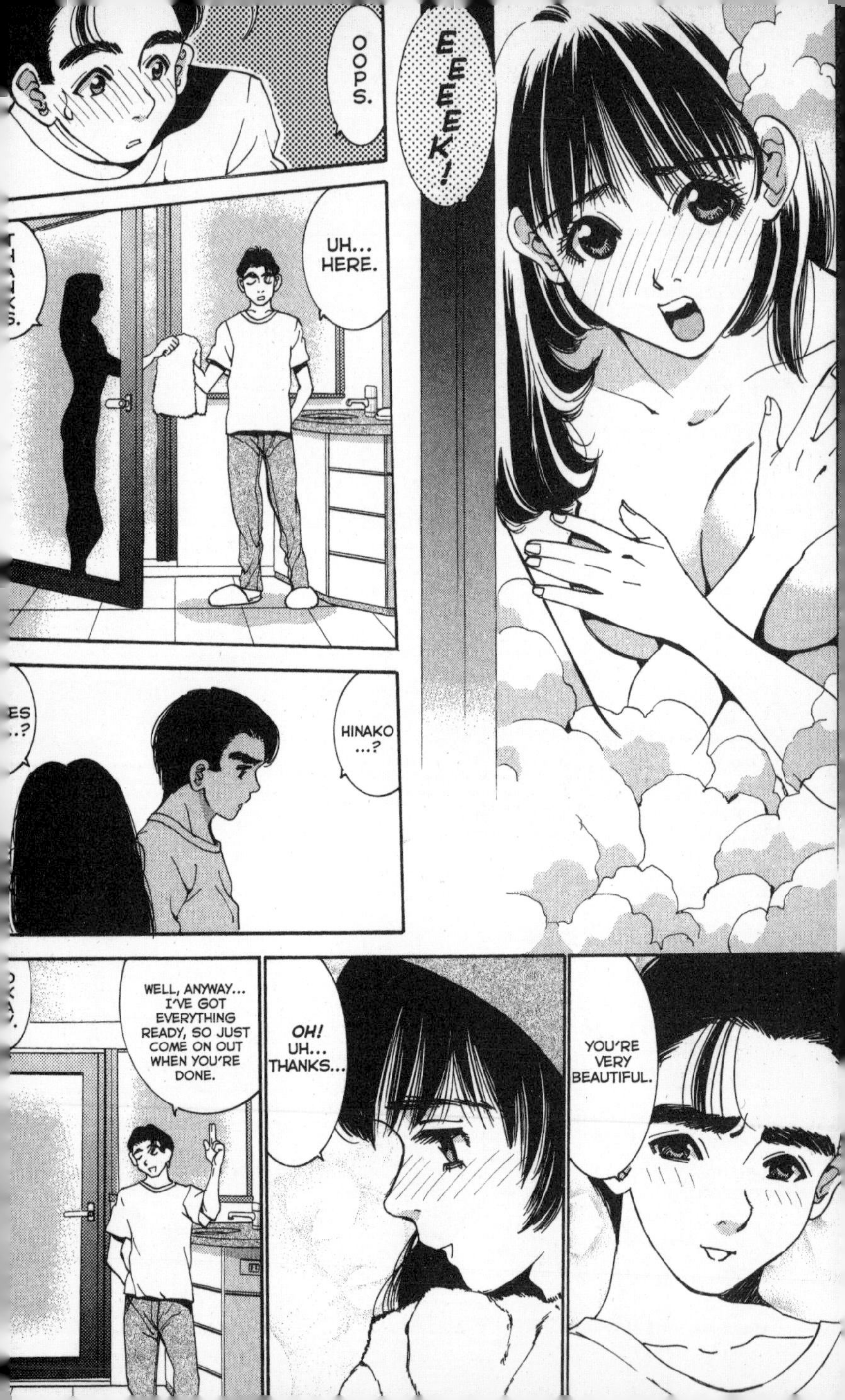
EEEEK!
OOPS.
UH... HERE.
HINAKO ...?
YOU'RE VERY BEAUTIFUL.
OH! UH... THANKS...
WELL, ANYWAY... I'VE GOT EVERYTHING READY, SO JUST COME ON OUT WHEN YOU'RE DONE.

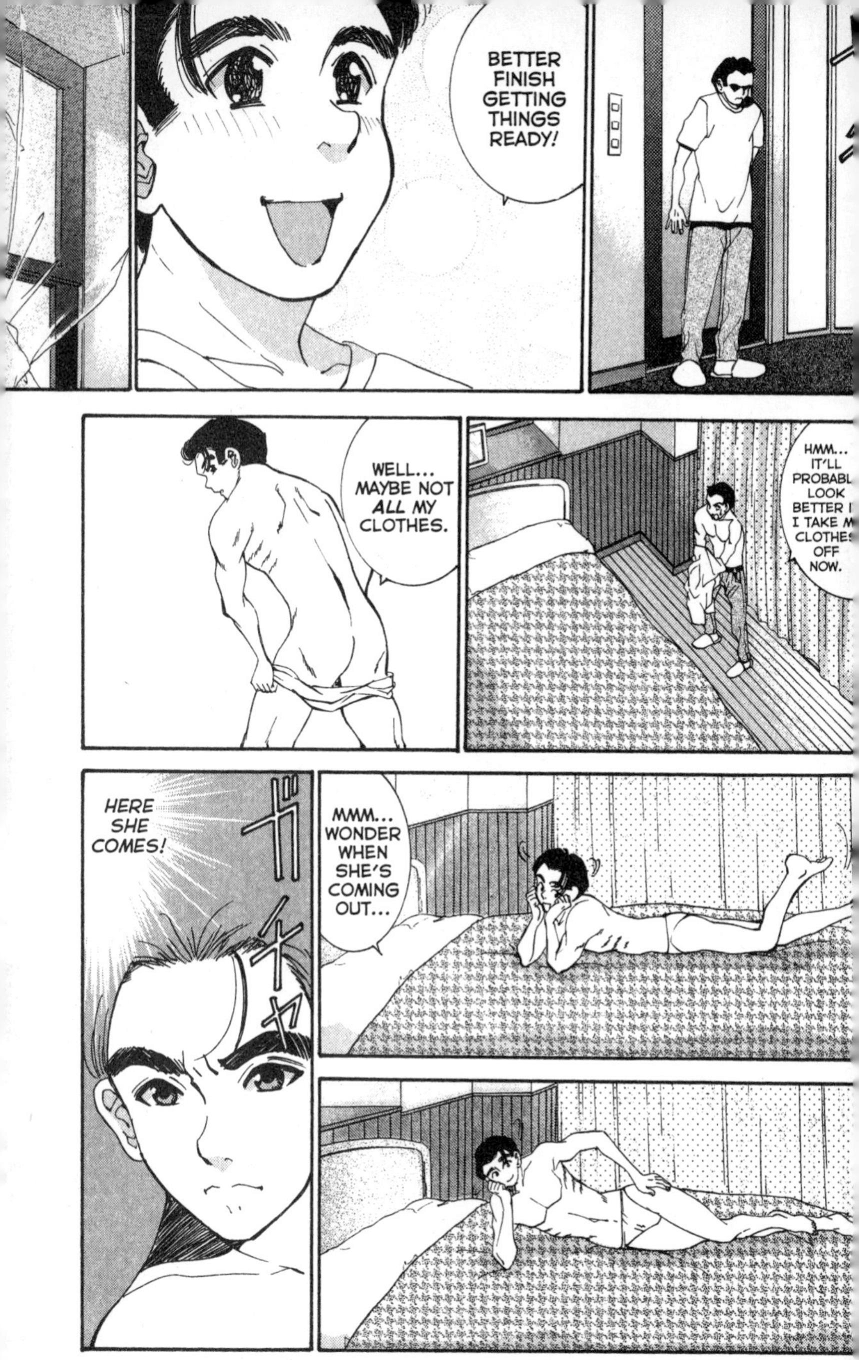
BETTER FINISH GETTING THINGS READY!
HMM... IT'LL PROBABL LOOK BETTER I I TAKE M CLOTHES OFF NOW.
WELL... MAYBE NOT *ALL* MY CLOTHES.
MMM... WONDER WHEN SHE'S COMING OUT...
HERE SHE COMES!

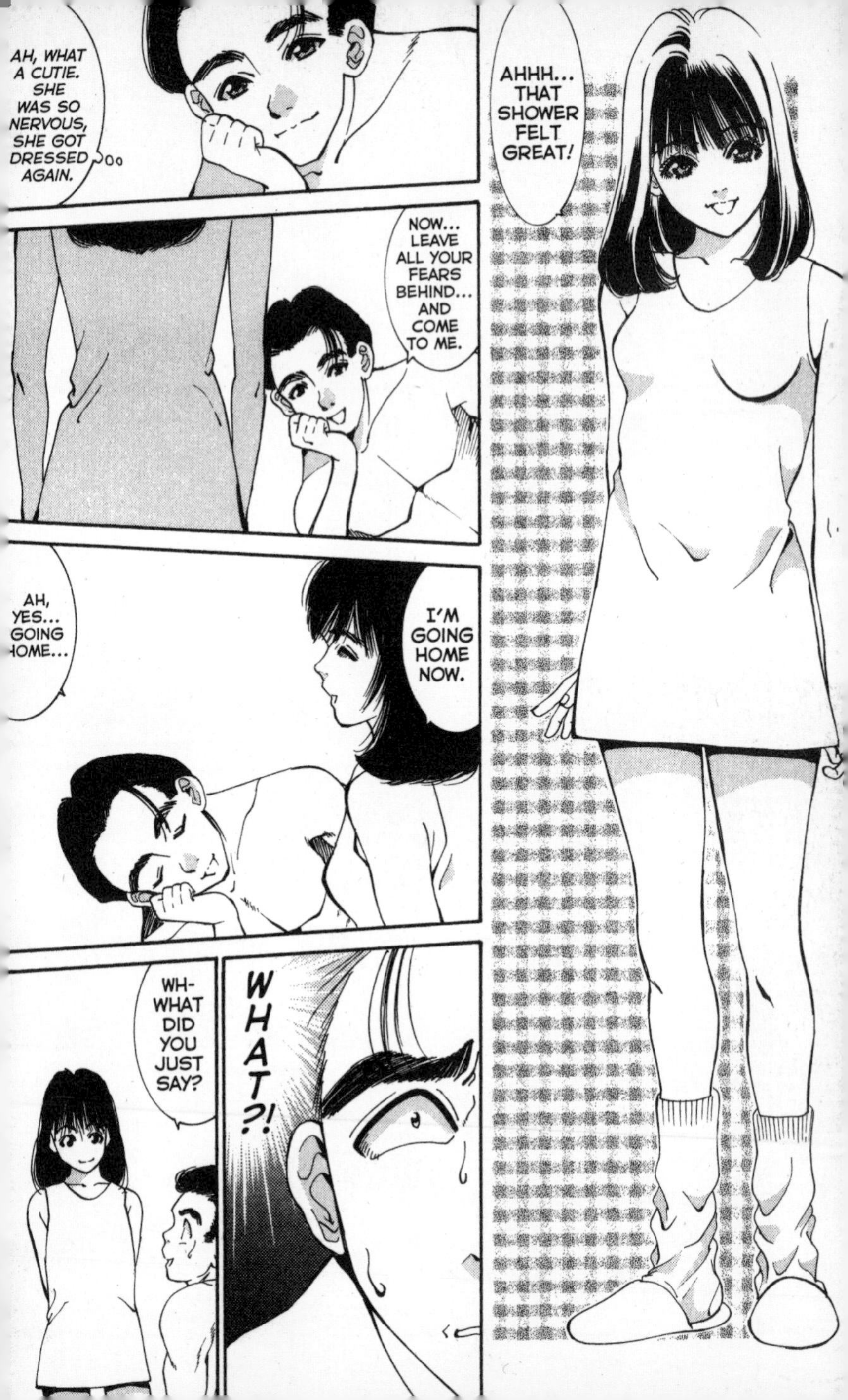
AHHH... THAT SHOWER FELT GREAT!
AH, WHAT A CUTIE. SHE WAS SO NERVOUS, SHE GOT DRESSED AGAIN.
NOW... LEAVE ALL YOUR FEARS BEHIND... AND COME TO ME.
I'M GOING HOME NOW.
AH, YES... GOING HOME...
WHAT?!
WH-WHAT DID YOU JUST SAY?

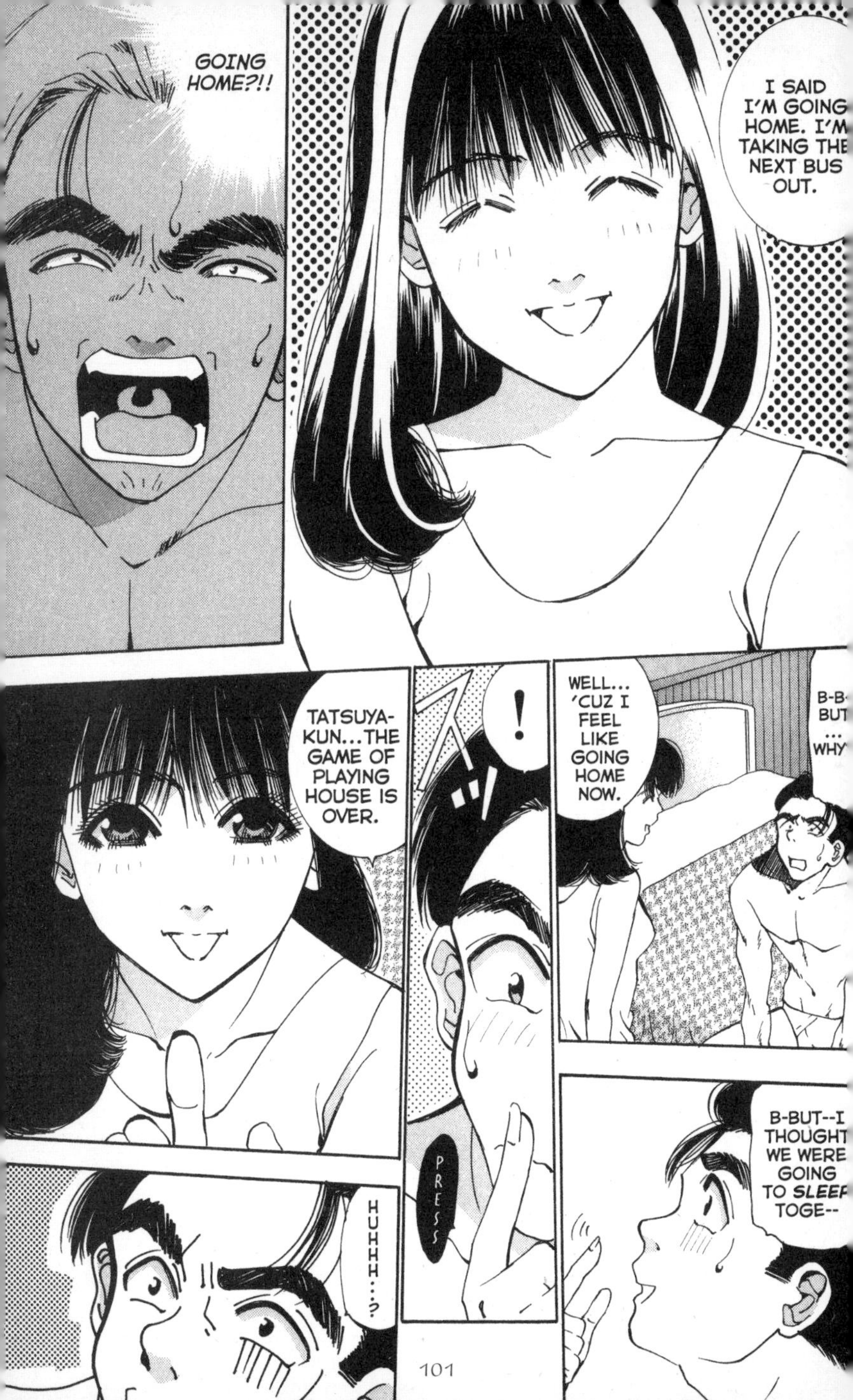
I SAID I'M GOING HOME. I'M TAKING THE NEXT BUS OUT.
GOING HOME?!!
B-B- BUT ... WHY
WELL... 'CUZ I FEEL LIKE GOING HOME NOW.
B-BUT--I THOUGHT WE WERE GOING TO *SLEEP* TOGE--
!
PRESS
TATSUYA-KUN...THE GAME OF PLAYING HOUSE IS OVER.
HUHHH...?

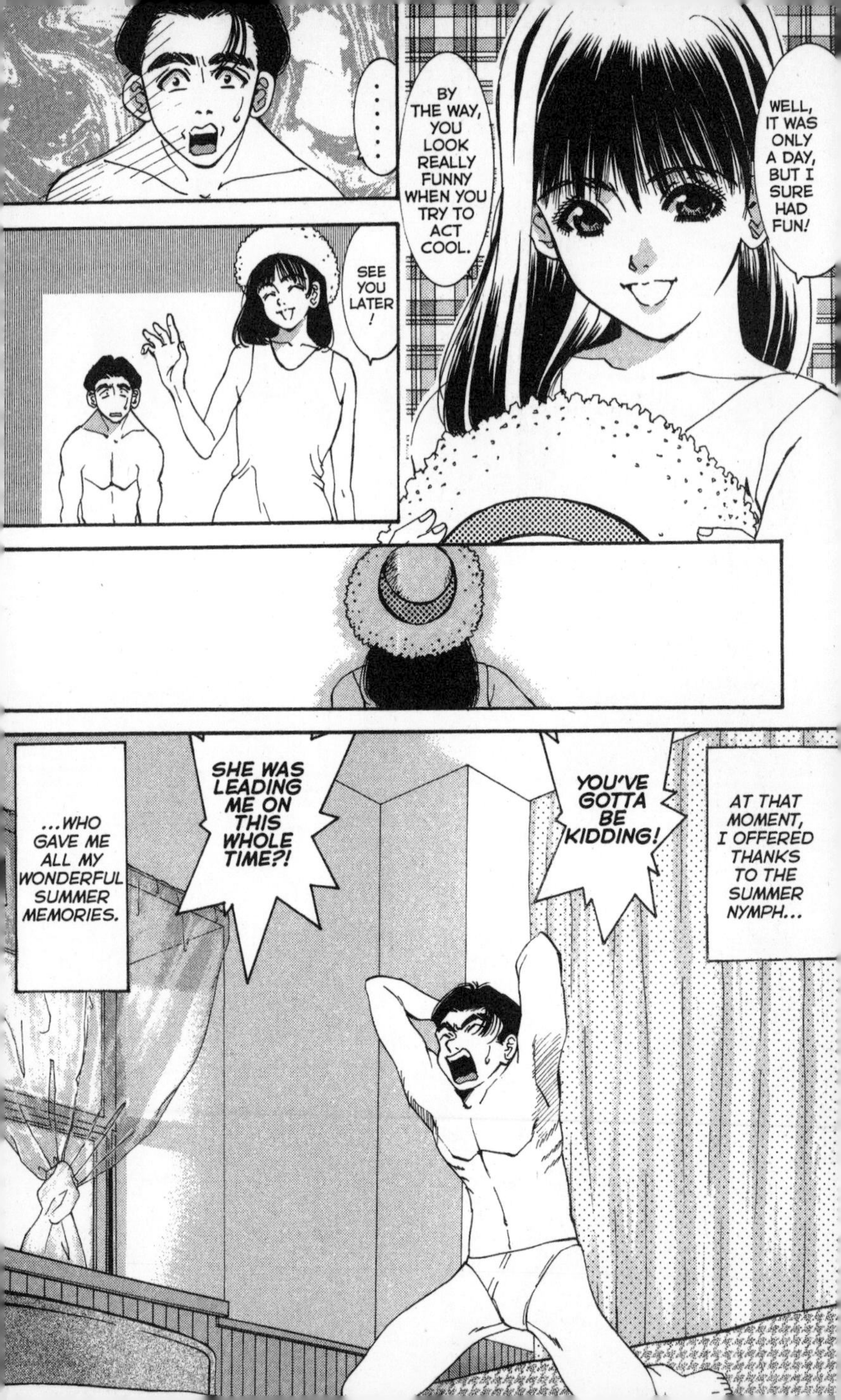
WELL, IT WAS ONLY A DAY, BUT I SURE HAD FUN!
BY THE WAY, YOU LOOK REALLY FUNNY WHEN YOU TRY TO ACT COOL.
......
SEE YOU LATER!
AT THAT MOMENT, I OFFERED THANKS TO THE SUMMER NYMPH...
YOU'VE GOTTA BE KIDDING!
SHE WAS LEADING ME ON THIS WHOLE TIME?!
...WHO GAVE ME ALL MY WONDERFUL SUMMER MEMORIES.

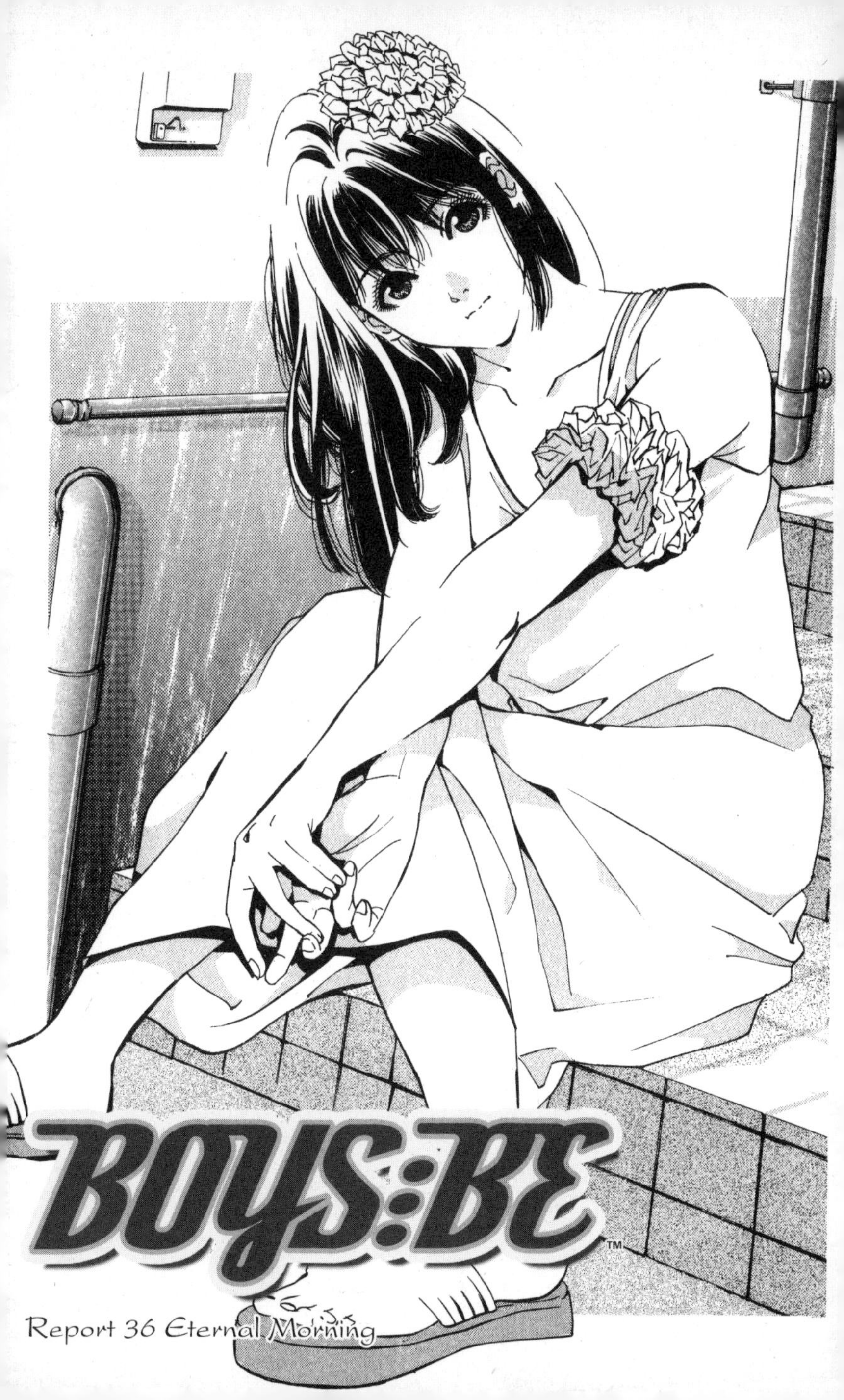
BOYS BE™
Report 36 Eternal Morning

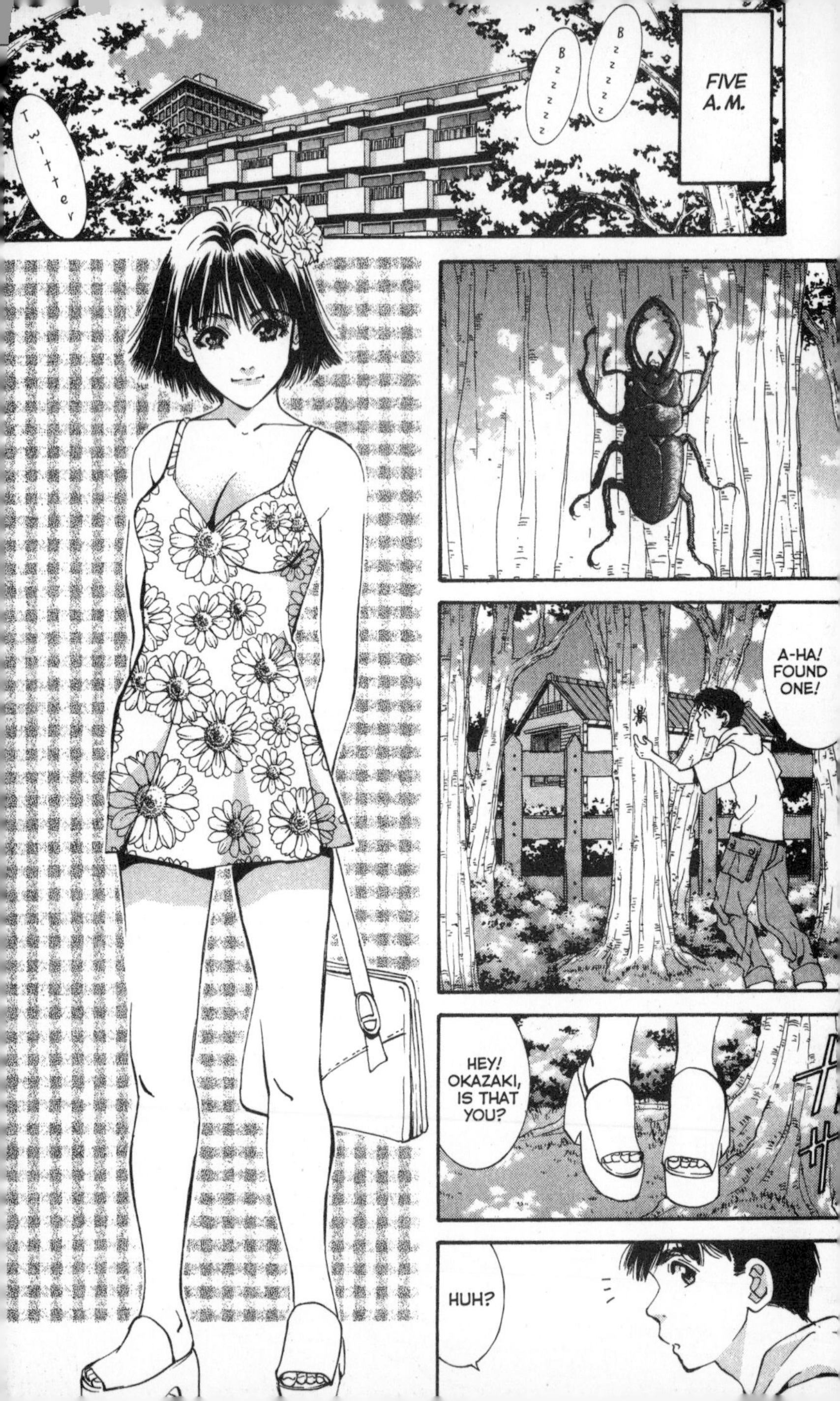
FIVE A.M.
Bzzzz
Bzzzz
Twitter
A-HA! FOUND ONE!
HEY! OKAZAKI, IS THAT YOU?
HUH?

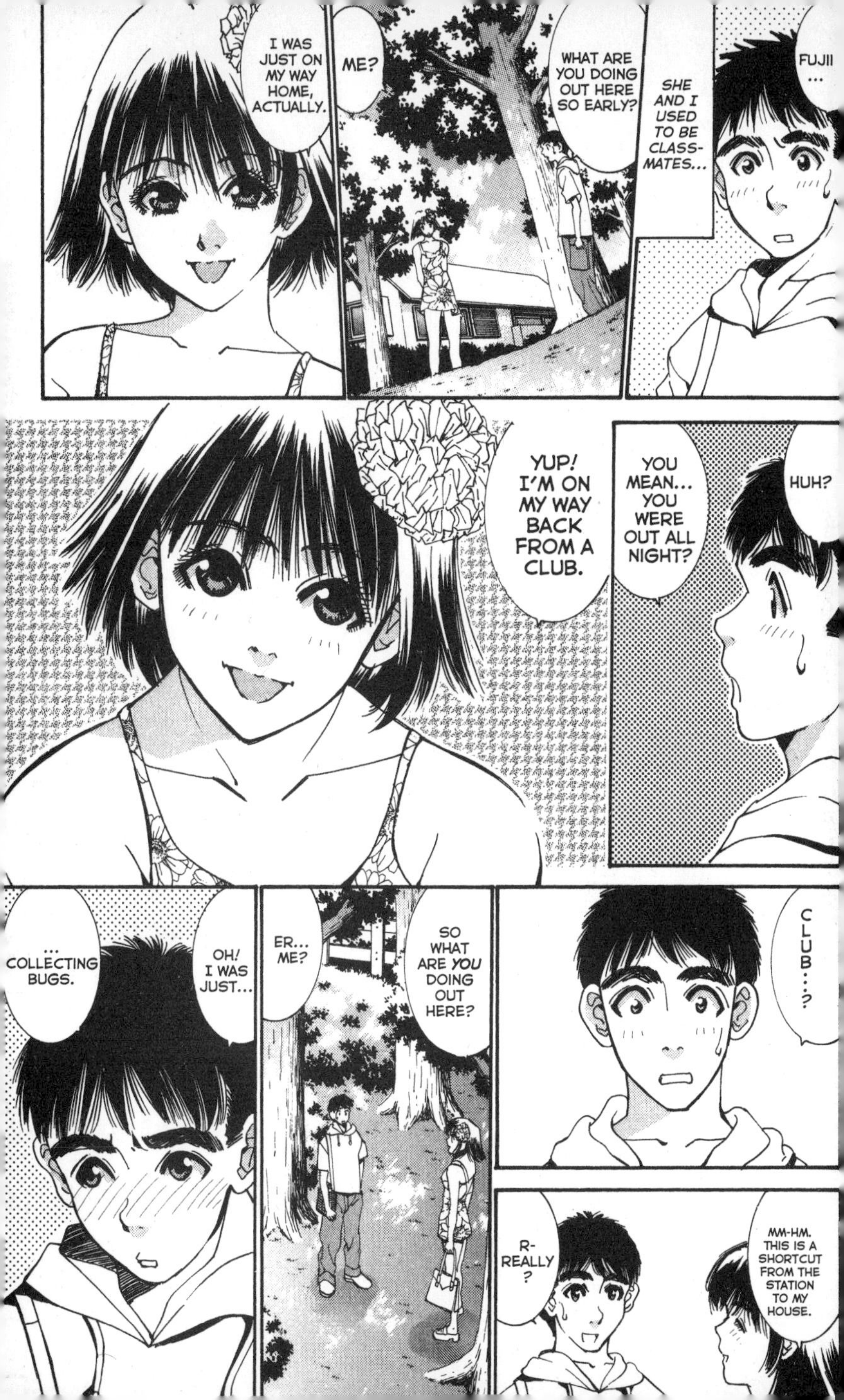
FUJII ...
SHE AND I USED TO BE CLASS-MATES...
WHAT ARE YOU DOING OUT HERE SO EARLY?
ME?
I WAS JUST ON MY WAY HOME, ACTUALLY.
HUH?
YOU MEAN... YOU WERE OUT ALL NIGHT?
YUP! I'M ON MY WAY BACK FROM A CLUB.
CLUB...?
MM-HM. THIS IS A SHORTCUT FROM THE STATION TO MY HOUSE.
R-REALLY?
SO WHAT ARE *YOU* DOING OUT HERE?
ER... ME?
OH! I WAS JUST...
... COLLECTING BUGS.

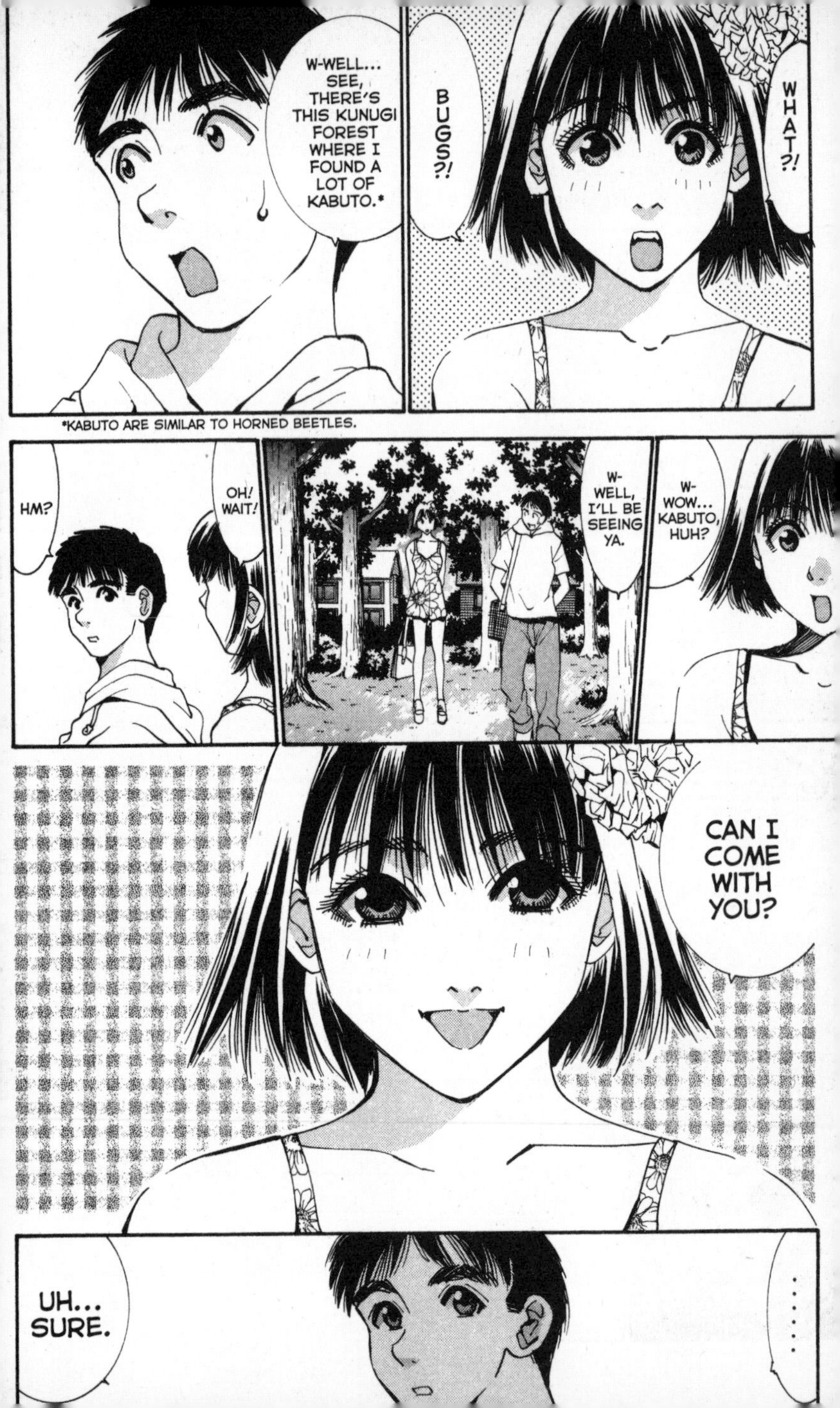
WHAT?!
BUGS?!
W-WELL... SEE, THERE'S THIS KUNUGI FOREST WHERE I FOUND A LOT OF KABUTO.*
W- WOW... KABUTO, HUH?
W- WELL, I'LL BE SEEING YA.
OH! WAIT!
HM?
CAN I COME WITH YOU?
......
UH... SURE.

*KABUTO ARE SIMILAR TO HORNED BEETLES.

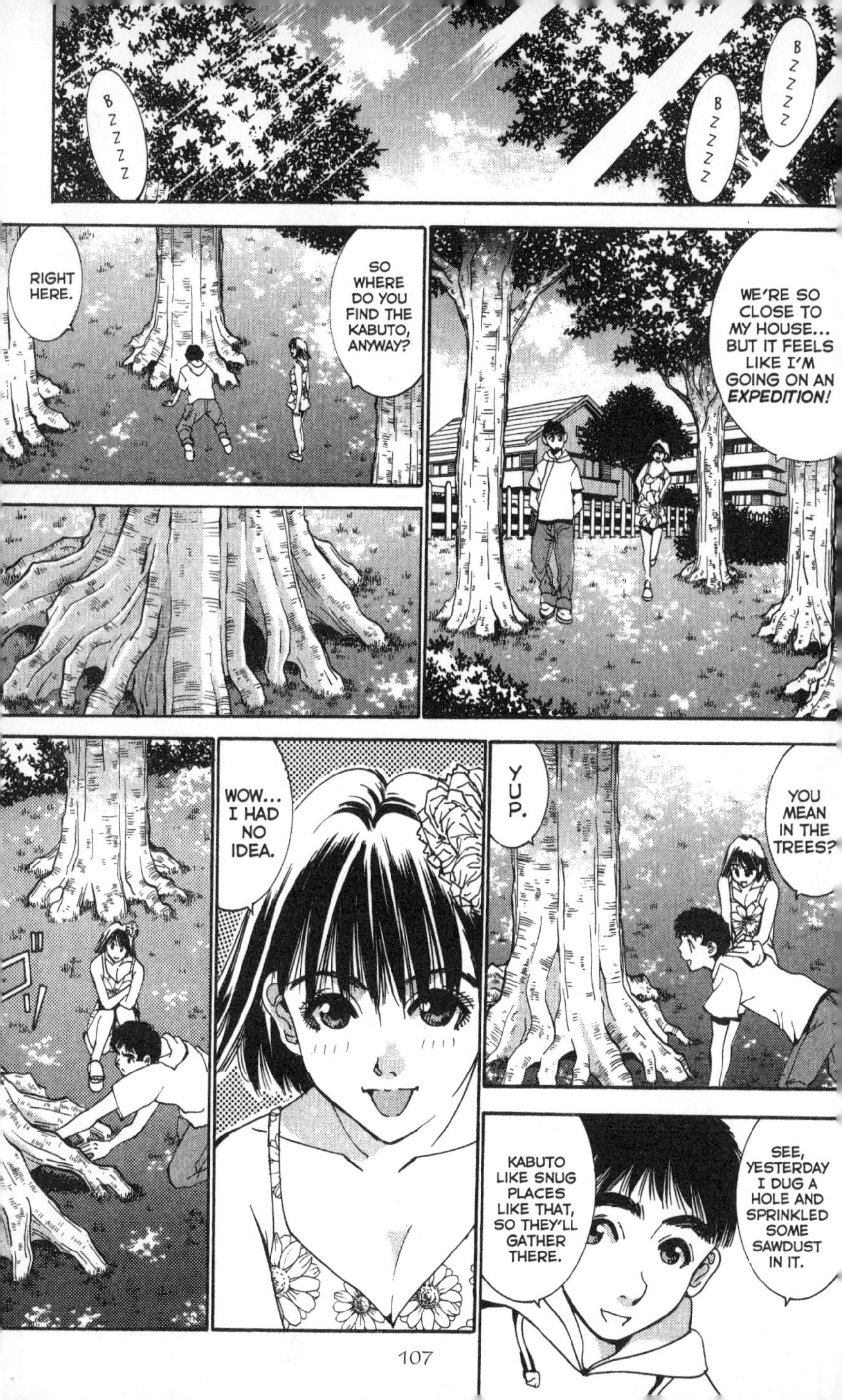
BZZZZ
BZZZZ
BZZZZ
WE'RE SO CLOSE TO MY HOUSE... BUT IT FEELS LIKE I'M GOING ON AN *EXPEDITION!*
SO WHERE DO YOU FIND THE KABUTO, ANYWAY?
RIGHT HERE.
YOU MEAN IN THE TREES?
YUP.
SEE, YESTERDAY I DUG A HOLE AND SPRINKLED SOME SAWDUST IN IT.
KABUTO LIKE SNUG PLACES LIKE THAT, SO THEY'LL GATHER THERE.
WOW... I HAD NO IDEA.

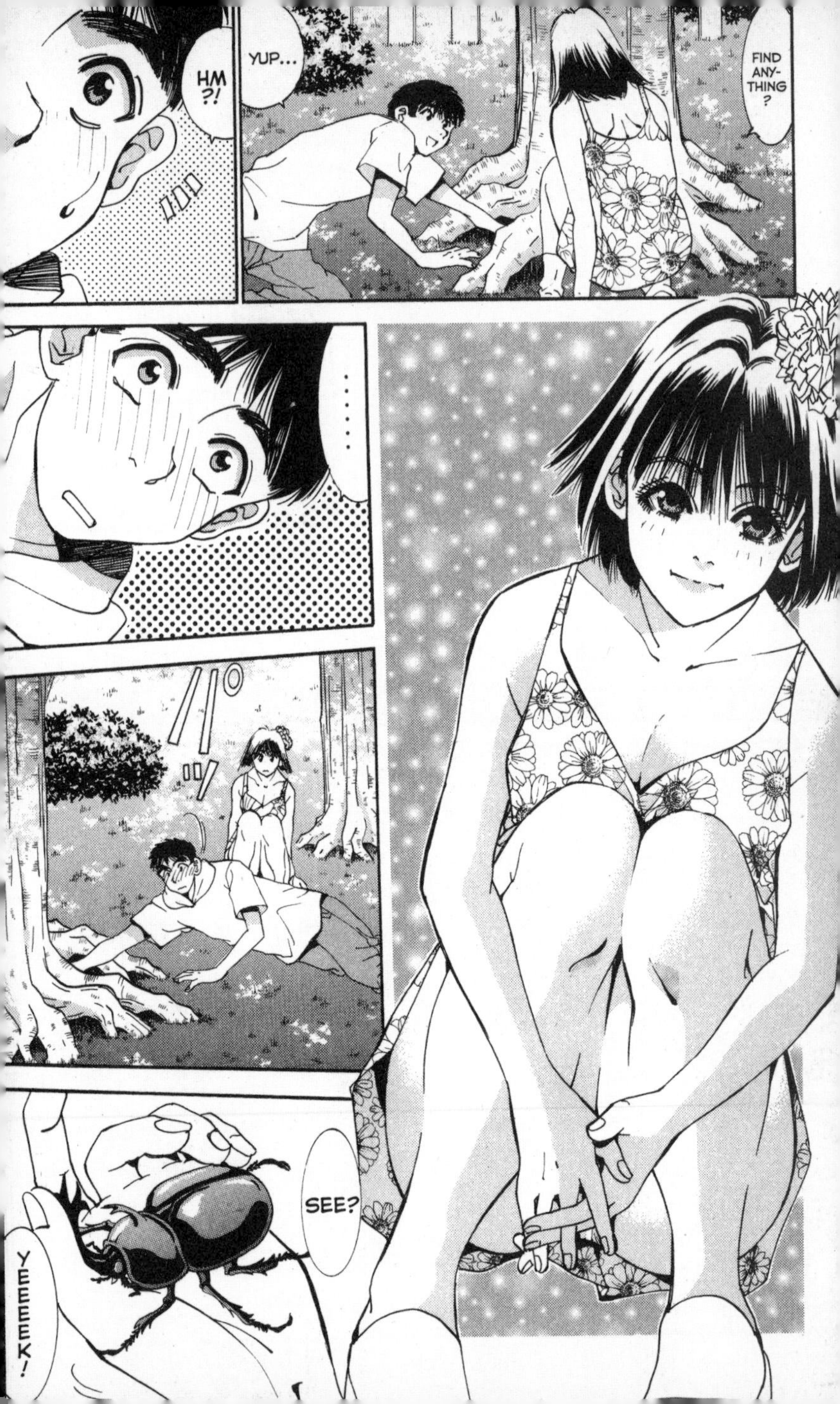
FIND ANYTHING?
YUP...
HM ?!
......
SEE?
YEEEEK!

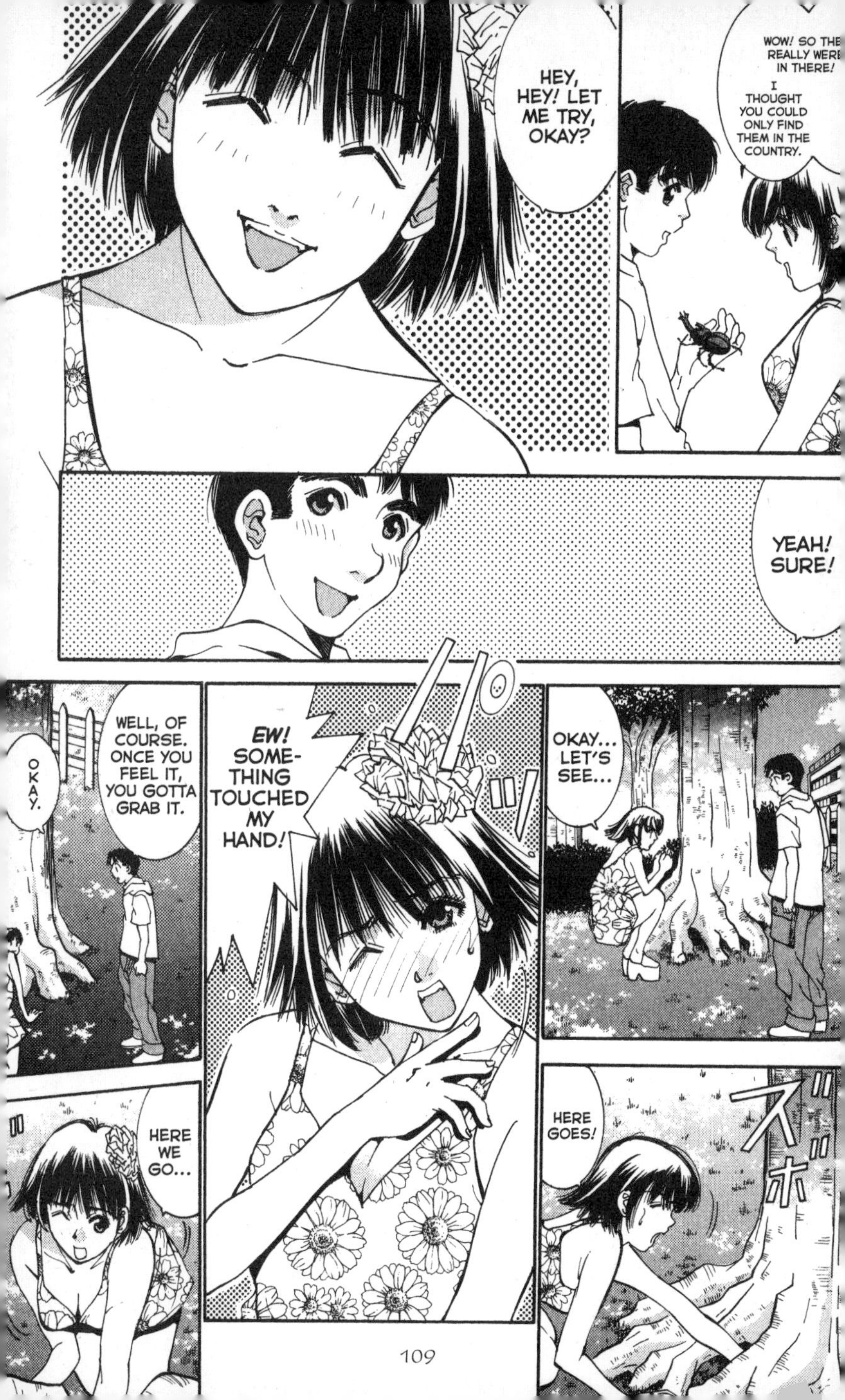
WOW! SO THE REALLY WERE IN THERE!
I THOUGHT YOU COULD ONLY FIND THEM IN THE COUNTRY.
HEY, HEY! LET ME TRY, OKAY?
YEAH! SURE!
OKAY... LET'S SEE...
HERE GOES!
EW! SOME-THING TOUCHED MY HAND!
WELL, OF COURSE. ONCE YOU FEEL IT, YOU GOTTA GRAB IT.
OKAY.
HERE WE GO...

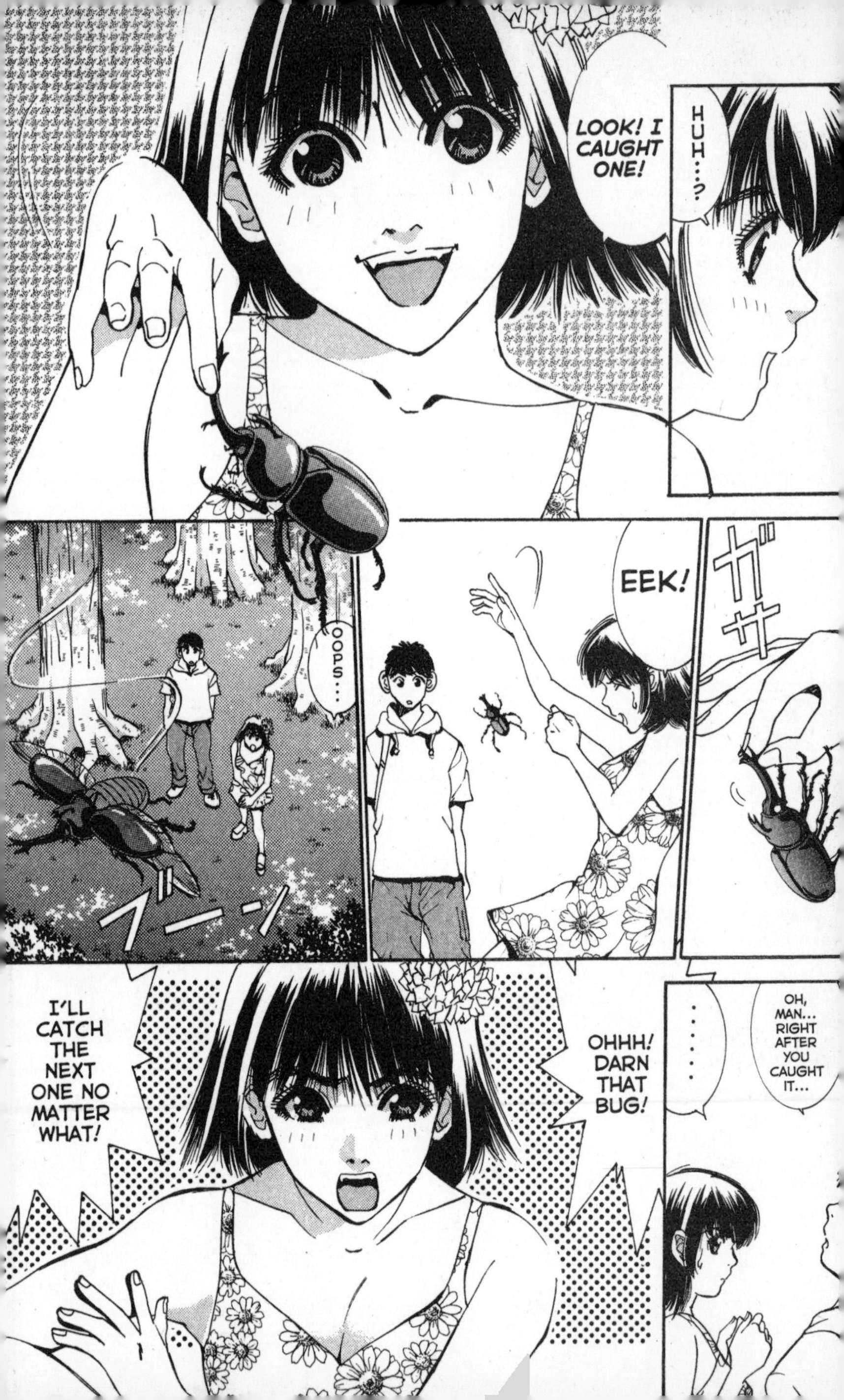

HUH...?
LOOK! I CAUGHT ONE!
ガサ
EEK!
OOPS...
ブーン
OH, MAN... RIGHT AFTER YOU CAUGHT IT...
......
OHHH! DARN THAT BUG!
I'LL CATCH THE NEXT ONE NO MATTER WHAT!

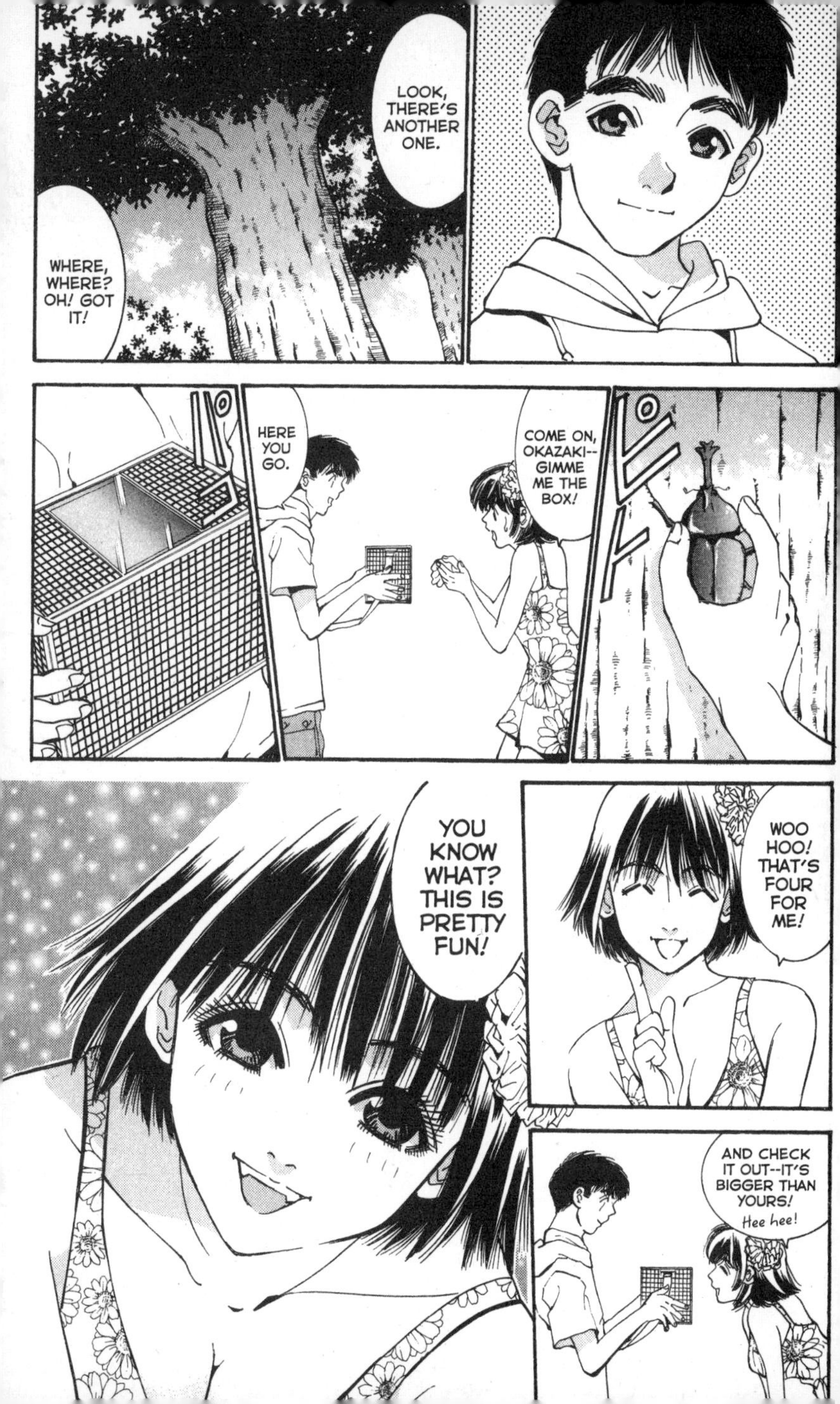
LOOK, THERE'S ANOTHER ONE.
WHERE, WHERE? OH! GOT IT!
COME ON, OKAZAKI--GIMME ME THE BOX!
HERE YOU GO.
WOO HOO! THAT'S FOUR FOR ME!
AND CHECK IT OUT--IT'S BIGGER THAN YOURS!
Hee hee!
YOU KNOW WHAT? THIS IS PRETTY FUN!

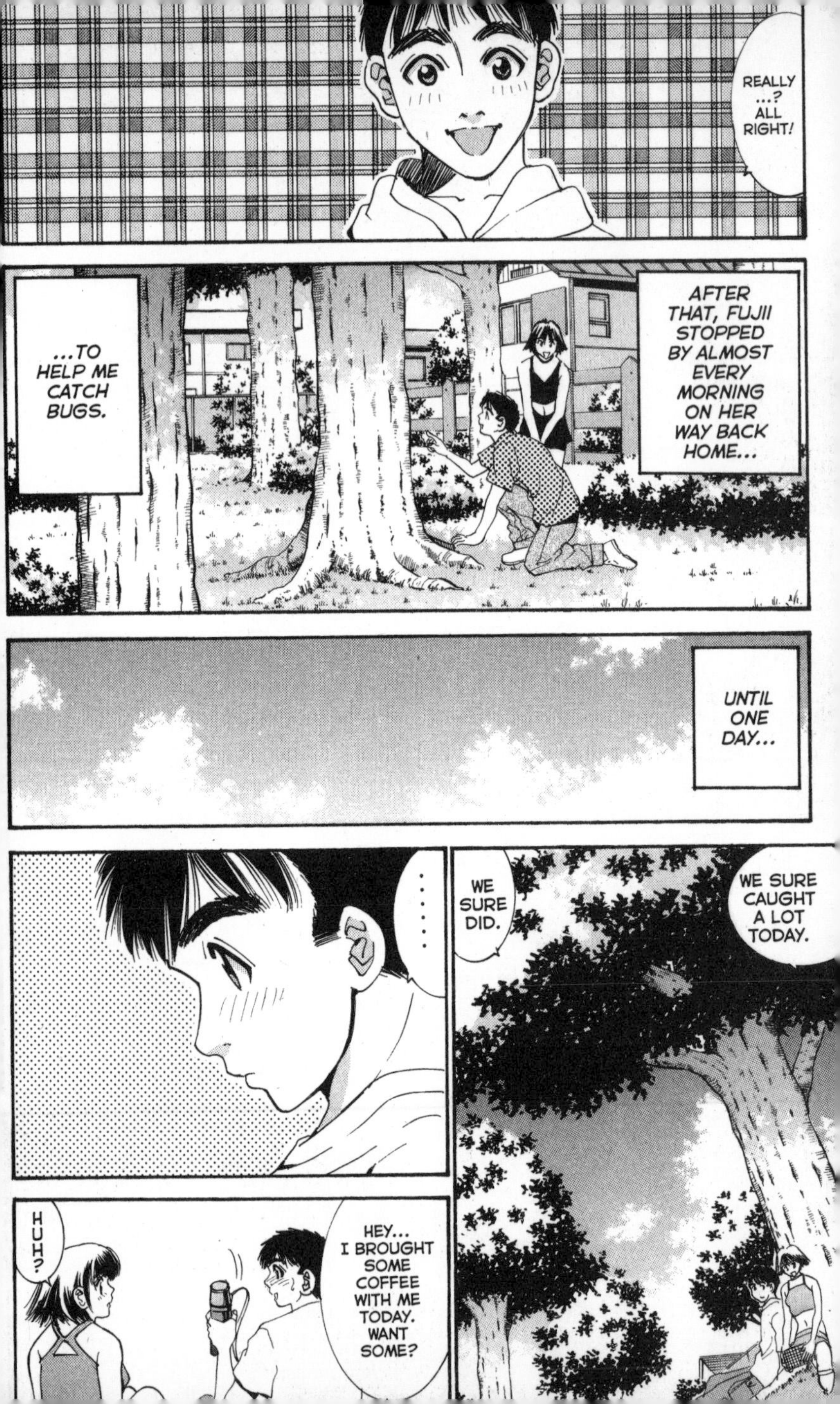
REALLY ...? ALL RIGHT!
AFTER THAT, FUJII STOPPED BY ALMOST EVERY MORNING ON HER WAY BACK HOME...
...TO HELP ME CATCH BUGS.
UNTIL ONE DAY...
WE SURE CAUGHT A LOT TODAY.
WE SURE DID.
......
HEY... I BROUGHT SOME COFFEE WITH ME TODAY. WANT SOME?
HUH?

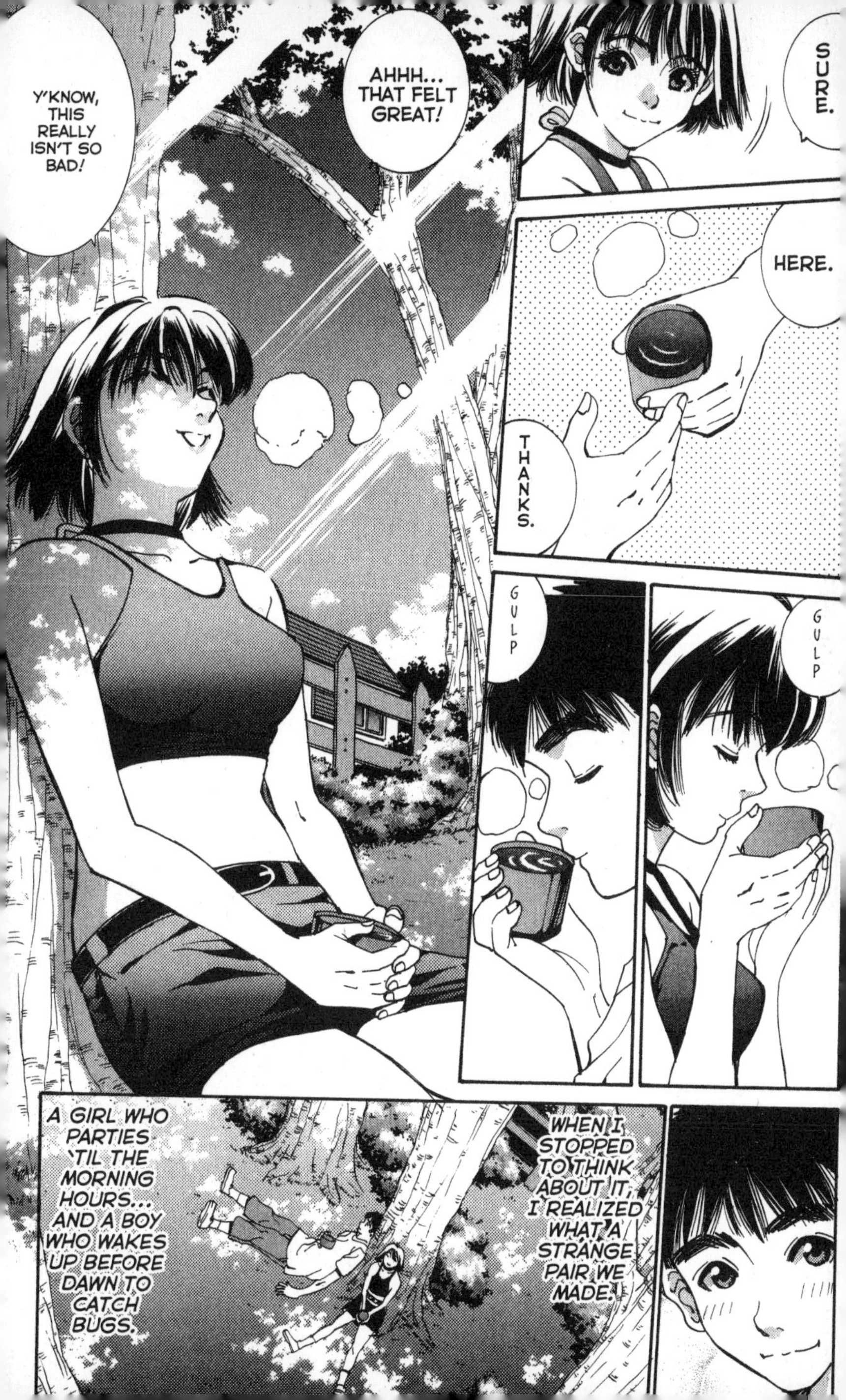
SURE.
HERE.
THANKS.
GULP
GULP
AHHH... THAT FELT GREAT!
Y'KNOW, THIS REALLY ISN'T SO BAD!
WHEN I STOPPED TO THINK ABOUT IT, I REALIZED WHAT A STRANGE PAIR WE MADE.
A GIRL WHO PARTIES 'TIL THE MORNING HOURS... AND A BOY WHO WAKES UP BEFORE DAWN TO CATCH BUGS.

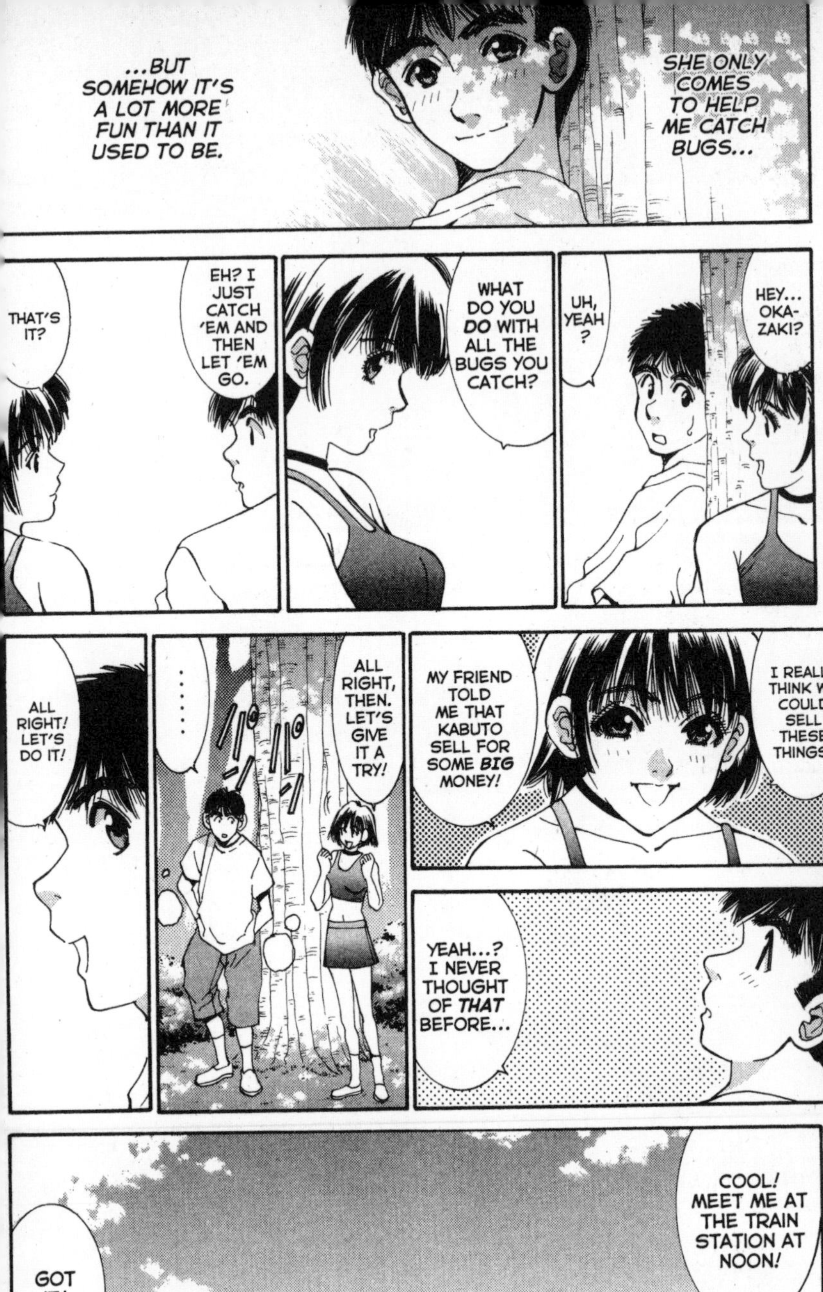

SHE ONLY COMES TO HELP ME CATCH BUGS...
...BUT SOMEHOW IT'S A LOT MORE FUN THAN IT USED TO BE.
HEY... OKA-ZAKI?
UH, YEAH?
WHAT DO YOU DO WITH ALL THE BUGS YOU CATCH?
EH? I JUST CATCH 'EM AND THEN LET 'EM GO.
THAT'S IT?
I REALLY THINK WE COULD SELL THESE THINGS!
MY FRIEND TOLD ME THAT KABUTO SELL FOR SOME BIG MONEY!
YEAH...? I NEVER THOUGHT OF THAT BEFORE...
ALL RIGHT, THEN. LET'S GIVE IT A TRY!
......
ALL RIGHT! LET'S DO IT!
COOL! MEET ME AT THE TRAIN STATION AT NOON!
GOT IT!

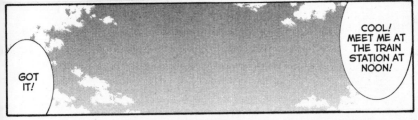

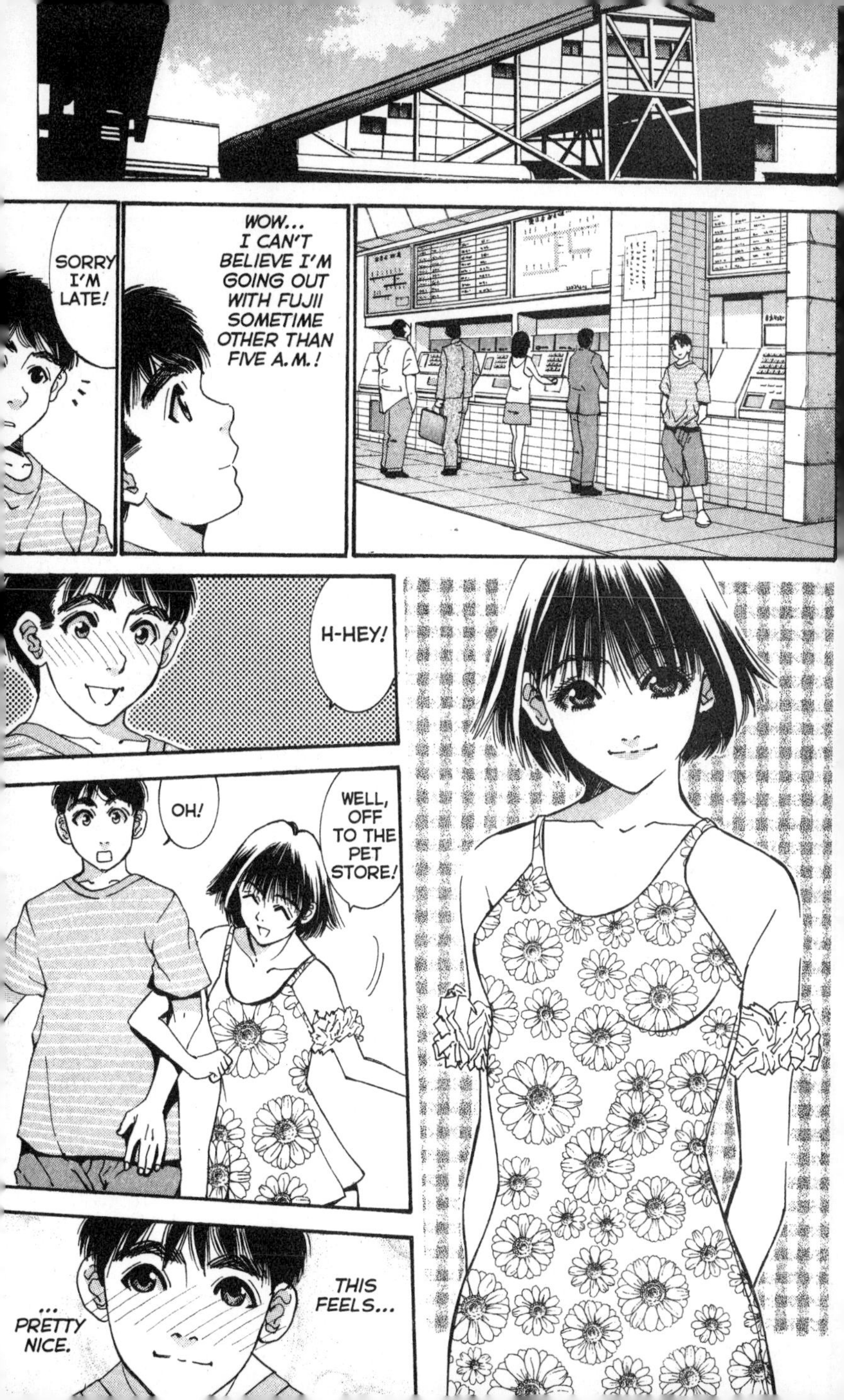
WOW... I CAN'T BELIEVE I'M GOING OUT WITH FUJII SOMETIME OTHER THAN FIVE A.M.!
SORRY I'M LATE!
H-HEY!
WELL, OFF TO THE PET STORE!
OH!
THIS FEELS...
...PRETTY NICE.

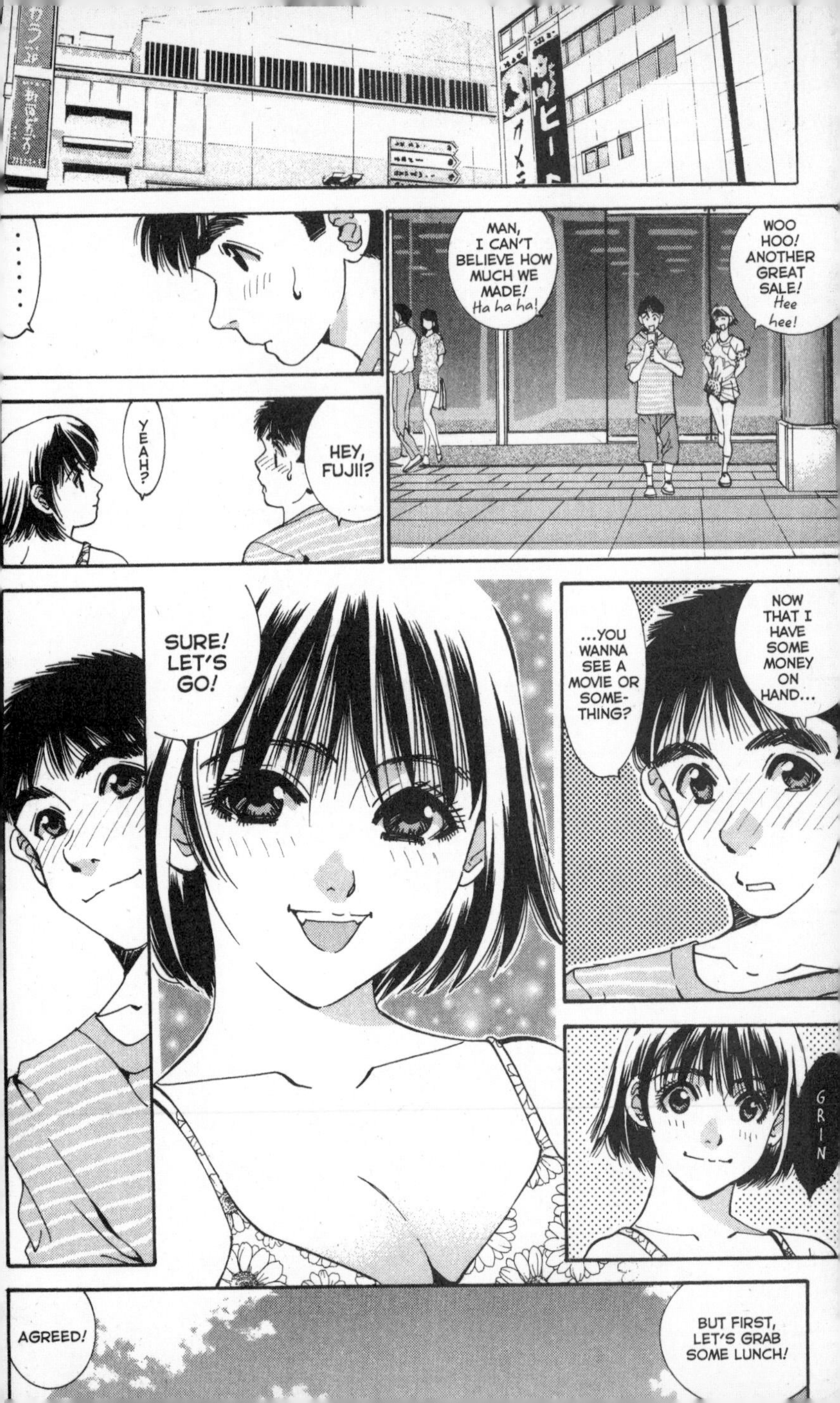
WOO HOO! ANOTHER GREAT SALE! Hee hee!
MAN, I CAN'T BELIEVE HOW MUCH WE MADE! Ha ha ha!
......
HEY, FUJII?
YEAH?
NOW THAT I HAVE SOME MONEY ON HAND...
...YOU WANNA SEE A MOVIE OR SOME-THING?
GRIN
SURE! LET'S GO!
BUT FIRST, LET'S GRAB SOME LUNCH!
AGREED!

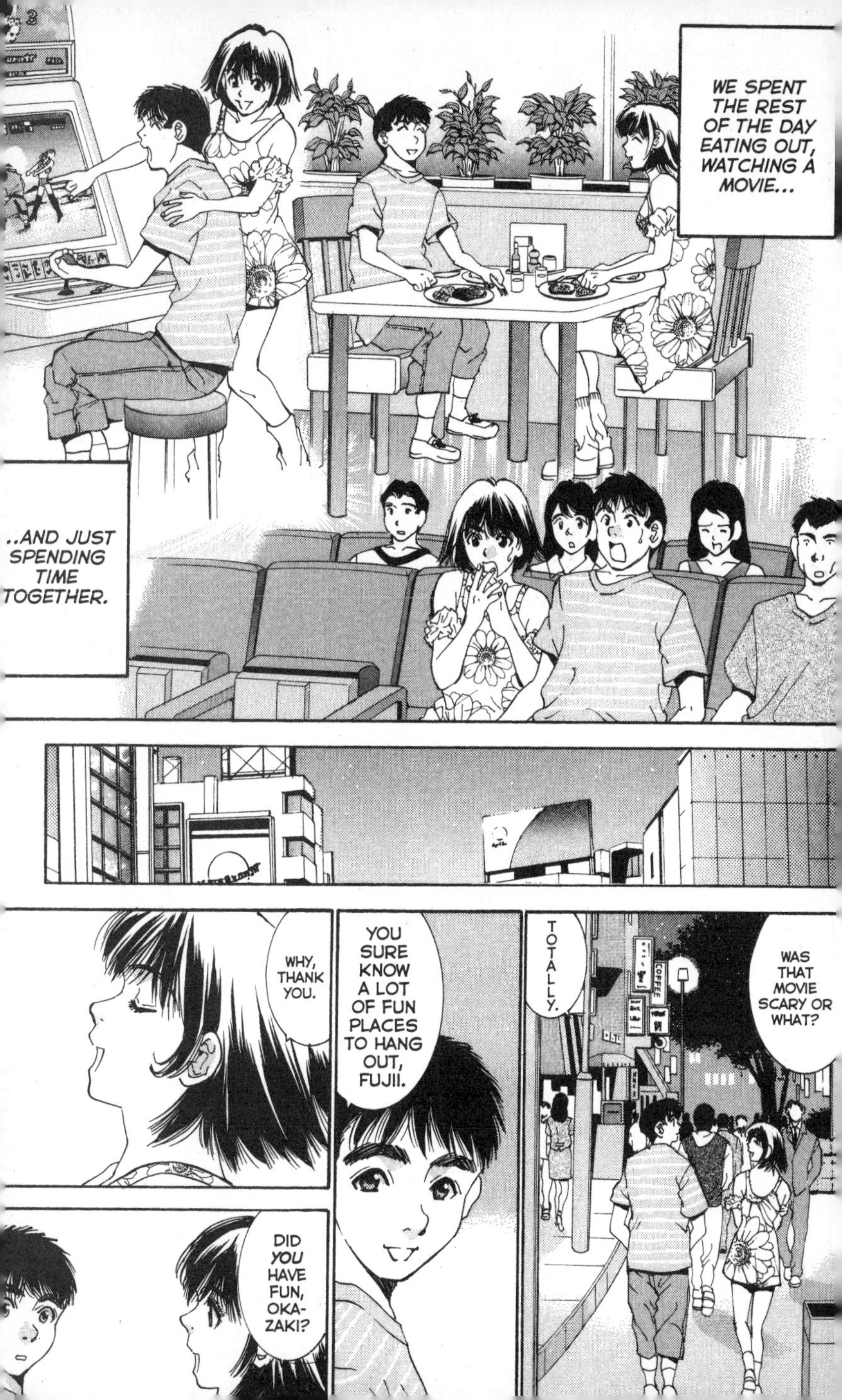
WE SPENT THE REST OF THE DAY EATING OUT, WATCHING A MOVIE...
..AND JUST SPENDING TIME TOGETHER.
WAS THAT MOVIE SCARY OR WHAT?
TOTALLY.
YOU SURE KNOW A LOT OF FUN PLACES TO HANG OUT, FUJII.
WHY, THANK YOU.
DID *YOU* HAVE FUN, OKA-ZAKI?

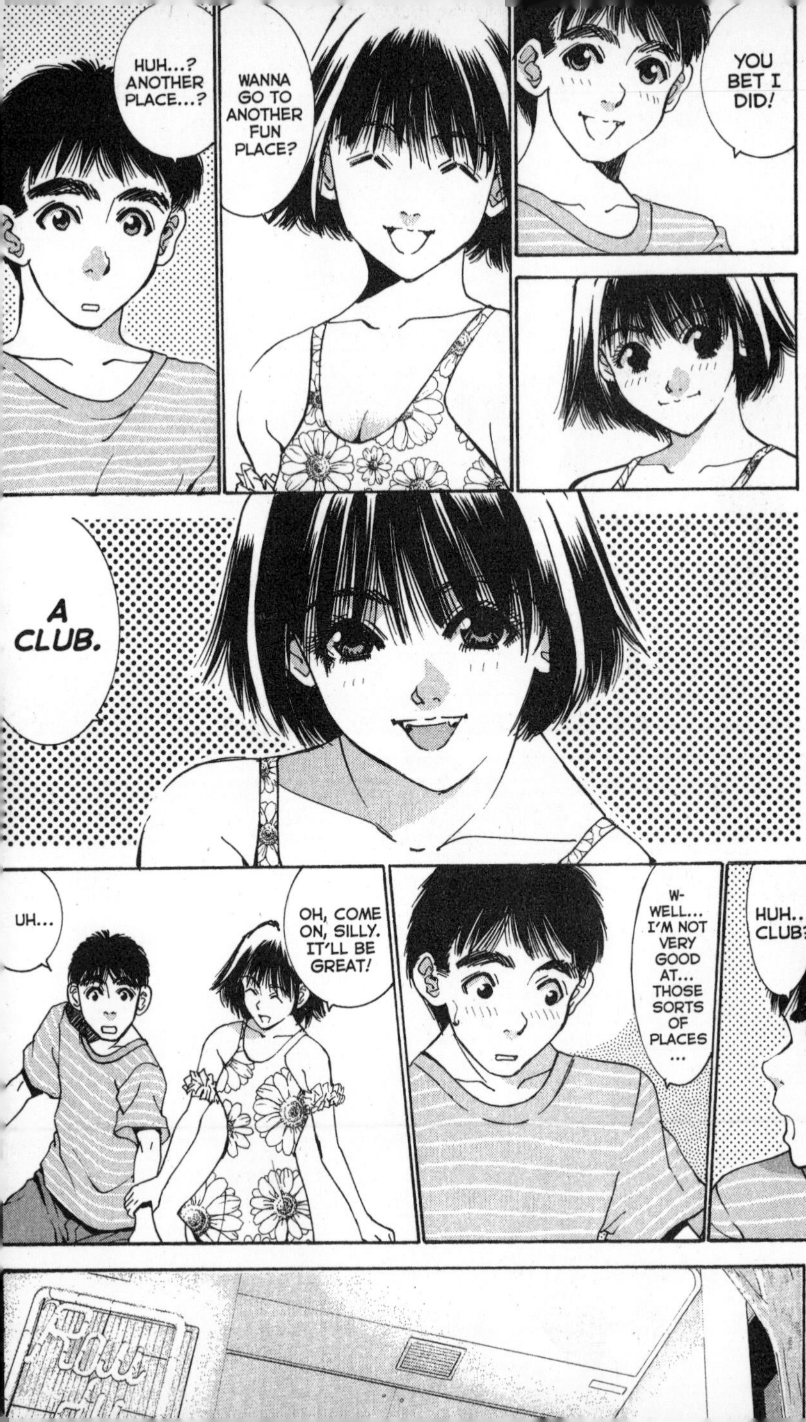
YOU BET I DID!
WANNA GO TO ANOTHER FUN PLACE?
HUH...? ANOTHER PLACE...?
A CLUB.
HUH... CLUB?
W-WELL... I'M NOT VERY GOOD AT... THOSE SORTS OF PLACES ...
OH, COME ON, SILLY. IT'LL BE GREAT!
UH...

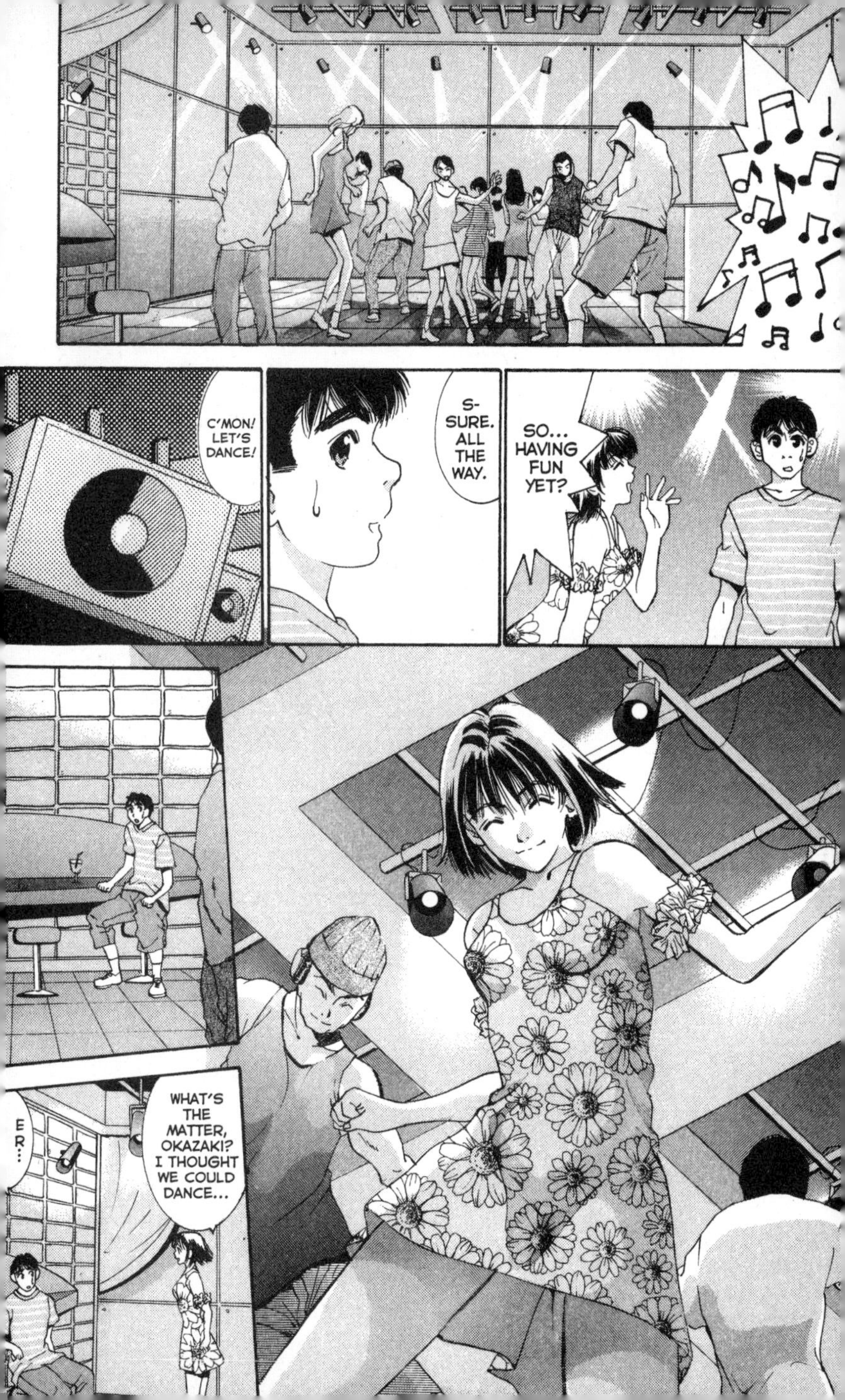
SO... HAVING FUN YET?
S-SURE. ALL THE WAY.
C'MON! LET'S DANCE!
WHAT'S THE MATTER, OKAZAKI? I THOUGHT WE COULD DANCE...
ER...

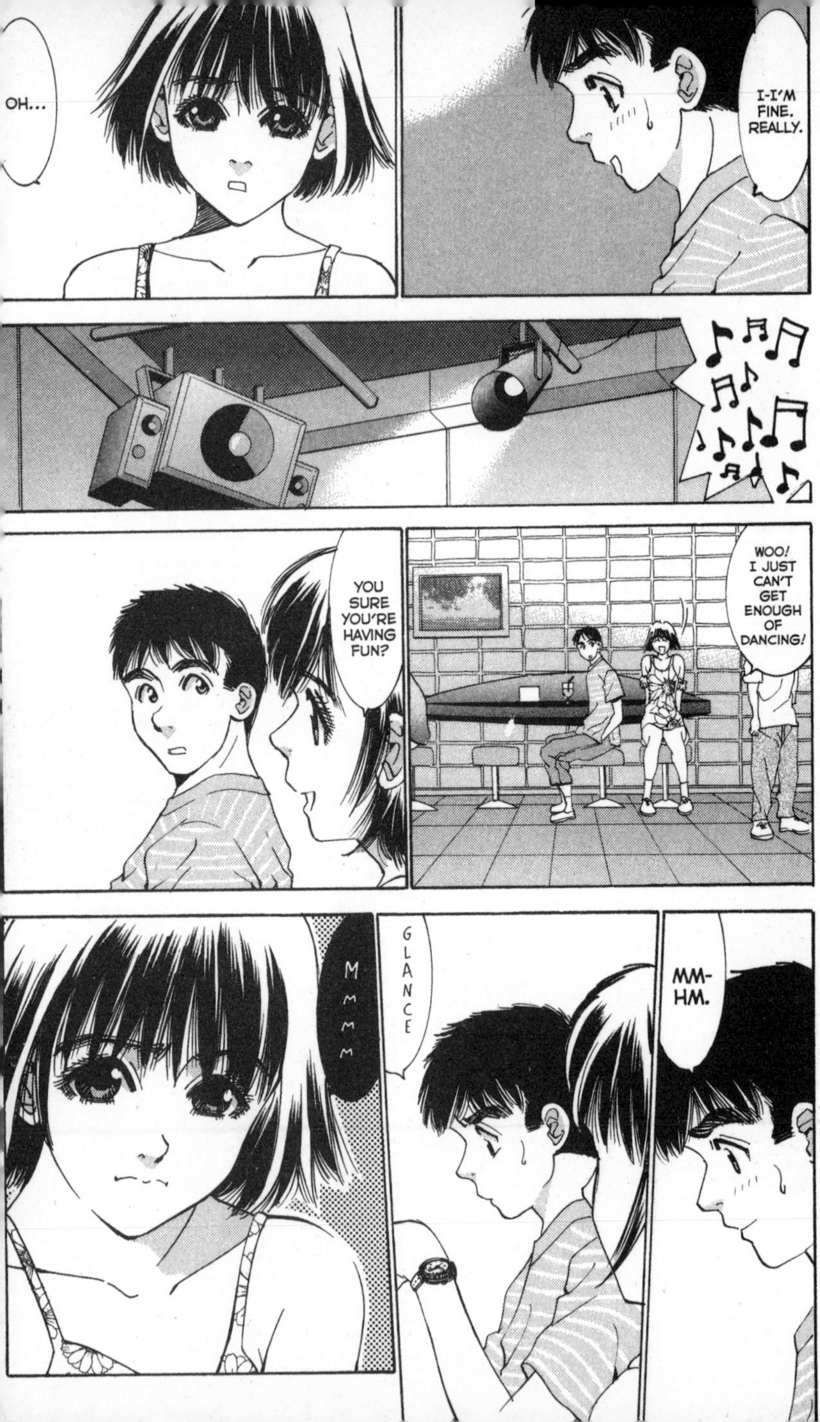
I-I'M FINE. REALLY.
OH...
WOO! I JUST CAN'T GET ENOUGH OF DANCING!
YOU SURE YOU'RE HAVING FUN?
MM-HM.
GLANCE
MMMM

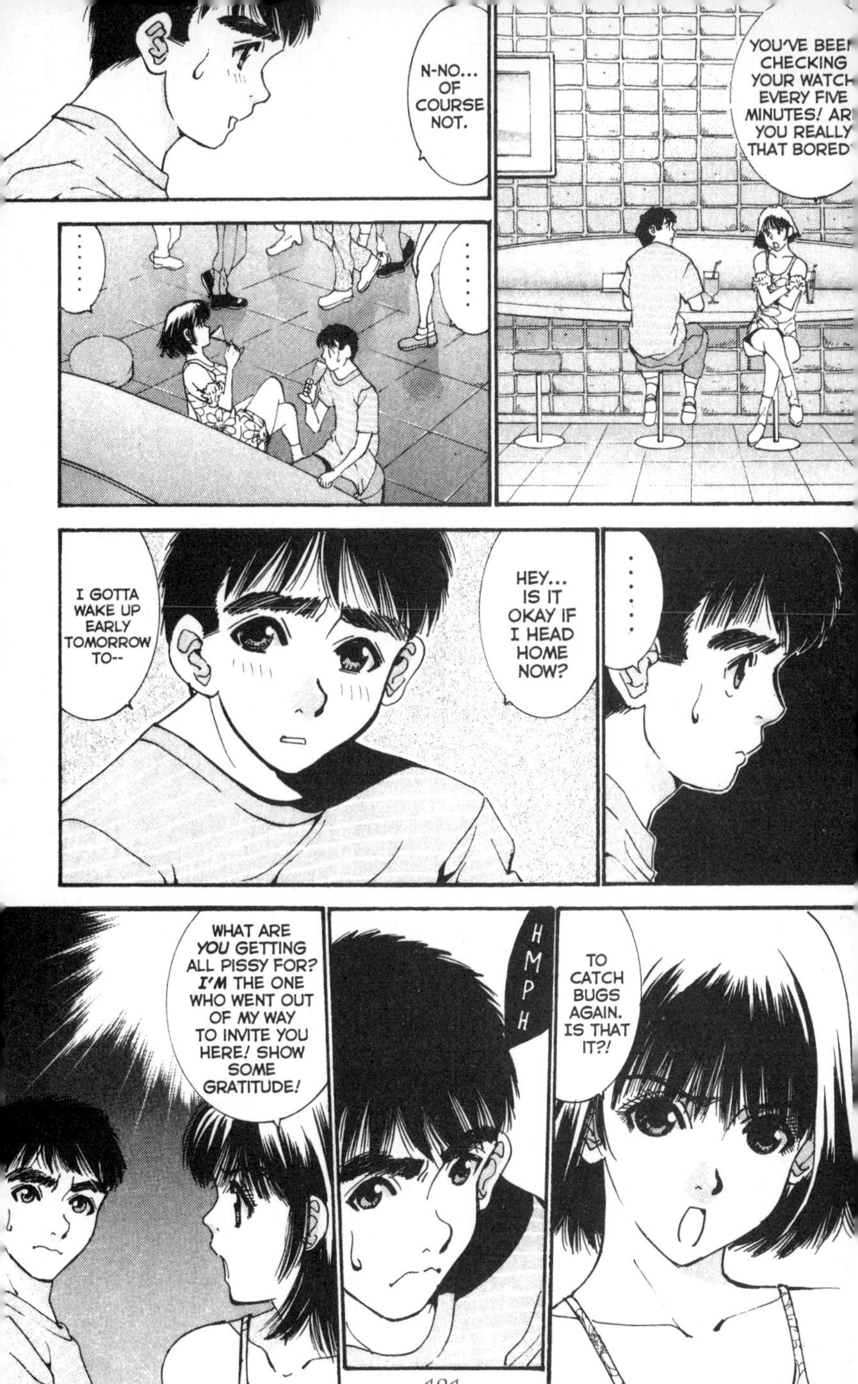
YOU'VE BEE CHECKING YOUR WATC EVERY FIVE MINUTES! AR YOU REALLY THAT BORED
N-NO... OF COURSE NOT.
......
......
......
HEY... IS IT OKAY IF I HEAD HOME NOW?
I GOTTA WAKE UP EARLY TOMORROW TO--
TO CATCH BUGS AGAIN. IS THAT IT?!
HMPH
WHAT ARE YOU GETTING ALL PISSY FOR? I'M THE ONE WHO WENT OUT OF MY WAY TO INVITE YOU HERE! SHOW SOME GRATITUDE!

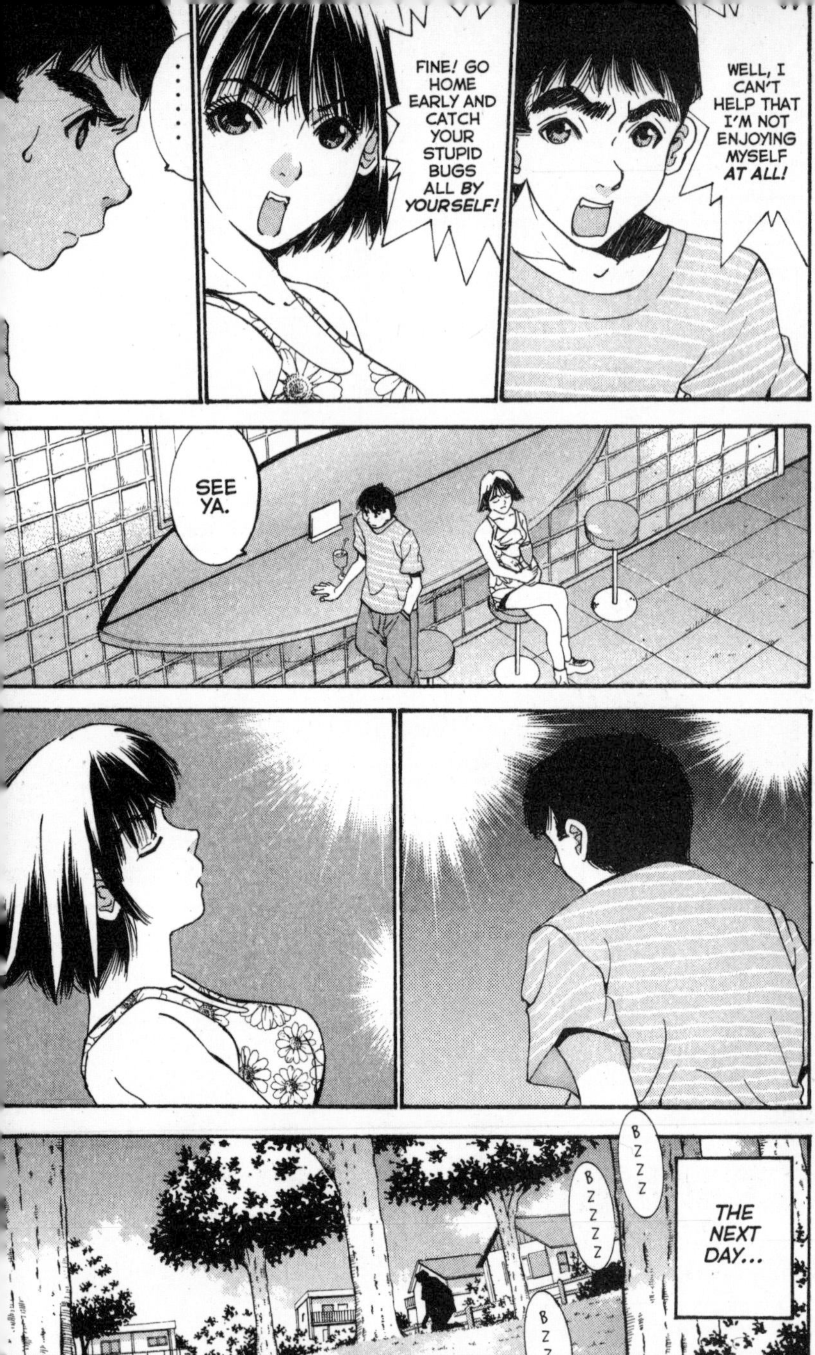
WELL, I CAN'T HELP THAT I'M NOT ENJOYING MYSELF AT ALL!
FINE! GO HOME EARLY AND CATCH YOUR STUPID BUGS ALL BY YOURSELF!
......
SEE YA.
THE NEXT DAY...
BZZZ
BZZZ
BZZZ

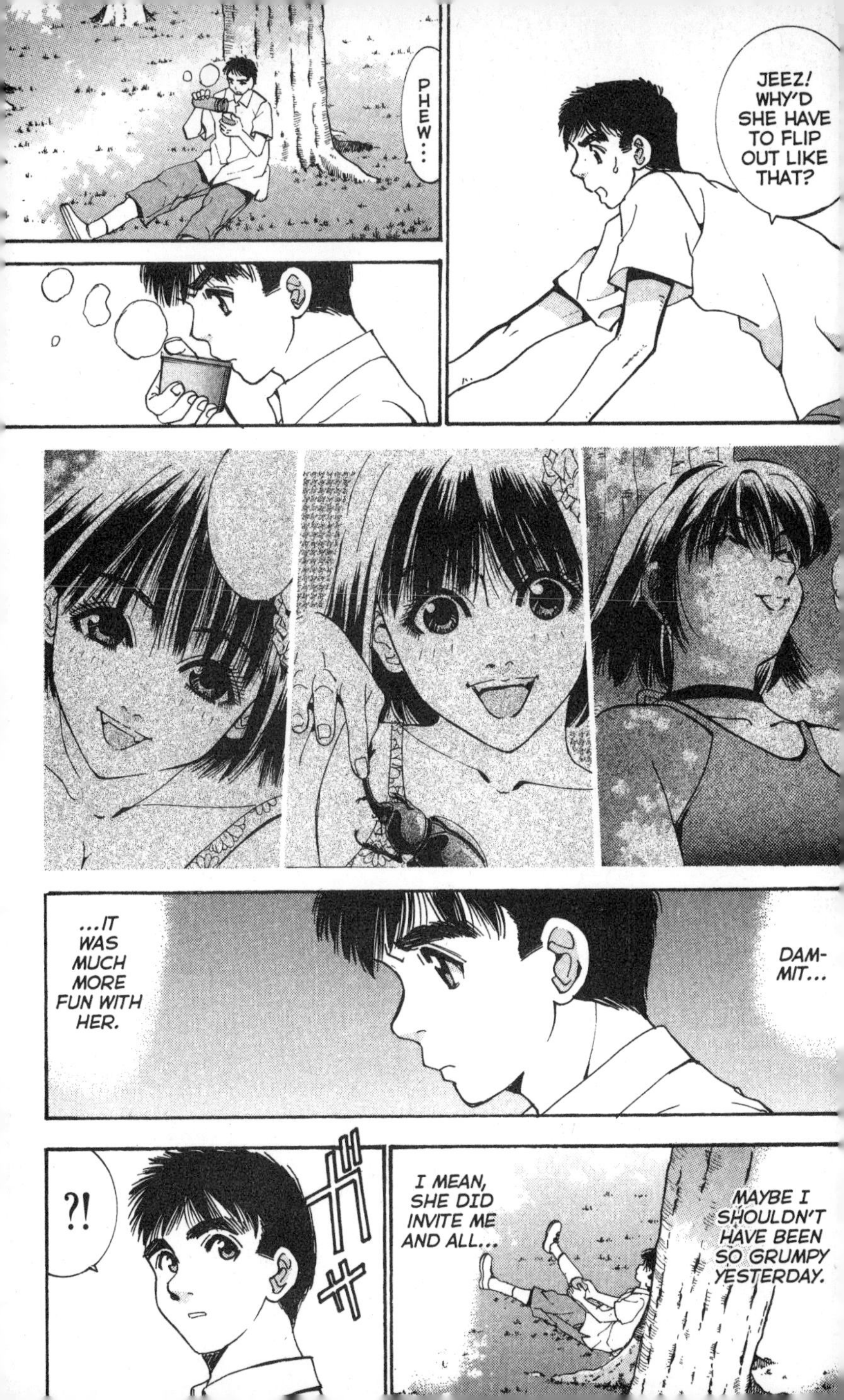
JEEZ! WHY'D SHE HAVE TO FLIP OUT LIKE THAT?
PHEW...
DAM-MIT...
...IT WAS MUCH MORE FUN WITH HER.
MAYBE I SHOULDN'T HAVE BEEN SO GRUMPY YESTERDAY.
I MEAN, SHE DID INVITE ME AND ALL...
?!

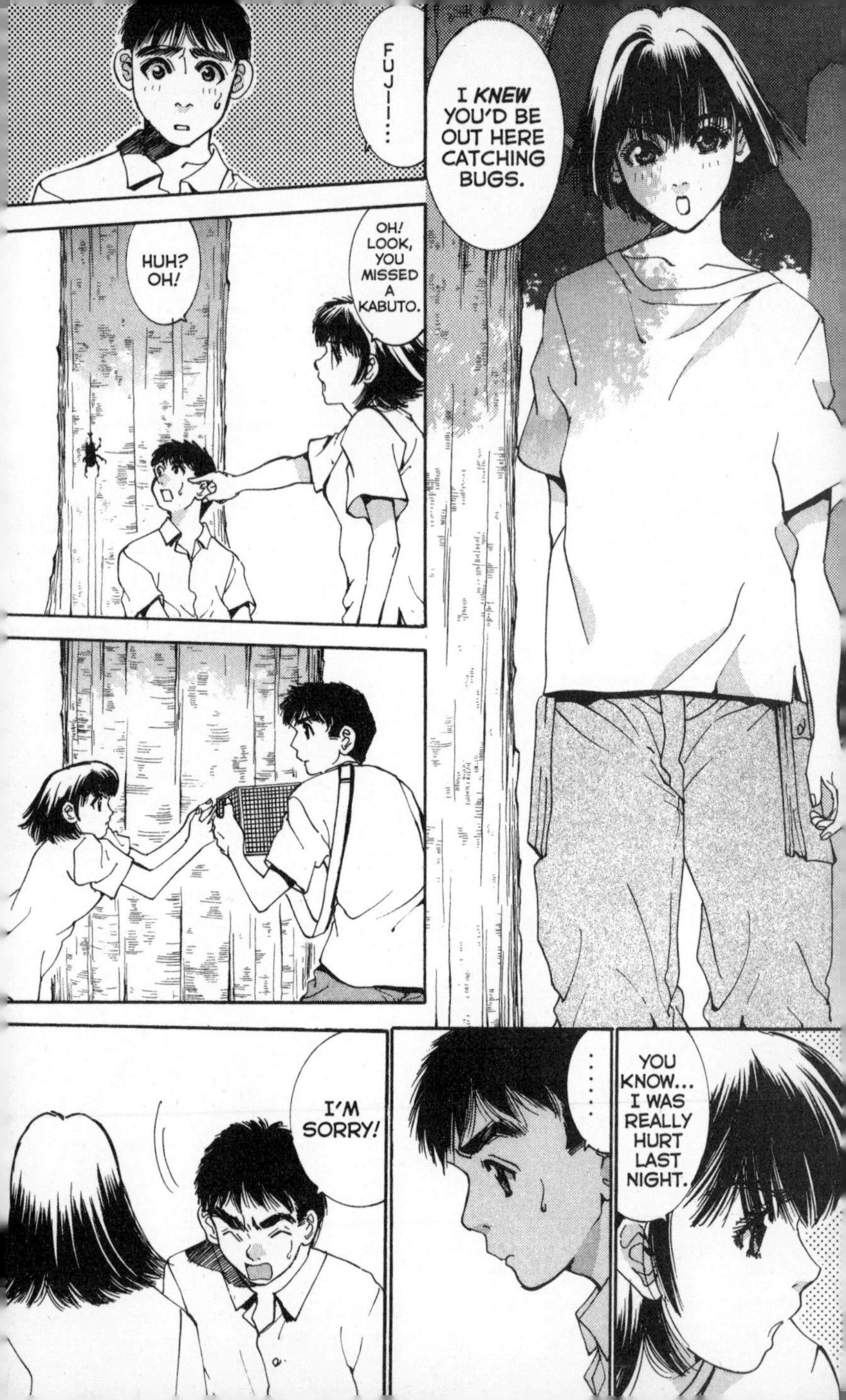
I KNEW YOU'D BE OUT HERE CATCHING BUGS.
FUJI...
OH! LOOK, YOU MISSED A KABUTO.
HUH? OH!
YOU KNOW... I WAS REALLY HURT LAST NIGHT.
......
I'M SORRY!

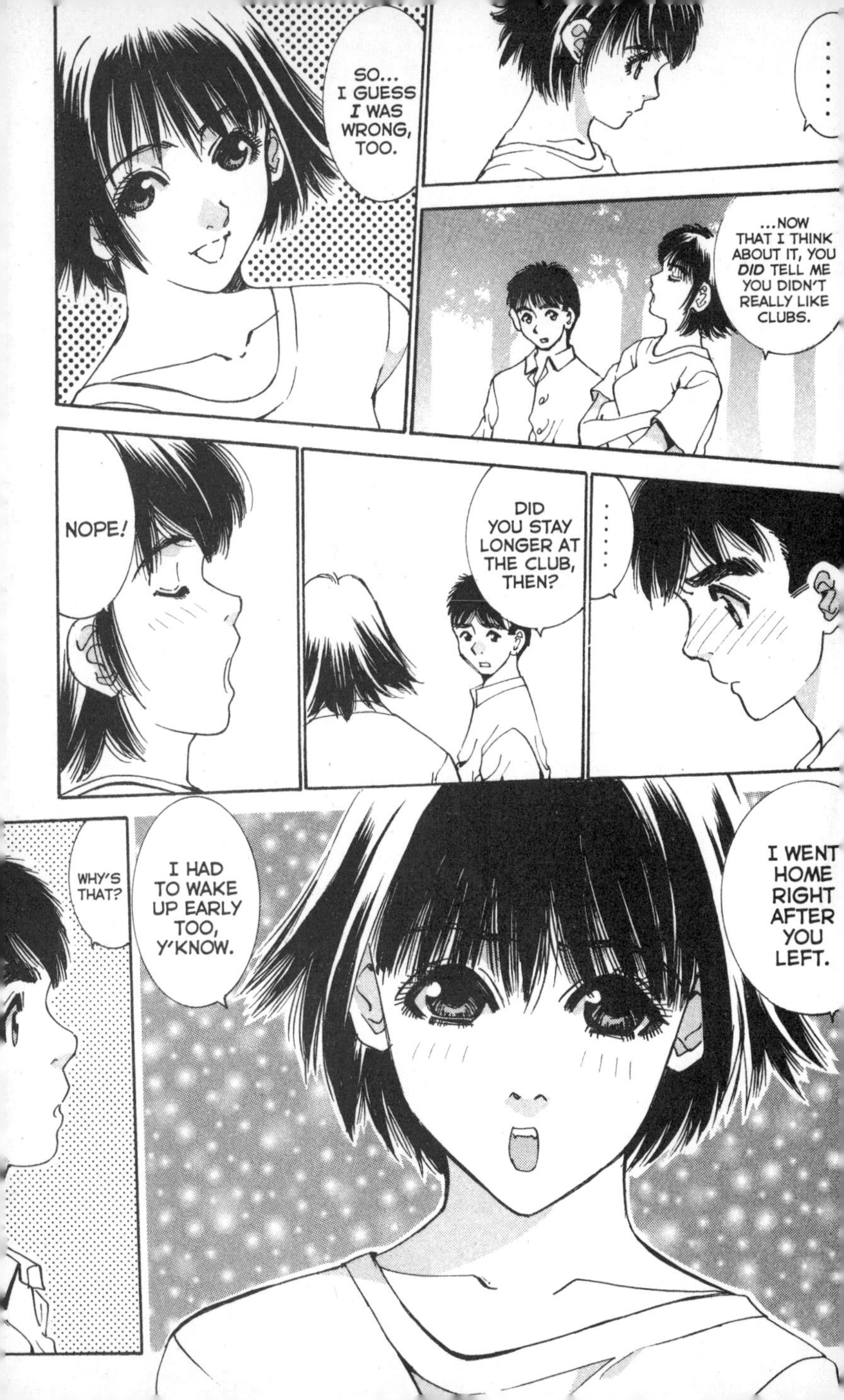
......
...NOW THAT I THINK ABOUT IT, YOU DID TELL ME YOU DIDN'T REALLY LIKE CLUBS.
SO... I GUESS I WAS WRONG, TOO.
......
DID YOU STAY LONGER AT THE CLUB, THEN?
NOPE!
I WENT HOME RIGHT AFTER YOU LEFT.
I HAD TO WAKE UP EARLY TOO, Y'KNOW.
WHY'S THAT?

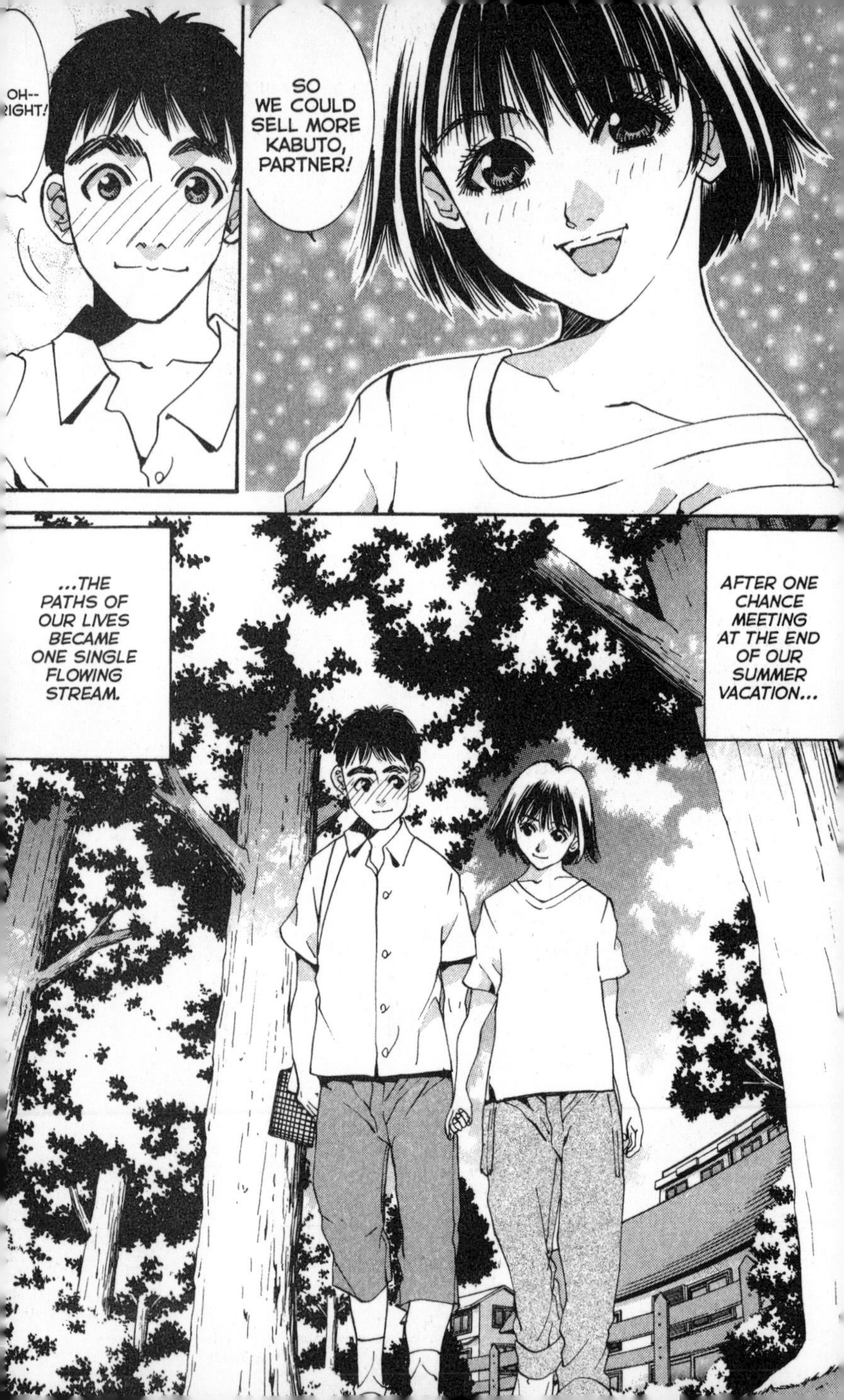
SO WE COULD SELL MORE KABUTO, PARTNER!
OH-- RIGHT!
AFTER ONE CHANCE MEETING AT THE END OF OUR SUMMER VACATION...
...THE PATHS OF OUR LIVES BECAME ONE SINGLE FLOWING STREAM.

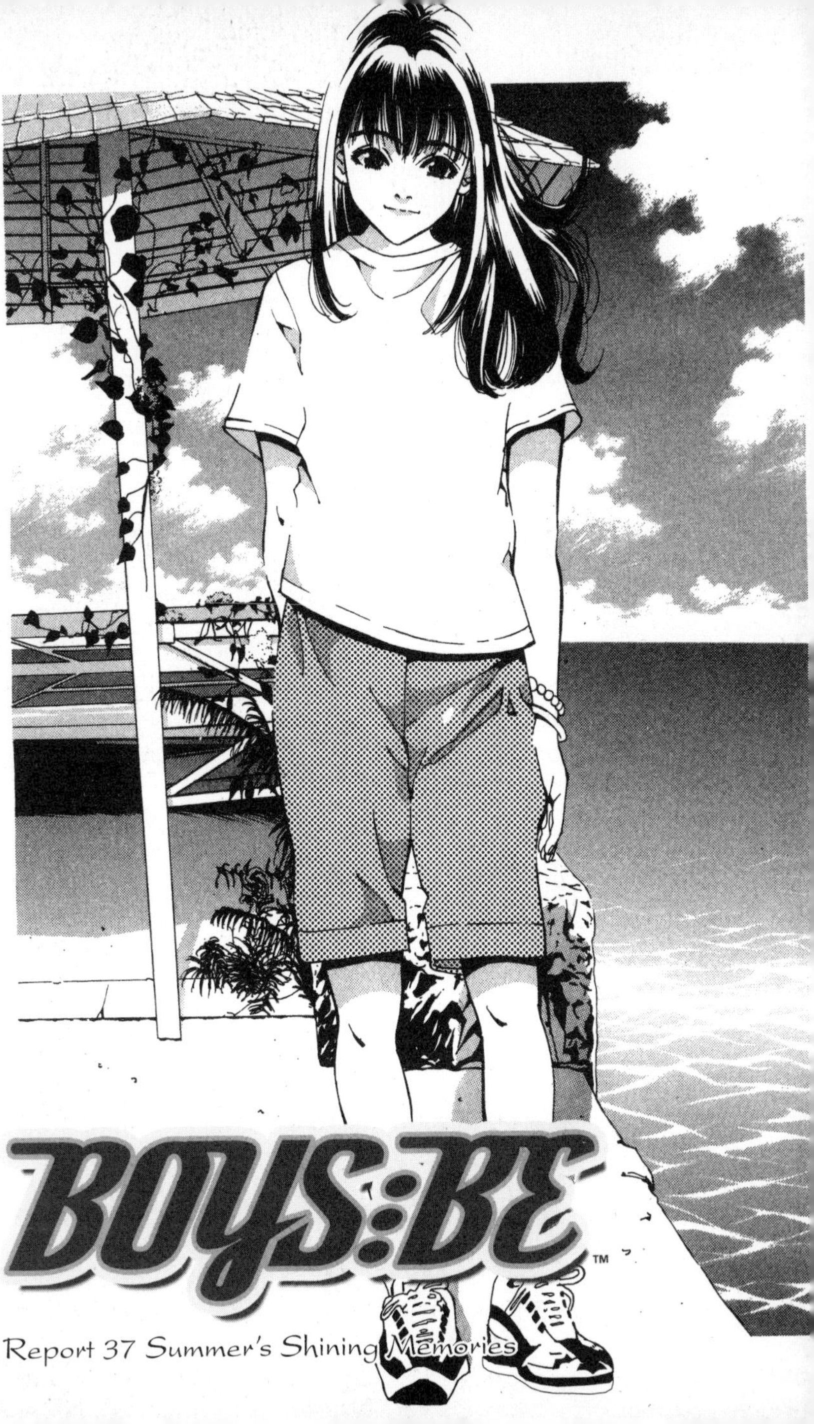
BOYS BE™
Report 37 Summer's Shining Memories

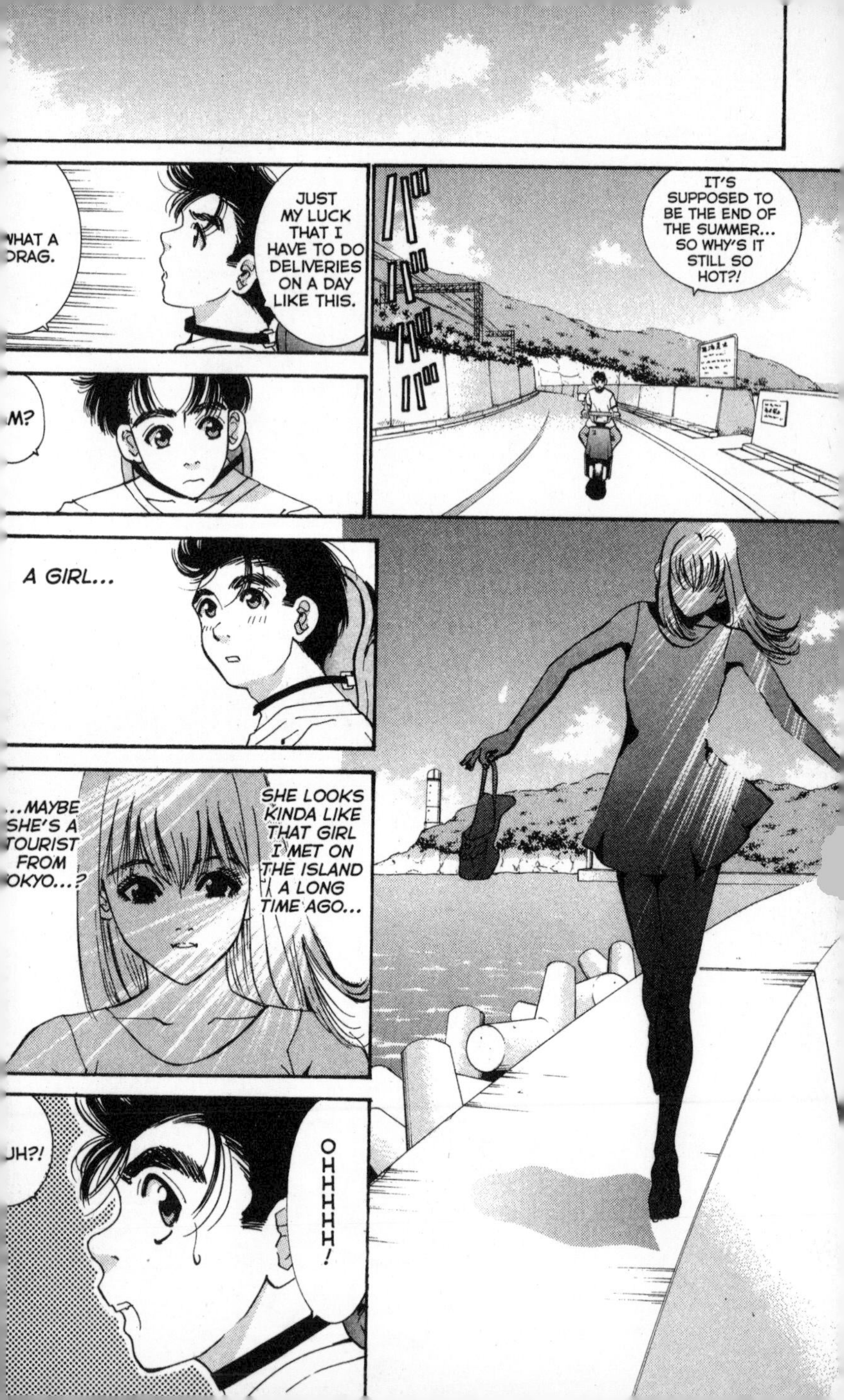
ババババ
IT'S SUPPOSED TO BE THE END OF THE SUMMER... SO WHY'S IT STILL SO HOT?!
JUST MY LUCK THAT I HAVE TO DO DELIVERIES ON A DAY LIKE THIS.
WHAT A DRAG.
M?
A GIRL...
SHE LOOKS KINDA LIKE THAT GIRL I MET ON THE ISLAND A LONG TIME AGO...
...MAYBE SHE'S A TOURIST FROM OKYO...?
OHHHHH!
JH?!

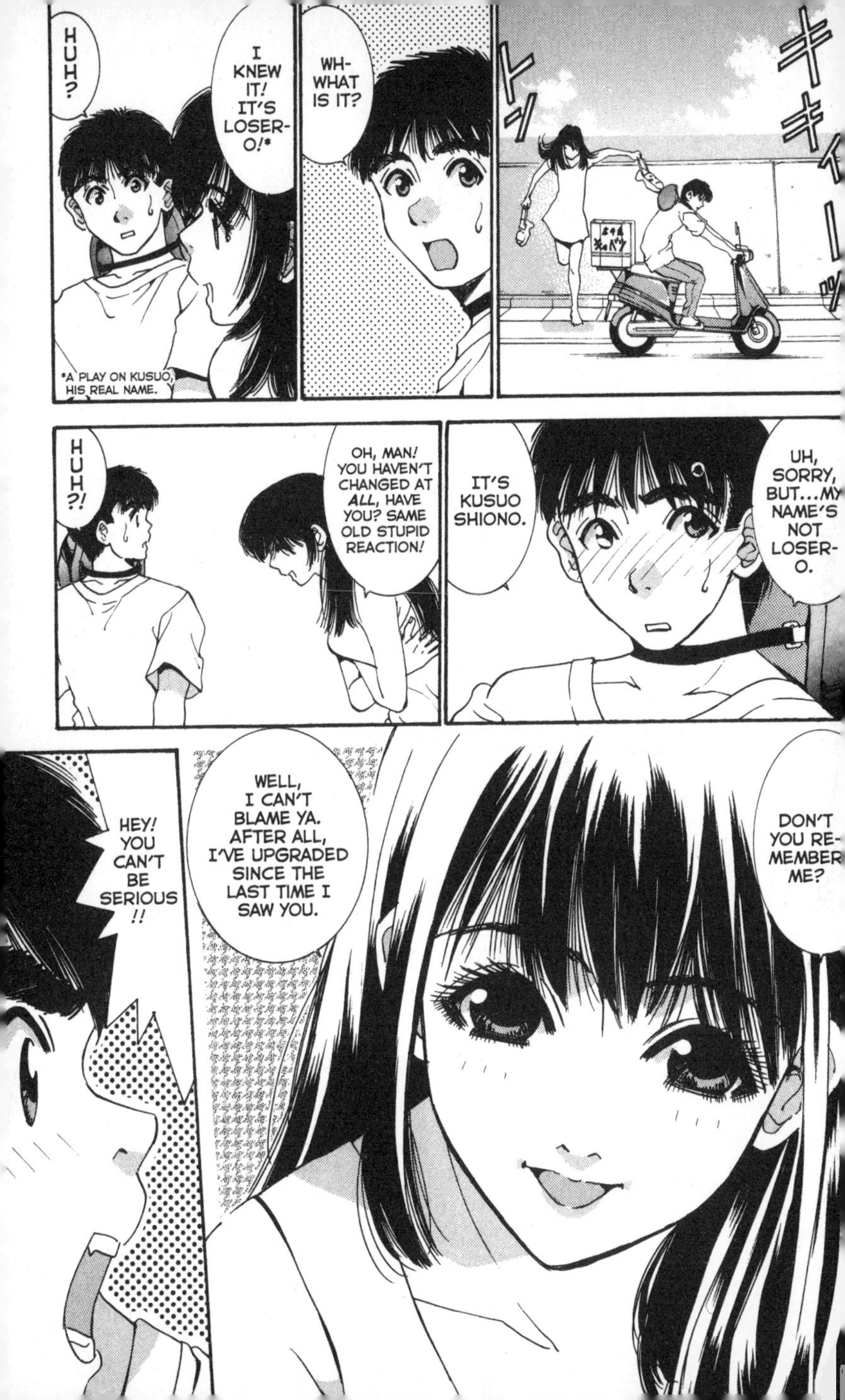
WH- WHAT IS IT?
I KNEW IT! IT'S LOSER-O!*
HUH?
*A PLAY ON KUSUO, HIS REAL NAME.
UH, SORRY, BUT...MY NAME'S NOT LOSER-O.
IT'S KUSUO SHIONO.
OH, MAN! YOU HAVEN'T CHANGED AT *ALL*, HAVE YOU? SAME OLD STUPID REACTION!
HUH?!
DON'T YOU RE-MEMBER ME?
WELL, I CAN'T BLAME YA. AFTER ALL, I'VE UPGRADED SINCE THE LAST TIME I SAW YOU.
HEY! YOU CAN'T BE SERIOUS!!

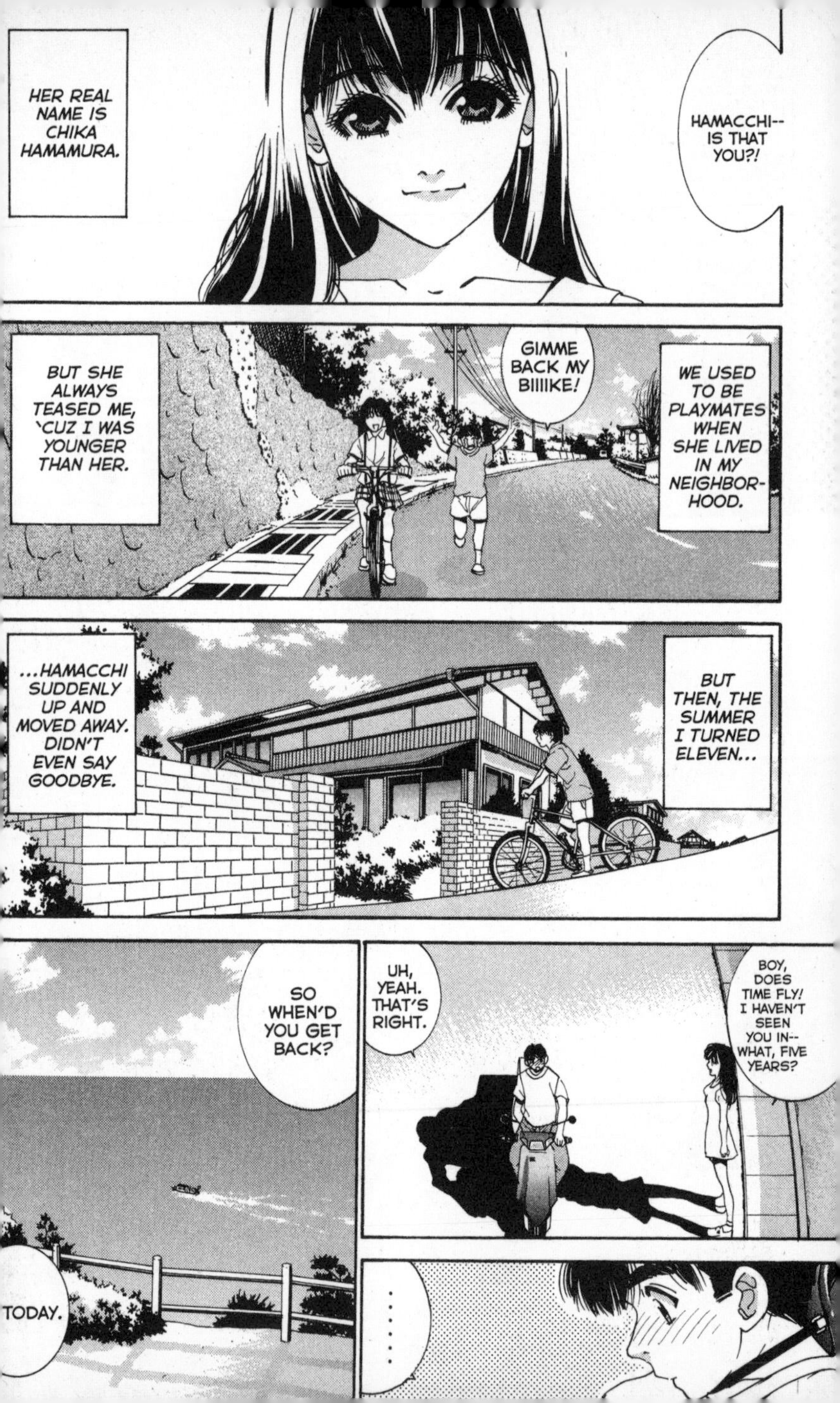
HAMACCHI-- IS THAT YOU?!
HER REAL NAME IS CHIKA HAMAMURA.
WE USED TO BE PLAYMATES WHEN SHE LIVED IN MY NEIGHBOR-HOOD.
GIMME BACK MY BIIIIKE!
BUT SHE ALWAYS TEASED ME, 'CUZ I WAS YOUNGER THAN HER.
BUT THEN, THE SUMMER I TURNED ELEVEN...
...HAMACCHI SUDDENLY UP AND MOVED AWAY. DIDN'T EVEN SAY GOODBYE.
BOY, DOES TIME FLY! I HAVEN'T SEEN YOU IN-- WHAT, FIVE YEARS?
UH, YEAH. THAT'S RIGHT.
.....
SO WHEN'D YOU GET BACK?
TODAY.

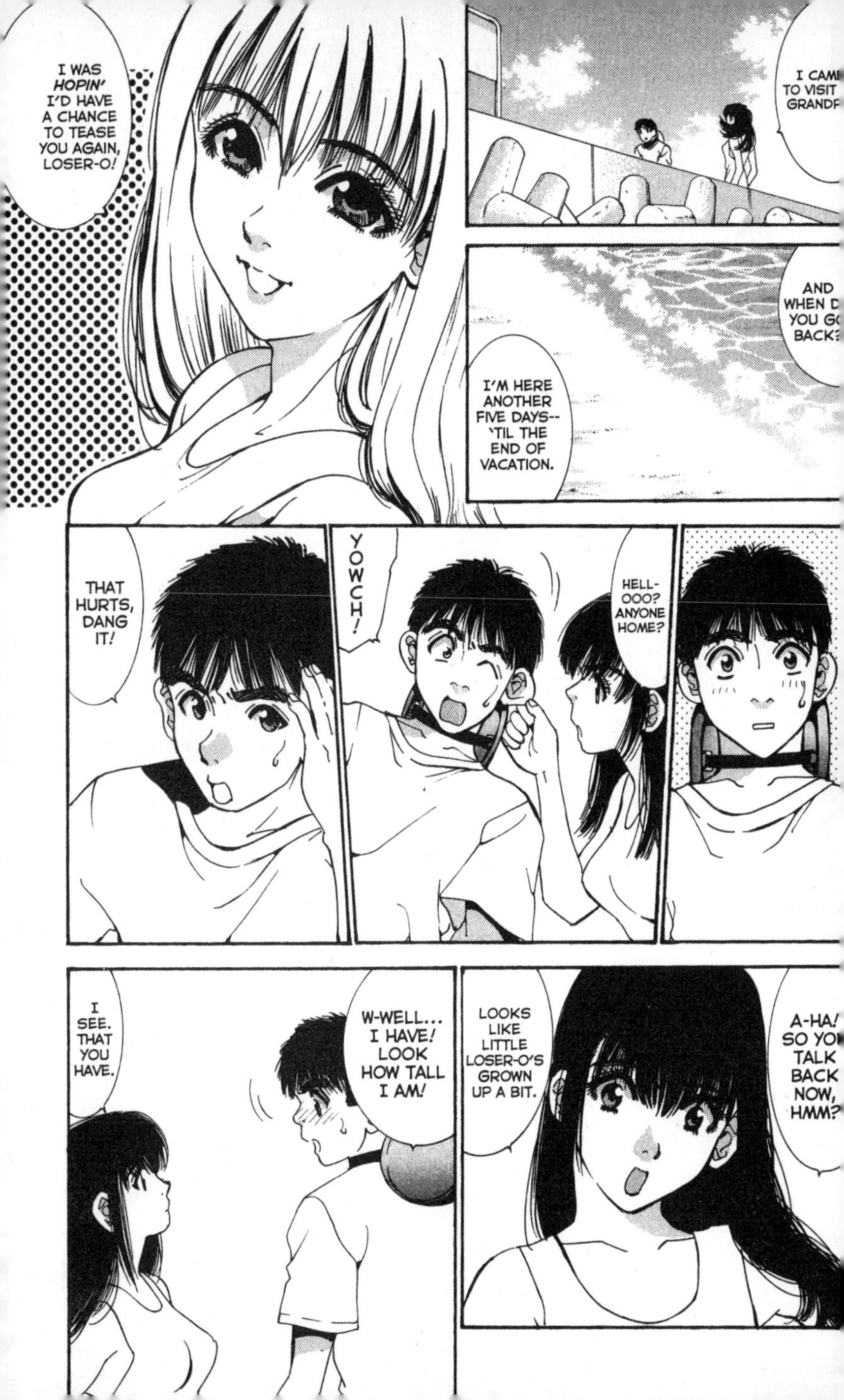
I CAM TO VISIT GRANDP
AND WHEN D YOU G BACK?
I'M HERE ANOTHER FIVE DAYS-- 'TIL THE END OF VACATION.
I WAS *HOPIN'* I'D HAVE A CHANCE TO TEASE YOU AGAIN, LOSER-O!
HELL-OOO? ANYONE HOME?
YOWCH!
THAT HURTS, DANG IT!
A-HA! SO YO TALK BACK NOW, HMM?
LOOKS LIKE LITTLE LOSER-O'S GROWN UP A BIT.
W-WELL... I HAVE! LOOK HOW TALL I AM!
I SEE. THAT YOU HAVE.

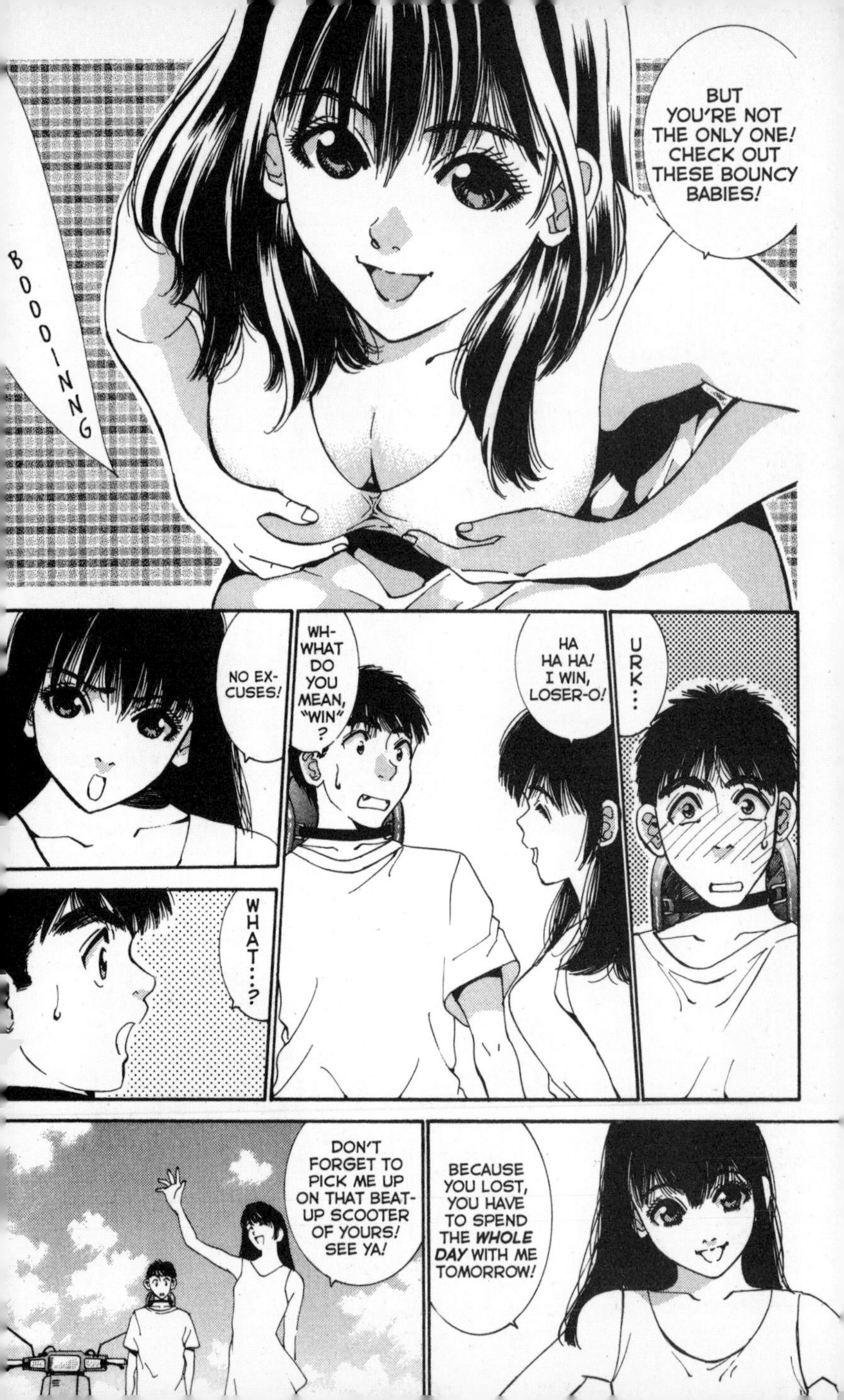
BUT YOU'RE NOT THE ONLY ONE! CHECK OUT THESE BOUNCY BABIES!
BOOOOINNG
URK...
HA HA HA! I WIN, LOSER-O!
WH- WHAT DO YOU MEAN, "WIN"?
NO EX- CUSES!
WHAT...?
BECAUSE YOU LOST, YOU HAVE TO SPEND THE *WHOLE DAY* WITH ME TOMORROW!
DON'T FORGET TO PICK ME UP ON THAT BEAT- UP SCOOTER OF YOURS! SEE YA!

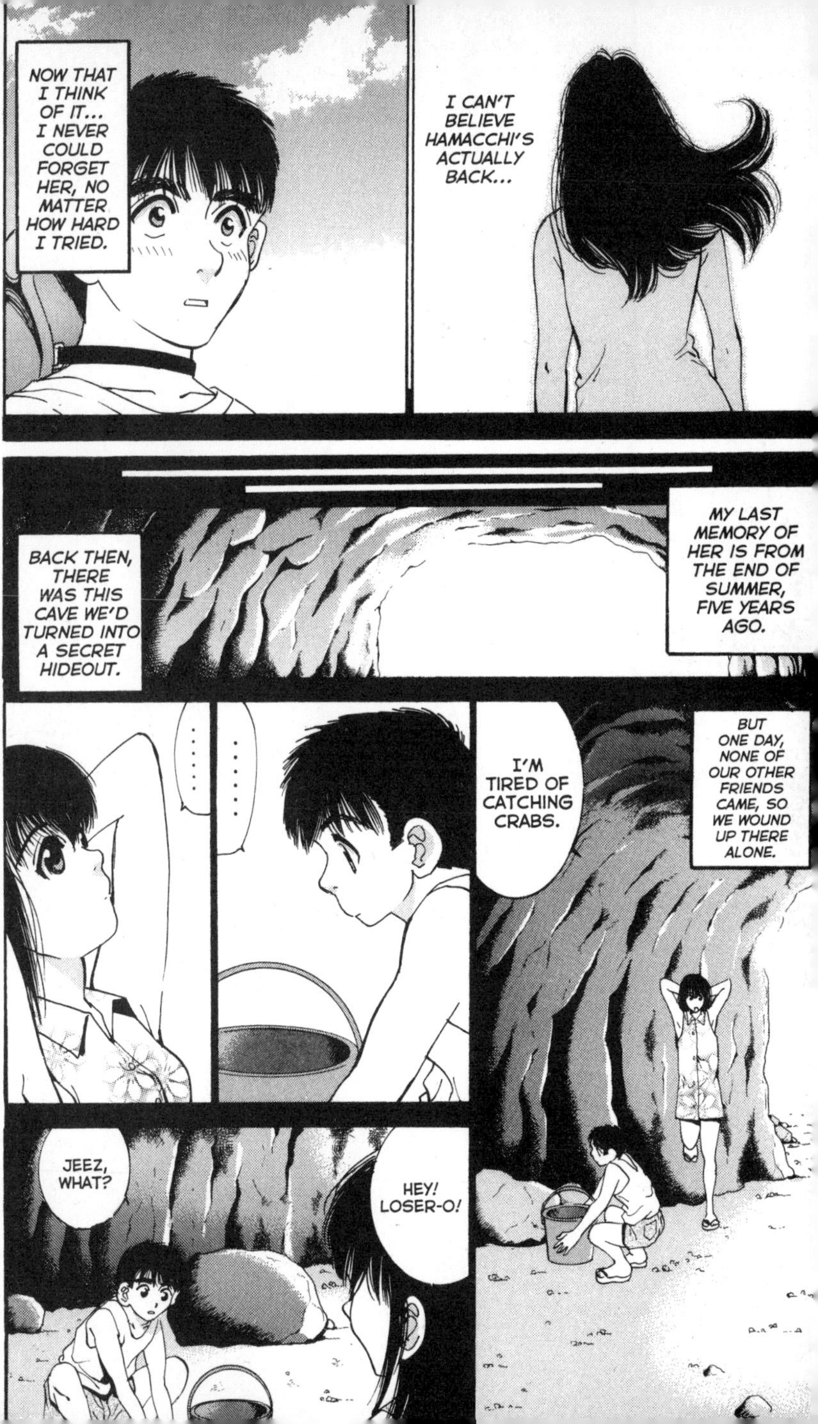
I CAN'T BELIEVE HAMACCHI'S ACTUALLY BACK...
NOW THAT I THINK OF IT... I NEVER COULD FORGET HER, NO MATTER HOW HARD I TRIED.
MY LAST MEMORY OF HER IS FROM THE END OF SUMMER, FIVE YEARS AGO.
BACK THEN, THERE WAS THIS CAVE WE'D TURNED INTO A SECRET HIDEOUT.
BUT ONE DAY, NONE OF OUR OTHER FRIENDS CAME, SO WE WOUND UP THERE ALONE.
I'M TIRED OF CATCHING CRABS.
......
......
HEY! LOSER-O!
JEEZ, WHAT?

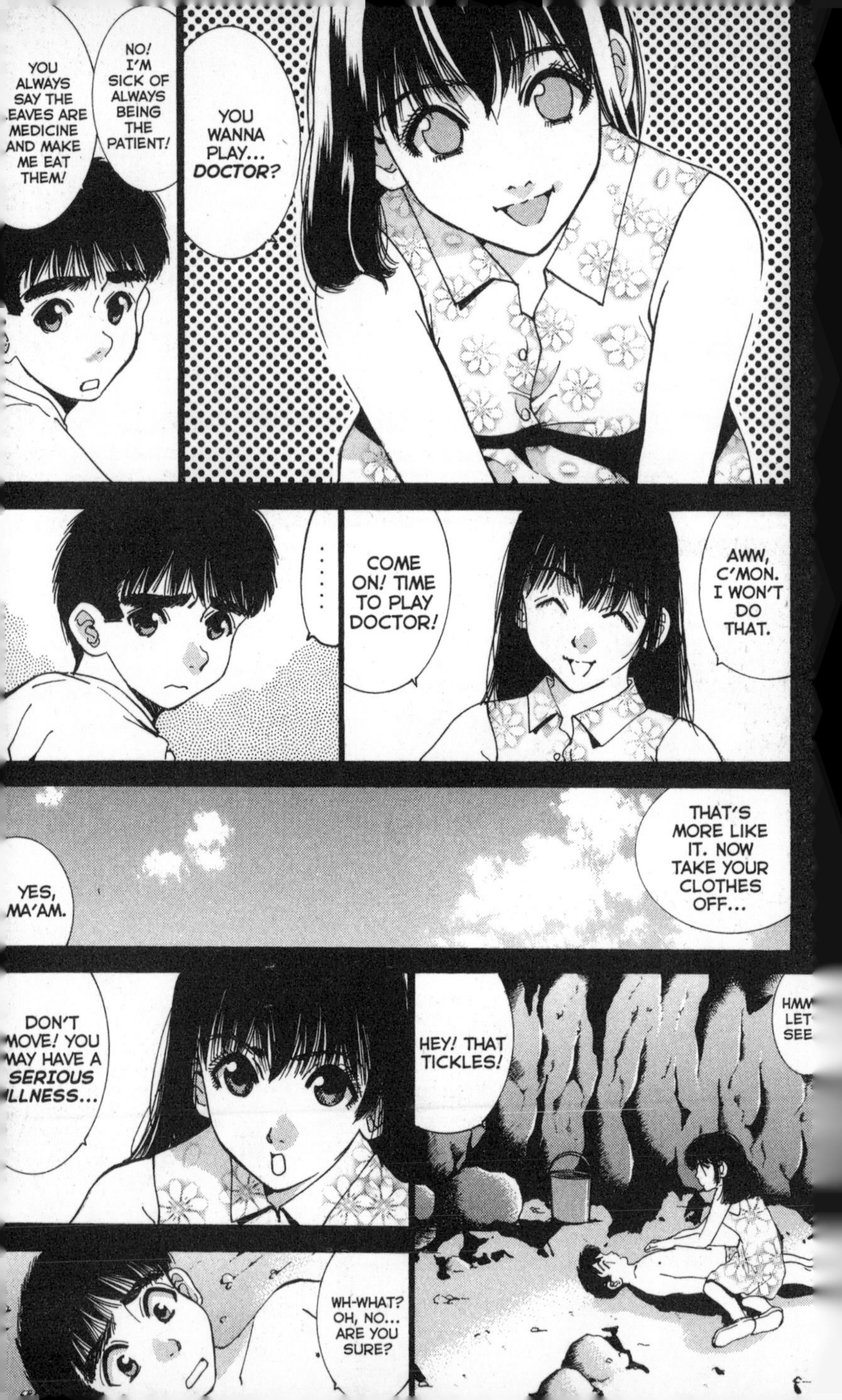
YOU WANNA PLAY... DOCTOR?
NO! I'M SICK OF ALWAYS BEING THE PATIENT!
YOU ALWAYS SAY THE EAVES ARE MEDICINE AND MAKE ME EAT THEM!
AWW, C'MON. I WON'T DO THAT.
COME ON! TIME TO PLAY DOCTOR!
......
THAT'S MORE LIKE IT. NOW TAKE YOUR CLOTHES OFF...
YES, MA'AM.
HMM LET SEE
HEY! THAT TICKLES!
DON'T MOVE! YOU MAY HAVE A SERIOUS LLNESS...
WH-WHAT? OH, NO... ARE YOU SURE?

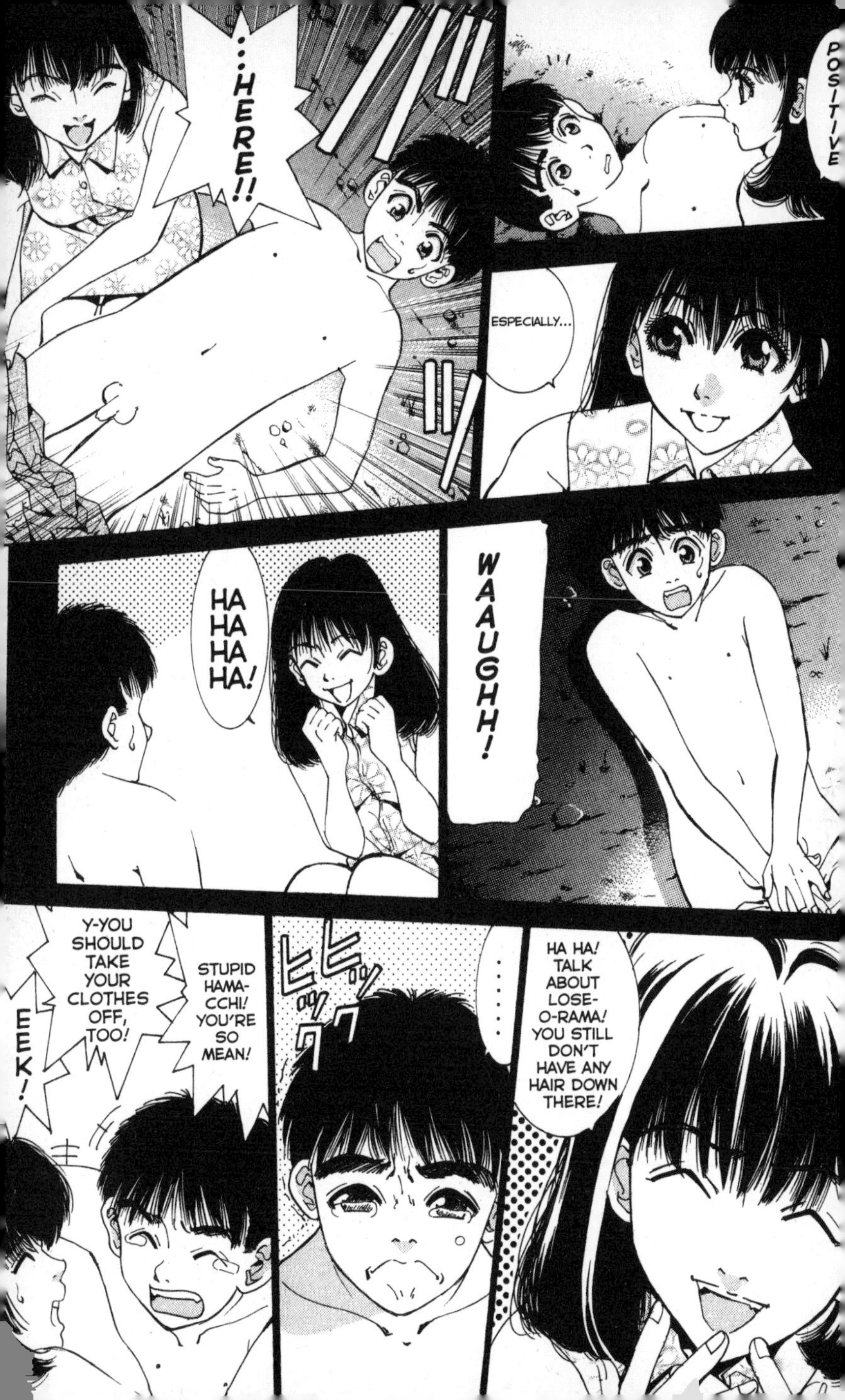
POSITIVE
ESPECIALLY...
...HERE!!
WAAAUGHH!
HA HA HA HA!
HA HA! TALK ABOUT LOSE-O-RAMA! YOU STILL DON'T HAVE ANY HAIR DOWN THERE!
......
STUPID HAMACCHI! YOU'RE SO MEAN!
Y-YOU SHOULD TAKE YOUR CLOTHES OFF, TOO!
EEK!

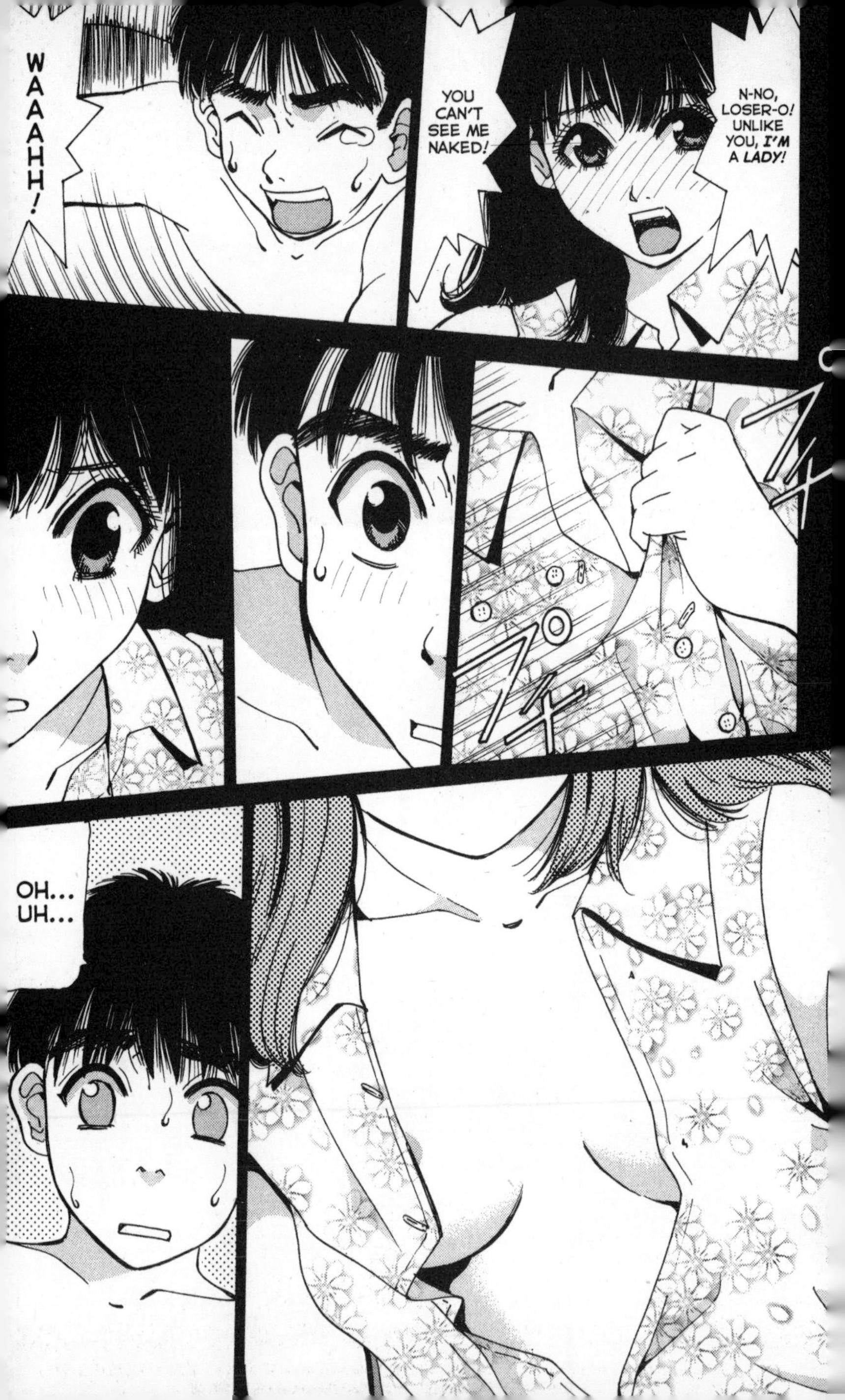
N-NO, LOSER-O! UNLIKE YOU, I'M A LADY!
YOU CAN'T SEE ME NAKED!
WAAAAHH!
OH... UH...

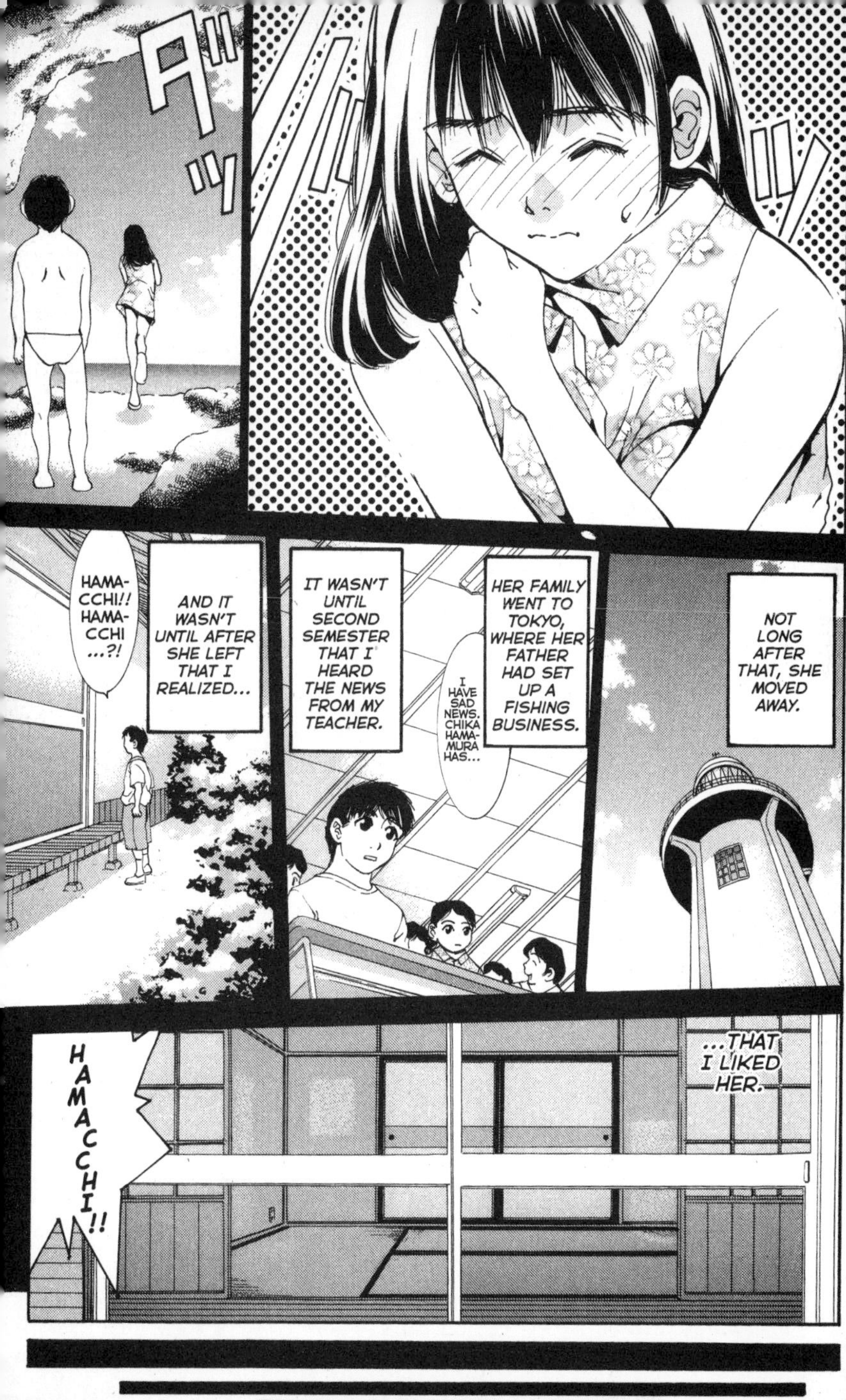

ダッ
NOT LONG AFTER THAT, SHE MOVED AWAY.
HER FAMILY WENT TO TOKYO, WHERE HER FATHER HAD SET UP A FISHING BUSINESS.
I HAVE SAD NEWS. CHIKA HAMAMURA HAS...
IT WASN'T UNTIL SECOND SEMESTER THAT I HEARD THE NEWS FROM MY TEACHER.
AND IT WASN'T UNTIL AFTER SHE LEFT THAT I REALIZED...
HAMACCHI!! HAMACCHI...?!
...THAT I LIKED HER.
HAMACCHI!!

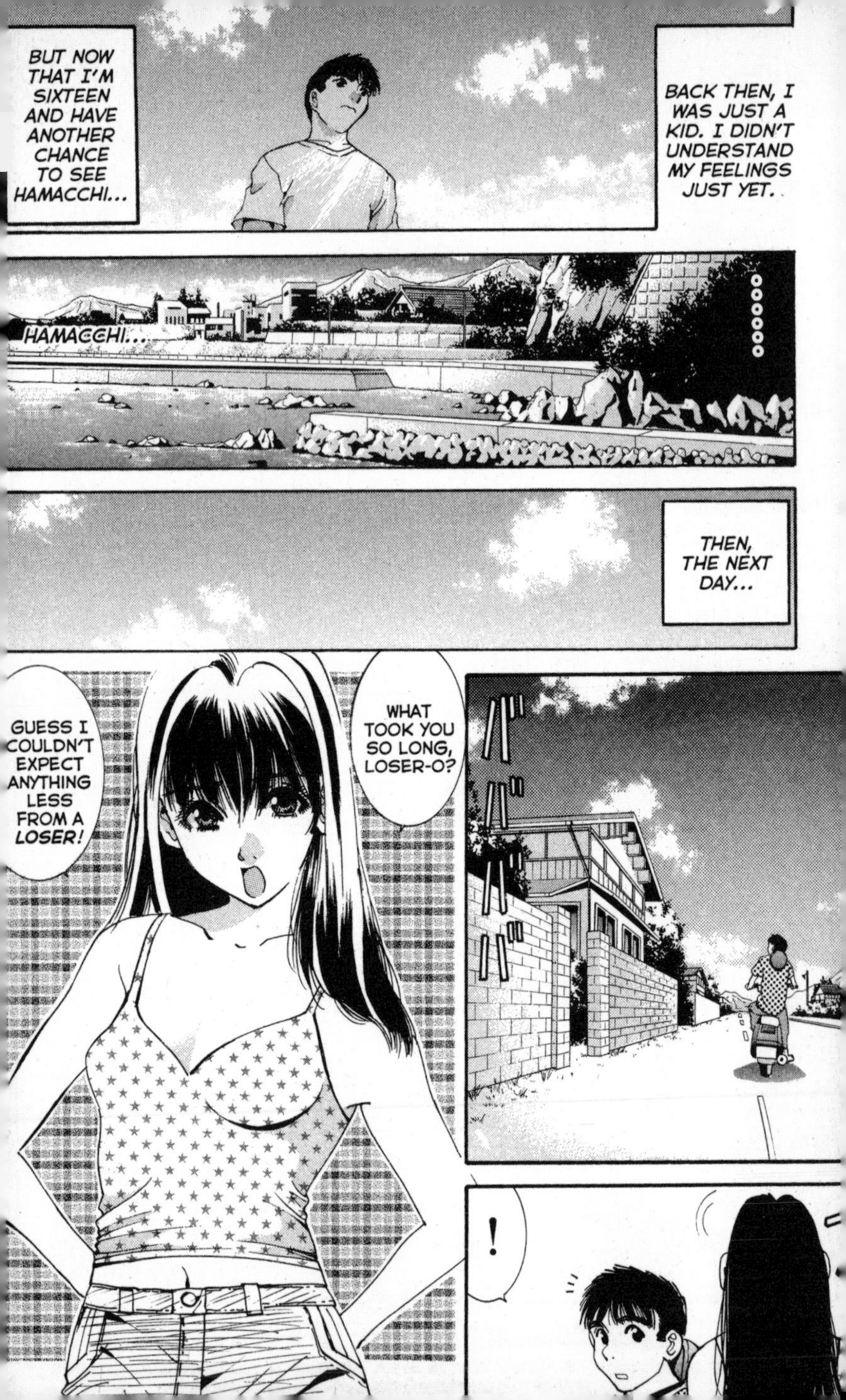
BACK THEN, I WAS JUST A KID. I DIDN'T UNDERSTAND MY FEELINGS JUST YET.
BUT NOW THAT I'M SIXTEEN AND HAVE ANOTHER CHANCE TO SEE HAMACCHI...
OOOOOO
HAMACCHI...
THEN, THE NEXT DAY...
WHAT TOOK YOU SO LONG, LOSER-O?
GUESS I COULDN'T EXPECT ANYTHING LESS FROM A LOSER!
!

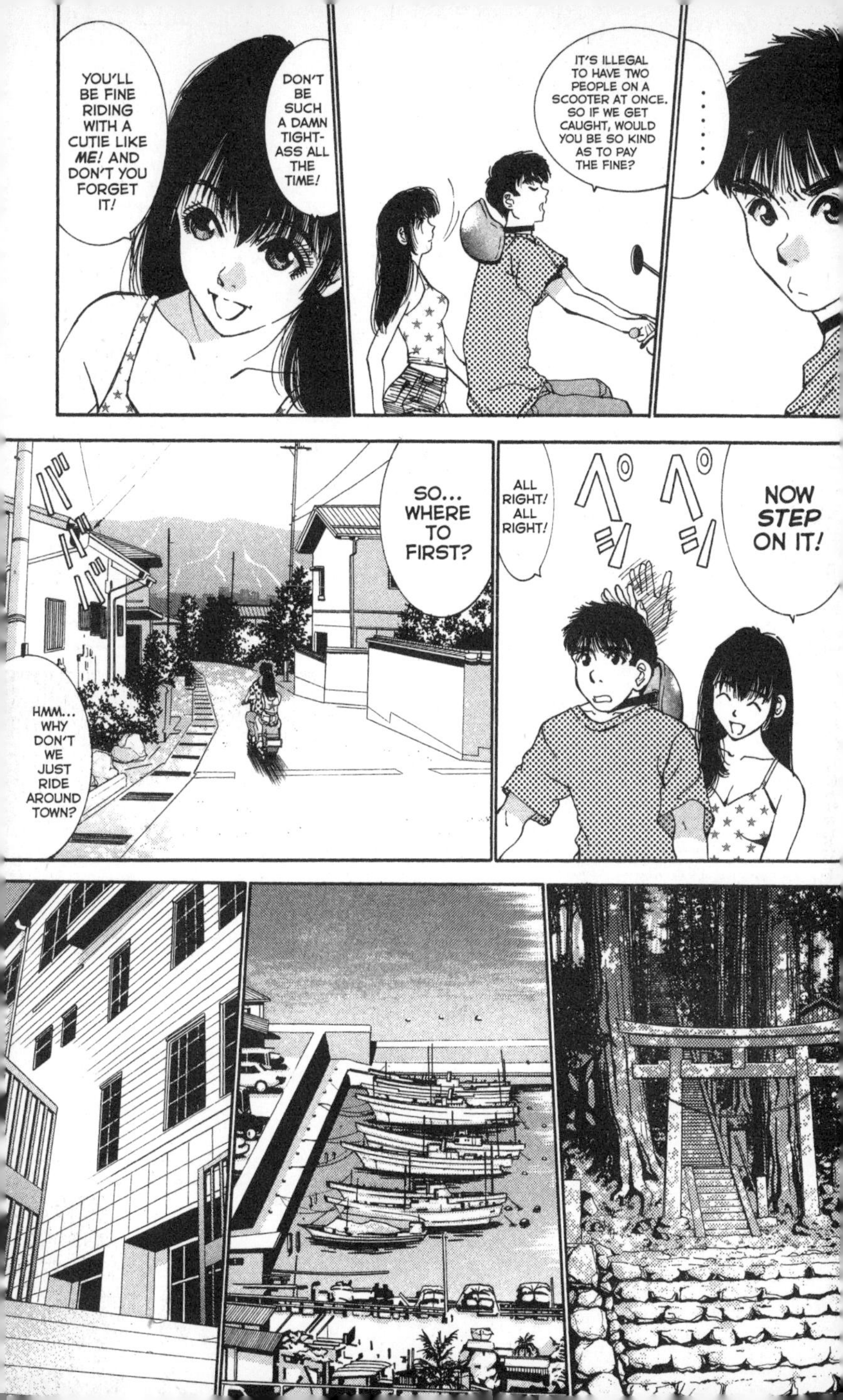
. . . . . .
IT'S ILLEGAL TO HAVE TWO PEOPLE ON A SCOOTER AT ONCE. SO IF WE GET CAUGHT, WOULD YOU BE SO KIND AS TO PAY THE FINE?
DON'T BE SUCH A DAMN TIGHT-ASS ALL THE TIME!
YOU'LL BE FINE RIDING WITH A CUTIE LIKE *ME!* AND DON'T YOU FORGET IT!
NOW *STEP* ON IT!
ALL RIGHT! ALL RIGHT!
SO... WHERE TO FIRST?
HMM... WHY DON'T WE JUST RIDE AROUND TOWN?

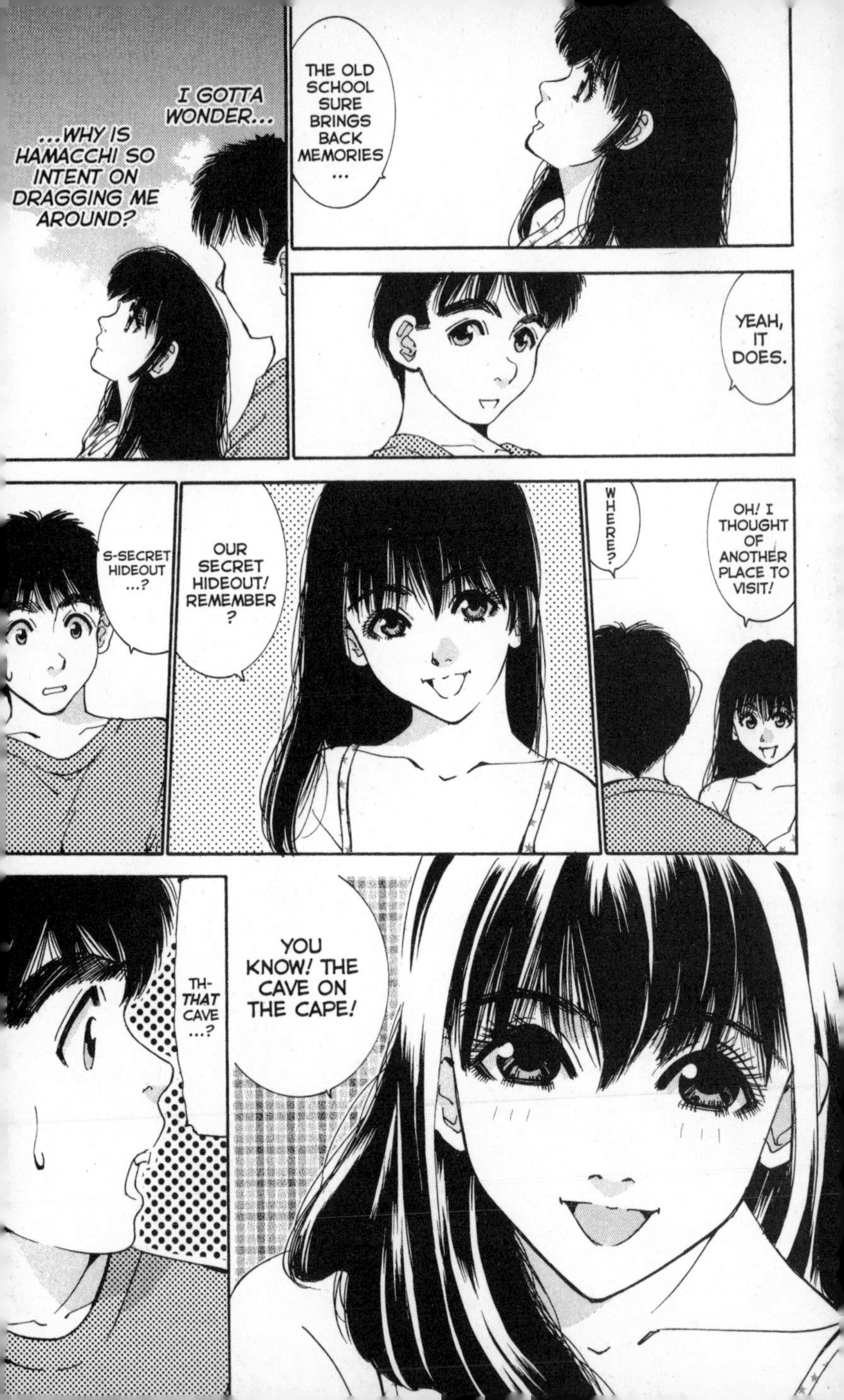
THE OLD SCHOOL SURE BRINGS BACK MEMORIES...
YEAH, IT DOES.
I GOTTA WONDER...
...WHY IS HAMACCHI SO INTENT ON DRAGGING ME AROUND?
OH! I THOUGHT OF ANOTHER PLACE TO VISIT!
WHERE?
OUR SECRET HIDEOUT! REMEMBER?
S-SECRET HIDEOUT...?
YOU KNOW! THE CAVE ON THE CAPE!
TH-*THAT* CAVE...?

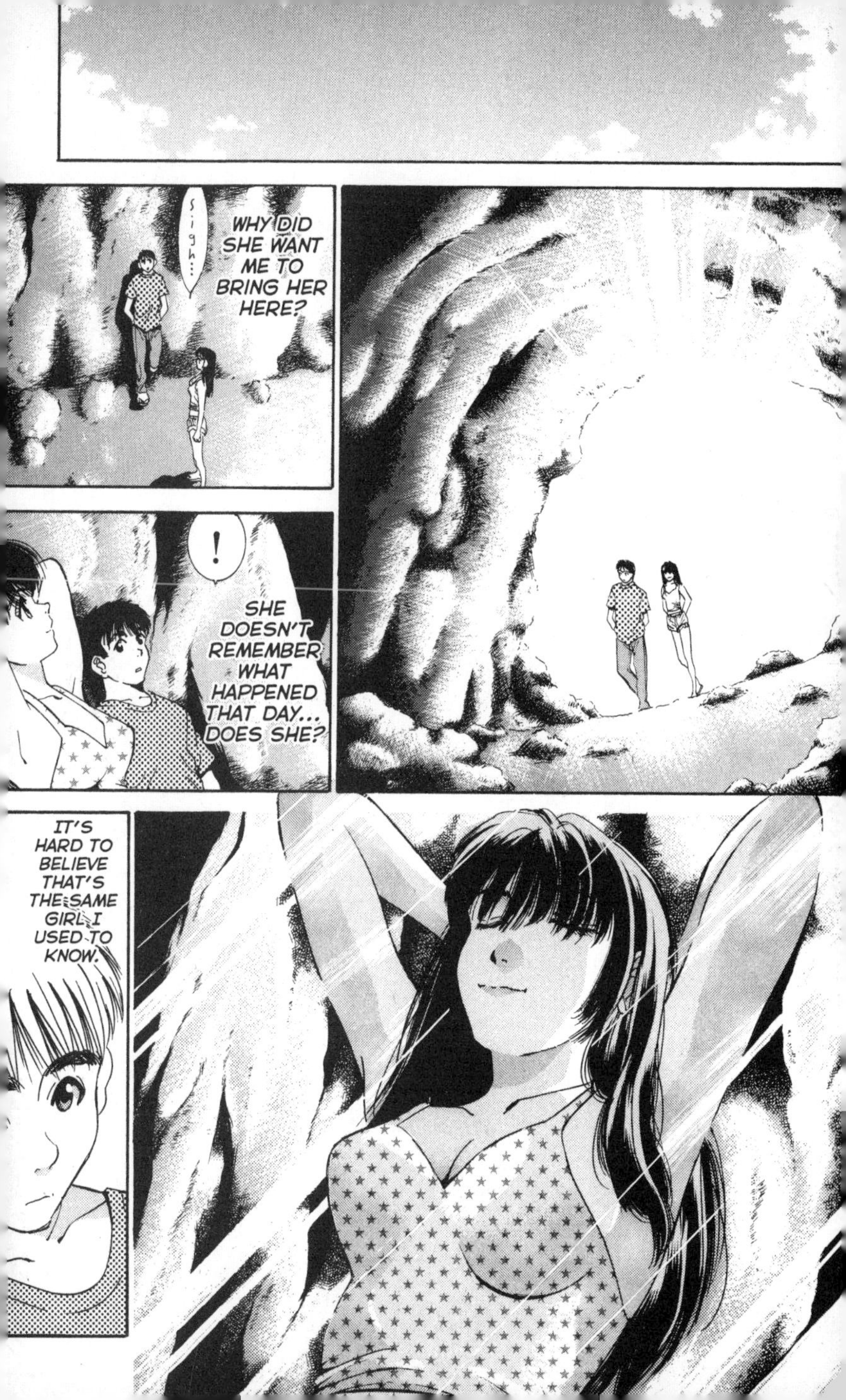
sigh...
WHY DID SHE WANT ME TO BRING HER HERE?
!
SHE DOESN'T REMEMBER WHAT HAPPENED THAT DAY... DOES SHE?
IT'S HARD TO BELIEVE THAT'S THE SAME GIRL I USED TO KNOW.

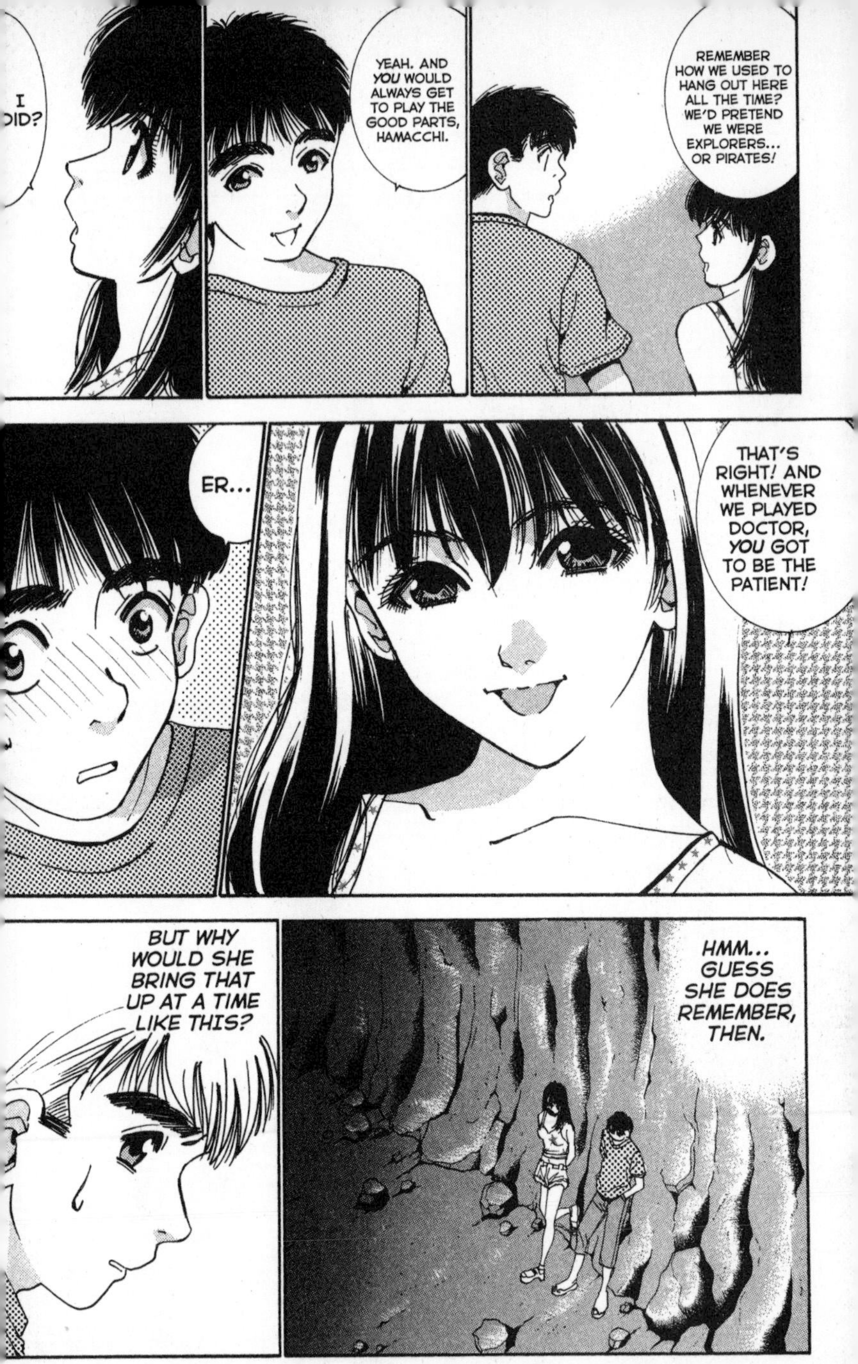
REMEMBER HOW WE USED TO HANG OUT HERE ALL THE TIME? WE'D PRETEND WE WERE EXPLORERS... OR PIRATES!
YEAH. AND *YOU* WOULD ALWAYS GET TO PLAY THE GOOD PARTS, HAMACCHI.
I DID?
THAT'S RIGHT! AND WHENEVER WE PLAYED DOCTOR, *YOU* GOT TO BE THE PATIENT!
ER...
HMM... GUESS SHE DOES REMEMBER, THEN.
BUT WHY WOULD SHE BRING THAT UP AT A TIME LIKE THIS?

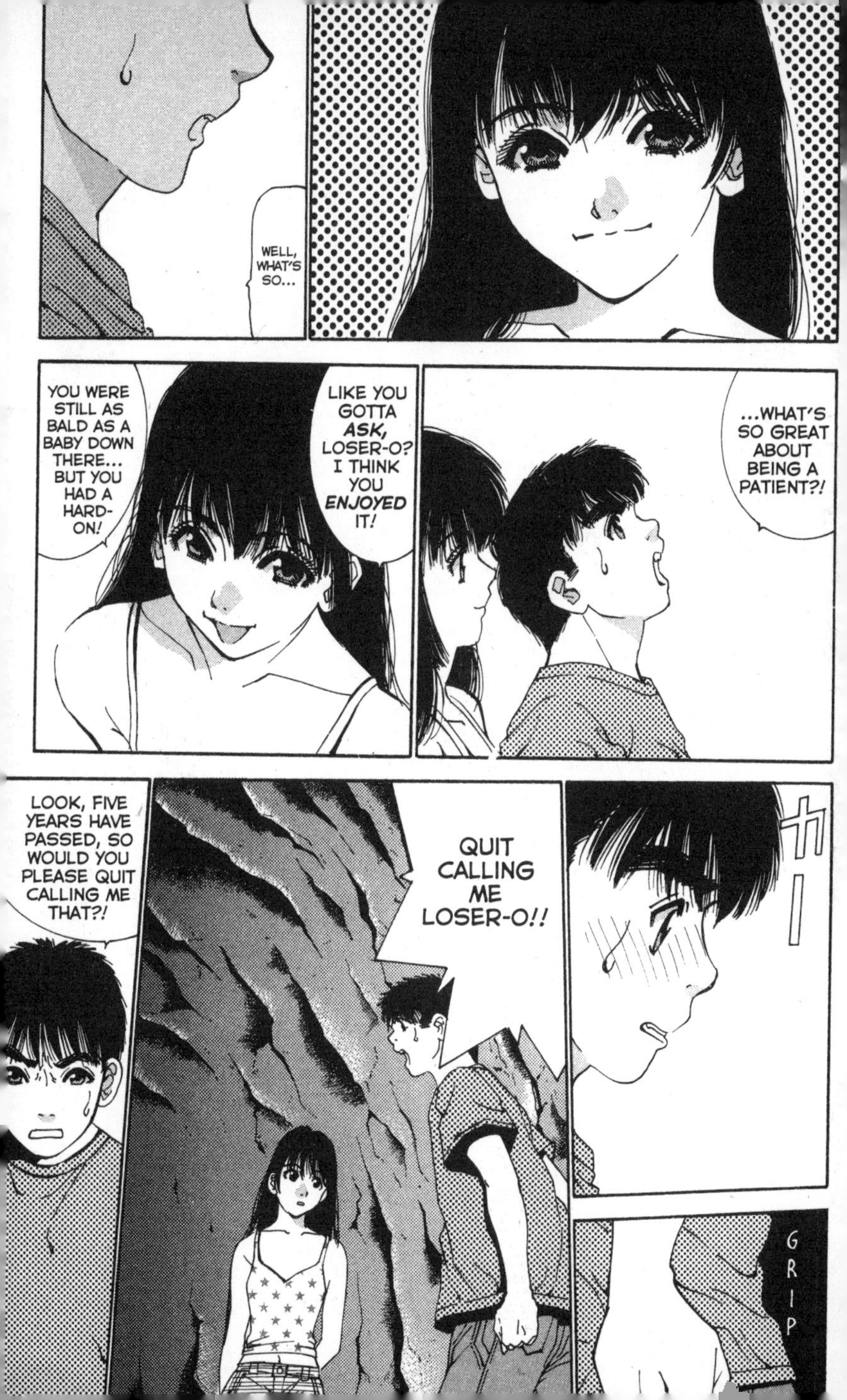
WELL, WHAT'S SO...
...WHAT'S SO GREAT ABOUT BEING A PATIENT?!
LIKE YOU GOTTA ASK, LOSER-O? I THINK YOU ENJOYED IT!
YOU WERE STILL AS BALD AS A BABY DOWN THERE... BUT YOU HAD A HARD-ON!
カー
GRIP
QUIT CALLING ME LOSER-O!!
LOOK, FIVE YEARS HAVE PASSED, SO WOULD YOU PLEASE QUIT CALLING ME THAT?!

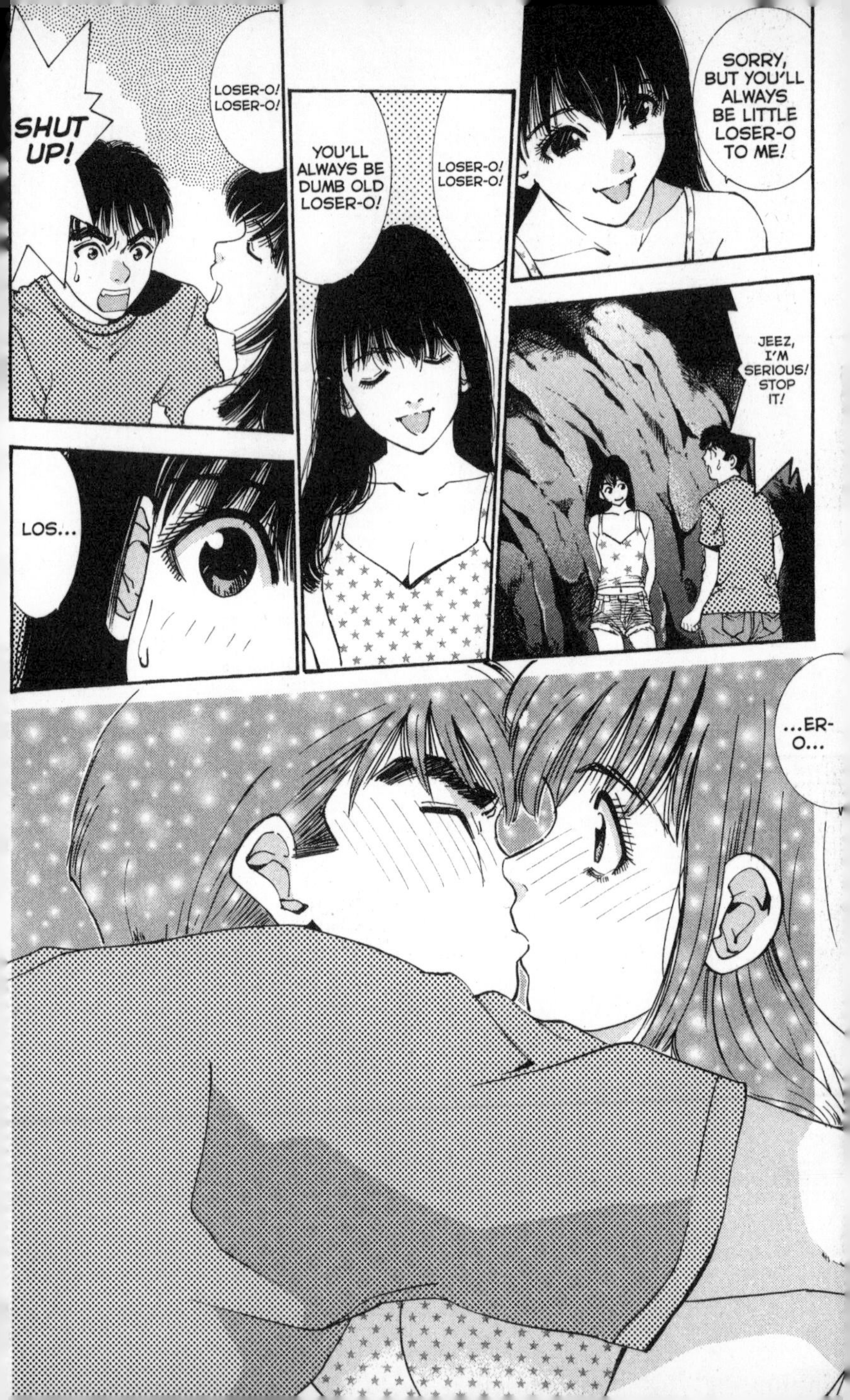
SORRY, BUT YOU'LL ALWAYS BE LITTLE LOSER-O TO ME!
JEEZ, I'M SERIOUS! STOP IT!
LOSER-O! LOSER-O!
YOU'LL ALWAYS BE DUMB OLD LOSER-O!
LOSER-O! LOSER-O!
SHUT UP!
LOS...
...ER-O...

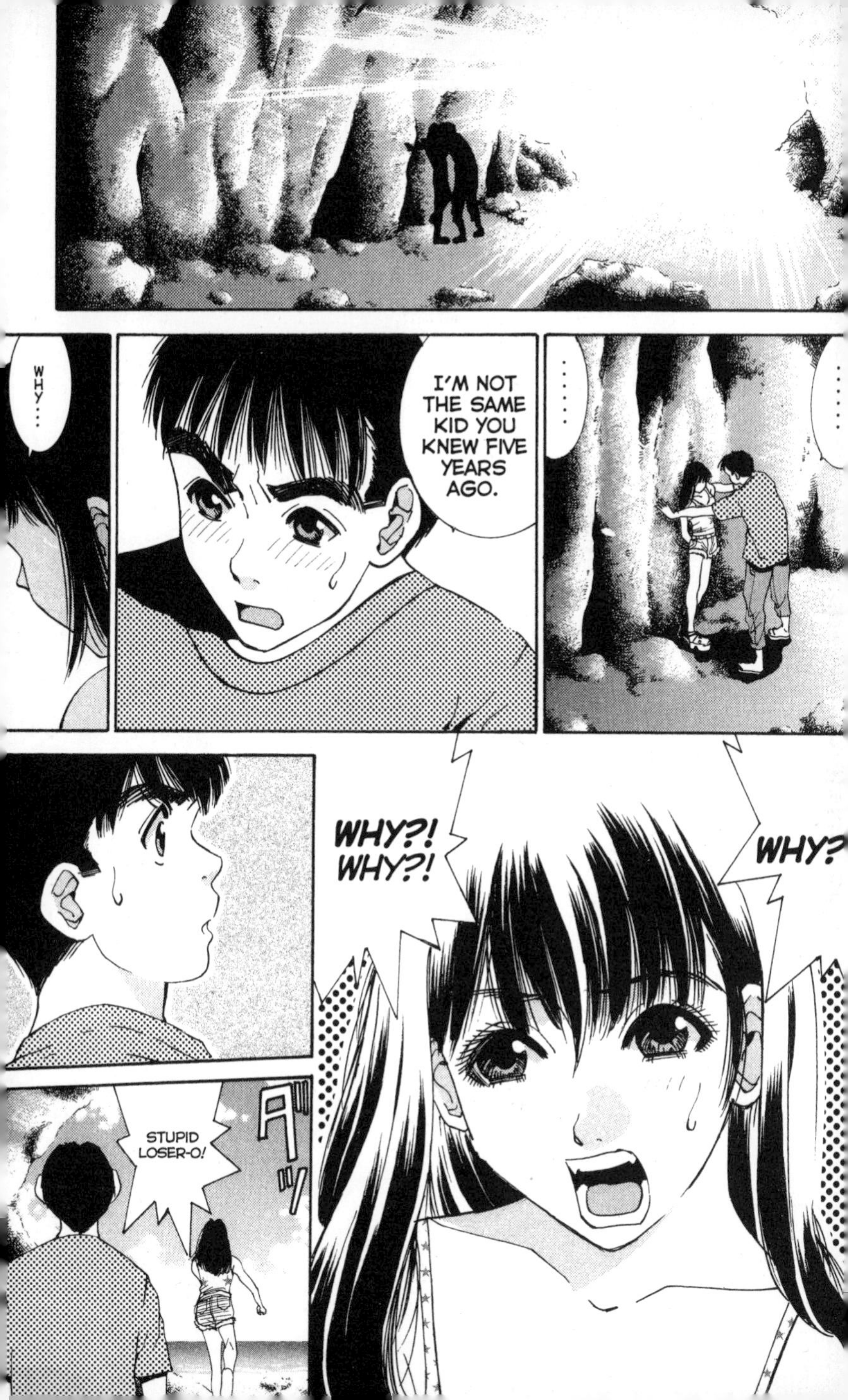
......
......
I'M NOT THE SAME KID YOU KNEW FIVE YEARS AGO.
WHY...
WHY?
WHY?! WHY?!
STUPID LOSER-O!

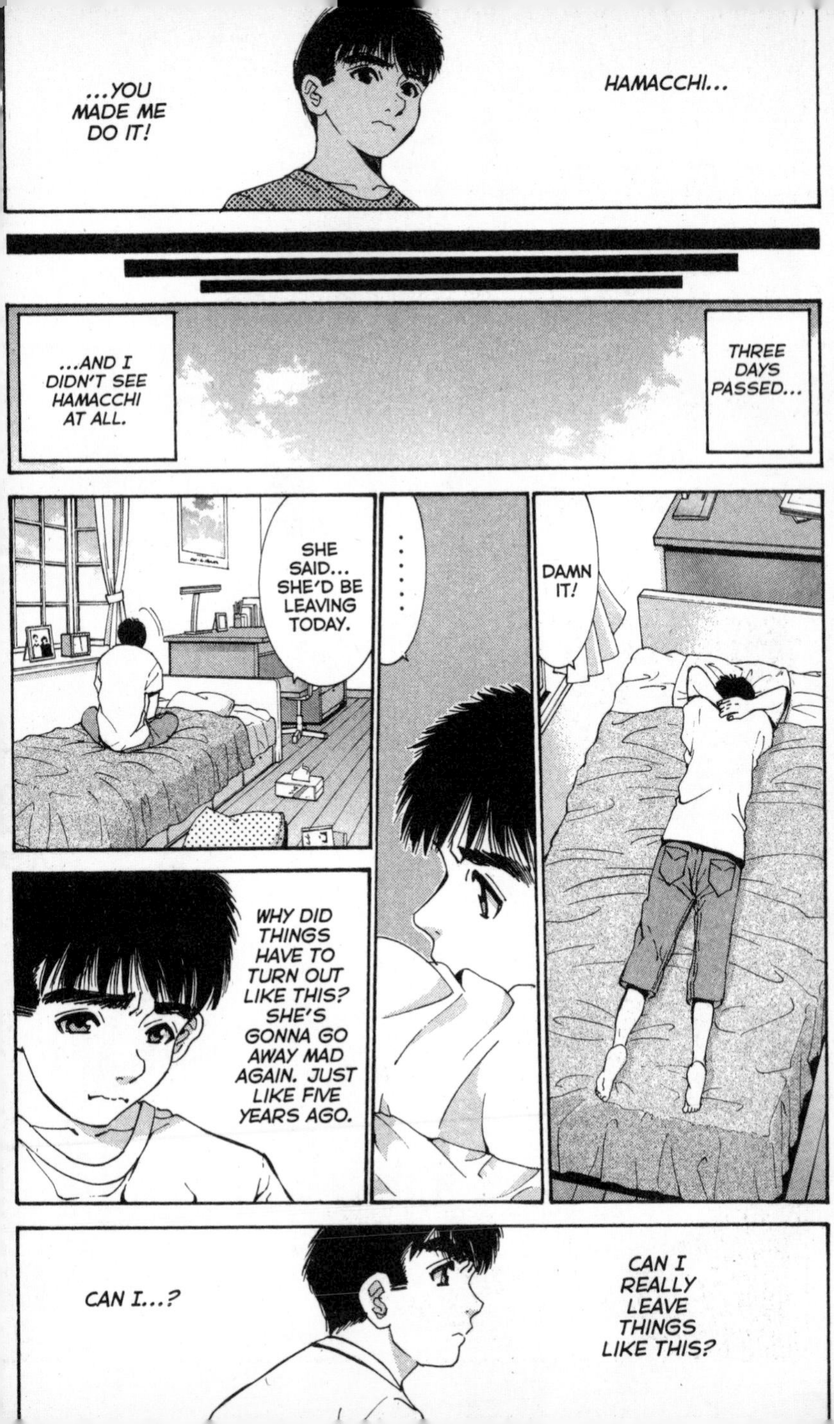
HAMACCHI...
...YOU MADE ME DO IT!
THREE DAYS PASSED...
...AND I DIDN'T SEE HAMACCHI AT ALL.
DAMN IT!
......
SHE SAID... SHE'D BE LEAVING TODAY.
WHY DID THINGS HAVE TO TURN OUT LIKE THIS? SHE'S GONNA GO AWAY MAD AGAIN. JUST LIKE FIVE YEARS AGO.
CAN I REALLY LEAVE THINGS LIKE THIS?
CAN I...?

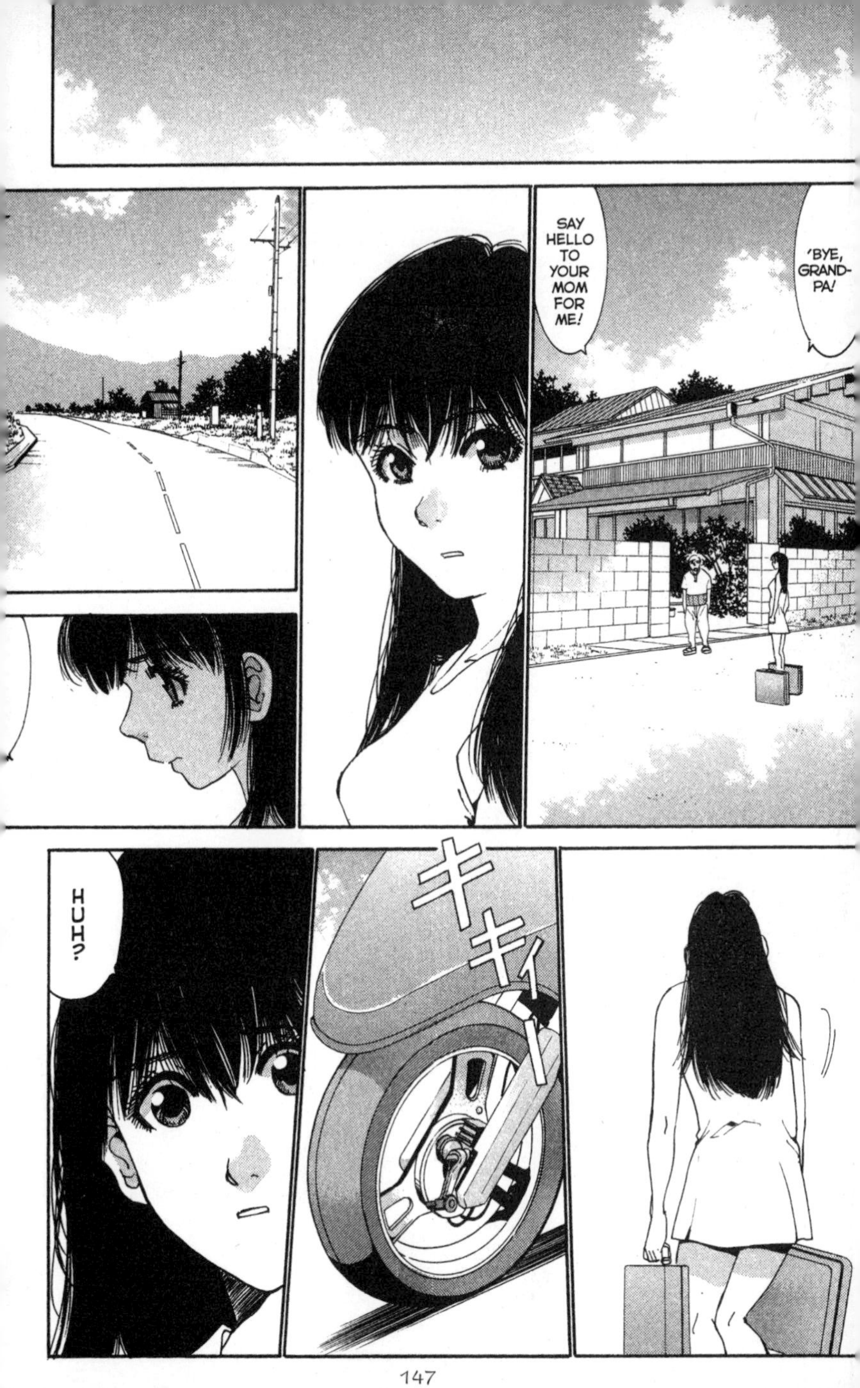
'BYE, GRAND-PA!
SAY HELLO TO YOUR MOM FOR ME!
キキィー
HUH?

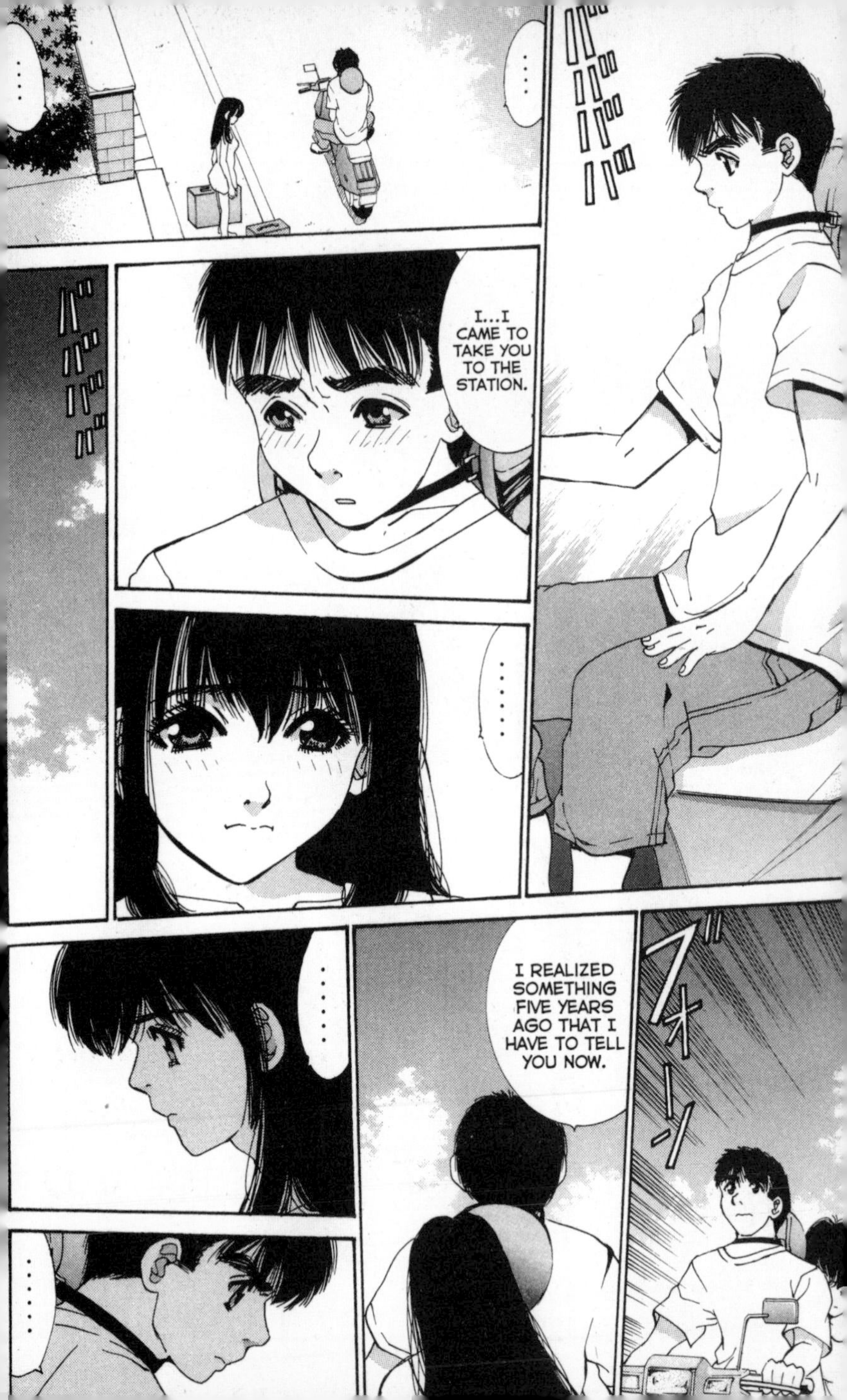

......
......
I...I CAME TO TAKE YOU TO THE STATION.
......
I REALIZED SOMETHING FIVE YEARS AGO THAT I HAVE TO TELL YOU NOW.
......
......

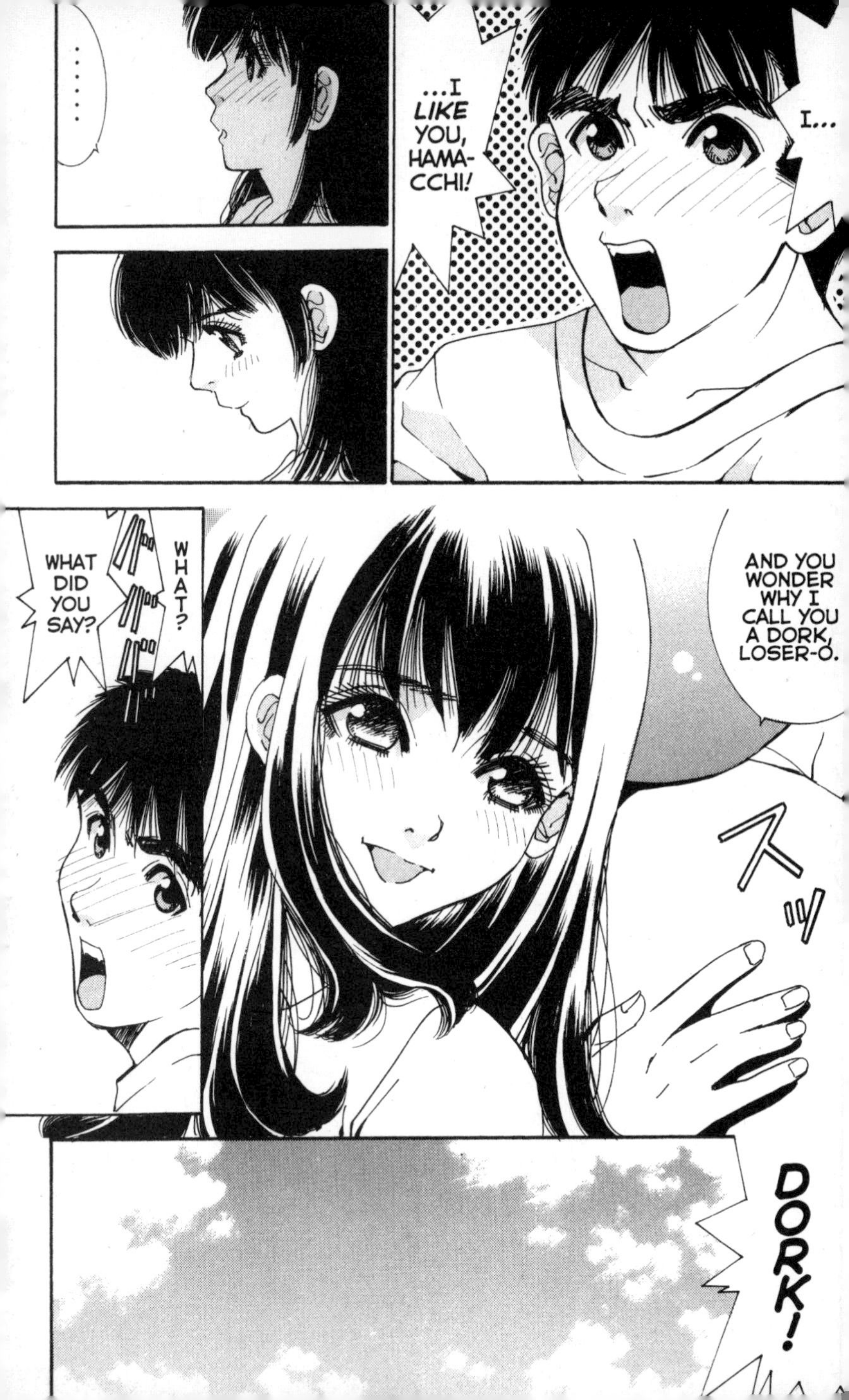
I...
...I LIKE YOU, HAMACCHI!
......
AND YOU WONDER WHY I CALL YOU A DORK, LOSER-O.
スッ
WHAT?
WHAT DID YOU SAY?
DORK!

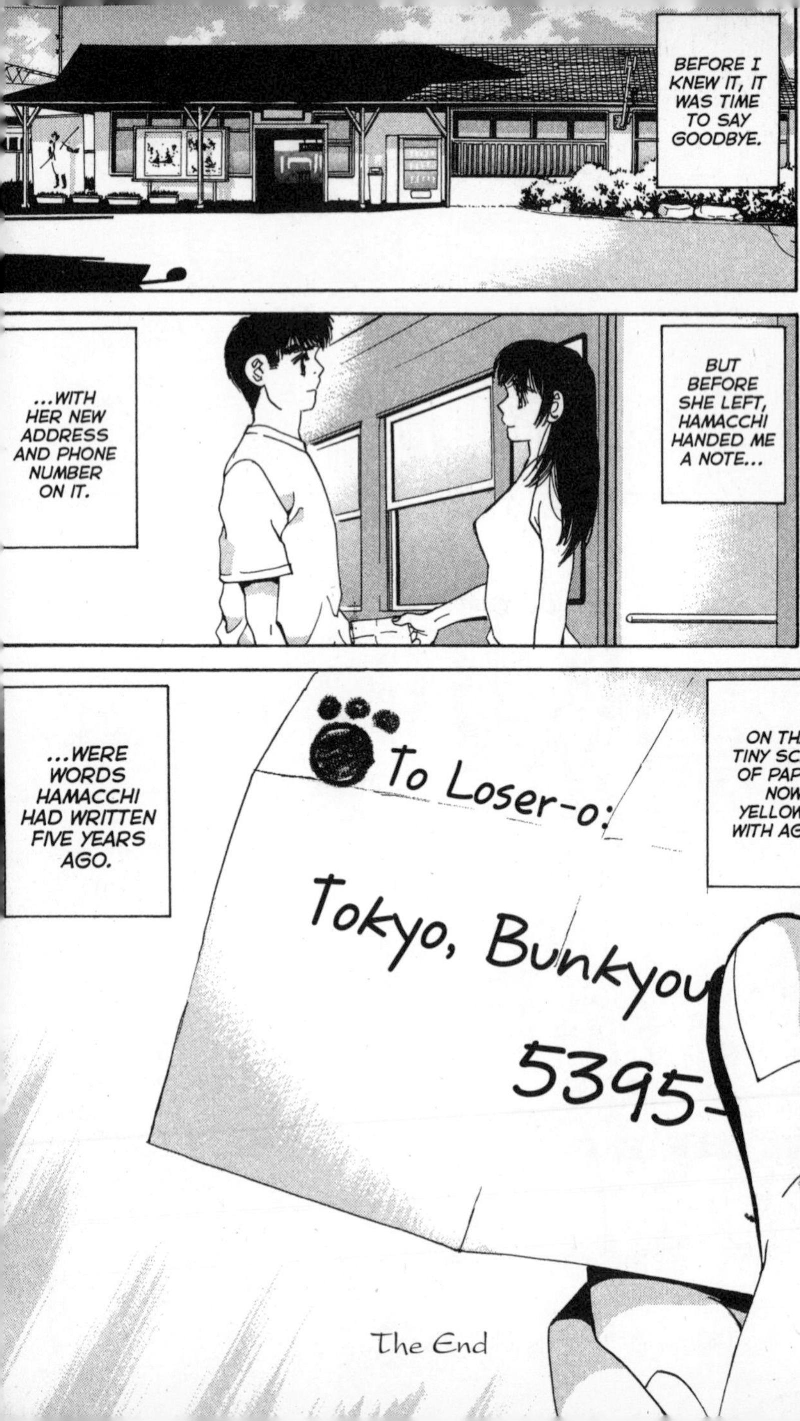
BEFORE I KNEW IT, IT WAS TIME TO SAY GOODBYE.
BUT BEFORE SHE LEFT, HAMACCHI HANDED ME A NOTE...
...WITH HER NEW ADDRESS AND PHONE NUMBER ON IT.
ON THAT TINY SCRAP OF PAPER, NOW YELLOWED WITH AGE...
...WERE WORDS HAMACCHI HAD WRITTEN FIVE YEARS AGO.
To Loser-o:
Tokyo, Bunkyou
5395-
The End

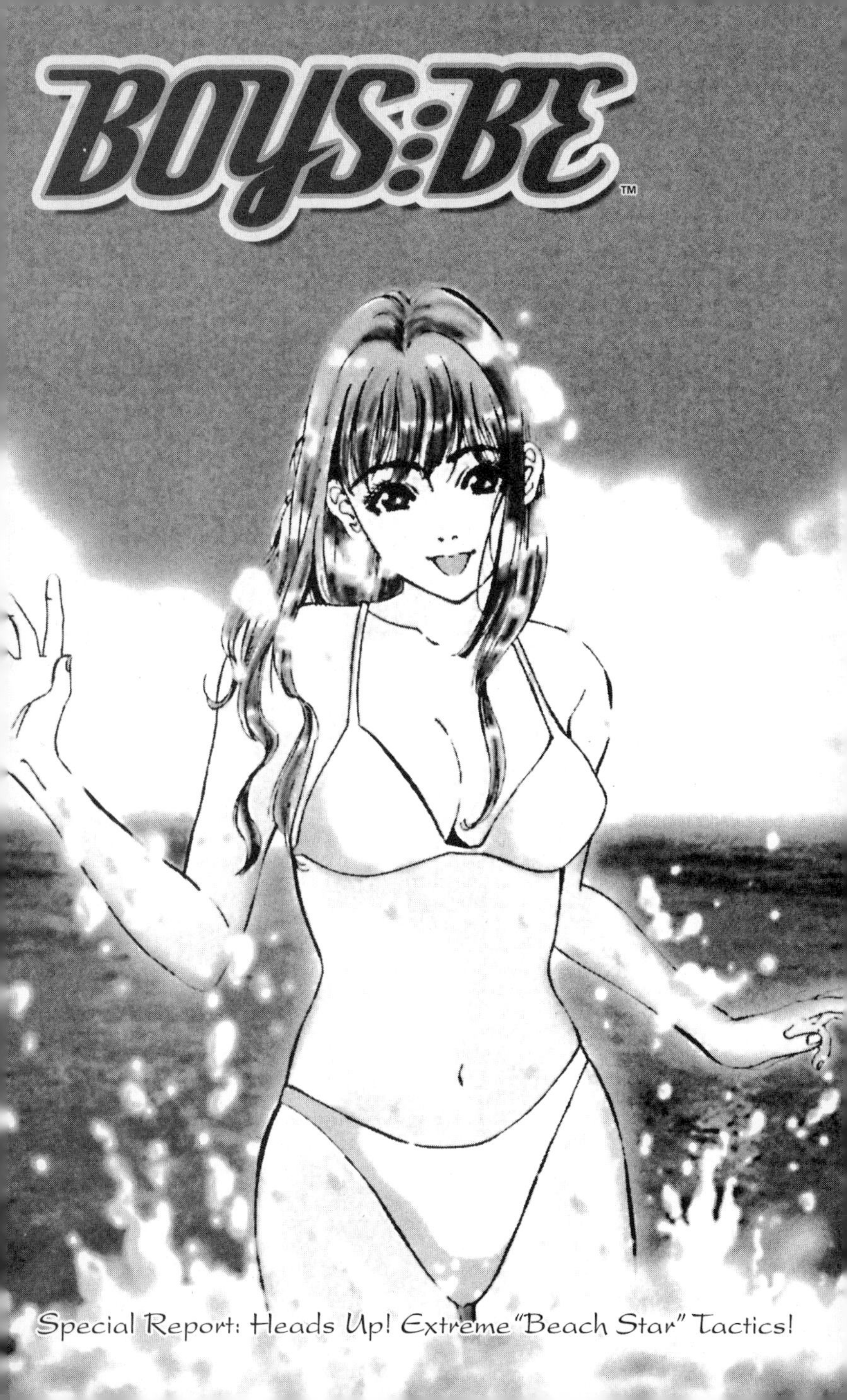
BOYS BE™
Special Report: Heads Up! Extreme "Beach Star" Tactics!

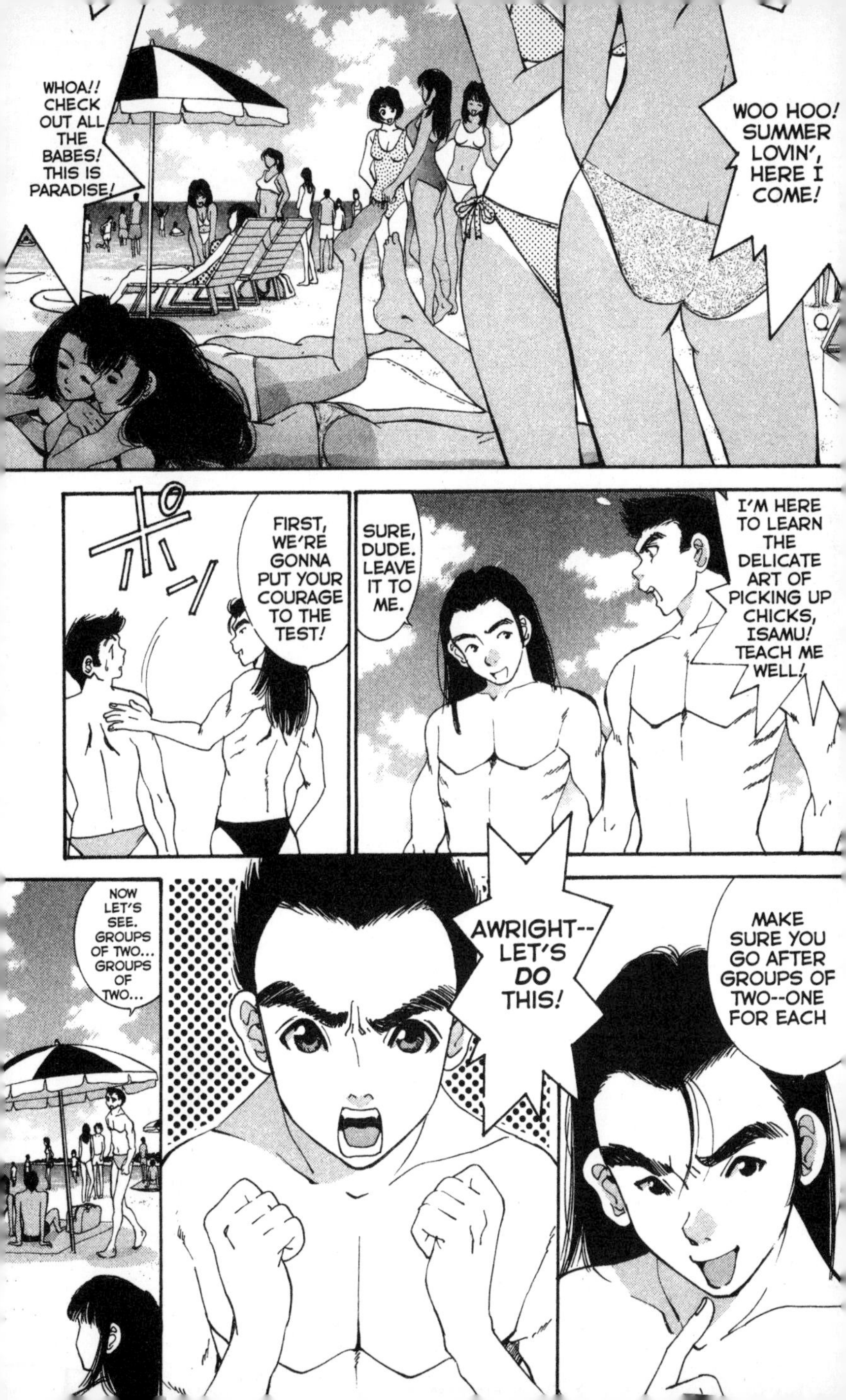
WOO HOO! SUMMER LOVIN', HERE I COME!
WHOA!! CHECK OUT ALL THE BABES! THIS IS PARADISE!
I'M HERE TO LEARN THE DELICATE ART OF PICKING UP CHICKS, ISAMU! TEACH ME WELL!
SURE, DUDE. LEAVE IT TO ME.
FIRST, WE'RE GONNA PUT YOUR COURAGE TO THE TEST!
MAKE SURE YOU GO AFTER GROUPS OF TWO--ONE FOR EACH
AWRIGHT-- LET'S *DO* THIS!
NOW LET'S SEE. GROUPS OF TWO... GROUPS OF TWO...

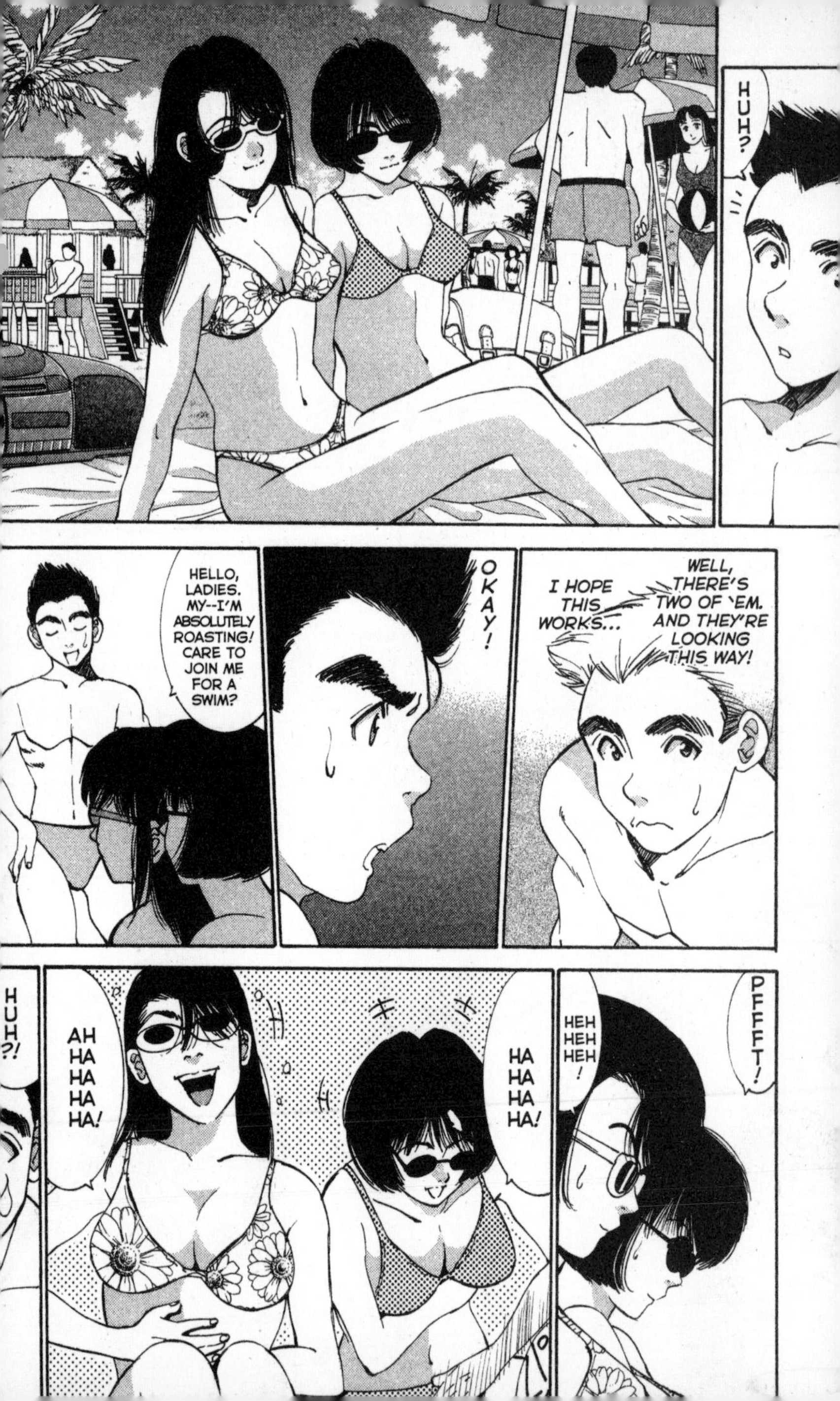
HUH?
WELL, THERE'S TWO OF 'EM. AND THEY'RE LOOKING THIS WAY!
I HOPE THIS WORKS...
OKAY!
HELLO, LADIES. MY--I'M ABSOLUTELY ROASTING! CARE TO JOIN ME FOR A SWIM?
PFFFT!
HEH HEH HEH!
HA HA HA HA HA!
AH HA HA HA HA HA!
HUH?!

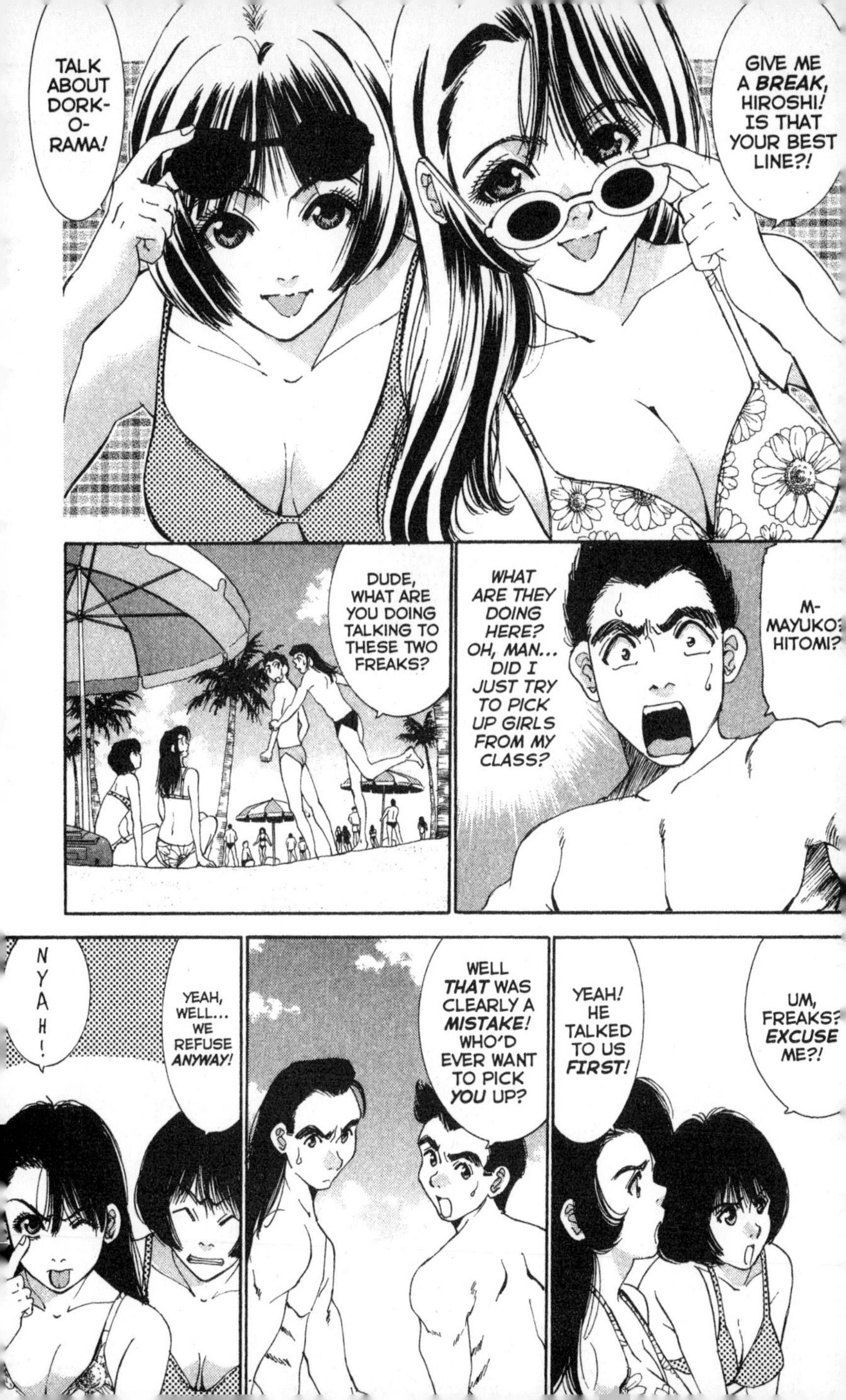
GIVE ME A *BREAK*, HIROSHI! IS THAT YOUR BEST LINE?!
TALK ABOUT DORK-O-RAMA!
M-MAYUKO? HITOMI?
WHAT ARE THEY DOING HERE? OH, MAN... DID I JUST TRY TO PICK UP GIRLS FROM MY CLASS?
DUDE, WHAT ARE YOU DOING TALKING TO THESE TWO FREAKS?
UM, FREAKS? *EXCUSE* ME?!
YEAH! HE TALKED TO US *FIRST*!
WELL *THAT* WAS CLEARLY A *MISTAKE*! WHO'D EVER WANT TO PICK *YOU* UP?
YEAH, WELL... WE REFUSE *ANYWAY*!
NYAH!

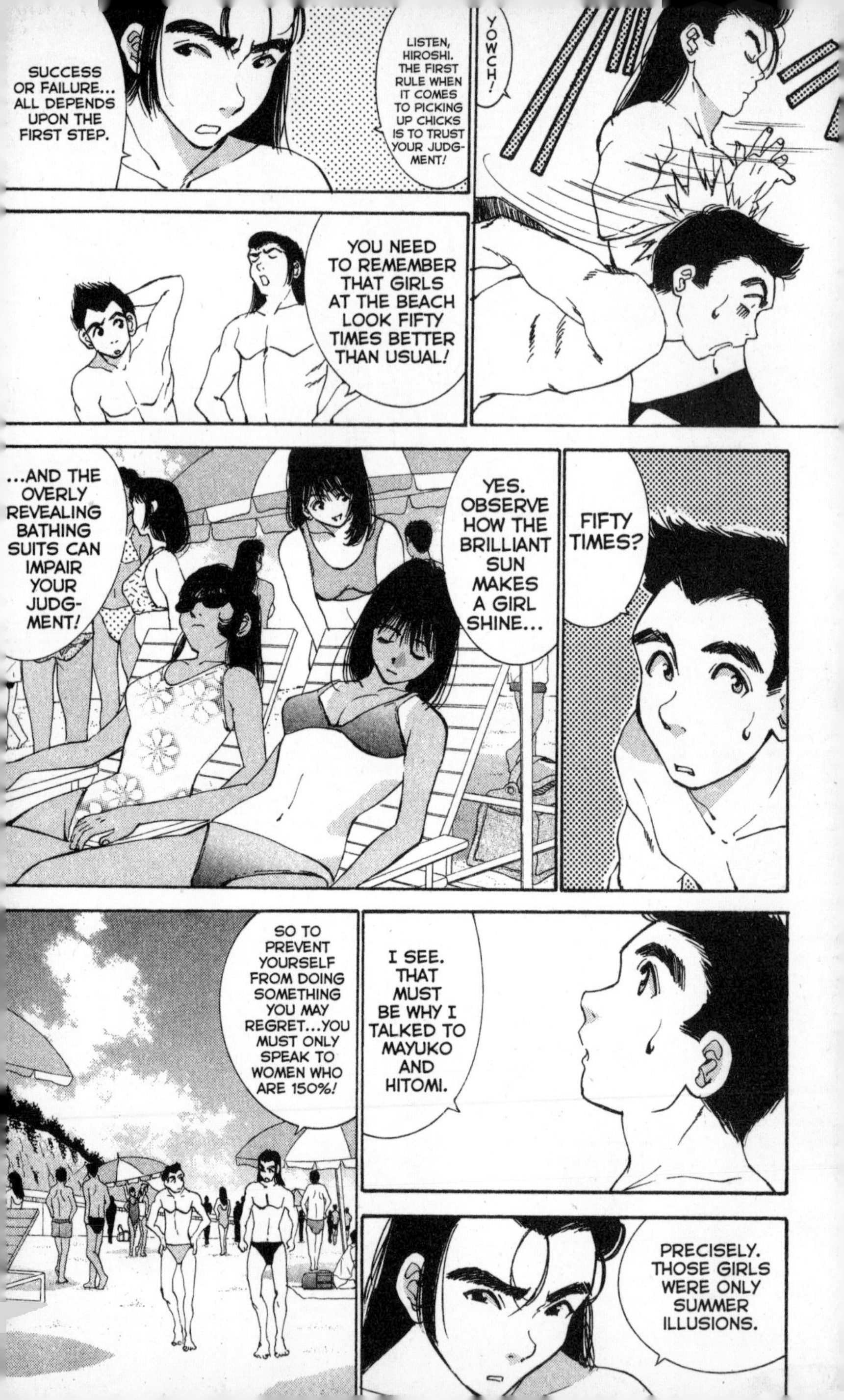
YOWCH!
LISTEN, HIROSHI. THE FIRST RULE WHEN IT COMES TO PICKING UP CHICKS IS TO TRUST YOUR JUDGMENT!
SUCCESS OR FAILURE... ALL DEPENDS UPON THE FIRST STEP.
YOU NEED TO REMEMBER THAT GIRLS AT THE BEACH LOOK FIFTY TIMES BETTER THAN USUAL!
FIFTY TIMES?
YES. OBSERVE HOW THE BRILLIANT SUN MAKES A GIRL SHINE...
...AND THE OVERLY REVEALING BATHING SUITS CAN IMPAIR YOUR JUDGMENT!
I SEE. THAT MUST BE WHY I TALKED TO MAYUKO AND HITOMI.
PRECISELY. THOSE GIRLS WERE ONLY SUMMER ILLUSIONS.
SO TO PREVENT YOURSELF FROM DOING SOMETHING YOU MAY REGRET...YOU MUST ONLY SPEAK TO WOMEN WHO ARE 150%!

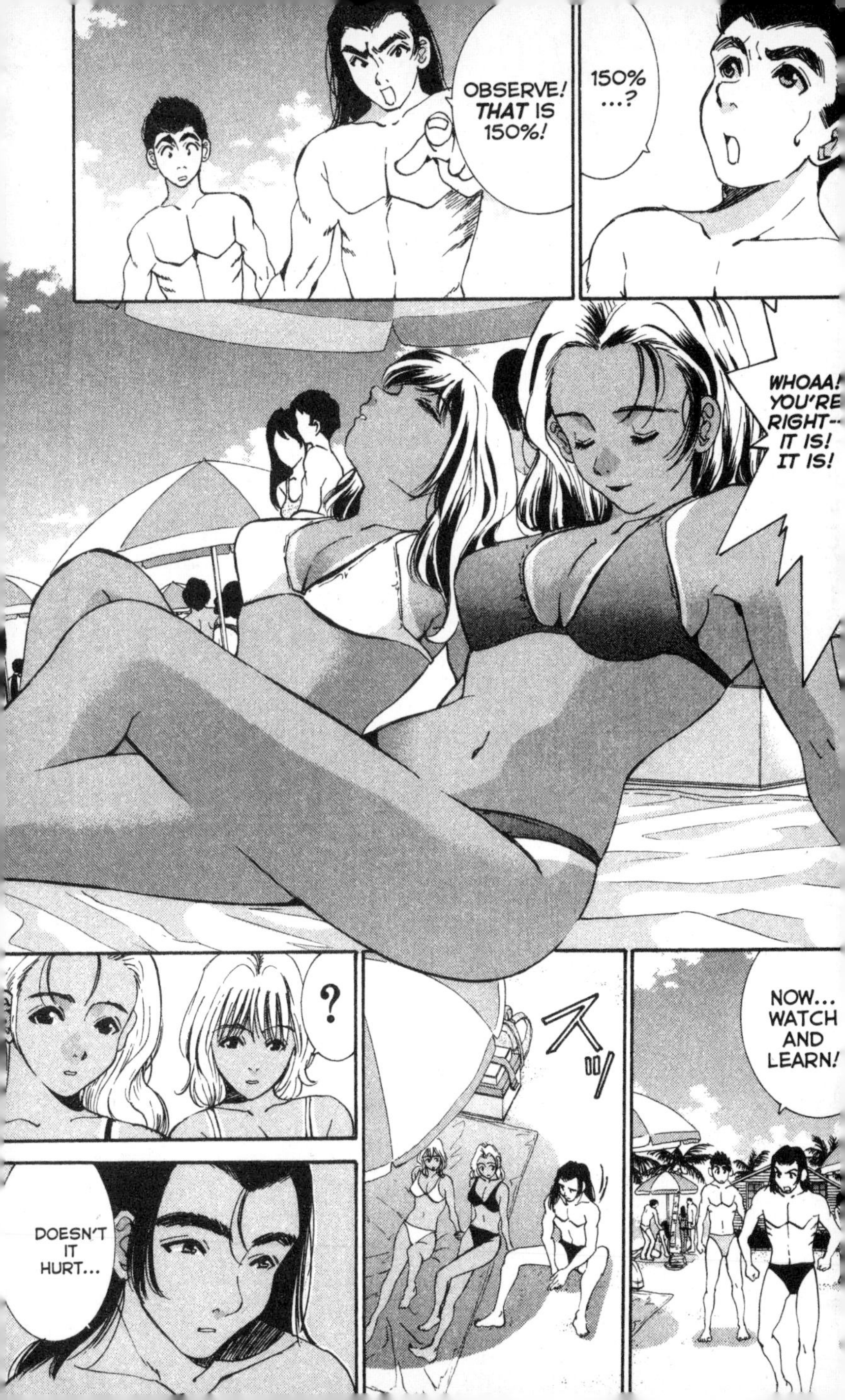
150% ...?
OBSERVE! THAT IS 150%!
WHOAA! YOU'RE RIGHT-- IT IS! IT IS!
NOW... WATCH AND LEARN!
?
DOESN'T IT HURT...

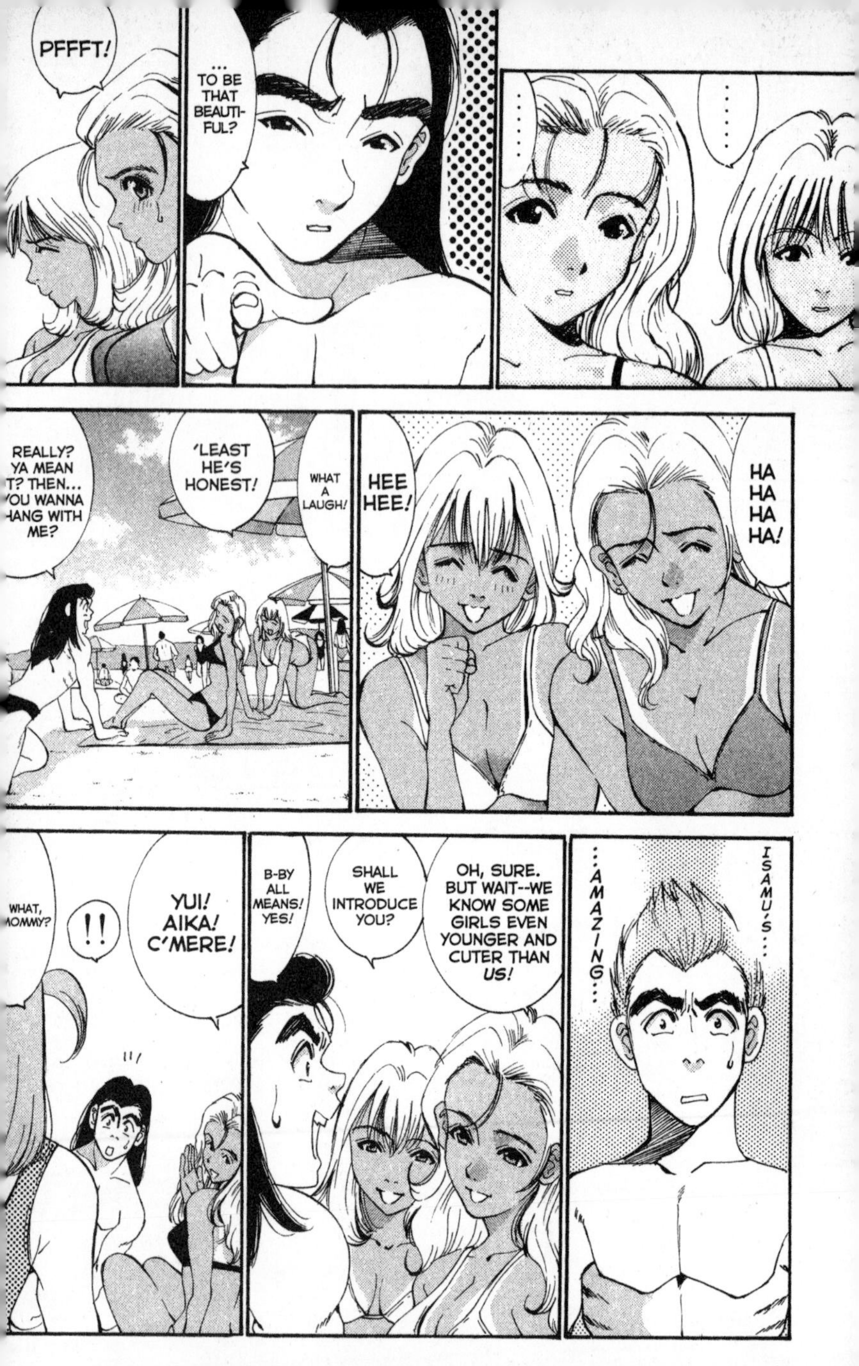
...
...
... TO BE THAT BEAUTI-FUL?
PFFFT!
HA HA HA HA!
HEE HEE!
WHAT A LAUGH!
'LEAST HE'S HONEST!
REALLY? YA MEAN T? THEN... OU WANNA HANG WITH ME?
ISAMU'S...
...AMAZING...
OH, SURE. BUT WAIT--WE KNOW SOME GIRLS EVEN YOUNGER AND CUTER THAN *US!*
SHALL WE INTRODUCE YOU?
B-BY ALL MEANS! YES!
YUI! AIKA! C'MERE!
!!
WHAT, OMMY?

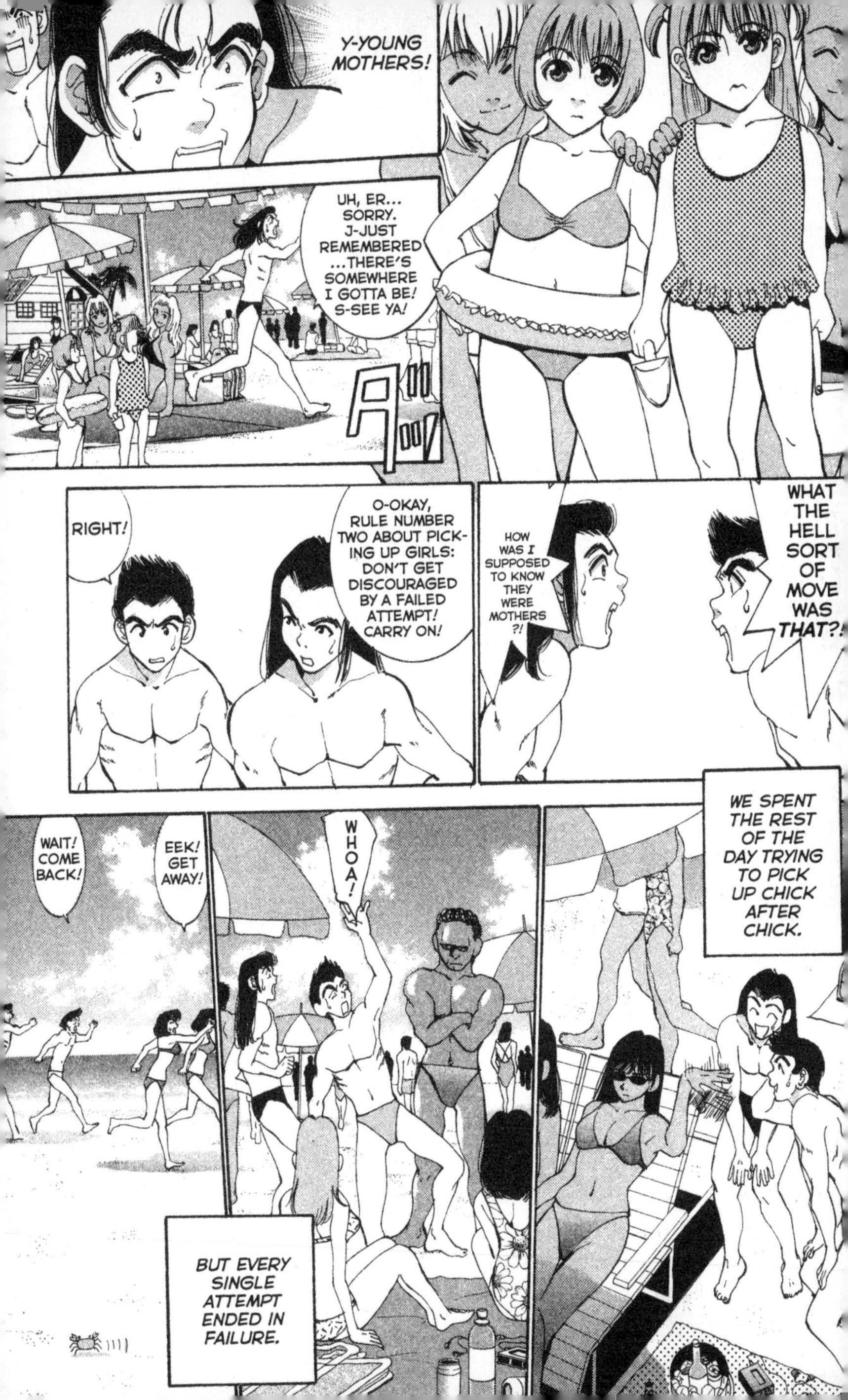
Y-YOUNG MOTHERS!
UH, ER... SORRY. J-JUST REMEMBERED ...THERE'S SOMEWHERE I GOTTA BE! S-SEE YA!
WHAT THE HELL SORT OF MOVE WAS *THAT*?!
HOW WAS *I* SUPPOSED TO KNOW THEY WERE MOTHERS ?!
O-OKAY, RULE NUMBER TWO ABOUT PICK-ING UP GIRLS: DON'T GET DISCOURAGED BY A FAILED ATTEMPT! CARRY ON!
RIGHT!
WE SPENT THE REST OF THE DAY TRYING TO PICK UP CHICK AFTER CHICK.
WHOA!
BUT EVERY SINGLE ATTEMPT ENDED IN FAILURE.
EEK! GET AWAY!
WAIT! COME BACK!

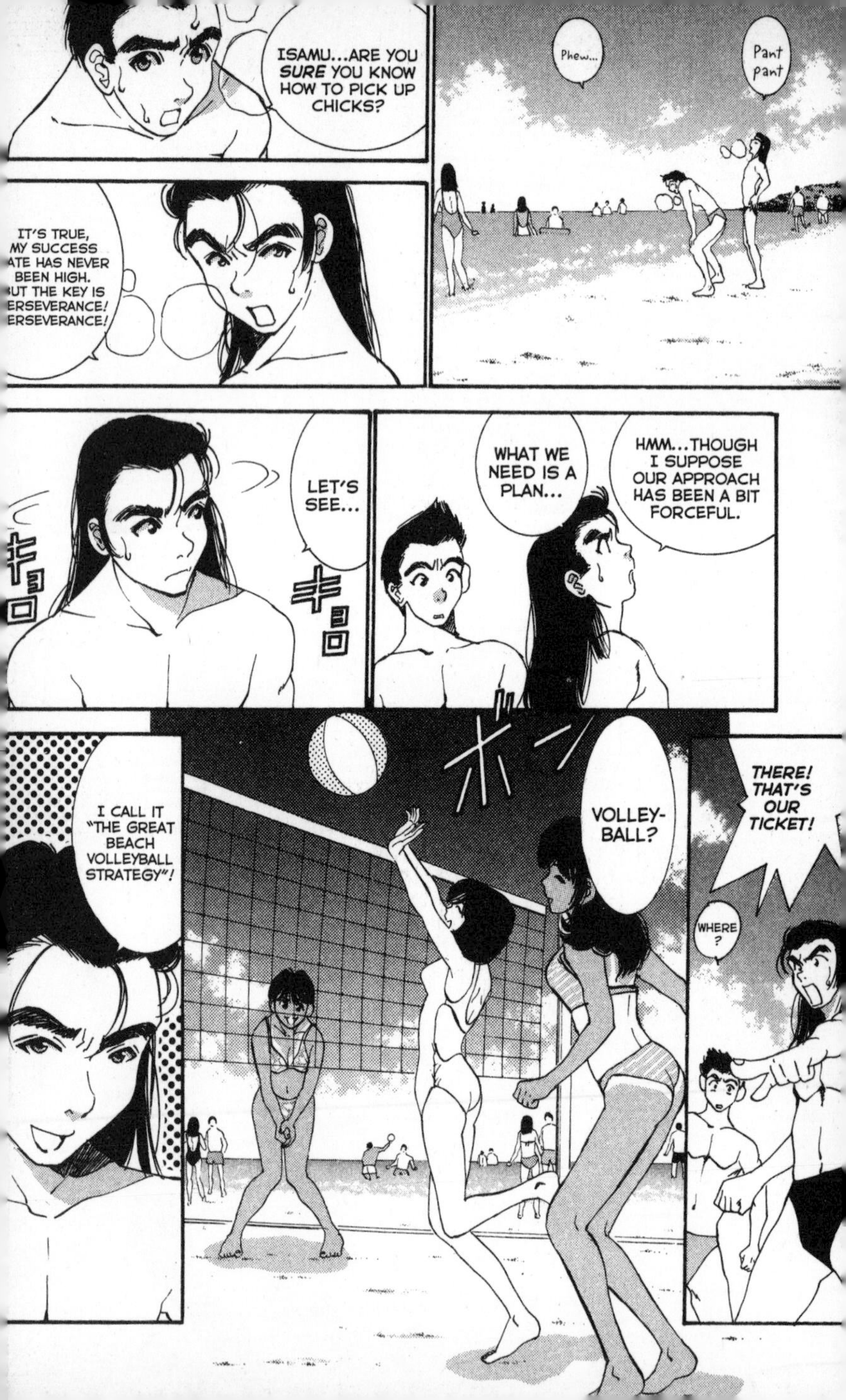
Pant pant
Phew...
ISAMU...ARE YOU *SURE* YOU KNOW HOW TO PICK UP CHICKS?
IT'S TRUE, MY SUCCESS ATE HAS NEVER BEEN HIGH. UT THE KEY IS ERSEVERANCE! ERSEVERANCE!
HMM...THOUGH I SUPPOSE OUR APPROACH HAS BEEN A BIT FORCEFUL.
WHAT WE NEED IS A PLAN...
キョロ
LET'S SEE...
キョロ
THERE! THAT'S OUR TICKET!
WHERE?
VOLLEY-BALL?
ボーン
I CALL IT "THE GREAT BEACH VOLLEYBALL STRATEGY"!

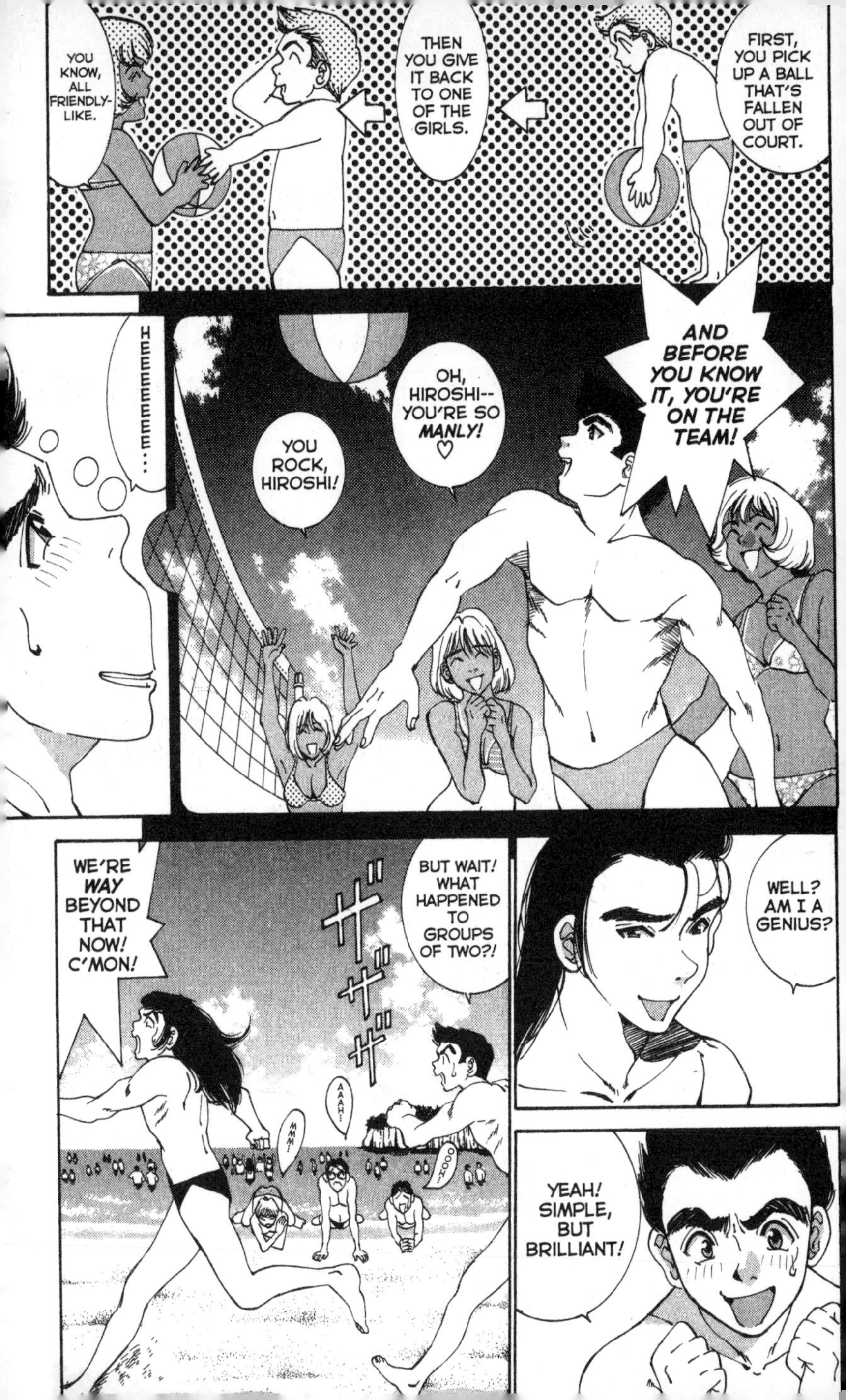
FIRST, YOU PICK UP A BALL THAT'S FALLEN OUT OF COURT.
THEN YOU GIVE IT BACK TO ONE OF THE GIRLS.
YOU KNOW, ALL FRIENDLY-LIKE.
AND BEFORE YOU KNOW IT, YOU'RE ON THE TEAM!
OH, HIROSHI-- YOU'RE SO *MANLY!* ♡
YOU ROCK, HIROSHI!
HEEEEEEEE...
WELL? AM I A GENIUS?
YEAH! SIMPLE, BUT BRILLIANT!
BUT WAIT! WHAT HAPPENED TO GROUPS OF TWO?!
WE'RE *WAY* BEYOND THAT NOW! C'MON!
AAAH...
MMM...
OOOH...

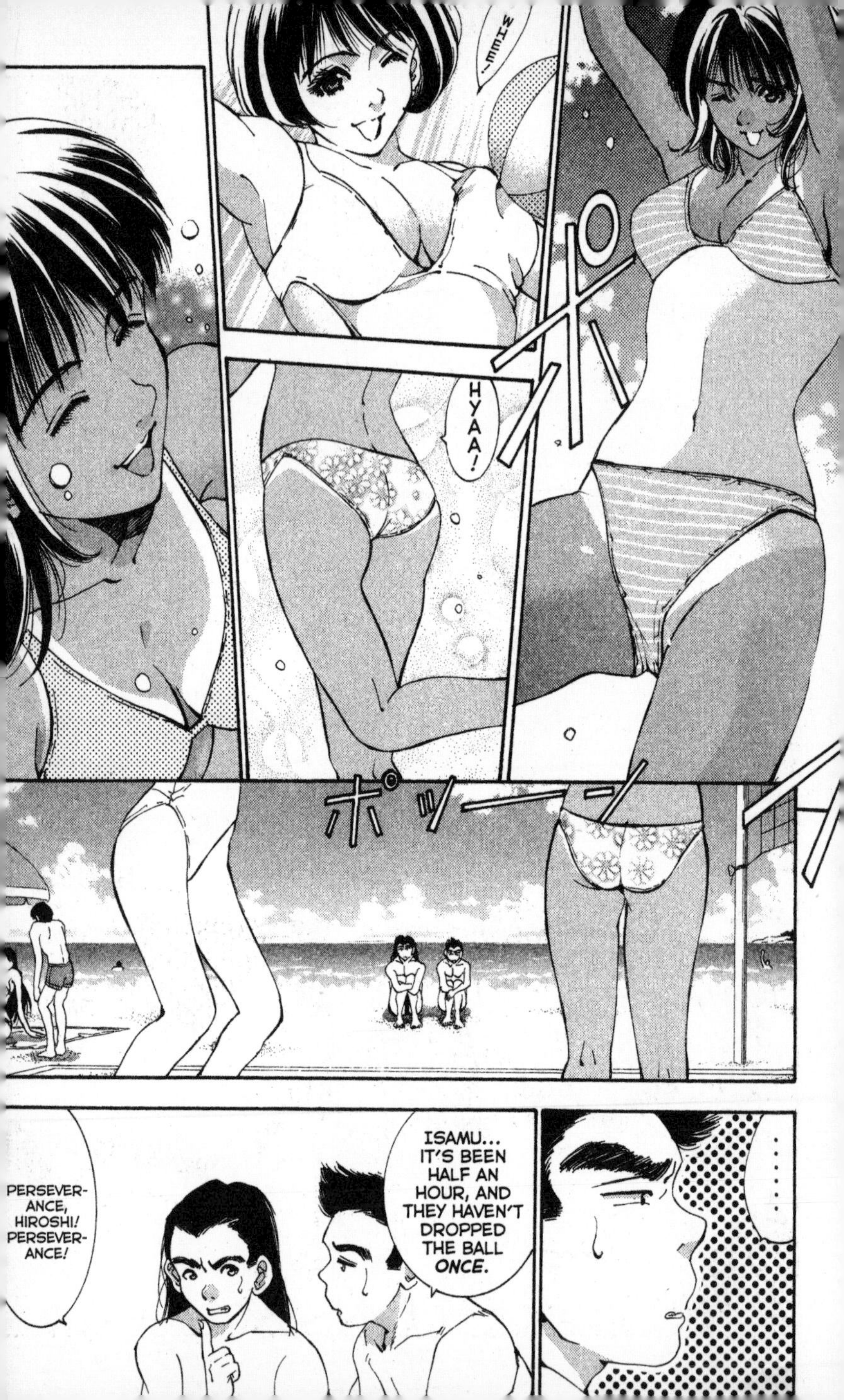
WHEE~!
HYAA!
......
ISAMU... IT'S BEEN HALF AN HOUR, AND THEY HAVEN'T DROPPED THE BALL *ONCE*.
PERSEVER-ANCE, HIROSHI! PERSEVER-ANCE!

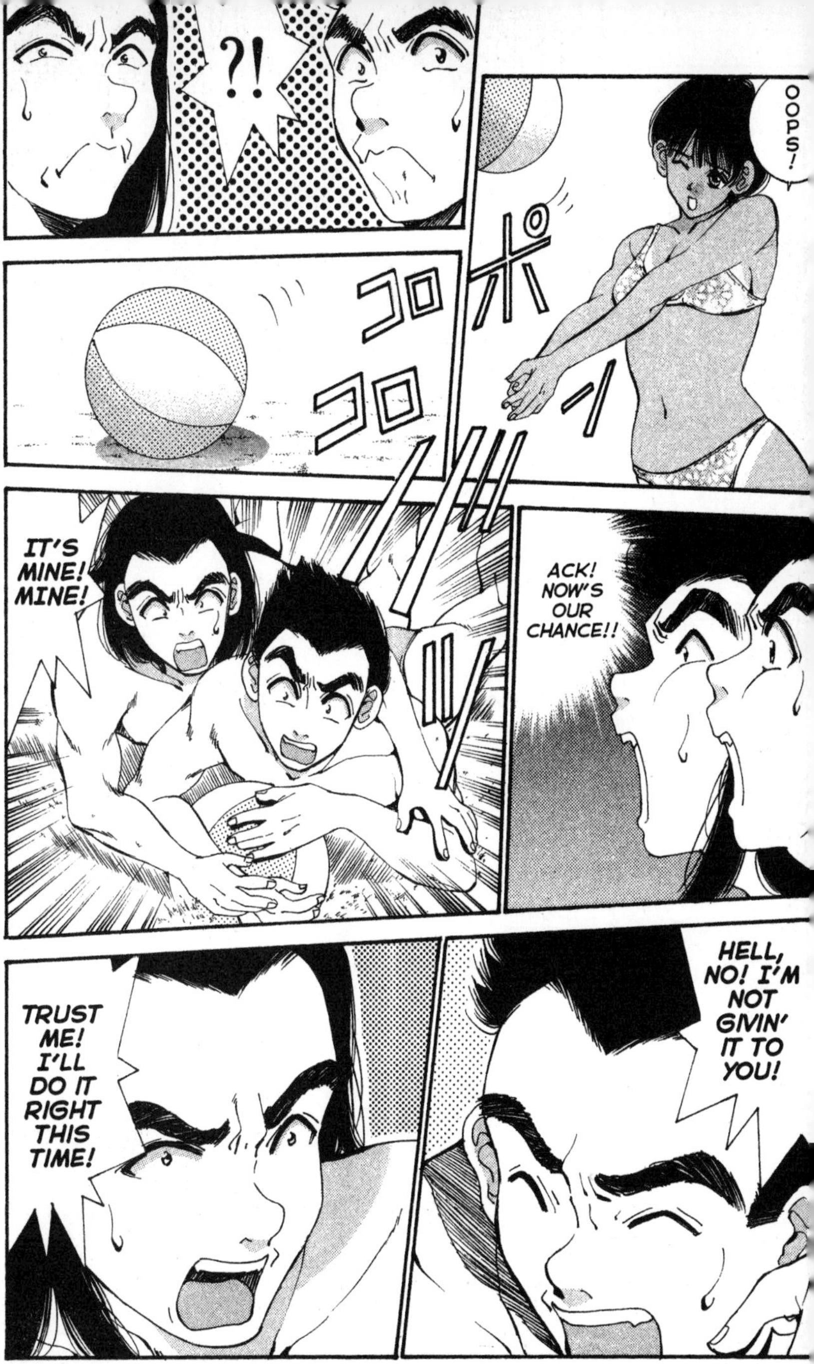
OOPS!
ポイ
?!
コロ
コロ
ACK! NOW'S OUR CHANCE!!
IT'S MINE! MINE!
HELL, NO! I'M NOT GIVIN' IT TO YOU!
TRUST ME! I'LL DO IT RIGHT THIS TIME!

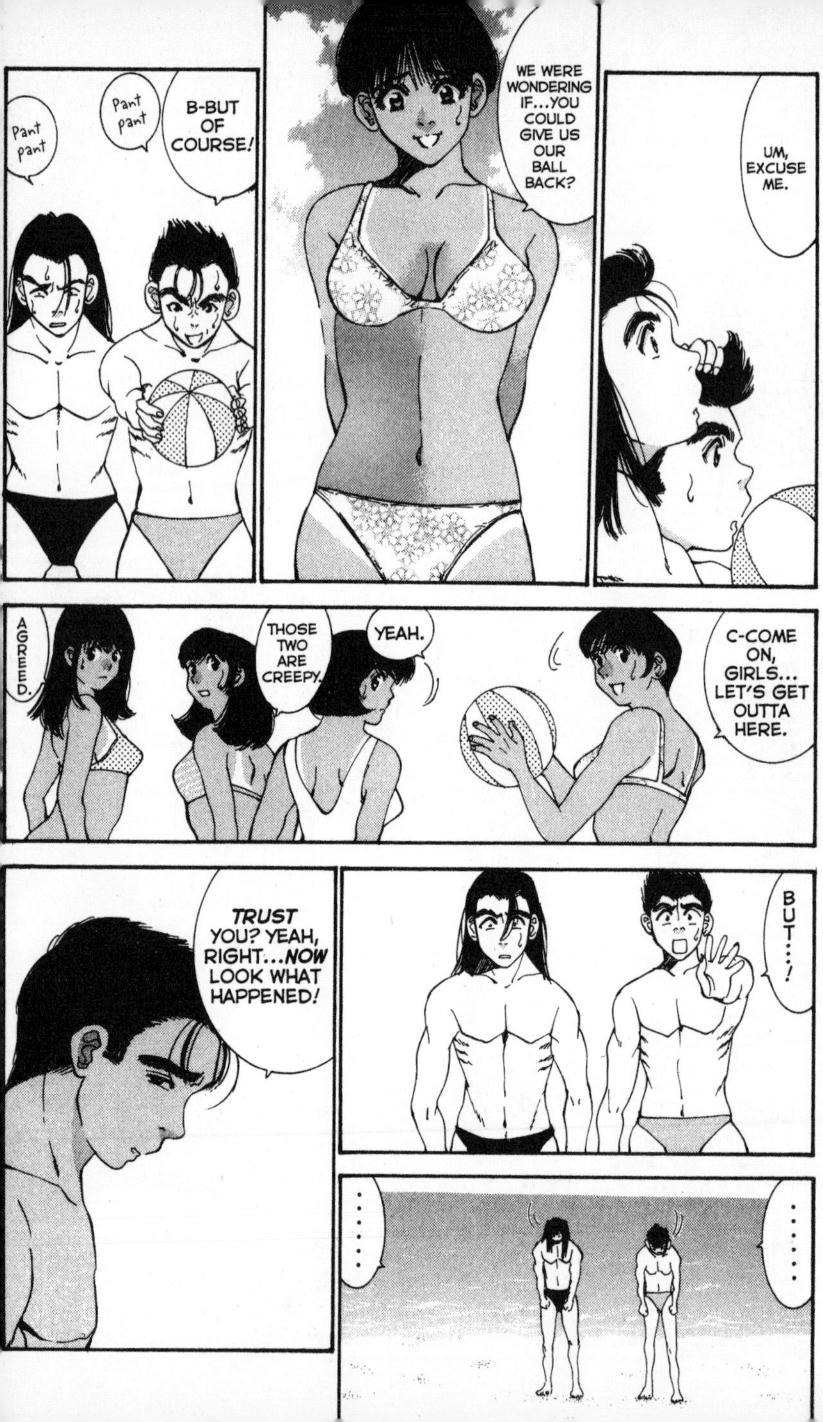
UM, EXCUSE ME.
WE WERE WONDERING IF...YOU COULD GIVE US OUR BALL BACK?
B-BUT OF COURSE!
Pant pant
Pant pant
C-COME ON, GIRLS... LET'S GET OUTTA HERE.
YEAH.
THOSE TWO ARE CREEPY.
AGREED.
BUT...!
......
......
TRUST YOU? YEAH, RIGHT...NOW LOOK WHAT HAPPENED!

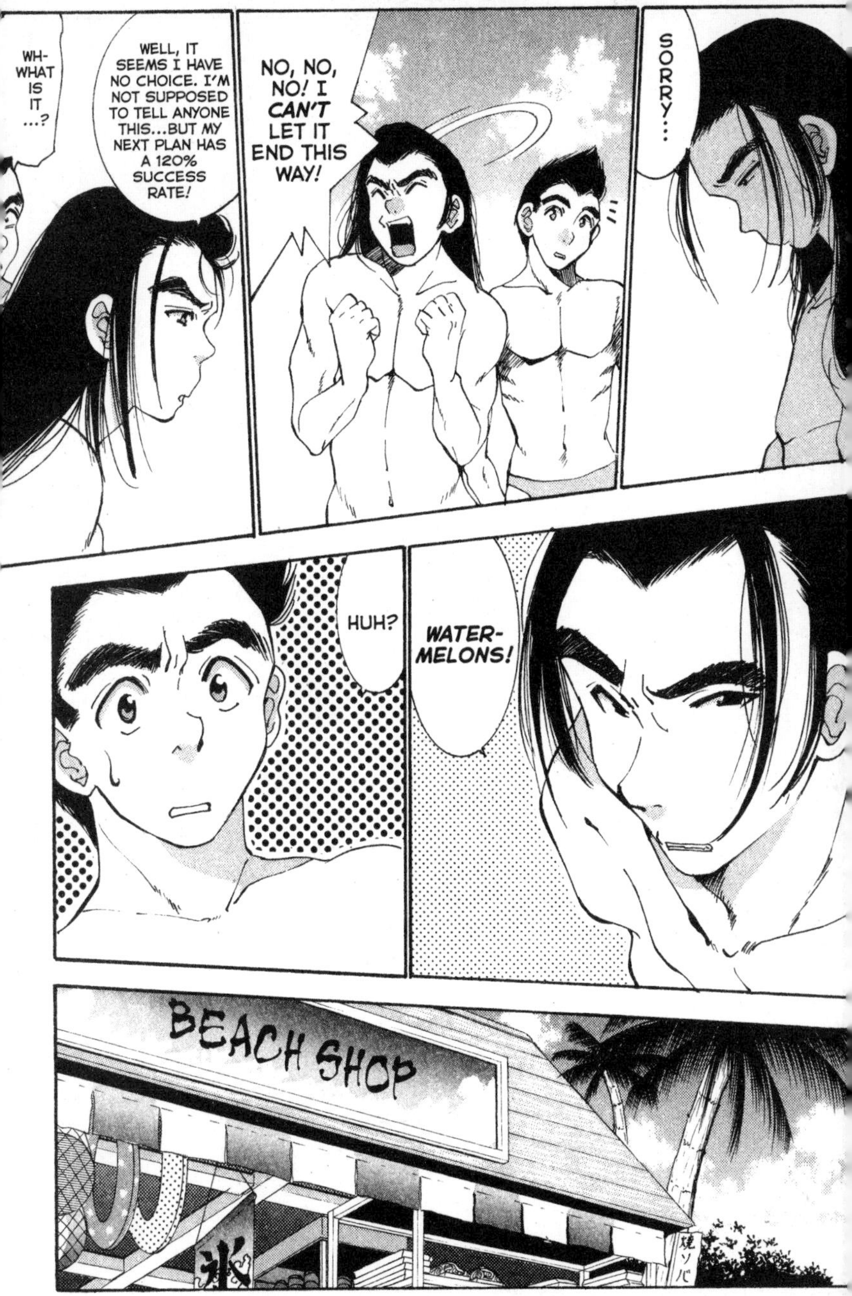
SORRY...
NO, NO, NO! I *CAN'T* LET IT END THIS WAY!
WELL, IT SEEMS I HAVE NO CHOICE. I'M NOT SUPPOSED TO TELL ANYONE THIS...BUT MY NEXT PLAN HAS A 120% SUCCESS RATE!
WH-WHAT IS IT ...?
WATER-MELONS!
HUH?
BEACH SHOP
焼ソバ
氷

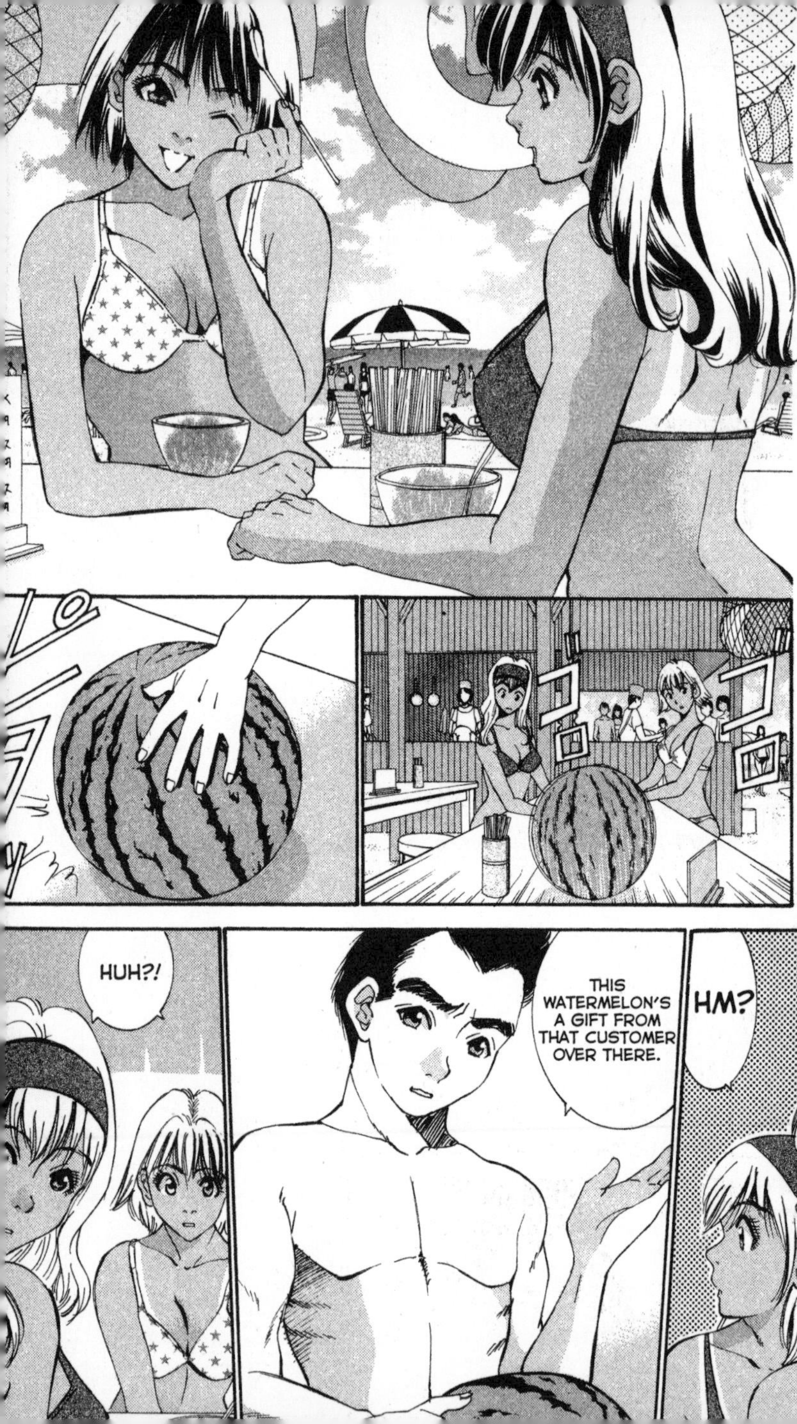
HM?
THIS WATERMELON'S A GIFT FROM THAT CUSTOMER OVER THERE.
HUH?!

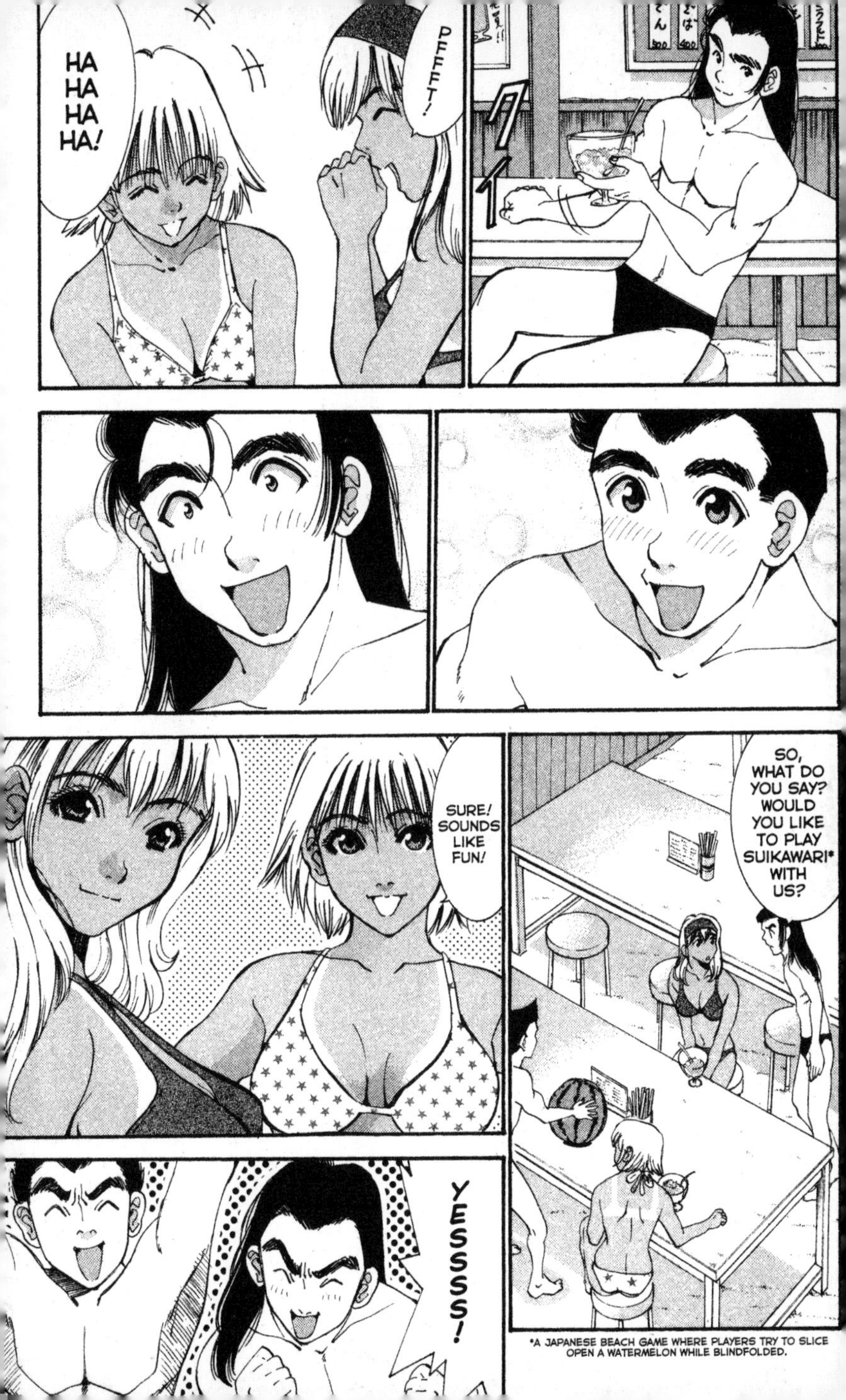
PFFFT!
HA HA HA HA!
SO, WHAT DO YOU SAY? WOULD YOU LIKE TO PLAY SUIKAWARI* WITH US?
SURE! SOUNDS LIKE FUN!
YESSSS!
*A JAPANESE BEACH GAME WHERE PLAYERS TRY TO SLICE OPEN A WATERMELON WHILE BLINDFOLDED.

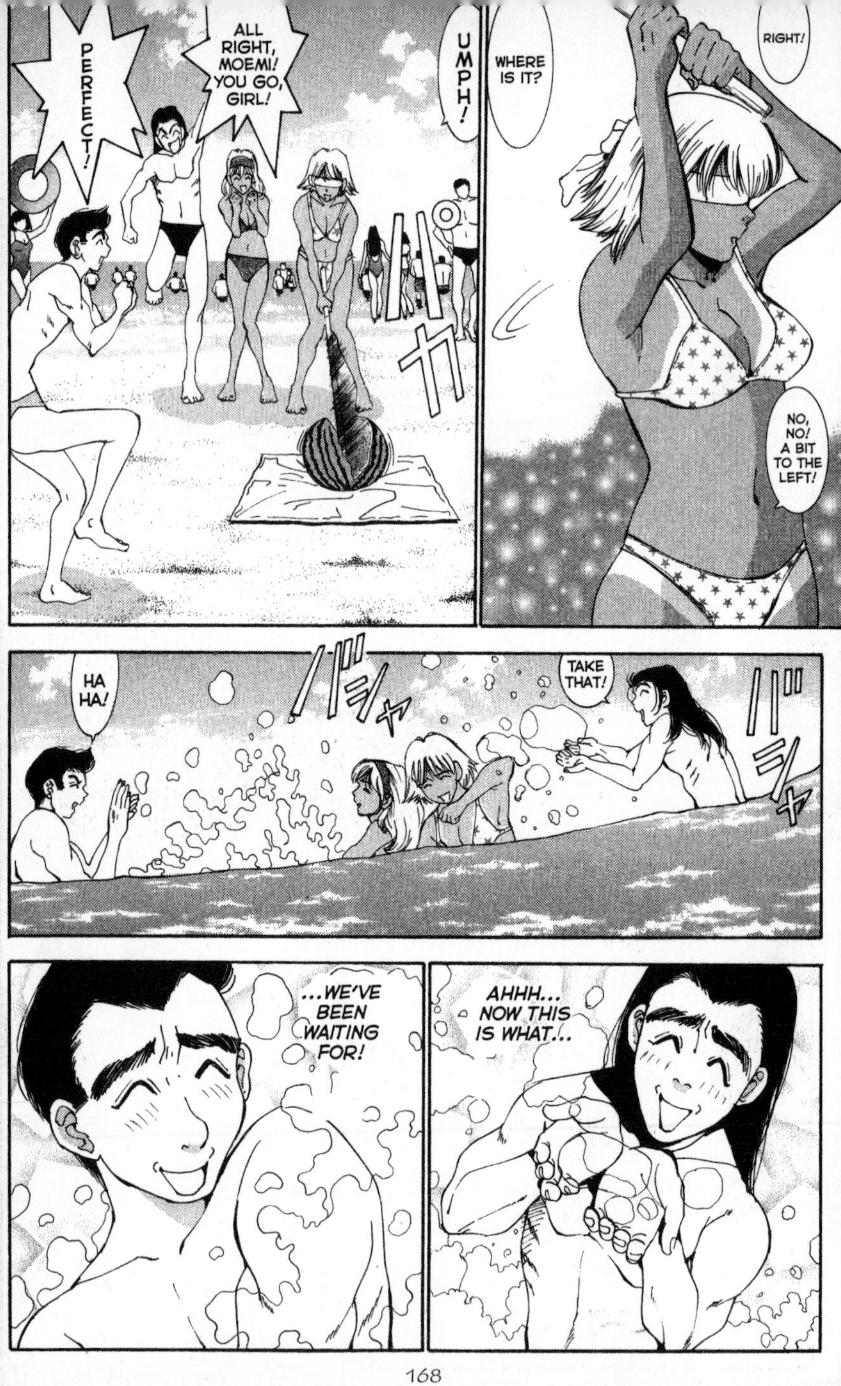
RIGHT!
WHERE IS IT?
NO, NO! A BIT TO THE LEFT!
UMPH!
ALL RIGHT, MOEMI! YOU GO, GIRL!
PERFECT!
パカ
バシャ
TAKE THAT!
バシャ
HA HA!
AHHH... NOW THIS IS WHAT...
...WE'VE BEEN WAITING FOR!

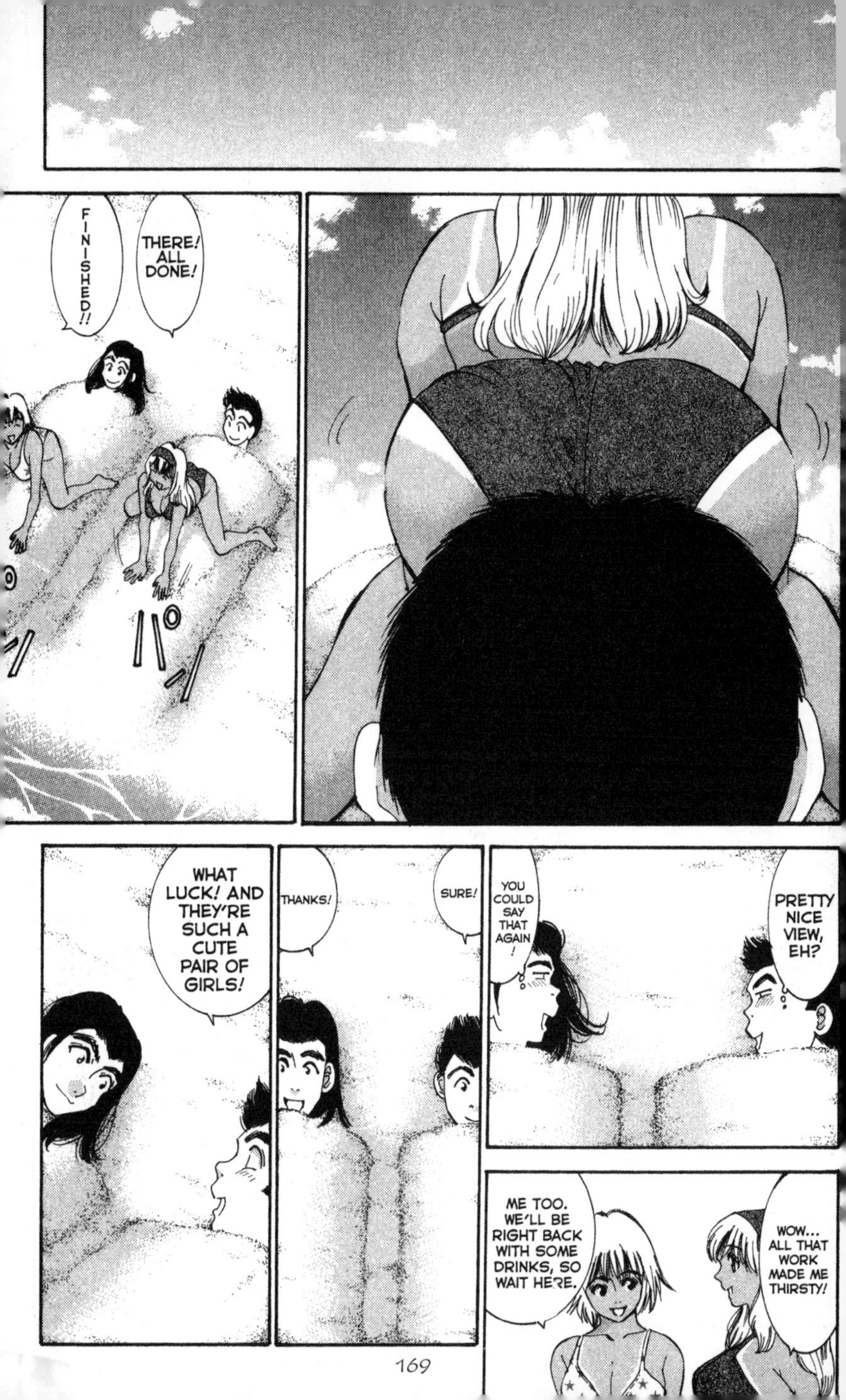
THERE! ALL DONE!
FINISHED!!
PRETTY NICE VIEW, EH?
YOU COULD SAY THAT AGAIN!
WOW... ALL THAT WORK MADE ME THIRSTY!
ME TOO. WE'LL BE RIGHT BACK WITH SOME DRINKS, SO WAIT HERE.
SURE!
THANKS!
WHAT LUCK! AND THEY'RE SUCH A CUTE PAIR OF GIRLS!

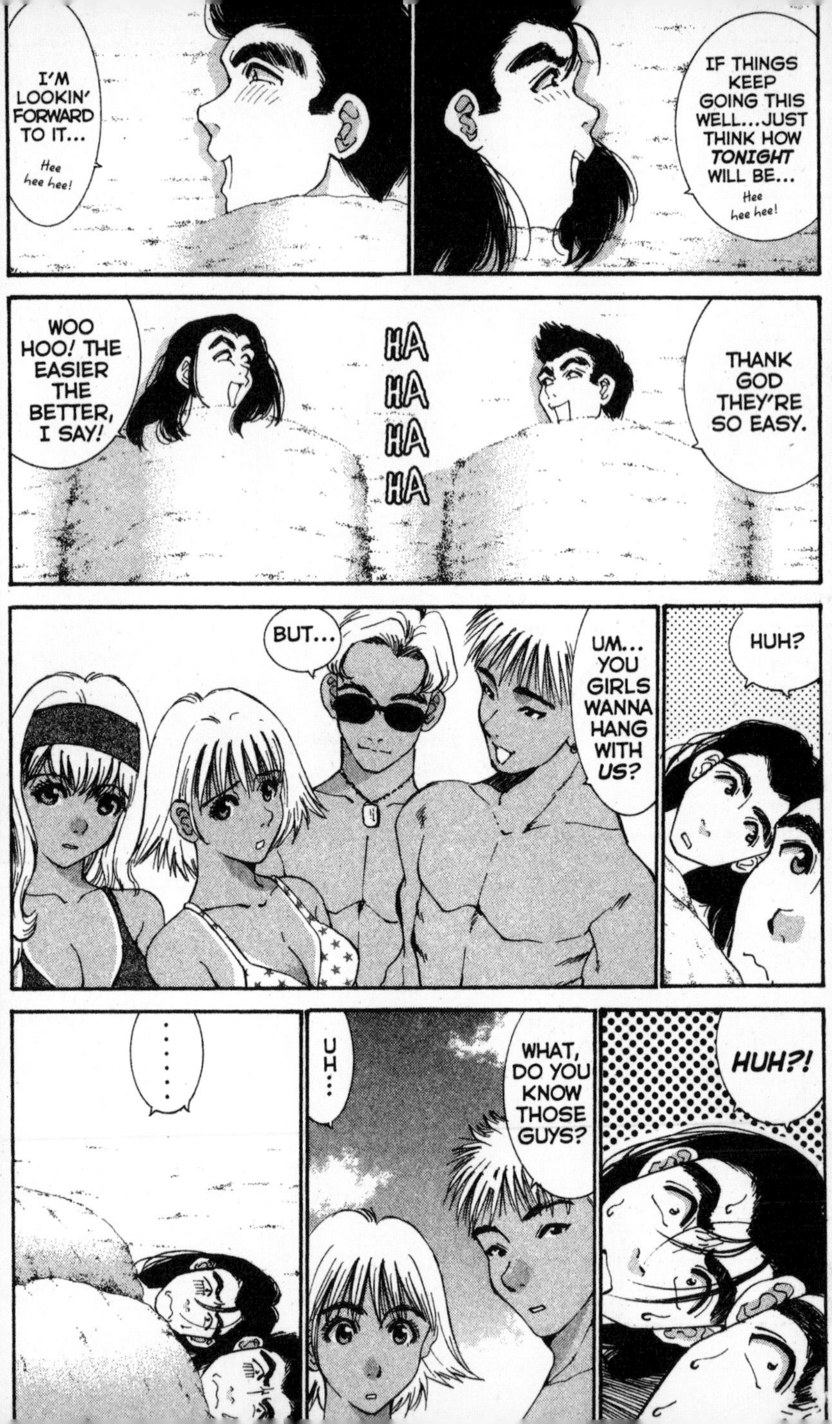
IF THINGS KEEP GOING THIS WELL...JUST THINK HOW *TONIGHT* WILL BE...
Hee hee hee!
I'M LOOKIN' FORWARD TO IT...
Hee hee hee!
THANK GOD THEY'RE SO EASY.
HA HA HA HA
WOO HOO! THE EASIER THE BETTER, I SAY!
HUH?
UM... YOU GIRLS WANNA HANG WITH *US*?
BUT...
HUH?!
WHAT, DO YOU KNOW THOSE GUYS?
UH...
......

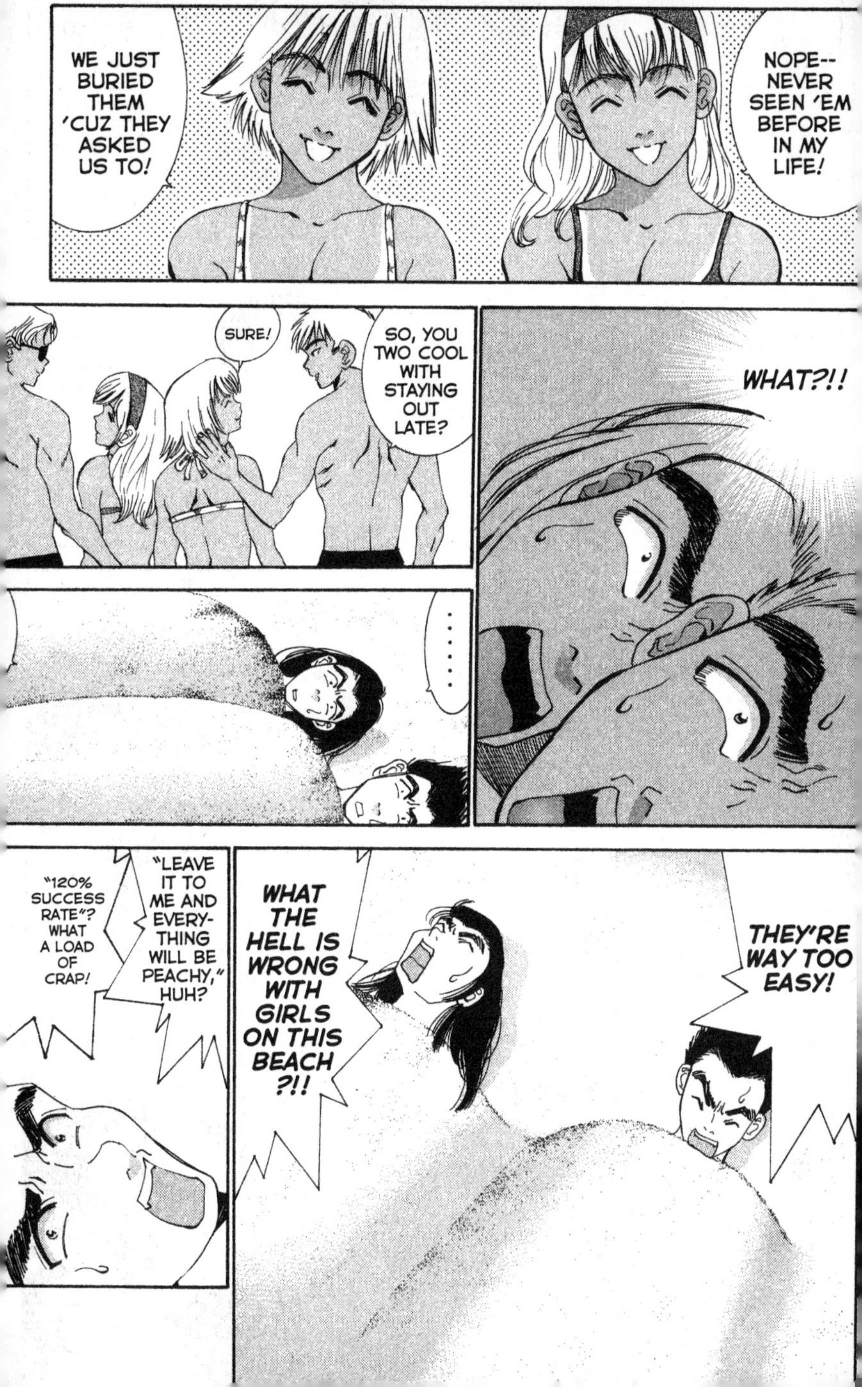
NOPE-- NEVER SEEN 'EM BEFORE IN MY LIFE!
WE JUST BURIED THEM 'CUZ THEY ASKED US TO!
WHAT?!!
SO, YOU TWO COOL WITH STAYING OUT LATE?
SURE!
......
THEY'RE WAY TOO EASY!
WHAT THE HELL IS WRONG WITH GIRLS ON THIS BEACH?!!
"LEAVE IT TO ME AND EVERY-THING WILL BE PEACHY," HUH?
"120% SUCCESS RATE"? WHAT A LOAD OF CRAP!

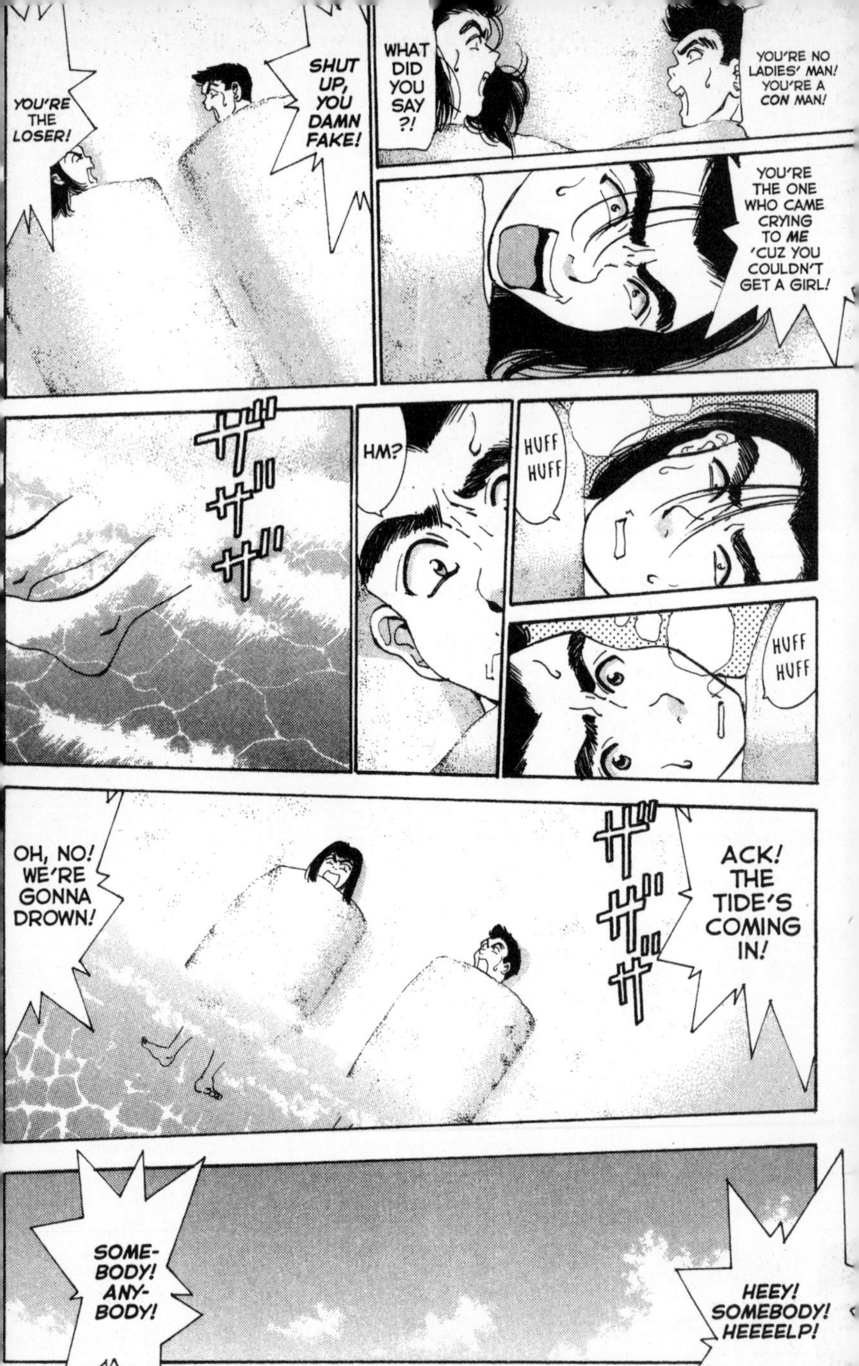

YOU'RE NO LADIES' MAN! YOU'RE A CON MAN!
WHAT DID YOU SAY ?!
YOU'RE THE ONE WHO CAME CRYING TO ME 'CUZ YOU COULDN'T GET A GIRL!
SHUT UP, YOU DAMN FAKE!
YOU'RE THE LOSER!
HUFF HUFF
HUFF HUFF
HM?
ザザザ
ACK! THE TIDE'S COMING IN!
ザザザザ
OH, NO! WE'RE GONNA DROWN!
HEEY! SOMEBODY! HEEEELP!
SOME-BODY! ANY-BODY!

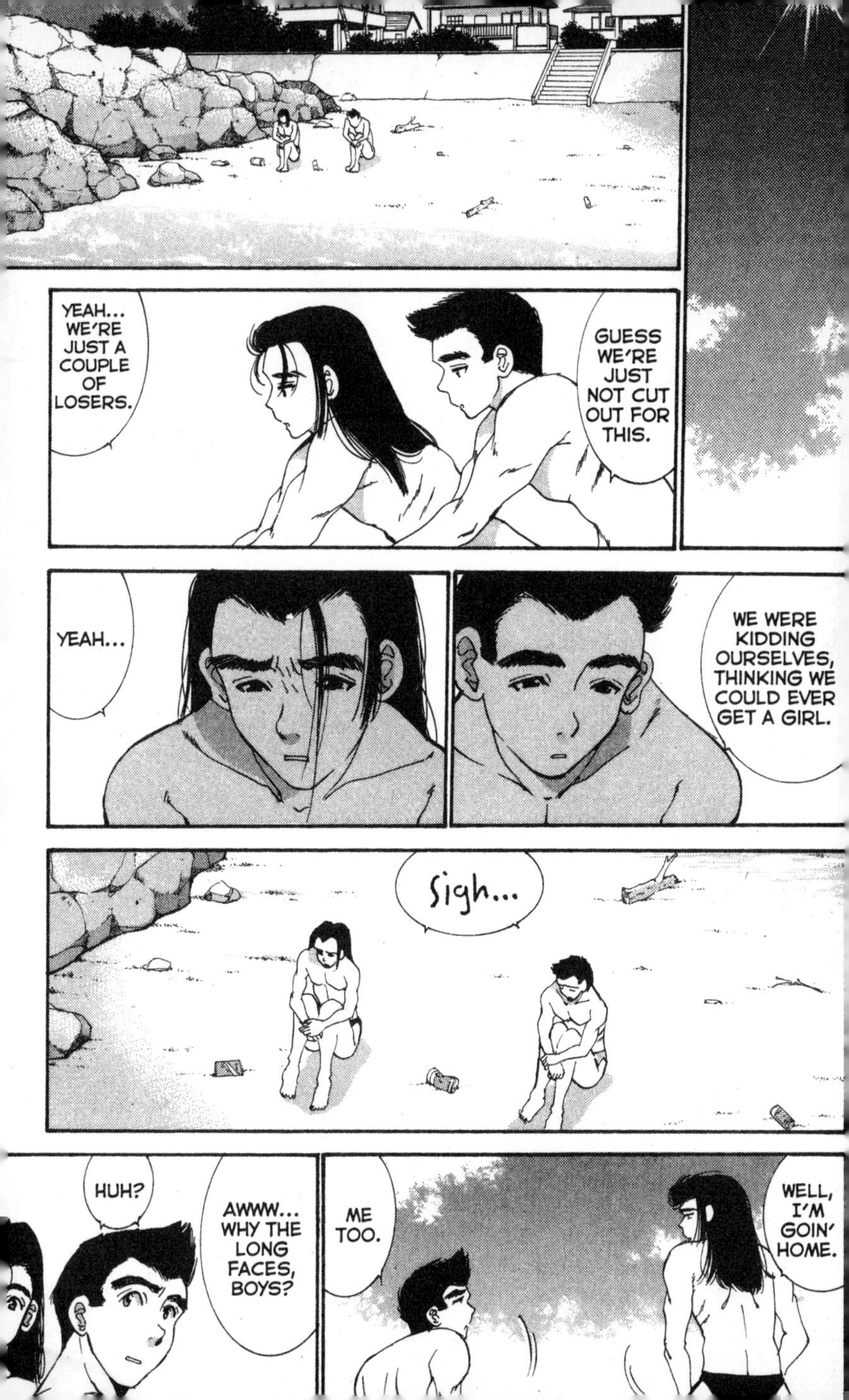
GUESS WE'RE JUST NOT CUT OUT FOR THIS.
YEAH... WE'RE JUST A COUPLE OF LOSERS.
WE WERE KIDDING OURSELVES, THINKING WE COULD EVER GET A GIRL.
YEAH...
Sigh...
WELL, I'M GOIN' HOME.
ME TOO.
AWWW... WHY THE LONG FACES, BOYS?
HUH?

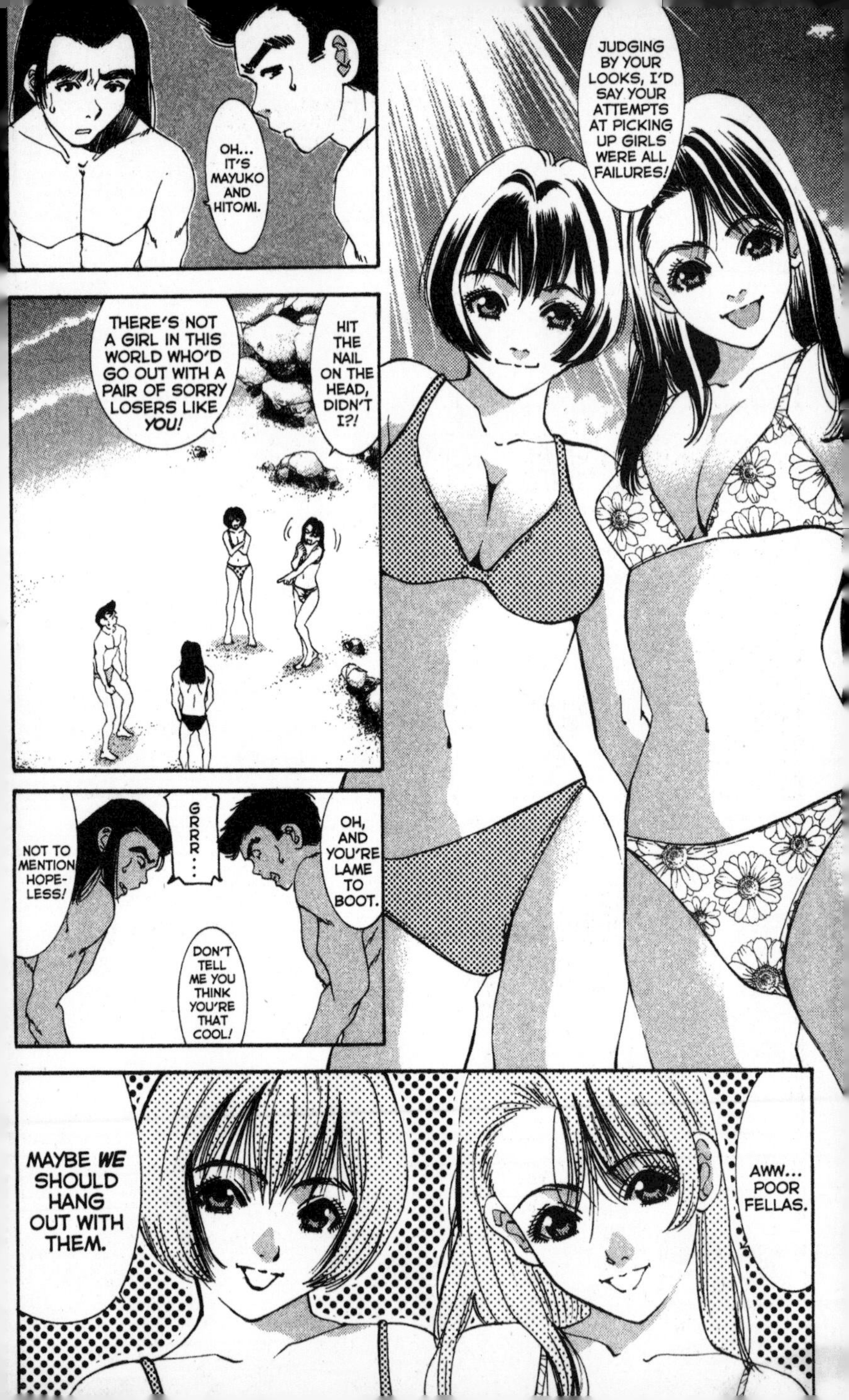
JUDGING BY YOUR LOOKS, I'D SAY YOUR ATTEMPTS AT PICKING UP GIRLS WERE ALL FAILURES!
OH... IT'S MAYUKO AND HITOMI.
HIT THE NAIL ON THE HEAD, DIDN'T I?!
THERE'S NOT A GIRL IN THIS WORLD WHO'D GO OUT WITH A PAIR OF SORRY LOSERS LIKE *YOU!*
OH, AND YOU'RE LAME TO BOOT.
GRRR...
NOT TO MENTION HOPELESS!
DON'T TELL ME YOU THINK YOU'RE THAT COOL!
AWW... POOR FELLAS.
MAYBE *WE* SHOULD HANG OUT WITH THEM.

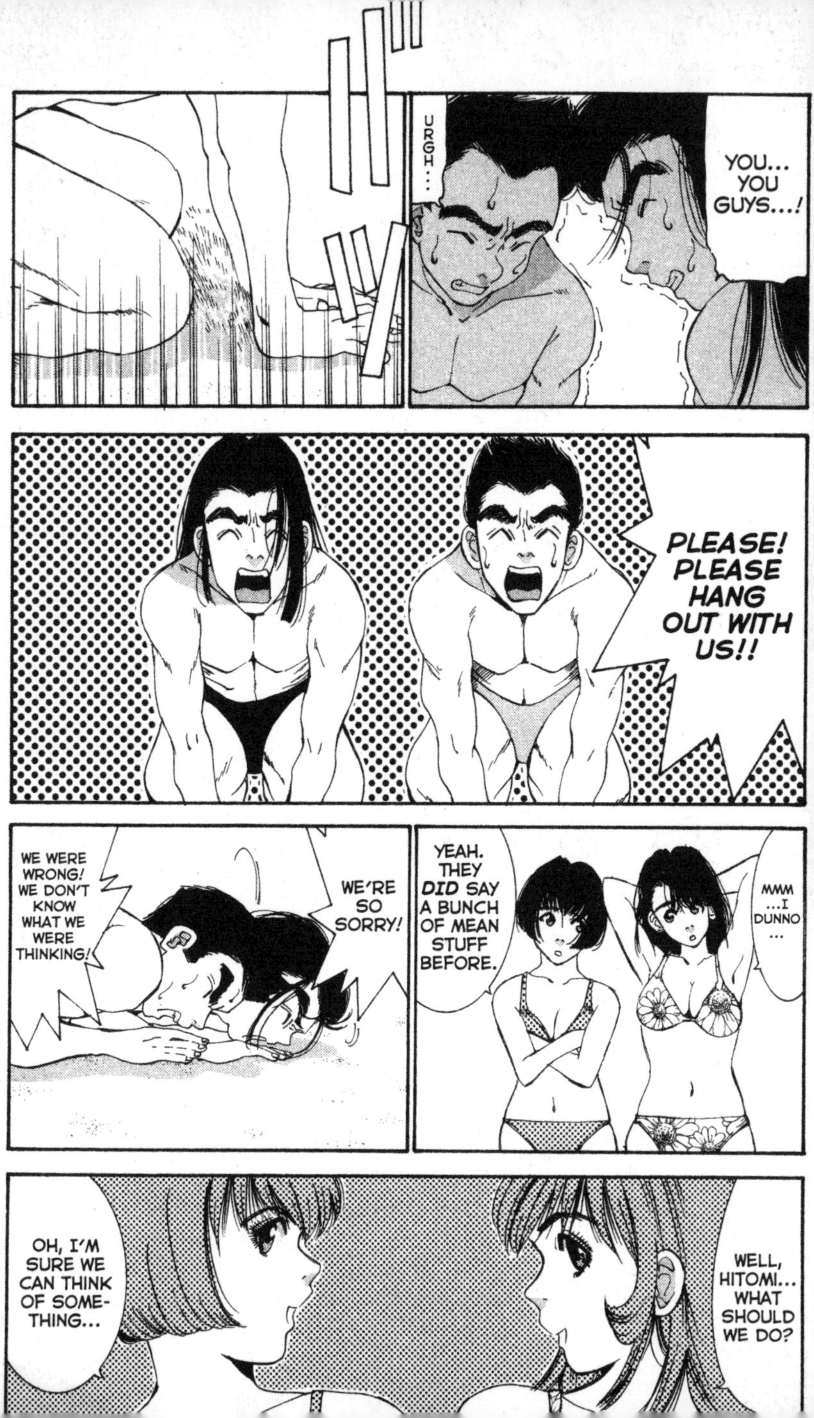
YOU... YOU GUYS...!
URGH...
PLEASE! PLEASE HANG OUT WITH US!!
MMM ...I DUNNO ...
YEAH. THEY *DID* SAY A BUNCH OF MEAN STUFF BEFORE.
WE'RE SO SORRY!
WE WERE WRONG! WE DON'T KNOW WHAT WE WERE THINKING!
WELL, HITOMI... WHAT SHOULD WE DO?
OH, I'M SURE WE CAN THINK OF SOME-THING...

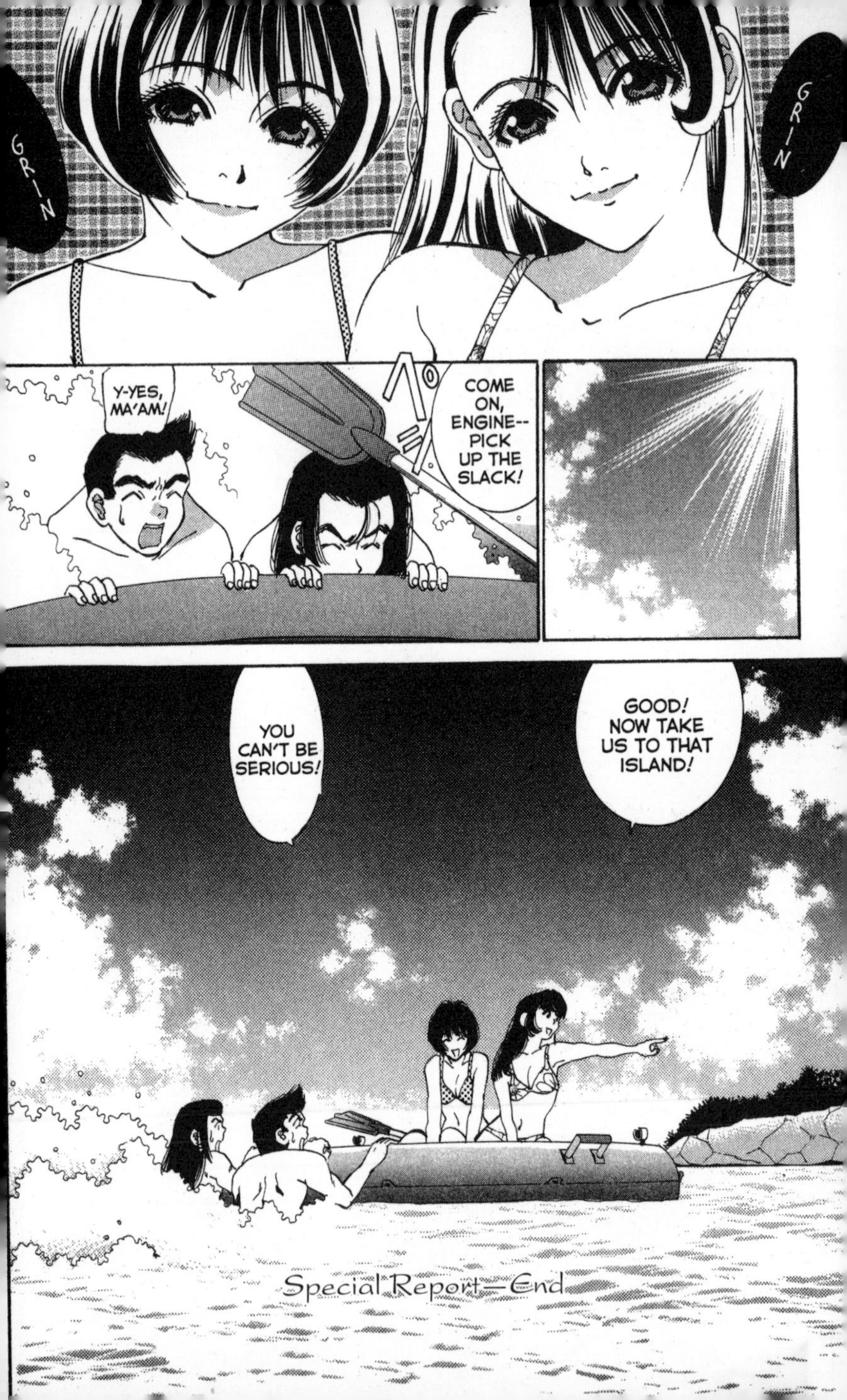
GRIN
GRIN
COME ON, ENGINE--PICK UP THE SLACK!
Y-YES, MA'AM!
GOOD! NOW TAKE US TO THAT ISLAND!
YOU CAN'T BE SERIOUS!
Special Report—End

Listen to Tamakoshi!

Hello! This is Tamakoshi!

This may be a little sudden, but I'd like to ask all of you out there what your definition of a beautiful woman is. Is it her style? Her hair? Her personality? I'm sure everyone has their own preferences, but for me, a woman's most important attribute is her manners. I mean, no matter how pretty she may be, or how kickin' her body is, a woman with good social graces is at the top of MY list!! Well, okay...I guess her smile is almost as important...

Antways, those are my thoughts!

Back when I was raised in Osaka, which is considered a very progressive city, social graces very quickly became something I took notice of. But my neighborhood convenience store is completely lacking in these graces. Many of the clerks are real babes...but they're always pissy and don't have a pinch of grace!

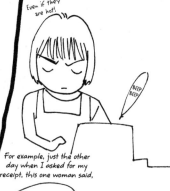

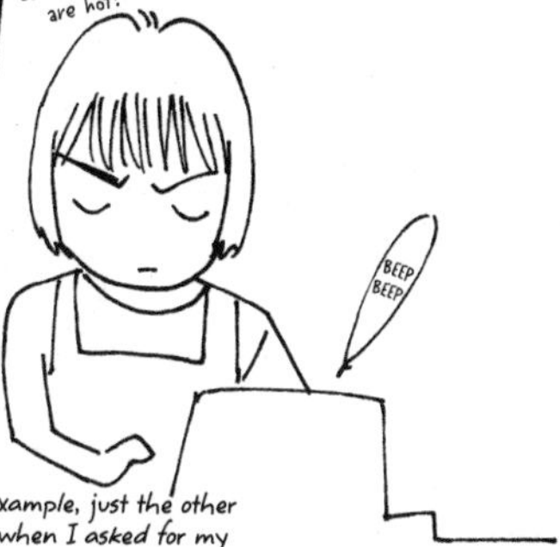
Even if they are hot!
BEEP BEEP

For example, just the other day when I asked for my receipt, this one woman said,

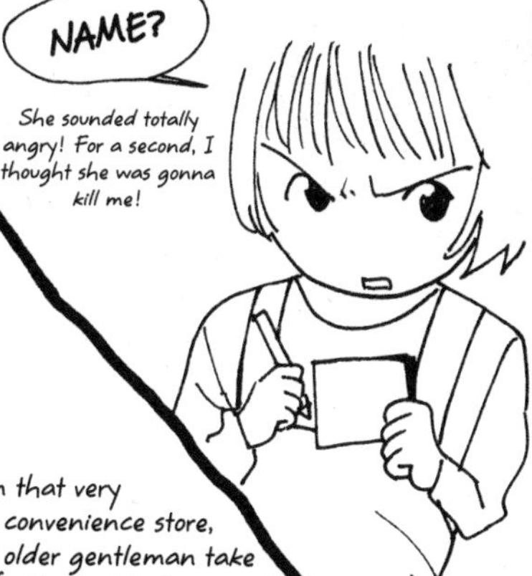
NAME?

She sounded totally angry! For a second, I thought she was gonna kill me!

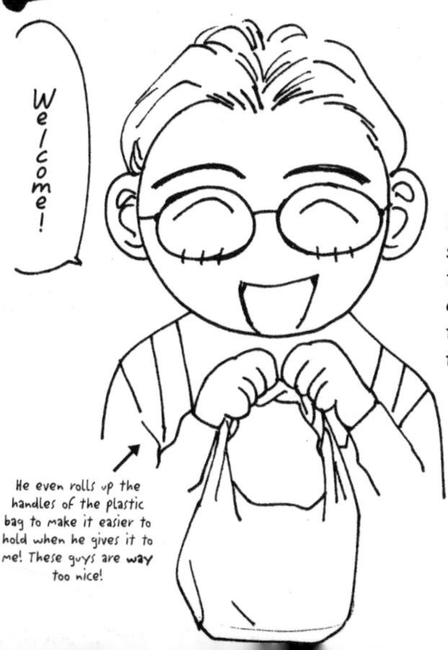
Welcome!

But in that very same convenience store, these older gentleman take over for the night. Compared to those nasty-tempered girls, these guys are beyond nice!

He even rolls up the handles of the plastic bag to make it easier to hold when he gives it to me! These guys are **way** too nice!

Itabashi's Space

All of my friends in my profession are old men. One day we all went to Sanin before they set the ban on crabs. So we're taking this rickety old train called the Tottori Line (whose name is the only fast thing about it). And as we're bumping along, this bunch of high school students gets on and sits across from us.

Eventually, one of them calls out to my friend and says, "Uh, isn't your sweatshirt on backwards?"

I wasn't sure if my friend was going to get flustered or upset. But he said, "Oh, I got a stain on the front of it," as if it were the most natural thing in the world. The kid seemed convinced, so he went over to a girl that had come on with him and started talking to her. They kept talking on and on so noisily...but anyway, I went over to my friend and said, "Hey, you're embarrassing us. Could you take that thing off?"

The thing is, he'd put his shirt on backwards on purpose, because when he was a kid, it was considered the cool thing to do. But that was a LONG time ago. I guess he was trying to keep the fad going.

Incidentally, the scene going in the box seat behind us had a very Boys Be... feel to it...and my friend was too stubborn to take off his sweatshirt.

Signing off from Kinosaki, right next to Takeno...
Masahiro "old man" Itabashi

Next Time in BOYS BE

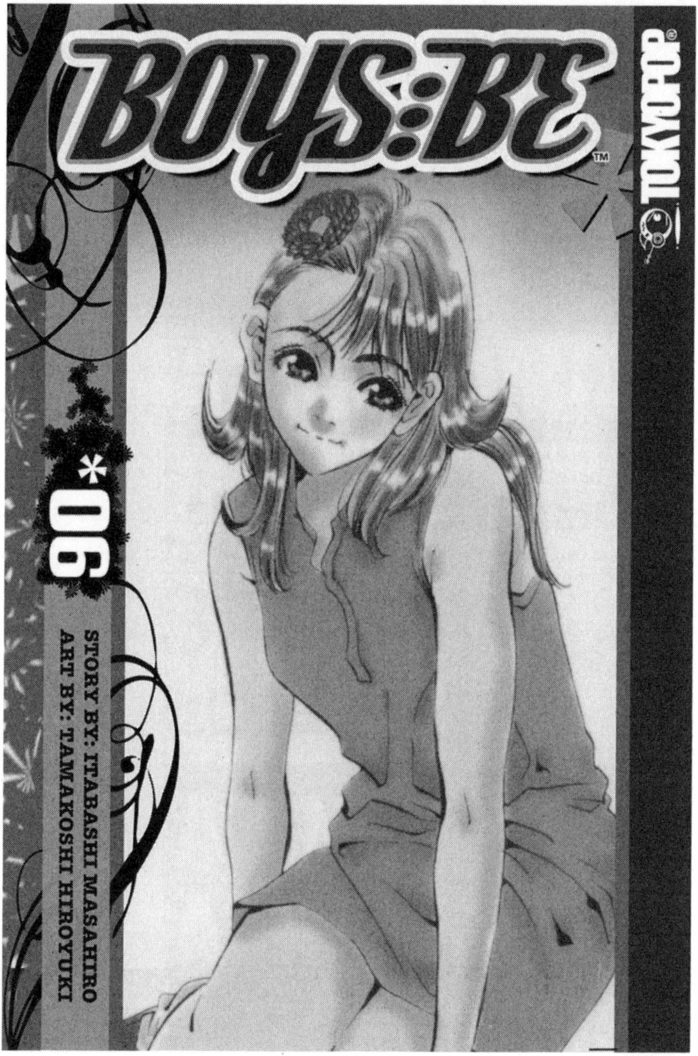
BOYS:BE
TOKYOPOP
06
STORY BY: ITABASHI MASAHIRO
ART BY: TAMAKOSHI HIROYUKI

A guy checking out porno in a video store is pounced on by three sexy classmates who coerce him into watching a video with them. What can a guy do? When a boy overhears his girlfriend's fears, he tries desperately to be the "perfect" boyfriend. And another boy's dream girl gives him nightmares when she starts getting tons of sweet gifts...but from whom? When it comes to love, things are not always what they seem!

Twin Talk

By Kathy and Chrissy Schilling

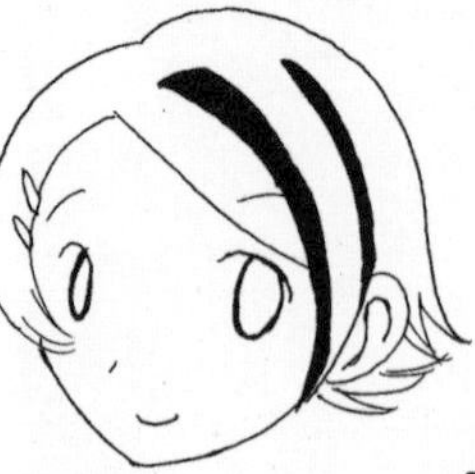

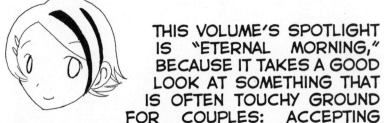

THIS VOLUME'S SPOTLIGHT IS "ETERNAL MORNING," BECAUSE IT TAKES A GOOD LOOK AT SOMETHING THAT IS OFTEN TOUCHY GROUND FOR COUPLES: ACCEPTING EACH OTHER'S INTERESTS. YOU MAY NOT BE A FAN OF YOUR PARTNER'S HOBBY, BUT IT'S ENOUGH IF YOU'RE WILLING TO ACCEPT IT AND MAYBE EVEN GIVE IT A TRY. WHO KNOWS--YOU MAY EVEN END UP LIKING IT. AND IF NOT, THEN WHATEVER.

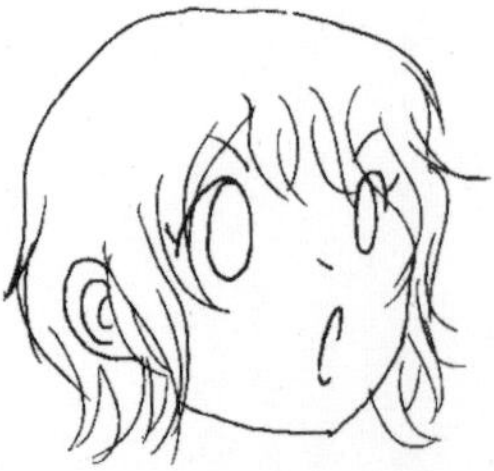

RIGHT. THAT'S WHAT FUJII COULDN'T SEE AT THE CLUB. LISTEN, GIRL, AT LEAST THE GUY GAVE IT A TRY! I MEAN, DON'T GET US WRONG--IT WAS GREAT THAT FUJII BROKE THE STEREOTYPE OF A DAINTY LITTLE GIRL BY GOING TO SEARCH FOR BUGS, LET ALONE HANDLING THEM--BUT SHE ALSO ENDED UP GENUINELY ENJOYING THE SPORT. SHE WASN'T JUST TRYING TO IMPRESS HER MAN.

IN DEFENSE OF OKAZAKI, WHILE TRYING OUT YOUR PARTNER'S HOBBY IS ONE THING, FEIGNING INTEREST ISN'T GOING TO GET YOU ANYWHERE IF YOU'RE LOOKING FOR A LONG-TERM RELATIONSHIP. YOU'LL JUST END UP LYING TO YOURSELF AND FEELING WORN OUT. THE BOY OR GIRL OF YOUR DREAMS IS GONNA HAVE TO ACCEPT YOU FOR WHO YOU ARE--EVEN IF IT MEANS YOU WON'T BE ABLE TO SHARE THE SAME TASTE IN MUSIC.

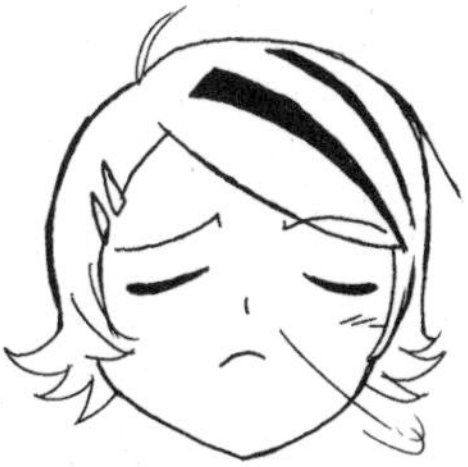

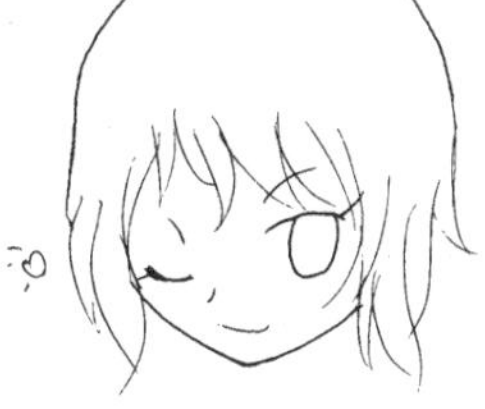

RIGHT. UPFRONT AND HONEST IS ALWAYS THE WAY TO GO. AND GOOD FOR OKAZAKI FOR BEING OPEN-MINDED ENOUGH TO TRY SOMETHING HE'D ALREADY SCRATCHED OFF HIS LIST! EVEN THOUGH CLUBBING DIDN'T FLOAT WITH HIM, AT LEAST HE CAN SAY HE DID IT. LIKE THE OLD SAYING GOES...THERE'S A FIRST TIME FOR EVERYTHING!

TOKYOPOP SHOP

WWW.TOKYOPOP.COM/SHOP

HOT NEWS!
Check out the
TOKYOPOP SHOP!
The world's best
collection of manga in
English is now available
online in one place!

SAKURA TAISEN

BECK: MONGOLIAN CHOP SQUAD

WWW.TOKYOPOP.COM/SHOP

Princess Ai
and other hot
titles are
available at
the store that
never closes!

PRINCESS AI VOL. 2: LUMINATION

- LOOK FOR SPECIAL OFFERS
- PRE-ORDER UPCOMING RELEASES
- COMPLETE YOUR COLLECTIONS

Princess Ai © & TM TOKYOPOP Inc. and Kitty Radio, Inc. Sakura Taisen © SEGA ©RED ©Ikku Masa. Beck: Mongolian Chop Squad © Harold Sakuishi.

SPOTLIGHT TOKYOPOP MANGA SUPPLEMENT

SAKURA TAISEN

BY OHJI HIROI & IKKU MASA

SOLDIERS, STEAM ROBOTS, SAMURAI GIRLS... OH, MY!

Imagine a Tokyo where monstrous steam-powered robots crash flower-viewing parties only to be cut down samurai-style by young girls in kimonos. It's eight years after the horrific Demon War, and Japan is a peaceful, prosperous place...or is it? Meet Ensign Ichiro Ogami —a recent graduate from the Naval Academy—who is about to be swept into this roiling world of robots, demons, and hot girls in uniform!

© SEGA © RED © Ikku Masa

T TEEN AGE 13+

THE HIGHLY ANTICIPATED MANGA RELEASE OF THE SUPER-POPULAR ANIME AND VIDEO GAME IS FINALLY HERE! (ALSO KNOWN AS *SAKURA WARS*.)

FOR MORE INFORMATION VISIT: WWW.TOKYOPOP.COM

that I'm not like other people...

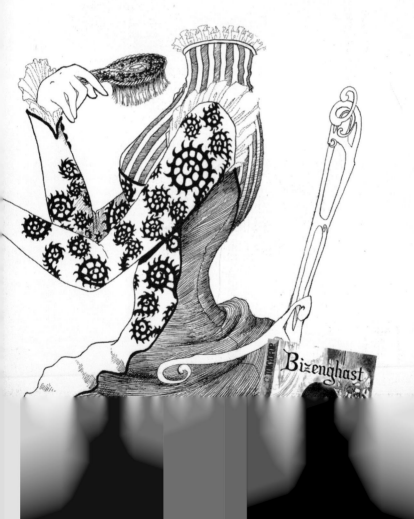

ENGHAST

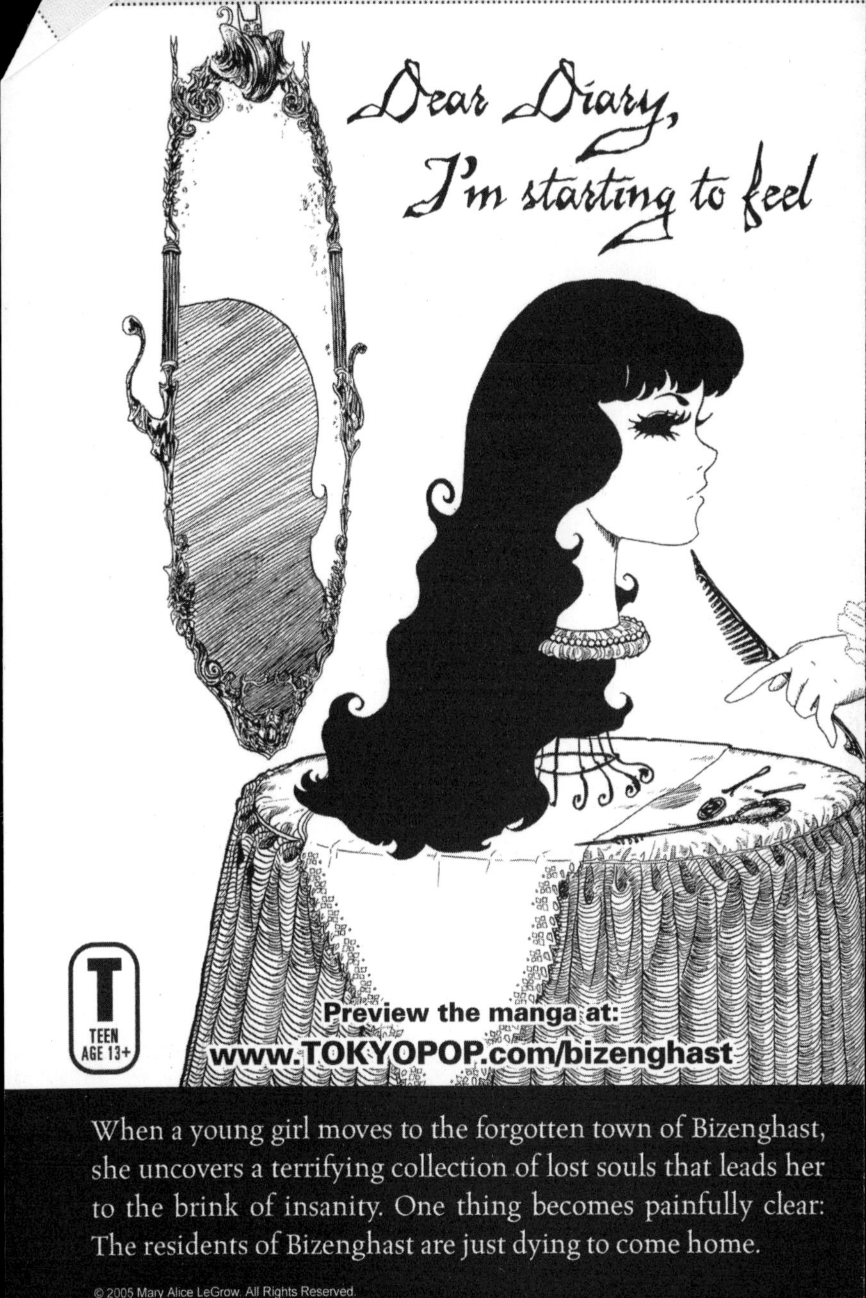
Dear Diary,
I'm starting to feel
T
TEEN
AGE 13+
Preview the manga at:
www.TOKYOPOP.com/bizenghast

When a young girl moves to the forgotten town of Bizenghast, she uncovers a terrifying collection of lost souls that leads her to the brink of insanity. One thing becomes painfully clear: The residents of Bizenghast are just dying to come home.

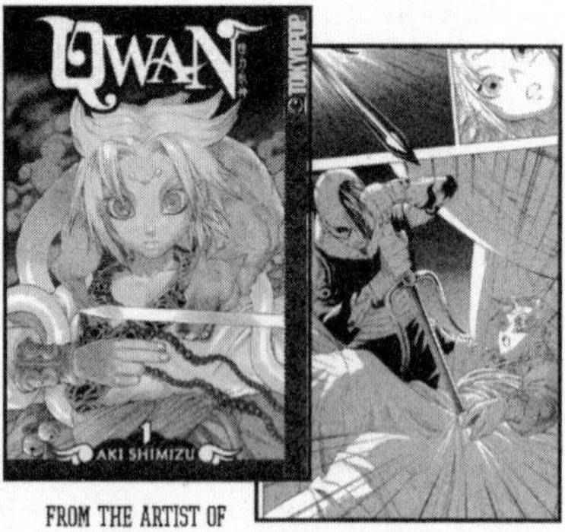
QWAN
1
AKI SHIMIZU
TOKYOPOP

FROM THE ARTIST OF SUIKODEN III

BY AKI SHIMIZU

QWAN

Qwan is a series that refuses to be pigeonholed. Aki Shimizu combines Chinese history, mythology, fantasy and humor to create a world that is familiar yet truly unique. Her creature designs are particularly brilliant—from mascots to monsters. And Qwan himself is great—fallen to Earth, he's like a little kid, complete with the loud questions, yet he eats demons for breakfast. In short, *Qwan* is a solid story with great character dynamics, amazing art and some kick-ass battle scenes. What's not to like?

~Carol Fox, Editor

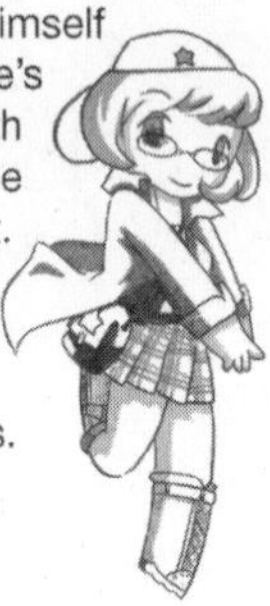

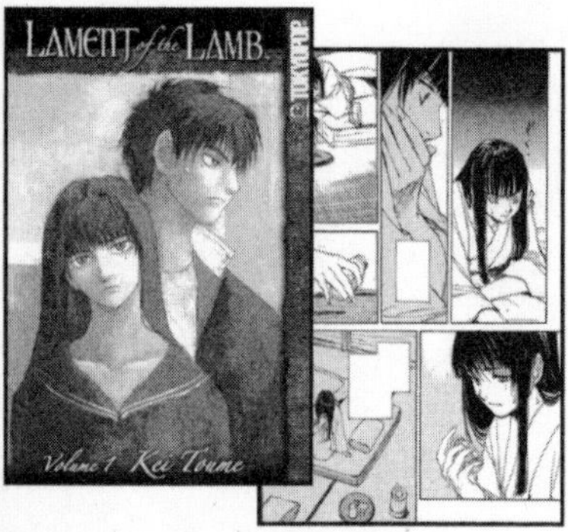
LAMENT of the LAMB
Volume 1 Kei Toume
TOKYOPOP

BY KEI TOUME

LAMENT OF THE LAMB

Kei Toume's *Lament of the Lamb* follows the physical and mental torment of Kazuna Takashiro, who discovers that he's cursed with a hereditary disease that makes him crave blood. *Lament* is psychological horror at its best—it's gloomy, foreboding and emotionally wrenching. Toume brilliantly treats the story's vampirism in a realistic, subdued way, and it becomes a metaphor for teenage alienation, twisted sexual desire and insanity. While reading each volume, I get goose bumps, I feel uneasy, and I become increasingly depressed. Quite a compliment for a horror series!

~Paul Morrissey, Editor

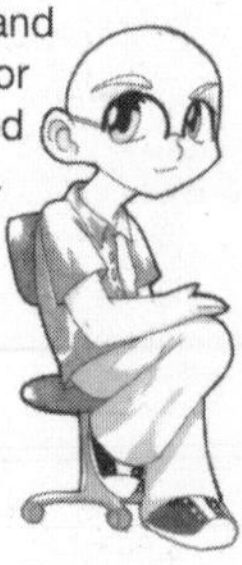

BY AYA YOSHINAGA, HIROYUKI
MORIOKA, TOSHIHIRO ONO, AND
WASOH MIYAKOSHI

THE SEIKAI TRILOGY

The Seikai Trilogy is one of TOKYOPOP's most underrated series. Although the trilogy gained popularity through the release of the anime, the manga brings a vitality to the characters that I feel the anime never did. The story is a heart-warming, exciting sci-fi adventure epic, the likes of which we haven't seen since *Star Wars*. *Banner of the Stars II*, the series' finale, is a real page-turner—a prison colony's security is compromised due to violent intergalactic politics. Each manga corresponds to the story from the novel...however, unless you read Japanese, the only way to enjoy the story thus far is through these faithful comic adaptations.

~Luis Reyes, Editor

BY SEIMARU AMAGI AND
TETSUYA KOSHIBA

REMOTE

Imagine Pam Anderson starring in *The Silence of the Lambs* and you've got a hint of what to expect from Seimaru Amagi and Tetsuya Koshiba's *Remote*. Completely out of her element, Officer Kurumi Ayaki brings down murderers, mad bombers and would-be assassins, all under the guidance of the reclusive Inspector Himuro. There's no shortage of fan-service and ultraviolence as Kurumi stumbles through her cases, but it's nicely balanced by the forensic police work of the brilliant Himuro, a man haunted by his past and struggling with suppressed emotions awakened by the adorable Kurumi.

~Bryce P. Coleman, Editor

The Seikai Trilogy © Hiroyuki Morioka, Hayakawa Publishing, Inc. © SUNRISE, WOWOW © Toshihiro Ono. Remote © Seimaru Amagi & Tetsuya Koshiba

.HACK//AI BUSTER - NOVEL
BY TATSUYA HAMAZAKI

In the epic prequel to *.hack*, the avatar Albireo is a solo adventurer in The World, the most advanced online fantasy game ever created. When he comes across Lycoris, a strange little girl in a dungeon, he soon comes to realize that she may hold a very deadly secret—a secret that could unhinge everything in cyberspace... and beyond!

Discover the untold origins of the phenomenon known as *.hack*!

© Tatsuya Hamazaki © Rei Izumi

CHRONO CODE
BY EUI-CHEOL SHIN & IL-HO CHOI

Time flows like a river, without changing its course. This is an escape from the river's flow...

Three people must cross time and space to find each other and change their destinies. However, a powerful satellite, a secret code and the future police impede their progress, and their success hinges on an amnesiac who must first uncover the true nature of her past in order to discover who her friends are in the future.

T
TEEN
AGE 13+

© IL-HO CHOI & EUI-CHEOL SHIN, DAIWON C.I. Inc.

SAIYUKI RELOAD
BY KAZUYA MINEKURA

Join Sanzo, Gojyo, Hakkai, Goku and their updated wardrobe as they continue their journey west toward Shangri-La, encountering new challenges and new adventures along the way. But don't be fooled by their change in costume: The fearsome foursome is just as ferocious and focused as before...if not more so.

The hit manga that inspired the anime, and the sequel to TOKYOPOP's hugely popular *Saiyuki*!

OT
OLDER TEEN
AGE 16+

© Kazuya Minekura

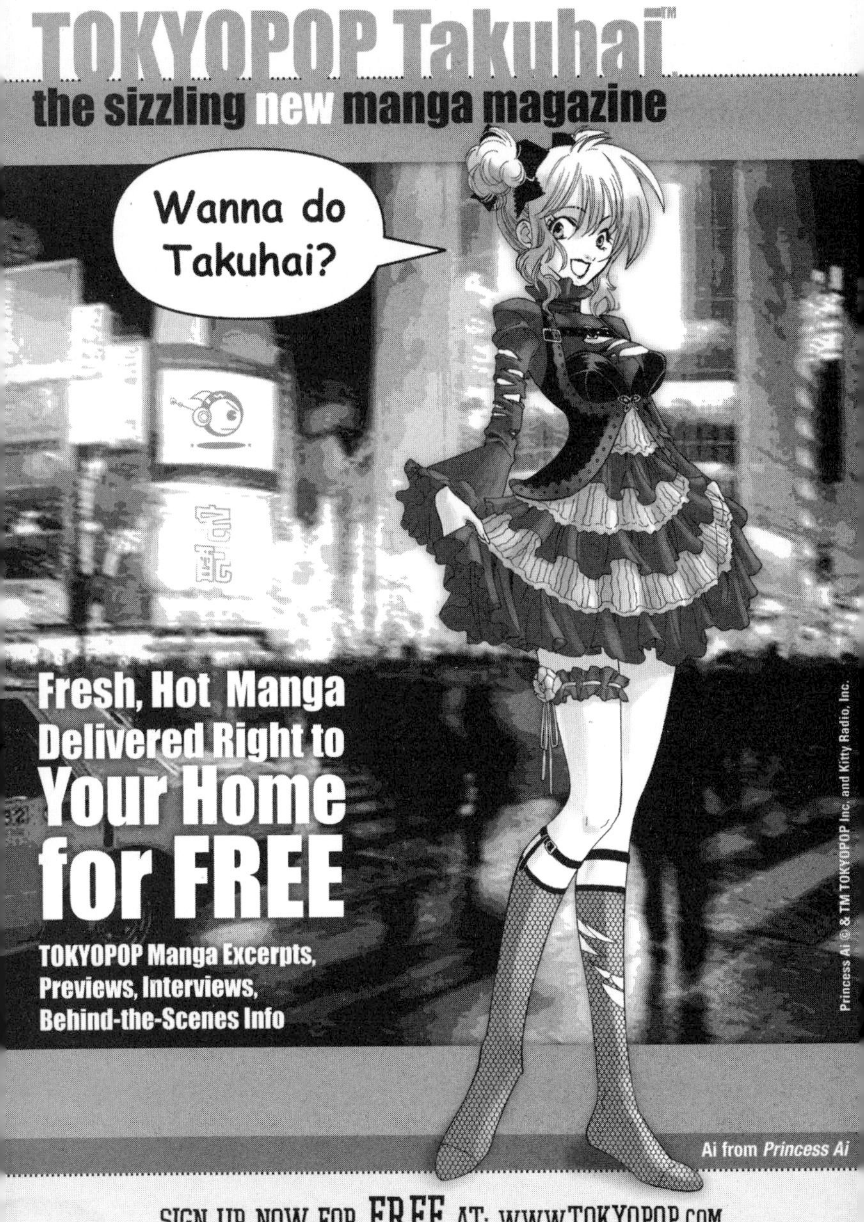

SIGN UP NOW FOR FREE AT: WWW.TOKYOPOP.COM

TOKYOPOP MANGA SUPPLEMENT

She crash-landed on earth...

now she has a thing or two to get off her chest.

DearS
ディアーズ

The hit series that inspired the anime and video game!

TEEN
AGE 13+

www.TOKYOPOP.com/dears

© PEACH-PIT.©2004 TOKYOPOP Inc. All Rights Reserved.

BLADE OF HEAVEN ™

THE ULTIMATE CLASH IS ABOUT TO BEGIN!

When Soma, a human, is accused of stealing the Heaven King's Sword, the otherwordly order is knocked out of balance. Heavenly beings and demons clash for ultimate supremacy. The hope for salvation rests with Soma, the heavenly princess, and the Blade of Heaven—each holds the key to preventing all Hell from breaking loose!

TEEN
AGE 13+

STOP!

This is the back of the book.
You wouldn't want to spoil a great ending!

This book is printed "manga-style," in the authentic Japanese right-to-left format. Since none of the artwork has been flipped or altered, readers get to experience the story just as the creator intended. You've been asking for it, so TOKYOPOP® delivered: authentic, hot-off-the-press, and far more fun!

DIRECTIONS

If this is your first time reading manga-style, here's a quick guide to help you understand how it works.

It's easy... just start in the top right panel and follow the numbers. Have fun, and look for more 100% authentic manga from TOKYOPOP®!